CAMBRIDGE STUDIES IN RELIGION AND
AMERICAN PUBLIC LIFE

GENERAL EDITOR: ROBIN W. LOVIN

The Virginia Statute for Religious Freedom

The Virginia Statute for Religious Freedom

Its Evolution and Consequences in American History

Edited by
MERRILL D. PETERSON
University of Virginia

AND

ROBERT C. VAUGHAN
Virginia Foundation for the Humanities and Public Policy

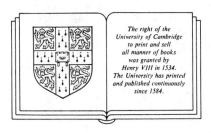

The right of the
University of Cambridge
to print and sell
all manner of books
was granted by
Henry VIII in 1534.
The University has printed
and published continuously
since 1584.

CAMBRIDGE UNIVERSITY PRESS

Cambridge
New York   New Rochelle   Melbourne   Sydney

Published by the Press Syndicate of the University of Cambridge
The Pitt Building, Trumpington Street, Cambridge CB2 1RP
32 East 57th Street, New York, NY 10022, USA
10 Stamford Road, Oakleigh, Melbourne 3166, Australia

First published 1988

Printed in the United States of America

Library of Congress Cataloging-in-Publication Data
The Virginia Satute for Religious Freedom.
(Cambridge studies in religion and American public
life)
Papers from a symposium held to commemorate the
two-hundredth anniversary of the Virginia Statute for
Religious Freedom at the University of Virginia on
September 19–21, 1985, and sponsored by the Virginia
Foundation for the Humanities and Public Policy.
Includes bibliographies and index.
1. Freedom of religion – Virginia – History – Congresses.
I. Peterson, Merrill D.   II. Vaughan, Robert C.
III. Virginia Foundation for the Humanities and
Public Policy.   IV. Series.
KFV2812.R45V57   1988   342.755'0852   87–13786
                            347.5502852

British Library Cataloguing in Publication Data
The Virginia Statute for Religious Freedom:
its evolution and consequences in American
history. – (Cambridge studies in religion
and American public life).
1. Religious liberty – United States –
History
I. Peterson, Merrill D.   II. Vaughan,
Robert C.
323.44'2'0973   BR516

ISBN 0 521 34329 1

Contents

Editors' Preface   *page* vii

List of Contributors   xiii

The Statute of Virginia for Religious Freedom   xvii

1   The Virginia Statute Two Hundred Years Later   1
    MARTIN E. MARTY

2   Colonial Religion and Liberty of Conscience   23
    EDWIN S. GAUSTAD

3   Religious Freedom and the Desacralization of Politics:
    From the English Civil Wars to the Virginia Statute   43
    J. G. A. POCOCK

4   The Political Theology of Thomas Jefferson   75
    THOMAS E. BUCKLEY, S.J.

5   James Madison, the Statute for Religious Freedom, and
    the Crisis of Republican Convictions   109
    LANCE BANNING

6   "The Rage of Malice of the Old Serpent Devil": The
    Dissenters and the Making and Remaking of the
    Virginia Statute for Religious Freedom   139
    RHYS ISAAC

7   "Quota of Imps"   171
    JOHN T. NOONAN, JR.

8   Jeffersonian Religious Liberty and American Pluralism   201
    CUSHING STROUT

v

9   Religion and Civil Virtue in America: Jefferson's
     Statute Reconsidered   237
     DAVID LITTLE

10   The Priority of Democracy to Philosophy   257
     RICHARD RORTY

11   Madison's "Detached Memoranda": Then and Now   283
     LEO PFEFFER

12   The Supreme Court and the Serpentine Wall   313
     A. E. DICK HOWARD

     Index   351

Editors' Preface

The papers in this volume stem from a symposium held to commemorate the two-hundredth anniversary of the Virginia Statute for Religious Freedom at the University of Virginia on September 19–21, 1985, planned and sponsored by the Virginia Foundation for the Humanities and Public Policy. Taken together, the papers treat the ideas and forces in the English and colonial background of the Virginia Statute, the making of the statute in Revolutionary Virginia, the place of the statute in the developing American tradition of religious culture, and the relevance of the statute to the contemporary perspectives of constitutional law, philosophy, and religion.

In his old age, Thomas Jefferson, author of the Virginia Statute for Religious Freedom, remembered the decade-long struggle that had culminated in its enactment as "the severest contest" in which he had ever engaged; and when he came to compose his epitaph, Jefferson included the statute, along with the authorship of the Declaration of Independence and the founding of the University of Virginia, among the testimonials of his life for which he wished most to be remembered. In 1776, having written the charter of the new nation in the Declaration, Jefferson returned to Virginia determined to establish the document's principles of freedom, equality, and self-government in the laws and institutions of the infant commonwealth. No reform was more important in his eyes than the overthrow of the Established Church – the Anglican Church – and the laying of a new foundation of civil and religious life. Everywhere in the world, church and state were united, and dissenters from the one true faith – the established religion – while they might be tolerated, suffered numerous pains and penalties. Jefferson proposed a revolutionary change based on two principles: first, absolute freedom of religious conscience and opinion; and second, the separation of church and state. Each

principle was dependent on the other, in his view. True religious freedom cannot exist as long as the state is a party to or adopts as much as
an opinion about religion; and the state cannot be disentangled from religious quarrels and hatreds except under conditions of freedom, wherein
no church or sect is dominant and each performs the office of a *censor
morum* on the others. There was a history behind these principles, of
course. Religious dissent had been a powerful force in the founding of
the American colonies. Roger Williams and William Penn, the founders
of Rhode Island and Pennsylvania respectively, had been early crusaders
in the cause of religious liberty. But unlike them, Jefferson was not a
religious dissenter, nor was he motivated primarily to secure the liberty
of his own faith. A philosopher of the Enlightenment, whose own deistic
natural religion reflected the ascendant rationalism of the age, Jefferson
laid the principles of freedom and separation on the broad liberal grounds
of reason and right, and thus made them accessible to – indeed, made
them a *right* of – all mankind.

Jefferson drafted the Virginia Statute in 1777, when he was a member
of the Virginia legislature, and it become law on January 16, 1786, when
he was United States minister to France. The achievement was made
possible by an unusual alliance: on the one side, liberals and rationalists
like Jefferson and his young colleague in this enterprise, as in so many
others, James Madison; on the other side, the various dissenting sects,
led by the evangelical Baptists. They shared a goal, although for different
reasons. By the unique logic of American history, the seekers after enlightenment and the seekers after salvation were allies in the cause of
religious liberty. Disestablishing the Anglican Church, as it turned out,
was only half the battle. Many Virginians feared the consequences of a
state without religion and of churches without public support. They proposed a halfway house in which all the citizens would be taxed to support
all the Christian ministers. Always in history, an "establishment of religion" had meant official sanction and support of a state church. Now in
the course of controversy in Virginia, it assumed a new meaning: the
civil support of Christianity without preference as to church or sect. Some
of the new states – South Carolina, for instance, where there had also
been an Anglican regime – adopted a plural establishment. But it was,
in part, to close off this fortuitous development in Virginia that Jefferson
drafted his bill; and it was to defeat the plan of a plural establishment that
Madison penned his great "Memorial and Remonstrance Against Religious Assessments."

The Virginia Statute is in three parts: the preamble, the enacting clause,
and the final, admonitory paragraph. The preamble, which is three-quar-
ters of it, is an eloquent manifesto of the sanctity of the human mind and

spirit – not only of religious liberty, but also of intellectual liberty in its widest latitude. Into the preamble, Jefferson poured all his rage against the cant and falsehood, the corruption and tyranny associated with the history of the alliance between church and state. He declared that religion and government are separate spheres, "that our civil rights have no dependence on our religious opinions," that to allow government to intervene is wrong and destructive both of liberty and of religion, and, finally, "that truth is great and will prevail if left to herself." Not only is it "sinful and tyrannical" to compel a man to support opinions he disbelieves, said Jefferson, but "even the forcing him to support this or that teacher of his own religious persuasion" is wrong. The enacting clause declares that no man shall be compelled to frequent or support any church and that all shall be free to hold and exercise their opinions in matters of religion without affecting their civil capacities. The final paragraph is curious. Jefferson was a rebel against the past; he believed that each generation should make its laws to suit itself. Yet he considered the principles of this statute so fundamental that he put generations on notice: "if any act shall be hereafter passed to repeal the present, or to narrow its operation, such act shall be an infringement of natural right."

On duty in France when the statute was enacted, Jefferson promptly saw to its publication and before the year was out reported to Madison on the acclaim it had received: "I do not mean by governments, but by the individuals which compose them. It has been translated into French and Italian, [and] has been sent to most of the courts of Europe. . . . It is inserted in the new *Encyclopédie,* and it is appearing in most of the publications respecting America. In fact it is comfortable," Jefferson concluded on a note of pride, "to see the standard of reason at length erected, after so many ages during which the human mind has been held in vassalage by kings, priests and nobles; and it is honorable for us to have produced the first legislature which has had the courage to declare that the reason of man may be trusted with the formation of his own opinions."

The Virginia Statute for Religious Freedom became the cornerstone of the unique American tradition of religious freedom and separation of church and state. It served as a model for other American states, both old and new. The last experiment with a plural establishment ended in Massachusetts in 1833. The principles of the statute entered into the United States Constitution by way of the First Amendment of the Bill of Rights, largely the work of James Madison: "Congress shall make no law respecting the establishment of religion, or prohibiting the free exercise thereof." Jefferson, as president of the United States, put a gloss on this clause that was destined to have great influence. In 1802, writing to a committee of Baptists in Danbury, Connecticut, he said,

> Believing with you that religion is a matter which lies solely between man and his God, that he owes account to none other for his faith or his worship, that the legislative powers of government reach actions only, and not opinions, I contemplate with sovereign reverence that act of the whole American people which declared that their legislature should "make no law respecting an establishment or religion, or prohibiting the free exercise thereof," thus building a wall of separation between Church and State.

At that time – indeed, until 1940 – the First Amendment, with all the other guarantees of civil liberty in the Bill of Rights, was held to apply against only the national government. And so it seldom came into play, since most matters touching religion came under the jurisdiction of the state governments. But beginning in 1940, the Supreme Court extended the guarantees of the First Amendment, ultimately of the Bill of Rights as a whole, to the state governments. The justices were much influenced in their understanding of the First Amendment by their understanding of the Virginia Statute for Religious Freedom and the circumstances that had produced it. As Justice Rutledge said, "The great instruments of the Virginia struggle . . . became warp and woof of our constitutional tradition." More than that, the justices picked up Jefferson's metaphor of "a wall of separation between Church and State." The metaphor, while simple, straightforward, and convenient, was not easily applied to the many and complex cases that now came before the Court; and in time, as Justice Jackson observed, that "wall of separation" began to look like one of Jefferson's serpentine walls at the University of Virginia.

It is one of the acknowledged pardoxes of American civilization that religion has flourished despite the absence of state support. In previous centuries, as Jefferson reflected before his death in 1826, the opinion was universal "that civil government could not stand without the prop of a religious establishment, and that the Christian religion would perish if not supported." But these assumptions were turned on their head in America. Alexis de Tocqueville, the young Frenchman who visited the United States in the 1830s and wrote his famous *Democracy in America,* was astonished by the coexistence of what he called "the spirit of liberty" and "the spirit of religion." In Europe, they stood opposed; in America, both flourished although completely separate. Twenty years later, the German theologian Philip Schaff studied the matter closely and came to the same conclusion. The vitality of religion in the United States, he thought, was owing to its self-reliance, its freedom, and its abstention from politics: "The voluntary system develops individual activity and liberality in the support of religion, while the state-church system has the opposite effect. . . . The United States are by far the most religious and Christian country in the world; and that, just because religion is there most free."

It was altogether fitting to commemorate this monumental document of the American founding at "Mr. Jefferson's University." The symposium was conceived and planned by the Virginia Foundation for the Humanities and Public Policy under the direction of the editors of this volume. The foundation was responding to the current intense public interest in the relationship between church and state. One need only point to recent and recurring debates and court cases on school prayer, tax exemption, and religious symbols – among many other issues – to confirm that the separation of church and state is a political, economic, and moral issue continually being redefined.

The state of scholarship in the field also argued the need for an intensive debate and scholarly volume accessible to a diverse audience. The literature on religious liberty in the United States is vast indeed. But the unbroken tradition of scholarship on the Virginia Statute did not include a comprehensive survey of the subject. What we sought was a range of historical, religious, and legal thought from the best scholars working in the field. We sought, as well, to construct the symposium and subsequent book in such a way that the reader would get at least a partial view of the eighteenth century, the context of the statute's composition and legislative passage.

The symposium generated lively discussion among a diverse audience of more than three hundred from around the state and country. Many perspectives were represented, and the questions and discussion reflected a broad range of opinion and thinking about religion and religious issues. All points of view were heard and appreciated. The plan of the symposium fostered such open exchange. Major papers were presented in an abridged form and followed by shorter commentaries. Audience discussion followed. In this way, the symposium moved through four sessions organized chronologically. A fifth session provided an overview of the Virginia Statute, Madison's contribution, and current issues.

The strength of these essays reflects the strength of the symposium, since the writers knew at the outset that they were working toward publication. For that reason, we regret that the limitations of publishing prevented our including the commentaries and several other fine essays presented at the symposium. We do acknowledge with a profound debt of gratitude the contributions that these participants made. Without them, the symposium would not have been successful, and this book would have been a very different collection. Their contributions are reflected in revisions made in these essays. We wish to thank Catherine L. Albanese,

Richard R. Beeman, Walter Berns, Patricia U. Bonomi, Robert F. Drinan, S.J., Kent Greenawalt, Alan Heimert, Winthrop S. Hudson, John H. Mansfield, Henry F. May, and Nicholas Wolterstorff. We were blessed with wonderful moderators: Henry J. Abraham, Helen Hill Miller, Nathan A. Scott, Jr., James H. Smylie, and Thaddeaus W. Tate, Jr.

We also acknowledge with grateful appreciation the work of many others who made the symposium possible. We relied on the wisdom and advice of an outstanding planning committee, especially William Lee Miller. Other active members included Henry Abraham, Keith Crim, Robert Cross, Jeffrey Hadden, Thomas Hall, A. E. Dick Howard, Kurt Leidecker, David Little, Erik Midelfort, K. L. S. Rao, and Robert Rutland. The excellent staff of the Virginia Foundation provided the resources necessary to organize an event of this scope. David Wyatt wrote the proposal that proved successful in raising the necessary funds; Linda Miller served as coordinator; and Susan Coleman and Hope Herring did the unobserved work essential to a conference. We are grateful to Robert O'Neil, President of the University of Virginia, for his enthusiastic support and dinner address to our participants, and to other university staff and faculty who helped things run smoothly.

Finally, of course, we would be remiss if we did not mention the generous support of the National Endowment for the Humanities, which funded the entire symposium and made possible this volume of essays.

We invite your interest and believe that this book will appeal to a large, general audience interested in the subject of religion and its expression in American life. Scholars and students in history, religious studies, law, philosophy, theology, and other disciplines should find it informative, provocative, and useful. We discovered through the planning, symposium, and editing that thought and feeling about religious liberty run very deep, and we hope that this volume will contribute to enlightened debate.

Contributors

Lance Banning is Associate Professor of History at the University of Kentucky. He is the author of *The Jeffersonian Persuasion: Evolution of a Party Ideology* (1978) as well as many articles and essays. He has received an NEH Fellowship for Younger Humanists and a Guggenheim Fellowship and was a Fellow at the National Humanities Center (1986–7).

Thomas E. Buckley, S.J., is Associate Professor of History at Loyola Marymount University. He has published many articles and book reviews and is the author of *Church and State in Revolutionary Virginia, 1776–1787* (1977).

Edwin S. Gaustad is Professor of History at the University of California, Riverside. His books include *The Great Awakening in New England, A Religious History of America,* and *George Berkeley in America.* He has been the editor of many publications, the most recent being *Documentary History of Religion in America,* vol. 1 (1982) and vol. 2 (1983).

A. E. Dick Howard is the White Burkett Miller Professor of Law at the University of Virginia. His publications include *Church, State and Politics* (1982) and *The Road from Runnymede: Magna Carta and Constitutionalism in America.* He was a Rhodes Scholar and received the Distinguished Professor Award from the University of Virginia in 1981.

Rhys Isaac is Professor of History at LaTrobe University in Melbourne, Australia. He is the author of *The Transformation of Virginia, 1740–1790,* which won the Pulitzer Prize for History in 1983, and has been a Fellow at the Wilson Center, the Institute of Early American History and Culture, and the Virginia Center for the Humanities.

David Little is a Professor of Religious Studies at the University of Virginia and has been the Henry R. Luce Visiting Professor of Ethics at

Haverford and Amherst colleges. His most recent book, along with authors Abdulaziz Sachedina and John Kelsay, *Human Rights and the Conflict of Cultures*, is scheduled for release in 1987. Dr. Little will be a Fellow at the United States Peace Institute in 1987 to 1989.

Martin E. Marty is the Fairfax M. Cone Distinguished Service Professor at the Divinity School of the University of Chicago and associate editor of *The Christian Century*. He was awarded the National Book award for *Righteous Empire* in 1972. His most recent work is *Pilgrims in Their Own Land: 500 Years of Religion in America* (1984). He is Fellow of the American Academy of Arts and Sciences.

John T. Noonan, Jr., is Judge, United States Court of Appeals for the Ninth Circuit Court and Robbins Professor of Law Emeritus, University of California, Berkeley. His publications include *A Private Choice: Abortion in America in the Seventies* (1981) and *Bribes* (1984) as well as numerous articles. He is a former editor of the *American Journal of Jurisprudence* and received the Laetare Medal from the University of Notre Dame in 1984.

Merrill D. Peterson, a member of the Board of the Virginia Foundation, is the Thomas Jefferson Memorial Foundation Professor of History at the University of Virginia and the author of many books, including *The Jefferson Image in the American Mind* (Bancroft Prize, 1961) and *Adams and Jefferson: A Revolutionary Dialogue*. His latest book is *The Great Triumvirate: Webster, Clay, and Calhoun* (1987).

Leo Pfeffer is Professor of Constitutional Law at Long Island University. His most recent books include *God, Caesar, and the Constitution* (1975), *Religious Freedom* (1977), and *Religion, State, and the Burger Court* (1984). He is a recipient of the Religious Freedom Award from Americans for Separation of Church and State (1955).

J. G. A. Pocock, Harry C. Black Professor of History, teaches at The Johns Hopkins University. He was a Fellow at the Woodrow Wilson International Center for Scholars in 1982 and is the author of numerous books and articles. He is at work on *Barbarism and Religion: Civil History in Gibbon's "Decline and Fall"* and *Languages of the Cave: Introducing the Historiograph of Political Thought*.

Richard Rorty is Kenan Professor of Humanities at the University of Virginia. His publications include *The Linguistic Turn* (1967), *Philosophy and the Mirror of Nature* (1979), and *Consequences of Pragmatism* (1982). He was awarded a MacArthur Prize Fellowship in 1981.

Cushing Strout is the Ernest I. White Professor of American Studies and Humane Letters at Cornell University. He has published numerous books and articles, including *The Veracious Imagination: Essays on American History, Literature, and Biography* (1981), *The Pragmatic Revolt in American History*, and *The New Heavens and New Earth: Political Religion in America* (1974).

Robert C. Vaughan is the President and founding Executive Director of the Virginia Foundation for the Humanities and Public Policy and of the Virginia Center for the Humanities. He has published frequently on public policy and the humanities and on American poetry. His dissertation was an exploration of poetry and religious belief.

The Statute of Virginia for Religious Freedom

DRAFTED BY THOMAS JEFFERSON IN 1777
AND ADOPTED BY THE GENERAL ASSEMBLY
IN 1786

Whereas almighty God hath created the mind free; that all attempts to influence it by temporal punishments or burthens, or by civil incapacitations, tend only to beget habits of hypocrisy and meanness, and are a departure from the plan of the Holy author of our religion, who being Lord both of body and mind, yet chose not to propagate it by coercions on either, as was in his Almighty power to do; that the impious presumption of legislators and rulers, civil as well as ecclesiastical, who being themselves but fallible and uninspired men, have assumed dominion over the faith of others, setting up their own opinions and modes of thinking as the only true and infallible, and as such endeavouring to impose them on others, hath established and maintained false religions over the greatest part of the world, and through all time; that to compel a man to furnish contributions of money for the propagation of opinions which he disbelieves, is sinful and tyrannical; that even the forcing him to support this or that teacher of his own religious persuasion, is depriving him of the comfortable liberty of giving his contributions to the particular pastor, whose morals he would make his pattern, and whose powers he feels most persuasive to righteousness, and is withdrawing from the ministry those temporary rewards, which proceeding from an approbation of their personal conduct, are an additional incitement to earnest and unremitting labours for the instruction of mankind; that our civil rights have no dependence on our religious opinions, any more than our opinions in physics or geometry; that therefore the proscribing any citizen as unworthy the public confidence by laying upon him an incapacity of being called to offices of trust and emolument, unless he profess or renounce this or that religious opinion, is depriving him injuriously of those privileges and advantages to which in common with his fellow-citizens he has a natural right; that it tends only to corrupt the principles of that religion it is meant to encourage, by bribing with a monopoly of worldly honours and emoluments, those who will externally profess and conform to it; that though indeed these are criminal who do not withstand such temptation, yet neither are those innocent who lay the bait in their way; that to suffer the civil magistrate to intrude his powers into the field of opinion, and to restrain the profession or propagation of principles on supposition of their ill tendency, is a dangerous fallacy, which at once destroys all religious liberty, because he being of course judge of that tendency will make his opinions the rule of judgment, and approve or condemn the sentiments of others only as they shall square with or differ from his own; that it is time enough for the rightful purposes of civil government, for its officers to interfere when principles break out into overt acts against peace and good order; and finally, that truth is great and will prevail if left to herself, that she is the proper and sufficient antagonist to error, and has nothing to fear from the conflict, unless by human interposition disarmed of her natural weapons, free argument and debate, errors ceasing to be dangerous when it is permitted freely to contradict them:

Be it enacted by the General Assembly, That no man shall be compelled to frequent or support any religious worship, place, or ministry whatsoever, nor shall be enforced, restrained, molested, or burthened in his body or goods, nor shall otherwise suffer on account of his religious opinions or belief; but that all men shall be free to profess, and by argument to maintain, their opinion in matters of religion, and that the same shall in no way diminish, enlarge, or affect their civil capacities.

And though we well know that this assembly elected by the people for the ordinary purposes of legislation only, have no power to restrain the acts of succeeding assemblies, constituted with powers equal to our own, and that therefore to declare this act to be irrevocable would be of no effect in law; yet we are free to declare, and do declare, that the rights hereby asserted are of the natural rights of mankind, and that if any act shall be hereafter passed to repeal the present, or to narrow its operation, such act will be an infringement of natural right.

1

The Virginia Statute
Two Hundred Years Later

MARTIN E. MARTY

For three reasons, it may seem strange to ask about the current fate of the Virginia Statute for Religious Freedom. First, most of the people who celebrated the bicentennial of the statute or who share the legacy of the statute are not Virginians. Second, the statute has no legal effect and never had one outside Virginia. Finally, most citizens have little historical awareness, we are told. It is a safe bet that a random poll would find that only a small percentage of the American people could name the document or would be aware of its contents. Certainly, it would not rank with the Declaration of Independence or the First Amendment to the Constitution of the United States as a charter for later liberties, as far as the public is concerned.

With good reason, the historical, legal, religious, and general publics, however, do commemorate the introduction of Thomas Jefferson's Bill for Establishing Religious Freedom in 1779 and the adoption under James Madison's tutelage of the Virginia Statute in January 1786.[1] The case for observance begins to fulfill the assignment of this contribution to a forum session on the statute today, or after two hundred years.

The Significance of the Statute

The Virginia event, by common consent, was the most decisive element in an epochal shift in the Western world's approach to relations between civil and religious spheres of life after fourteen centuries. Often cited is the summary by Winfred E. Garrison:

> For more than fourteen hundred years . . . it was a universal assumption that the stability of the social order and the safety of the state demanded the religious solidarity of all the people in

1

The Old Capitol in Richmond where the General Assembly of Virginia met from 1780 to 1788. Here the Virginia Statute for Religious Freedom was passed in 1786. A bronze tablet now marks the site at Fourteenth and Cary streets. Courtesy of the Virginia Historical Society.

one church. Every responsible thinker, every ecclesiastic, every ruler and statesman who gave the matter any attention, held it as an axiom. There was no political or social philosophy which did not build upon this assumption . . . all, with no exceptions other than certain disreputable and "subversive" heretics, believed firmly that religious solidarity in the one recognized church was essential to social and political stability.[2]

For those who like to speak of an "Age of Constantine" that began in the fourth century, there is reason to regard the Virginia act as the key moment of the end of that age and the beginning of a new one. Virginia was the oldest of the Atlantic coast colonies of Britain; in the late eighteenth century, it still had the most people. The Establishment there was that of the Church of England, favored in Britain as New England Con-

gregational establishments, of course, were not. Several other colonies –
notably Rhode Island and Pennsylvania, which had been founded on largely
Baptist and Quaker models – never had an established church, so they
may have had reason to claim priority on disestablishment and on promoting religious freedom. It was precisely because Virginia was the key
Establishment colony that the Establishment had defenders as notable as
Patrick Henry and George Washington; that there had to be an argument
for removing ecclesiastical privilege and ensuring free exercise of religion; that comparable notables, such as Thomas Jefferson and James
Madison, did the arguing; and that the Assembly, after struggles and
maneuvers, passed the bill with such a decisive majority that people can
see the Virginia Statute as a hinge between ages.

A second reason for celebration after two hundred years is that the
statute and its precedent had an effect on the First Amendment to the
Constitution, and thus on the measure that did acquire legal status and
still has it. We shall note that the two main concerns of the statute parallel
the two clauses of the First Amendment that concern religion. The parallel is by no means coincidental. Whoever wishes to engage in archaeol-
ogy to understand the text and context of the First Amendment does well
to focus on the Virginia Statute. To reinforce this theme: Many Supreme
Court decisions and much public philosophical debate about the First
Amendment focus on the minds and intentions of the drafters. That tends
to mean Madison, who advocated but did not draft the statute. Yet Jefferson was himself drafting "a fulfillment of the philosophy of the Declaration of Independence,"[3] and Jeffersonian precedents are much debated by those who examine later developments in relations between
civil and religious spheres and authorities. When the Catholic social philosopher John Courtney Murray spoke of "the American proposition,"[4]
the assumptions and stipulations of the Virginia Statute had to be included as prime elements.

The Persuasive–Coercive Distinction

None of these reasons goes so far as to establish the statute as
part of the enforceable legal tradition of the United States. As such, it
belongs to what we may call the *persuasive*, as opposed to the *coercive*,
part of national charters and covenants. This distinction arises from Jefferson's and Madison's own view about the nature of religious "opinions," "belief," "mind," "reason," "modes of thinking," "sentiments,"
"principles," and "truth" – to borrow eight characteristic terms from
the statute itself. It is also a distinction often forgotten by those who
would like to make some set of religious opinions or beliefs – for ex-

ample, the "Judeo-Christian" – into a legally privileged and at least lightly established component of the nation's system. Jefferson saw that religion had or should have only a persuasive character. Law existed to coerce people from establishing religion and to ensure its free exercise, in later First Amendment terms. There coercion stopped, for the sake of licensing and protecting persuasion.[5]

The statute, then, is located with the Declaration of Independence as part of the necessarily informal and ill-defined but enormously potent "American creed." People, Jefferson would insist, cannot be coerced into accepting or agreeing with a creed. If a person wishes to become a naturalized citizen, to hold public office, or to enter the military, he or she is "coerced" into supporting the Constitution of the United States. Such a person is never coerced, only "persuaded," into agreeing with the opinions and beliefs – indeed, the "self-evident" "truths" – of the Declaration of Independence and the classic documents of Abraham Lincoln or the Virginia Statute. Thus when British author G. K. Chesterton claimed to have been run through a kind of catechism of beliefs at the time he applied for a passport, a quizzing that put him off and then inspired him to create the famous phrase that America was "a nation with the soul of a church"[6] – a phrase regularly cited by those who wish to see religion, including a particular religion like the "Judeo-Christian," legally privileged – something strange was going on. Either the passport and other entrance laws were particularly elaborate at the time or the officer in charge exceeded his bounds or Chesterton confused, as often do those who quote him, those elements that make their way through persuasive means and those that have at least implicit support of law and coercion.

Let it be noted that in Jefferson's letter of January 1, 1802, to the Danbury [Connecticut] Baptist Association, in which he coined a metaphor about the building of "a wall of separation between Church and State," he was not quoting or effecting anything of legal and coercive force.[7] When the Supreme Court quotes it, the metaphor remains nothing more than a guide to the reasoning of the Court; it is not the law of the land. How, then, does the statute help produce its effects "persuasively" today?

"Today": The Period Since the 1940s

Even the word "today" or the phrase "two hundred years later" demands some examination. Because the Virginia Statute is so closely connected to the First Amendment clause, it is fair to say that "today" began in 1940 in *Cantwell* v. *Connecticut,* a Supreme Court decision that started the modern practice of making decisions about religion on the basis of the First Amendment in a national context. Justice Owen Roberts drafted the decision; the key words are:

> The First Amendment declares that Congress shall make no law respecting an establishment of religion or prohibiting the free exercise thereof. The Fourteenth Amendment has rendered the legislatures of the states as incompetent as Congress to enact such laws.[8]

Technically, this became known as "incorporation." Until 1940, with respect to the "religion" clauses, the First Amendment provisions were considered to apply only to the the national government, not to the states. Now the "due-process" clause of the Fourteenth Amendment, framed in 1866, would be extended in First Amendment cases to individual states. While it is the First Amendment and not the Virginia Statute that is directly at stake, it is safe to say that the implications of the statute are "in trouble" today because incorporation is. Attorney General Edwin Meese, III, in an address to the American Bar Association in the summer of 1985, explicitly questioned and attacked incorporation reasoning. Secretary of Education William Bennett regularly questions the notion of using such approaches to limit federal aid to parochial education.[9]

The Attack on Incorporation

For years, some organized forces in American Protestantism have tried to "de-federalize" the First Amendment "religion" clauses to turn back to the states the power to determine legal matters concerning religion. The effect of this would be to quarantine Virginia and its influence, as we have seen them here, and perhaps to pose the question whether Virginia itself would live up to the statute and the First Amendment in the current political and religious climate. The purpose of such anti-incorporation thinking is clear: Wherever religious majorities prevail, they could determine the legal expression of religion. The Supreme Court decisions prohibiting prayer in public schools, for example, would have no effect because individual state courts have not necessarily concurred with them. Where a religious group or cluster dominates, it could establish religion and limit free exercise. Thus Utah, overwhelmingly Mormon, and Alabama or Mississippi, overwhelmingly Baptist, could have their own way in determining religious support and exercise. Only "Congress" is included in the First Amendment.

Typical of the religious right's attacks on incorporation is the work of attorney John W. Whitehead, author of best-sellers on the subject. "It is apparent," he writes, "that if the southern states had been represented in

Congress there would have been no Fourteenth Amendment," and with the Court's "utilization of Section 1 of the Fourteenth Amendment, the Bill of Rights has come to apply to the states, thereby imposing on them the restrictions meant originally for the federal government." Therefore, says Whitehead, "the Supreme Court by ignoring history and by employing the due-process clause to nationalize the Bill of Rights has accomplished just the opposite of what was intended by the framers." A "liberal, relativistic interpretation" by the Court engages in "legal semantics juggling" and "sleight of hand" to effect a "shift" to a "highly centralized, octopean, bureaucratic system. It is no longer America, but post-America. . . . In consequence, the totalitarian state stands beckoning for its curtain call, and Orwell's *1984* becomes more of a reality moment by moment."[10]

Less strident and less directly motivated by a particular religious outlook are scholars like Northeastern University political science professor Robert L. Cord, who writes at book length against the incorporation theory with respect to the First and Fourteenth Amendments and the "religion" clauses. With many other scholars, he notices that it was *Everson* v. *Board of Education* (1947) that used the Fourteenth Amendment to "restrain" state legislative power. "Since *Everson* . . . in all of the Fourteenth Amendment Establishment Clause cases, no opinion of the U.S. Supreme Court has held that the constitutional religious restraints on the States have been less than on the United States Government." Thus, "*Everson* v. *Board of Education* is the single most important American constitutional law case in the realm of the Establishment of Religion Clause."[11] Cord follows with many chapters that criticize the pernicious effects on religion, law, and society that result from the incorporation approach. The influence of such argument seems to be growing, and its effect may be one of the most important aspects of life "today," or "two hundred years later." If the Supreme Court could or would reverse its direction after 1940 or 1947, as it may well do if radically different kinds of appointments are made, we could say that this is the most potentially dramatic trend of our day. Virginia could go back and cherish the statute, and citizens of the other forty-nine states could assent or dissent in the same spirit they might use with respect to charters in the history of other nations, not of their own.

The Precise Enactments of 1786, Vied in 1985

If Whitehead assumes that the trend has been "totalitarian," while others foresee regression and repression if incorporation no longer prevails, there are other issues connected with the Virginia Statute as a persuasive document, an element in the informal American "proposition" or "creed." One way to assess the ethos "two hundred years later" is to engage in the historical task of revisiting the Virginia Statute of 1786. Exactly what did it "enact"? The words merit citation: "no man shall be compelled to *frequent* [emphasis added] or support any religious worship, place, or ministry whatsoever."

"Frequenting" and "Supporting" Clauses

This "frequenting" clause and its corollary "support" feature parallel the first, or "establishment," clause of the First Amendment: "Congress shall make no law respecting an establishment of religion." To raise the question of the statute today would be to revisit all "establishment" clause cases pending or decided, a task clearly beyond our scope.

In the narrowest sense, the one to which Jefferson's work in 1779 and Madison's in 1785 and 1786 were directed, things go splendidly. The "ecclesiastical" powers comparable with the Anglican Church in Virginia lack the power and, ordinarily, the will to coerce the frequenting of their "worship, place, or ministry." On a slightly broader scale, vestiges of old establishment have only recently disappeared or still linger. Cord, for instance, noted that "until a recent policy change, cadets at national military academies were required to attend their own religious worship services." He went on: "In those instances the Federal Government, through the regulations of the academies, could easily be charged with forcing or influencing persons to attend church."[12]

It is difficult to cite other violations of the Virginia Statute ethos to match that one. It is in the broadest sense that the statute argument goes on today. This has to do with religious frequentation at least implicitly coerced not by specific religious bodies or creeds, but under the aegis of general "civil" or "public" or "national" religion. Arguments concern the propriety of state and federal chaplains in legislative sessions; the Court has been friendly to the perpetuation of this practice, and said so in a case that came before it from Nebraska.

The most controversial extension of the Virginia Statute stricture against requiring the frequenting of "worship, place, or ministry" since the incorporation approach came to dominate has to do, of course, with school prayer. This is a topic of such vast dimension, exacting such extensive and emotional debate on many sides, that it would be folly to attempt to elaborate on it here. Suffice it to say that those who reject the Supreme Court decisions in *Engel* v. *Vitale* (1962) and *Abington School District* v. *Schempp* (1963) and who now seek either Court reversals or a constitutional amendment licensing some form of prayer in public schools are challenged to ignore what the statute is about. Their other choice is to find arrangements whereby such prayer could occur without even the mildest "compelling" of children to "frequent" such worship occasions in schools under the ministry of fellow students, teachers, or guest religious leaders. Those who support the Court decisions, oppose reversals, and work against an amendment, on the contrary, contend that they are simply living in the spirit and out of the ethos of the Virginia Statute. Without arguing the case here, I would simply go on record as saying that I agree with the latter, although I would also have to remind that the Virginia Statute cannot be legally determinative.

The Assembly also enacted that "no man shall be compelled to . . . *support* [emphasis added] any religious worship, place, or ministry whatsoever." This also belongs to the debate over the "establishment" clause. The Whiteheads and Cords, the Meeses and Bennetts, and the millions who, according to polls, agree with them want to remove this question from federal governmental and Supreme Court concerns and give the issue of compelled support back to the states, where, they argue, things were before 1940 and 1947. Or they may argue, and some do, that a number of proposals or practices not yet supported by vote or permitted by courts do not represent "support." Among these, as Bennett regularly makes clear, are what have come to be called "tuition tax credits," which are usable in church schools, plus any number of other arrangements wherein some elements of religious education benefit from tax support.

Once one opens the "support" question, of course, the boundaries grow quickly beyond the school. When, in 1985, there were controversies in New York City over whether the Salvation Army and the Catholic Archdiocese could receive, administer, and disperse governmental funds for humane purposes, using their religious agencies and personnel, while rejecting city demands that they not discriminate against homosexuals, some questioned the legal propriety of having millions of tax dollars thus routed. Did not this mean "support"? Similarly, through the years, some have questioned whether the tax exemption of church property and practices, not only in the broader sense, where a semisecular zone is involved (as in providing meal services that compete with those of restaurants, or staging entertainment that competes with that in theaters – for example, the "Crystal Cathedral" case in California) but also in the narrower sense, where the spiritual zone alone is implicated (tax exemption for sanctuary and educational space), should be legitimized. Is not the removal of ecclesiastical properties from tax rolls a burden to taxpayers who do not support such "worship, place, or ministry"? Is it not thus a violation of the intent and ethos of the Virginia Statute?

The Argument over Jefferson

Rather than do more than report on the persistence of such discontents and debates, and eschewing all temptations to enter the argument myself, let me be content only to report one interesting feature of the Virginia-based references. Both sides have gone to great lengths to ponder the practices of Jefferson in later years – as president, as proponent of various practices at the University of Virginia, and in his correspondence and statements. These practices, it is said, color somewhat the principles of the bill of 1779 and the statute of 1786.

In one of the most far-reaching and searching elaborations, Robert M. Healey, with few axes to grind, concluded that Jefferson's views after 1779 remained "fairly stable throughout his life" and that "all of his subsequent writings on the problem of religious liberty are commentary upon the Bill for Establishing Religious Freedom." Again, his views "remained consistent." Yet "his practice in attempting to implement these beliefs about freedom of conscience is, by contrast, startlingly varied." He did refuse to proclaim days of fast, thanksgiving, or other religious observance, added Healey, "or even to recommend them as desirable to the nation."[13] Thus in his second inaugural address, Jefferson said:

> In matters of religion, I have considered that its free exercise is placed by the constitution independent of the powers of the general government. I have therefore undertaken, on no occasion, to prescribe the religious exercises suited to it; but have left them, as the constitution found them, under the direction or discipline of State or Church authorities acknowledged by the several religious societies.[14]

Yet, said Healey, he "seems proud of having used religion blithely for purely political purposes"[15] in 1774, when "he cooked up a resolution . . . for 'a day of fasting, humiliation & prayer' " during the war, "under conviction of the necessity of arousing our people from the lethargy into which they had fallen." He and his colleagues thought "that the appointment of a day of general fasting & prayer would be most likely to call up & alarm their attention." Therefore, they "rummaged over the revolutionary precedents & forms of the Puritans of that day." This is hardly a noble charter, but it does show that Jefferson did, on occasion, allow for acts that clearly contradicted the bill of 1779 and the statute of 1786. So did some other acts, which had what Healey called "real teeth." Jefferson vacillated over the question whether clergy could hold public office. He proposed a complex variety of solutions to the problem of religion at the University of Virginia.[16]

It is this checkered pattern that leads lawyer Whitehead and political scientist Cord to argue that the practices of Jefferson suggest that only narrow interpretations of the bill are legitimate.

> If Jefferson [had been an advocate of the absolute separation of church and the federal state] he would not have made a treaty with the Kaskaska Indians in 1803 – a year after the Danbury Baptist letter – pledging federal money to build them a Roman Catholic Church and to support their priest. . . . Apparently only the Madison and Jefferson of 1785 and 1786 in Virginia were important to the U.S. Supreme Court's quest to understand and interpret the First Amendment of 1791.[17]

Thus writes Cord, who permits the interpretation that the Jefferson of 1774 and 1803 was a different man from the Jefferson of 1786. Some might write off 1774 and 1803 to the cynicism that Jefferson confessed to in 1774 and the expediency necessary in 1803. Similarly, vacillations concerning clergy in politics or religious policies at the University of Virginia can be written off as the result of political necessity or indeterminacy, since Jefferson was dealing with uncharted and unprecedented issues and had to work his way through them. In the camp of religious militants who favor some sort of license for at least state government to "support" religion, it is the practices, not the bill and the statute, that are determinative.

Anticipating "Free Exercise"

The second part of what was enacted parallels the second, or "free-exercise," clause of the First Amendment: "Congress shall make no law . . . prohibiting the free exercise [of religion]." The statute reads:

> nor shall [any man] be enforced, restrained, molested, or burthened in his body or goods, nor shall otherwise suffer on account of his religious opinions or belief; but that all men shall be free to profess, and by argument to maintain, their opinion in matters of religion, and that the same shall in no wise diminish, enlarge, or affect their civil capacities.

There are four passive verbs: "enforced" ("to bring force to bear upon," whether physically or in any other way, according to the *Oxford English Dictionary*), "restrained," "molested," and "burthened." All relate to both "opinions and belief"; there is here no mention of practices. It was "opinions and belief" that, by nature and natural law and natural rights, belonged to religious freedom, although these verbs clearly relate to practices of the state and not to mere "opinions and belief." It was not the opinions of officials that brought force to put dissenting ministers into Virginia prisons. It was not opinions that restrained the unlicensed from preaching freely. It was action that molested and burthened them. The "free-exercise" clause brought the force of these verbal pretensions into the congressional realm, and incorporation, after the Fourteenth Amendment "liberties" were connected with First Amendment "freedom," carried them to the states. The intention of the Virginia Statute, then, clearly lives on – for now.

Arguments over enforcing, restraining, molesting, and burthening continue, and cases over these regularly reach the courts. It was the rights of Jehovah's Witnesses to propagate without restraint that issued in *Cantwell* v. *Connecticut*. It was the fights of the Amish to go unmolested in their educational policies that climaxed in *Wisconsin* v. *Yoder* (1972). It is the rights of the Unification Church and the Hare Krishna people and any number of other "sects and cults" to be unburthened for their "religious opinions or belief" – but, in practice, for their practices – that occupy lawyers, religious groups, and courts in our time.

So constant are these complaints above government intrusion and resistance to it that symposiums are held and proceedings are printed on religious reaction. Dean M. Kelley has edited *Government Intervention in Religious Affairs,* which reports on a major conference on the subject in 1981.[18] It was probably as broadly ecumenical or interreligious a gathering as could be assembled on any issue. A sequence of case studies came from Missouri Synod Lutherans and southern Baptists, bodies that do not bring many appeals or cases to other church bodies. There were worries expressed over religious solicitation, government surveillance, obtaining information compulsorily from religious bodies, "de-conversion," IRS crackdowns, personnel policies, and the like. Certainly in such cases, one side of the Virginia Statute is alive and well! William Lee Miller felt impelled to enter a dissenting note: "Responsible Government, Not Religion, Is the Endangered Species."

Affecting "Civil Capacities"

The second, or positive, half of the statute's "free-exercise" clause is also implied in the debates of two hundred years later: "all men shall be free to profess, and by argument to maintain, their opinion in matters of religion, and that the same shall in no wise diminish, enlarge, or affect their civil capacities." The first part of the clause adds little new to the second: Profession and argumentative maintenance of opinion are ensured if there is no enforcement, restraint, molestation, or burthening. It is the second part that adds nuances to the debate. The three verbs are at issue: shall one's religious profession or opinion in any way "diminish, enlarge, or affect . . . civil capacities"?

Debates over diminishing occurred, for example, when President Jimmy Carter put to work his Baptist-born views of human rights in his executive policies. Similarly, when President Ronald Reagan named 1983 the "Year of the Bible" and appeared on (privately funded) television commercials to promote the cause, there were those who claimed that it is illegal for the chief executive to promote one or two of numerous Scriptures and faiths in a pluralistic society. Here the statute would side with the defenders of the presidents. The public that does not like the policies should not have elected the presidents. Politicians are "package deals." Should only the agnostic 5 percent of the (polled) electorate be eligible for office? Should others in the 95 percent, if elected, be required to chop up their lives and leave the religious roots of their ethics and the spiritual color of their moral systems behind? It may be injudicious, but it is not illegal – in the spirit of the statute and the First Amendment – for citizens, even First Citizens, to be explicit about their religion.

In this argument, I concur with Paul J. Weber's comment on Madison, who

> would not forbid religiously motivated public officials either singly or in voluntary associations from making religious (or any other) recommendations – as long as they did so in their individual and not in their official capacities. . . . He had high praise for public functionaries performing religious duties . . . as long as it was unofficial, voluntary and financed by private donations.

This, Weber calls a policy of "equal separation": "While Madison did not deny that sound religion is necessary to civil government, he flatly denied that establishment is. Establishment had three components: coercion, disabilities (for those not established), and privilege. Equal separation meant the destruction of these components." Removal of disabilities after disestablishment was a consistent policy of Madison and Jefferson alike.[19]

Similarly, religious opinions or beliefs, when expressed, might lead to an enlargement of one's popularity, but not of one's legal capacities. Once again, when the matter belongs to the sphere of the persuasive and not the coercive dimensions of civil life, efforts to "enlarge" are legitimate, if not always politically well advised. Some editorialists argued that it "violated the separation of church and state" when President Reagan, soon after the 1984 Republican National Convention, went to a hotel to identify with militant Christians who had a particular vision for America. Nothing in the Virginia Statute would have led Jefferson to find legal grounds for complaint, although one pictures him totally opposed to the substance of Reagan's remarks and assumes that he would have found the context uncongenial and the policy ill-advised, if one goes by his record.

It goes without saying that if there is to be neither legal diminishing nor enlarging, there would not likely be other kinds of affecting of civil capacities. Yet there is still some controversy over the subject, not simply when it applies to public figures. Those who have begun to advocate that America give formal and legal privilege to the Judeo-Christian tradition, for example, often ally with those who would thereby be ready to give second-class status to nonbelievers. For Jefferson, "religious opinions or belief" included antireligious or nonreligious opinions or belief, since the alternative would have meant coercion, which would not have been legal or effective in any case. This is completely compatible with Jefferson's view in *Notes on the State of Virginia* that whether the neighbor said there were twenty gods or none, this "neither picks my pocket nor breaks my leg." Neither the presence nor the absence of a belief in God dared limit civil capacities.[20]

The Ethos Associated with the Statute: Opinion and Action

So much for the specific enactments. There remains what we have been calling the ethos of the bill and the statute; how does it fare after two hundred years? There has been a shift from the Enlightenment assumptions of Jefferson and, to some extent, Madison. Religion, in the Virginia Statute, is chiefly a cognitive or intellectual, not a behavioral or existential, matter. More than ten times, religion has to do with "opinions," and five with "mind" and "truth," while there are also references to "belief," "reason," "modes of thinking," "sentiments," and "principles," as we have already noted. There is only one reference to "will," one to "body," and one to "faith," to counter these.

In this respect, with the waning of Enlightenment philosophy – is it taught as the truth about life in any major academic philosophy department today? – and with some questioning of the power of reason, definitions of religion used in contemporary anthropology, psychology, sociology, or theology have vastly changed. Most problems dealing with religious freedom in our time have to do not with "opinions" of individuals in isolation, but of persons in groups or of groups themselves, where practice is what matters. Compare with Jefferson's the undoubtedly most widely used anthropological definition of religion, one that (with Paul

Tillich's concept of "ultimate concern") has informed the Supreme Court. It is that of Clifford Geertz. Religion is "(1) a system of symbols which acts to (2) establish powerful, pervasive, and long-lasting moods and motivations in men by (3) formulating conceptions of a general order of existence and (4) clothing these conceptions with such an aura of factuality that (5) the moods and motivations seem uniquely realistic."[21]

The nearest one comes to the Enlightenment picture is the "conceptions," but the contexts show that something much different is involved. It is on the basis of this "system" that humans, often in groups, act, thus creating problems in civil societies when their actions collide with the laws and interests of others in the society.

The legal development of First Amendment reasoning also appears in Justice Roberts's opinion in *Cantwell* v. *Connecticut*. Until 1940, the courts distinguished between belief, which was protected, and action, which was not. Here old Enlightenment notions of separation between the two were challenged. Roberts wrote:

> Thus the Amendment embraces *two* [emphasis added] concepts – freedom to believe and freedom to act. The first is absolute but, in the nature of things, the second cannot be. Conduct remains subject to regulation for the protection of society. The freedom to act must have appropriate definition to preserve the enforcement of that protection. In every case the power to regulate must be so exercised as not, in attaining a permissible end, unduly to infringe the protected freedom.[22]

Roberts thus introduced not a simple alternative to the old distinction, but left things up in the air. Now the "free-exercise" clause may or may not be construed to provide protection for some kinds of practice and behavior, protection that is special in the case of religion compared with freedom of the press, assembly, and speech. Religion seems henceforth to have moved beyond those freedoms, beyond what Richard E. Morgan called "the secular regulation." Morgan speculated that some justices accidentally invoked this "higher" principle, while others may have intended to go further to support religious practice than mere "free-speech" guarantees may have done. Could suppression of religion in Europe in the 1940s have led Americans to give even more attention than before to religion?[23] In any case, henceforth action and behavior came to be a more controversial issue in free-exercise cases than had the older, rarer, more congenial issues having to do with individual "opinion." In this respect, there has been movement beyond and, some would say, away from what the Virginia Statute more simply provided.

The Debate About God

One of the major and surprising debates over issues raised by the statute has to do with its focus and base in God. There are only three references: one to "Almighty God," one to the "Holy author of our religion," and one to "his Almighty power." There are some possibly diplomatic, politically astute identifications with "our religion" as compared with "false religion." Such references have helped feed the debate over the religious views of Jefferson, Madison, and other Founding Fathers, especially as these views have a bearing on the issue of religious privilege today.

There are basically four camps. One, which argues that the First Amendment (and, behind it, the Virginia Statute) simply wants government to have nothing to say and do about religion, need not concern us in this context. A second, a secular–neutral interpretation (viewed as hostile to religious interests by some, especially conservative Protestants, or as muddled by others, including Robert Cord, whose book is a full criticism of the position)[24] is associated with Leo Pfeffer, who well represents himself in this book. That leaves two.

The Deist–Humanist School of Thought

Proponents of the deist–humanist school argue that the Enlightenment fathers, among them not least of all Jefferson, worked with assumptions that did and should represent a privileged religion or quasi-religion on its own. They argue that a society cannot cohere without some more or less spiritual core, some minimal *consensus juris,* some common religious faith that admits of great variety and permits dissent, but still provides a framework. They further argue that the churches and sects, divided as they are, cannot provide this. They are too particular. One must reach for religion that aspires to be universal, inclusive, and at least legally, if not intellectually, tolerant. They argue that the hidden, and not always quite so hidden, assumption behind Jefferson's bill and statute was a particular view of the world that has to be called religious.

One recent, ingenious, typed-as-neoconservative argument of this sort studiously goes out of its way to call the coordinating philosophy nonreligious, but then defines it in a way that Geertzians and most others in the religious-studies field would call religious. It is an analysis by Walter Berns, who does not believe that Jefferson, Madison, and the First Amendment imply "strict," or "absolute," separation of church and state. Yet Berns does not give an acceptable gift to most religionists when he reminds them where the Enlightenment era polity located religious interests.

> Instead of establishing religion, the Founders established religious *freedom,* and the principle of religious freedom derives from a nonreligious source. Rather than presupposing a Supreme Being, the institutions they established presuppose the rights of man, which were discovered . . . in the state of nature, to be precise. . . . The rights presuppose the state of nature, and the idea of the state of nature is incompatible with Christian doctrine. . . .
>
> In the beginning was the state of nature, and the word was with the philosophers of natural rights. . . .
>
> The origin of free government in the modern sense coincides with and can *only* coincide with, the solution of the religious problem, and the solution of the religious problem consists in the subordination of religion. In prior times, it was thought to matter whether a nation believed in twenty gods or one God or no God, or whether the one God was this God or that God.[25]

Berns may be correct when he says that such a polity subordinates religion, however uncongenial that assignment of place may sound to those who profess religion. Yet he is not likely to escape the criticism of those who would say that the only way to get to a subground beyond the grounded religion is with another religion; that the "opinions" and "beliefs" as well as the practices of the "philosophers of natural rights" and Founders were weighted with metaphysical and theological (or deological) assumptions. There seems to be no universal place to stand above the battle. Robert Healey, for instance, a moderate in every respect, judges that "on several counts Jefferson may fairly be charged with being as sectarian as the Trinitarians whom he opposed." The critics in Jefferson's own time regularly dismissed his universal-rights philosophy as Unitariansim, and Jefferson himself owned up to finding himself in sympathy with it, which all others regarded as a sect among the sects, a competitor.[26]

Among the other disciples of John Dewey – whose *Common Faith* showed the need for religious, if "a-theistic," terms for this basis – was J. Paul Williams, who believed that what we must call a Jeffersonian-democratic view of life demanded "metaphysical sanctions" and "ceremonial reinforcement."[27] Historian Sidney Mead argued eloquently for support of "the religion of the Republic." Such a religion, deriving from Jefferson and others, might fight for the freedom of others, but would find them too sectarian and particular. He spoke of his "quest to discover and delineate *the* religion of the pluralistic culture in which I have lived and moved and had my being." Using Franklin, not Jefferson, as a reference point, he detailed a Jeffersonian religion with which he agreed, and then concluded:

> This is the theology behind the legal structure of America, the theology on which the practice of religious freedom is based and its meaning interpreted. Under it, one might say, it is religious particularity, Protestant or otherwise, that is heretical and schismatic – even un-American![28]

A problem with this religion is that it has few articulators like Dewey, Williams, and Mead. Few Unitarians have devoted themselves to this, despite their roots in the Enlightenment ethos and outlook. Philosophy departments relegate teaching of it to history departments, which can point to its potency in 1785, but not to philosophers or theologians who will propagate it as true and valid today. Yet it is bonded to much of the legal structure of America. As the Enlightenment advocacy weakens and a cultural vacuum has developed, militant religionists have more and more seized the moment to make counterclaims.

The Theist and "Judeo-Christian" School

In this camp, the call is for the privileging of what are usually called "Judeo-Christian tradition" opinions and beliefs. Finding that tradition to be more an invention for the purposes of a pluralist society than a traditional term,[29] I prefer to call this the "biblical" tradition. American Christians always did get more of their civil views from the Hebrew Scriptures – which they call the Old Testament – than from the New. Here they are with Jews. This biblical tradition is, of course, in philosophical and civil terms, "theistic." So the advocates who are not content with its placement in the persuasive sphere, where it has been since Jefferson and 1786, would like to privilege it and, in rudimentary ways, establish it and thus locate it, in part, in the zone of the coercive, the legally based. Education is, of course, the main field of contention, although this advocacy must also deal with legal, governmental, clinical, and similar worlds.

On the scholarly level, something of this sort appears throughout Cord's writing, and it is a relatively constant theme among most of the intellectuals typed and self-typed as neoconservative. They often speak up for the "sacred" or "tradition" because not all of them invest the religious commitment with content, yet these are code words for religion. Secretary of Education William Bennett typifies humanities figures with governmental power who make the case for such privileging.

Their populist allies are chiefly, but by no means only, on the Protestant right. A whole militant literature has grown, some of it exemplified by John W. Whitehead, to whom we have already referred. It is important for members of this camp to determine whether to call Jefferson a theist or a deist or something else, since it is important to them to claim that his principles and policies not only allow for, but also charter what they are after. They have not yet agreed, and the disagreements derive chiefly from what use they wish to make of him. Thus C. Gregg Singer, in *A Theological Interpretation of American History,* is blunt: "That Jefferson was a Deist is almost universally admitted." But he complains that not many historians have seen "the intimate relationship existing between his Deism on the one hand and his political and social creed on the other."[30] It becomes necessary for Singer to rescue the American tradition *from* Jefferson!

Whitehead and the prevalent school need a different reading of Jefferson:

> The argument has been raised that deism played a very large role in the founding of America. It has also been said that the early fathers were, as a collective, deists. This is an erroneous assumption that has been fostered by many non-Christian historians. . . . Such assumptions deny the early Christian character of our country. . . . In its essence deism denies the deity of Christ and the existence of the Trinity. . . . The two men among the early fathers who are most cited as being deists are Thomas Jefferson and Benjamin Franklin. However, neither of these men fits the definition of a deist. . . .
>
> Although both Franklin and Jefferson were influenced by deism (among other things), . . . it is equally clear they were not deists. In plain and forthright language these two men set forth Calvinism's doctrines of predestination and total providence while including a Unitarian view of the subordination of Christ's person in the Godhead.[31]

One passes up the temptation to criticize this analysis of Jefferson in order to concentrate on the use made of him. To Whitehead and the conservative Protestants allied with him, and they number in the millions, it is necessary to take America back from the secularists and the deists and give it to the theists, the Judeo-Christians.

In an often used article, Whitehead was again clear: "Jefferson was a theist in the traditional sense, believing in a personal God with whom one could communicate. He was not, therefore, a deist." Whitehead focused on the Supreme Court's decision of *Torcaso v. Watkins* (1961), in which the Court, in a "stark turnabout," promoted "the humanistic belief of deifying the individual and the rationalization of Man's mind qualifies as a religion." That decision cited "secular humanism" as a religion, alongside Buddhism, Taoism, and Ethical Culture, other nontheistic religions. "It is clear that Secular Humanism is a religious belief system subject to first amendment protection and prohibition" in the Court's eyes, said Whitehead, who disagreed.

Now, "the Court's acceptance of belief-as-religion has virtually eliminated theism from the public educational system while the religion of Secular Humanism has become entrenched in the public schools." Whitehead and more popular apologists claim that it must be disestablished; Justice Clark, in a school-prayer decision, had said that the state "may not establish a 'religion of secularism' " in the sense of "affirmatively opposing or showing hostility to religion, thus 'preferring those who believe in no religion over those who do believe.' "[32] A whole belligerent campaign, popularized on Christian television and promoted through extensive mailing programs and organizational efforts, is based on this presupposition as interpreted by Whitehead.

Why Resolution Is Difficult Today

The Virginia Statute of 1786 as a background and tone-setting document is typical of founding texts that lie behind these debates over "who owns America," who should be privileged. Part of the problem stems from its intractability: How would one permanently settle the question of who should receive privilege in a fluid, dynamic, pluralist society? Part of it may be Jefferson's fault for not having recognized that his critique of sectarian religion in the name of universalism turned out to be another sectarianism. Still more may reside in the politics and practices of Jefferson and Madison in 1779 and 1785 to 1786, when the First Amendment was written, and during their presidencies. In the statute, there is language that broadly and dimly favors the language of "our" religion, Enlightenment of a Protestant sort with biblical faith, especially Christian style. At the same time, there are efforts here and elsewhere to transcend such particularisms. Also, the early presidents and other people of influence took years of sometimes inconsistent action to come to practical terms with the theoretical revolution of which they had been a part. This is a way of saying that if after two centuries we may debate the two minds they often showed on subjects of this sort, we should recognize that they came to those two minds quite naturally on historical, personal, and philosophical grounds.

The debates we have today on the subjects they raised are compliments to them for the way they seized their moment and read their callings and opportunities. They were fated to stand at a moment of transition between ages. Their revolution toward religious freedom may have occurred without the firing of shots or the cost of life and limb. Yet in some ways, it was more radical than was the armed American Revolution, the War of Independence, with respect to the assumptions and innovations that lay behind it and issued from it. They were not wrong to put on the Great Seal of the United States their understanding and claim that this was *Novus Ordo Seclorum,* a new order of ages.

NOTES

1 Thomas Jefferson's Bill for Establishing Religious Freedom (1779), to which regular reference without page citation will be made, is in Julian P. Boyd, ed., *The Papers of Thomas Jefferson* (Princeton, N.J.: Princeton University Press, 1950), 2: 545–7. It is a convention to italicize phrases that were omitted from the bill when it became the Virginia Statute in 1786.

2 Winfred E. Garrison, "Characteristics of American Organized Religion," *Annals of the American Academy of Political and Social Science* 256 (March 1948): 17.

3 Leonard W. Levy, *Jefferson and Civil Liberties: The Darker Side* (Cambridge, Mass.: Belknap Press of Harvard University Press, 1963), p. 6.

4 This is the title of Part 1 of John Courtney Murray, S.J., *We Hold These Truths: Catholic Reflections on the American Proposition* (New York: Sheed and Ward, 1960). Murray speaks of this "proposition" as a term used "with conceptual propriety" to refer to something that is "at once doctrinal and practical, a theorem and a problem. It is an affirmation and also an intention" (p. vii).

5 This distinction draws on the chapter title "From Coercion to Persuasion: Another Look at the Rise of Religious Liberty and the Emergence of Denominationalism" in Sidney E. Mead, *The Lively Experiment: The Shaping of Christianity in America* (New York: Harper & Row, 1963), pp. 16–37.

6 Quoted in Raymond T. Bond, ed., *The Man Who Was Chesterton* (Garden City, N.Y.: Doubleday, 1960), pp. 125–6.

7 Andrew A. Lipscomb and Albert E. Bergh, eds., *Writings of Thomas Jefferson* (Washington, D.C., 1903), 16: 281–2.

8 *Cantwell* v. *Connecticut,* 310 U.S. 296 (1940), at 303–4.

9 Discussions of statements by Edwin Meese, III, and William Bennett were frequent in the United States press in the summer of 1985.

10 John W. Whitehead, *The Separation Illusion: A Lawyer Examines the First Amendment* (Milford, Mich.: Mott Media, 1977), pp. 73, 81–3.

11 Robert L. Cord, *Separation of Church and State: Historical Fact and Current Fiction* (New York: Lambeth Press, 1982), pp. 101, 109.

12 Ibid., p. 112.

13 Robert M. Healey, *Jefferson on Religion and Public Education* (New Haven, Conn.: Yale University Press, 1962), pp. 128–9.

14 Thomas Jefferson, Second Inaugural Address, March 4, 1805, in ibid., p. 134, and Paul L. Ford, ed., *Writings of Thomas Jefferson* (New York, 1892–9), 8: 341.

15 Healey, *Jefferson on Religion and Public Education,* p. 135.

16 Jefferson, quoted in ibid., p. 134, and Jefferson, *Autobiography,* in *Writings of Jefferson,* ed. Ford, 1:9–11.

17 Cord, *Separation of Church and State,* pp. 115–16, 121.

18 Dean M. Kelley, ed., *Government Intervention in Religious Affairs* (New York: Pilgrim Press, 1982), pp. 41–56.

19 Paul J. Weber, "James Madison and Religious Equality: The Perfect Separation," *Review of Politics* 44 (April 1982): 185.

20 Thomas Jefferson, *Notes on the State of Virginia,* ed. William Peden (Chapel Hill: University of North Carolina Press, 1955), p. 159.

21 Clifford Geertz, *The Interpretation of Cultures* (New York: Basic, 1973), p. 90.

22 *Cantwell* v. *Connecticut,* at 303–4.

23 Richard E. Morgan, *The Supreme Court and Religion* (New York: Free Press, 1972), pp. 62–4.

24 Cord, *Separation of Church and State,* p. 19 and passim.

25 Walter Berns, *The First Amendment and the Future of Democracy* (New York: Basic, 1976), pp. 15–16, 18, 26.

26 Healey, *Jefferson on Religion and Public Education,* pp. 114–16.

27 John Dewey, *A Common Faith* (New Haven, Conn.: Yale University Press, 1934), and J. Paul Williams, *What Americans Believe and How They Worship,* rev. ed. (New York: Harper & Row, 1962), p. 491; see chap. 18, "The Role of Religion in Shaping American Destiny," pp. 472–92.

28 Sidney E. Mead, *The Nation with the Soul of a Church* (New York: Harper & Row, 1975), p. 5.

29 Arthur A. Cohen, *The Myth of the Judeo-Christian Tradition* (New York: Harper & Row, 1969), pp. xi–xxi and passim.

30 C. Gregg Singer, *A Theological Interpretation of American History* (Nutley, N.J.: Craig, 1964), p. 38.

31 Whitehead, *The Separation Illusion,* pp. 19, 21.

32 John W. Whitehead and John Conlan, "The Establishment of the Religion of Secular Humanism and Its First Amendment Applications," *Texas Tech Law Review* 10 (Winter 1978) 1:12–13, 17–18.

Bruton Parish, the Anglican church built in 1715 in Williamsburg to serve both citizens and the colonial government as the official place of worship. Courtesy of Colonial Williamsburg Foundation.

2

Colonial Religion and Liberty of Conscience

EDWIN S. GAUSTAD

In the world of exploration and discovery, Cross and Crown sailed in the same ships and shared a similar, although not identical, zeal. In the colonies and settlements, the trading posts and military forts, the interests of state and church could not readily be distinguished. Nor was anyone particularly interested in doing so. The prevailing pattern of religion in colonial America combined political and ecclesiastical interests so intimately that we still have difficulty defining precise limits of and making clear distinctions among the respective roles of governors, legislators, ministers, teachers, and the voting members of the public. Historians of the twentieth century put questions to the seventeenth century that the colonists themselves might not have been able to answer, often because the questions would seem pointless or obscure or absurd. In that earlier day, it was a "self-evident" truth that church and state must labor side by side for their mutual benefit and for the sake of all those placed in their care.

In the most natural and casual of ways, the Church of England would go where England went; the quasi-nationalized Catholicism of Spain and France would follow, or plant, the flags of these countries in whatever New World territories became available to them. No one defended the practice, because no one had to: It was a given of European and of Europein-American life. It was also a given that savages, so long denied the blessings of the Christian gospel, should have that blessing bestowed on them. And for savages to reject that great gift made as little sense as for starving multitudes to turn away from freely offered food. To attack the church as it went about its proper mission, whether to savages or to civilized, was to attack the state and to threaten the survival of the entire social order. Error had no rights, anymore than deadly viruses have rights.

One was either part of a society – politically, morally, theologically – or one was the enemy of that society.

It *was* a different world, this world that prevailed in England's colonies no less than in the colonies of other European powers. On the continent of North America, this world view manifested itself in two powerful versions: the Congregational Way of New England, and the Anglican Way of most of the other colonies. Risking a scandalous superficiality, one might argue that these were merely two versions of the same Christian establishment, the chief difference being that one looked to London for direction and support, while the other did not. It is far more complicated that that, of course, but for our present purposes, it is useful to see these two establishments as sharing an all-pervading world view. So did the Lutherans who came to America, the Presbyterians, the Dutch and German Reformed, and the Roman Catholics; these groups, however, never had the opportunity in colonial America to transform their establishmentarian assumptions into political realities of consequence. So Anglicanism and Congregationalism more or less divided the territory between them – the former making concessions to the Dutch in New York and New Jersey, and the latter presenting at times a united front with Presbyterianism. In between or all around these state churches were pockets of dissent and distraction: believers who either fled from society altogether or were determined to organize it on assumptions that were disturbingly different from those of the established churches. We shall return to the dissenters later.

The majority, these dominant consensus religionists, knew that society prospered, the state advanced, and the gospel was made secure only as sacred and secular realms coalesced. In Virginia, the Church of England had its earliest start, and there it achieved its greatest colonial presence. With legislative backing by 1619 and, with the passive support of the Bishop of London and the more active support of missionaries from England a century later, Anglicanism was by 1750 stronger in the Chesapeake region than anywhere else in the British colonies of North America. Maryland and Virginia had more than half the Anglican parishes (about 150) that were to be found in British America. About 60 such parishes were in the Middle Colonies in 1750, and even New England by this time had been successfully invaded – although not without protest – by more than 40 churches. In both these regions, the Church of England's expansion was directly due to the efforts of the Society for the Propagation of the Gospel and, to a lesser extent, the Society for Promoting Christian Knowledge.

The significance or impact of an Anglican Establishment extending from Georgia to New York varied enormously from colony to colony as well as from decade to decade. In the South, Virginia, as noted, had both the oldest and the strongest Anglican presence. Nonetheless, the complaints of Virginia's Established clergy (as well as those of the laity against the clergy) portray a rather gloomy picture. Of course, no bishop was present to enforce discipline, to facilitate ordination, and to defend clerical prerogatives and power. The long tenure of Commissary James Blair (in Virginia from 1689 to his death in 1743) should have filled the episcopal vacuum more effectively than it did; unfortunately, however, Blair and a succession of royal governors more often worked against one another than in harmony. More crippling even than the hierarchical weakness was the parish structure. A dispersed population prevented the creation of the typical English parish, as minister after minister complained about the long distances they were required to travel and the meager congregations they found at the end of an arduous journey.

The legislature, moreover, seemed unsympathetic to the fluctuation in clerical salaries as the price of tobacco rose or fell. While the law saw to it that parishes were laid out, the success of the parish and the comfort of the minister were left in other hands. Those other hands, normally the vestry, assumed control of the parish with such authority that the clergy felt itself to be manipulated more than benefited by this arrangement. The vestry had its complaints too: about clergymen who left England to escape debts or wives or onerous duties, seeing Virginia as a place of retirement or refuge. It is certainly true that seventeenth-century Virginia had limited appeal for England's wealthy or well-to-do. A pamphlet published in 1663 even asserted that criminals given the choice of hanging or being sent to Virginia often chose the former.[1] One can therefore speak of Anglican "rule" in Virginia only in two limited senses: (1) Anglicans before 1750 had a virtual monopoly on the institutional religious life of Virginia; and (2) Anglicans were more "at home," more pervasive, and more deeply rooted in Virginia than anywhere else.

Maryland, the other southern colony where the Church of England was quite strong by 1750, had started out, of course, under quite different religious auspices: those of English Catholics. Lord Baltimore's proprietorship was repeatedly challenged and ultimately lost when Maryland became a royal colony in the final decade of the seventeenth century. In 1696, the three Anglican clergy already in the colony petitioned the Bishop of London to strike while the iron was hot, strengthening the "Ecclesiastical rule here" with enough power and authority to thwart Lord Baltimore's authority permanently. If this were not done, the clergymen warned, Maryland would be overrun by "enthusiasts" (meaning the Quakers), "idolaters" (meaning the Roman Catholics), and "atheists" (meaning all nonchurchgoers in general).[2] Thomas Bray, founder of the missionary societies noted above, did in fact go to Maryland, although his greatest influence was back in London as a successful promoter of the Anglican cause in all of Britain's colonies. While Maryland continued to be a Catholic center in North America, by the mid-eighteenth century, there were three times as many Anglican churches as Catholic ones there.

Elsewhere in the South, Anglicanism had a firm foothold in South Carolina, especially in and around the Charleston area. North Carolina was regarded as wild and inhospitable country, suitable for settlement only by Quakers and New Light enthusiasts. Anglicans by 1750 were outnumbered there, and Anglican itinerants regarded North Carolina as the best possible example of what happens to a society that does not have a national or an established church: Drunkenness, immorality, ignorance, false teaching, and scandalous worship prevail. True religion was insulted, along with all reason and common sense, by that which pretended to be religion but which was, in fact, the grossest "Exhibition of Folly that has yet appear'd in the World."[3] Georgia, so recently founded, had by 1750 only three Anglican parishes, and all Anglicans were prepared to agree with the 1768 comment of one of their own: that the settlers there "seemed in general to have but very little more knowledge of a Savior than the aboriginal natives."[4] In all the southern colonies except Maryland, the Church of England had been favored from the beginning; yet in all the southern colonies except Virginia, Establishment was more hope than reality. And even in Virginia, one could claim effectiveness only in comparative terms.

In the Middle Colonies, Anglicanism had not been in on the ground floor but, by 1750, seemed to be making up for lost time in an effective manner. The Dutch had, of course, initiated the settlements and the trade in the New York–New Jersey regions. After about only forty years of Dutch control, however, the English seized power in 1664. Since the Dutch Reformed Church was, like the Anglican Church, a national establishment, the conquerors extended a courteous toleration to the conquered. Dutch Reformed parishioners continued, therefore, to be a significant presence in the eastern portions of these two states, their churches still outnumbering the Anglican ones in 1750 by more than two to one. Quite apart from the Dutch, however, Anglican authorities were unable to resist the encroachment of Congregationalists, Presbyterians, and Baptists; in the early eighteenth century, they even cooperated with political authorities in England in arranging for German refugees from the Palatinate to settle along the Hudson River. Pennsylvania, launched under Quaker supervision, proved receptive to Anglicanism, as it did to all religions under a deliberate policy of liberty; and tiny Delaware (or the "lower counties") had by 1750 more Anglican churches than did North Carolina and Georgia combined. But Anglicanism in all these colonies, although it enjoyed legal privilege in New York and New Jersey, never enjoyed the security of numerical dominance in any of them. Dissent, diversity, heterogeneity – these nipped at the heels of a national church unaccustomed to so disorderly a bounty of religions.

To correct what was clearly an irregular state of affairs, Anglicans in the Middle Colonies more than anywhere else argued passionately, then desperately, for a bishop to reside in their midst. A bishop would set things right; a bishop would bring order out of chaos; a bishop would put enthusiasts, idolaters, and atheists in their place. Ironically, by pressing the episcopacy issue with such fervor, Anglicans nullified much of the hard-won gains they had achieved in the early eighteenth century. As the passion of the patriots increased in the 1760s and early 1770s, the obsession of Anglicans in the Middle Colonies for strong bishops called attention to their Tory stance as well as to their assumption that episcopacy and monarchy went hand in hand. New York Anglican Thomas Bradbury Chandler, in his *Appeal to the Public* (1767), alarmed more than he persuaded when he noted that

> Episcopacy and Monarchy are, in their Frame and Constitution best suited to each other. Episcopacy can never thrive in a Republican Government, nor Republican Principles in an Episcopal Church. For the same Reasons, in a mixed Monarchy, no Form of Ecclesiastical Government can so exactly harmonize with the State, as that of a qualified Episcopacy.[5]

Two years after the Stamp Act had been passed and the Stamp Act Congress called was hardly a propitious time to remind the citizens of New York (and elsewhere) that the Church of England was inextricably wed to the king of England.

The problems of Anglican Establishment in the Middle Colonies were different from those in the southern colonies, but no less severe. Diversity was rampant: by design in Pennsylvania, by default elsewhere. The roots of Anglicanism were shallow, most of the clergy being temporary missionaries in the employ of the Society for the Propagation of the Gospel. And the patriotism of this church came increasingly into question as most Anglican spokesmen here, unlike in the South, made clear their disapproval of Revolutionary sentiment. When the Revolution did break out, Charles Inglis of New York's Trinity Church called it "certainly one of the most causeless, unprovoked, and unnatural [rebellions] that ever disgraced any country."[6] No wonder, then, as one Anglican missionary reported in 1776, that these unsympathetic clergy were, on occasion, "dragged from their horses, assaulted with stones & dirt, ducked in water; obliged to flee for their lives, driven from habitations & families, laid under arrest and imprisoned!"[7] In an effort to make Establishment more real, these Anglican clergy had succeeded only in making it more terrifying.

In New England, Anglicanism never really had a chance to win wide public favor. Puritans and Pilgrims had come to the New World for the express purpose of getting as far away as possible from a corrupt (as they saw it) Church of England, this fact setting a certain tone. When the Church of England did arrive in Boston, it arrived at the point of a sword. Sir Edmund Andros, surely one of the most unpopular royal governors ever to rule in North America, had the pointedly unpopular assignment of reducing the independent New Englanders into a confederation. To this, he added the insult of forcing on Boston a church suitable for his own worship: King's Chapel, which opened in 1689. This thrust of Anglicanism into New England, more political than religious, did not represent the start of any surge. But the sending of missionaries in the early eighteenth century did. Rhode Island – which, like Pennsylvania, welcomed all religions – became the first significant Anglican center, with James Honeyman settling in Newport in 1704 for a stay of almost fifty years. Less than two decades after Honeyman's arrival, Anglicanism erupted in the very citadel of Congregationalism: Yale College. There in 1722, the rector and two tutors suddenly, scandalously, abandoned their Congregational heritage to become Anglicans and, soon thereafter, to seek their ordination in England. Anglican missionaries could hardly take credit for this stroke of good fortune, but they could not conceal their glee over what Honeyman called a "grand revolution." No wholesale defections followed; but Anglicanism now grew in Connecticut as it was growing in Rhode Island, which became ever more obviously a center of promise when not a bishop, but a dean, George Berkeley (Dean of Londonderry), took up residence in Newport from 1729 to 1732. If Parliament had come through with a grant of twenty thousand pounds that had been promised, Rhode Island – rather than New York – would probably have been the site of the first Anglican school north of Virginia. But Parliament did not pay off. When philosopher and churchman Berkeley left America, the Anglican Establishment lost its brightest colonial luminary. Nonetheless, by 1750, Anglicanism could boast of nineteen churches in Connecticut, seventeen in Massachusetts, and seven in tiny Rhode Island.

By that time, the agents of the Society for the Propagation of the Gospel were widely scattered throughout New England, much to the dismay of Congregationalists in general and the disgust of Boston pastor Jonathan Mayhew in particular. Mayhew had no objection to the general purposes of the society; indeed, he applauded them insofar as they resulted in religion reaching areas that were totally bereft of Christianity. But by the 1760s, Mayhew noted, the society seemed far more interested in competing with other Christian groups than in preaching to the unconverted. The society, for example, had many more missionaries in New England in 1761 (about thirty) than in all the southern colonies, "where they were so much needed." And, strangely, the society had no missionaries at all in the West Indies, "where there are so many Negro slaves in total ignorance of Christianity." Moreover, in New England, the society did not send its agents into the hinterlands or poorer towns; on the contrary, they "have generally been station'd in the oldest, most populous and richest towns, where the best provision was before made for ministers; where the public worship of God was constantly and regularly upheld, and his word and sacraments duly administered according to the congregational and presbyterian modes." Anglicanism, Mayhew concluded, was not interested in spreading the gospel, but only in "setting up altar against altar."[8] Mayhew's data appeared to support his charge, as once more the issue was one of national establishment and episcopal control – not one of Christianity, on the one hand, or paganism, on the other.

In the mainland colonies, however, genuine episcopal control remained more the ideal than the reality. Where the church was strongest, in Maryland and Virginia, so was the local and lay control. By the mid-eighteenth century, the church was reduced to minority status elsewhere in the South and, indeed, in all the other colonies. In New England itself, notwithstanding Mayhew's anxieties and protestations, the Anglicans were outnumbered by the Congregationalists in 1750 by about ten to one. For in New England, something akin to real establishment did prevail – but it was Puritan, not Anglican.

In Massachusetts and Connecticut, the Congregational churches numbered around four hundred in 1750 – a degree of saturation unmatched by any other denomination at any time in any colony. While the term "theocracy" cannot properly be applied to these two colonies, the term "establishment" surely can. The alliance between civil and ecclesiastical forces was intimate, meaningful, and enduring. Society, politics, and education were imbued with the unmistakable imprint of the "New England mind." In the seventeenth century, homogeneity had been maintained with a success also unmatched elsewhere in North America. In the eighteenth century, dissent made some inroads, but toleration (chiefly of Quakers, Baptists, and Anglicans) came slowly, reluctantly, and quite unevenly. The American Revolution, which had such disastrous consequences for Anglican Establishment, left the Congregational connection in these two colonies unsevered until well into the nineteenth century. Official religion in Massachusetts and Connecticut, therefore (and to a lesser degree in New Hampshire), did constitute colonial America's most effective alliance between church and state. In this respect, it may be contrasted with Anglicanism, whose effectiveness was limited by geography, by diversity, by a shackled polity, and by an often passive but sometimes passionate opposition.

But if Congregationalism comes out the winner in this comparison, it emerges as loser from the perspective of its regional limitation. Anglicanism tried, especially with the help of Thomas Bray's private societies, to be a religious presence in all thirteen colonies, and by 1750, it had penetrated all thirteen. Congregationalism, on the contrary, was a powerful presence only in New England at that late date, a pitiful presence in New York and New Jersey (seven churches altogether), a modest entry in South Carolina (four churches), and a total void everywhere else. True, some of this parochialism was mitigated by the close association between the Congregationalists and the Presbyterians, who were strong in the Middle and southern colonies. But between the two denominations there existed no institutional bond or grand strategy of conquest. Congregationalism, therefore, while it offered a model of what establishment in America might become, lacked the capacity to bestow on that model a universal appeal. And where the model had proved effective, it had done so at a cost of intolerance and a resort to persecution that left deep scars in the social memory.

The two most powerful religious bodies in the American colonies, Anglicanism and Congregationalism, had by far the greatest number of churches by the mid-eighteenth century. Indeed, if the Presbyterian churches are counted with the Congregational and Anglican ones, the total number approached one thousand. All other denominations together had less than half that number of churches in 1750.[9] It would seem, therefore, that the pattern of establishment would prevail, that dissenting voices would be drowned out, that the only real choice after the Revolution would not be between establishment of religion and disestablishment, but of which establishment would prevail. We know that this turned out not to be the case, and we know that Thomas Jefferson and James Madison had a lot to do with that turn of events. Dissenters also had a lot to do with it, however, well beyond their mere passive presence as contributors to diversity and, therefore, to the difficulty of elevating any single church to established status. Their contribution was more active, more deliberate, more self-conscious than that. So we turn to those who, on theological grounds, resisted all establishment of religion, arguing in its stead for "a full liberty in religious concernments" – in the words of the charter of Rhode Island.

Resitance to religious conformity came early. The New World implied for many who set out for it a time when and a place where new light might yet break forth. It implied, even invited, experimentation, novelty, a readiness to heed the Spirit and follow wherever it led. This was characteristic of Puritanism itself, of course, which is one reason why the early Puritans felt that they must deal severely with those who surrendered too readily to their own private whims, their idiosyncratic fancies. But neither alternative life style nor variant theology could be restrained, especially in a wilderness. Not the broad tolerance of the rationalist, but the narrow conviction of the zealot would first test freedom's limits in the New World. In the Old World as well, John Milton would argue in *Areopagitica* (1644) that truth is not set and fixed, but still unfolding: truth, even biblical truth, is a "streaming fountain," and if oppressive authorities try to cramp one's search, then Scriptural truths will "sick'n in a muddy pool of conformity and tradition."[10] There must be "perpetuall progression," "further light," endless unfolding, as Milton found the line from freedom in religion to freedom of the press to be straight and clear.

Along with Milton's English voice, some American voices were raised against any cramping of mind or soul or spirit. Ejected from Massachusetts in 1636, Roger Williams had occasion to reflect at length on the relationship between civil and churchly powers, on the demands for conformity, and on the horrors of religious persecution in human history. England's history should have been enough to show the folly of enforced conformity, for "it hath been England's sinful shame to fashion and change their garments and religions with wondrous ease and lightness, as a higher power, a stronger sword, hath prevailed; after the ancient pattern of Nebuchadnezzar's bowing the whole world in one most solemn uniformity of worship to his golden image."[11] But Massachusetts had learned no lesson; rather, this government would, if possible, continue to bind people's consciences, would continue to allow the wilderness of the world to invade the garden of Christ's church, would continue to persecute – not knowing or caring whether it might not be persecuting Christ. "I must profess," Williams exclaimed, "while heaven and earth last, that no one tenet that either London, England, or the world doth harbor is so heretical, blasphemous, seditious, and dangerous to the corporal, to the spiritual, to the present, to the eternal good of all men as the bloody tenent . . . of persecution for cause of conscience."[12]

This was not merely Roger Williams's private quarrel with John Cot-

ton over who was right and who was wrong about the way in which
Massachusetts sought to run its own affairs and the way in which Williams had been treated. Here was a principle, not an apologia; a conviction, not a calculated defense. When an uneducated and powerless Baptist named Obadiah Holmes left Rhode Island in 1651 on a private
preaching mission to Massachusetts, that lowly man was arrested, tried,
convicted, and publicly whipped in Boston with thirty lashes. Holmes
had not the eloquence to defend himself; Williams supplied the eloquence, together with the passion, in a letter to the colony's governor
condemning this outrageous violation of conscience. "The Maker and
Searcher of our hearts knows," Williams wrote, "with what bitterness I
write." Now, fifteen years after his own involuntary exile, Williams learned
that the Bay Colony had learned nothing. It would still follow the bloody
and unsavory path that England had for one hundred years or more pursued. And to what end? Pure religion? True Christianity? Nonsense! "Sir,
I must be humbly bold to say that 'tis impossible for any man or men to
maintain their Christ by their sword and to worship a true Christ . . .
and not to fight against God . . . and to hunt after the precious life of the
true Lord Jesus Christ." Williams concluded by calling for a spirit of
moderation together with a resolve, "in these wonderful searching, dis-
puting, and dissenting times," for those in authority to search, listen,
pray, fast, and "tremblingly to enquire what the holy pleasure and the
holy mysteries of the most Holy are."[13]

Obadiah Holmes returned to Newport, whipped but not whipped
down, to join once more with John Clarke in leading a Baptist church
that would keep consciences free. John Clarke accompanied Roger Williams to England in order to secure for Rhode Island a charter that would
promise "a full liberty in religious concernments" to all its citizens.
This charter, secured in 1663, offered the most explicit guarantee of religious liberty that the New World had yet seen: no one should be molested, punished, or disquieted for "any difference of opinion in matters
of religion," but all persons shall "freely and fully have and enjoy . . .
their own judgments and consciences."[14] Rhode Island would differ as
sharply as possible from neighboring Connecticut and Massachusetts not
simply in being more tolerant, not merely in adjusting to diversity, but,
far more than that, in proclaiming a religious liberty as complete and
unflinching as has been achieved anywhere in the world more than three
centuries later. Government did not exist to destroy liberty of conscience, but to preserve and protect it.

So Rhode Island would protect even the Quakers who came to live
there and who soon came to dominate the government. Roger Williams
did not like the Quakers; he despised their theology and distrusted their

motives. In this, he was not alone. He *was* alone in asserting that their consciences should nonetheless be left free. In Quakerism's early decades of the 1650s and 1660s, the Spirit-filled enthusiasts were deemed to be as much a political and social threat as a theological one. Massachusetts could not abide in its midst those fanatics who pretended to a private revelation from God, those zealots who paid no heed to biblical reproof or clerical censure. No government could long stand in the face of anarchists who accepted no authority except that within their own breasts. So Massachusetts jailed and fined and whipped them; then the Bay Colony exiled them; then it hanged them. In the eyes of establishment, any religious establishment, once again, error had no rights. And once again, the pattern had been set in the Old World over and over, in countless inquisitions, tortures, condemnations, and burnings at the stake. During its Civil War, England had experienced more diversity in religion than it had ever cared to dream of. With the Restoration in 1660, the nation again moved to contain, suppress, or eradicate the more extreme forms of nonconformity to the Church of England. Quakerism was such an instance of extremism; it had to be suppressed.

Quakers, along with such revolutionaries as the Fifth Monarchists, terrified the forces of law and order. With the Restoration came a resolve to set English society on a safe and sober course once more. The Clarendon Code was designed to do precisely that, since it stipulated fines, imprisonment, social ostracism, and other forms of discouragement to dissent. Perhaps the most famous prisoner of Clarendon's several measures, John Bunyan, achieved his first notoriety by attacking the Quakers. Even that was insufficient to endear him to the Crown, however, for he, too, dissented from the Church of England, its theology, its polity, its liturgy. Bunyan could attack the Quakers in print; he had no other weapon. The government, however, could move with force against those naked revolutionaries whose principal crime was to call England back to righteousness. By restoring the king and his bishops, most Englishmen believed they had already come back to righteousness. In any case, they had during the Protectorate endured all the enthusiastic bombast that they cared to. Quakers must be brought to heel. Except for the prestige and conviction of William Penn, together with the inviting wilderness of the New World, this might indeed have happened.

Quakers in the 1660s and 1670s proved to be an easy and vulnerable target for persecution in England and Ireland. Their presence was obvious, and their preaching was obnoxious; no more than that was needed to make the case against them. Penn, who had difficulty with such reasoning, presented in 1670 a striking attack against it: *The Great Case of Liberty of Conscience*. Here he freely acknowledged his status as a religious dissenter, but how did this offend the civil government or dishonor the nation? Although his argument implicitly defends all dissenters, it is the "poor despised Quakers" he would specifically rescue.

> For mine own part, I publickly confess myself to be a very hearty Dissenter from the established worship of these nations. . . . [I believe Quakers] to be the undoubted followers of Jesus Christ, in his most holy, strait, and narrow way, that leads to the eternal rest. In all which I know no treason, nor any principle that would urge me to a thought injurious to the civil peace. If any be defective in this particular, it is equal [just] both individuals and whole societies should answer for their own defaults; but we are clear.[15]

Arguing from every basis that he could expect rational and Christian rulers to acknowledge, Penn patiently explained that every violation of liberty of conscience managed only "to impeach the honor of God, the meekness of the Christian religion, the authority of scripture, the privilege of nature, the principles of common reason, the well being of government" and to aggravate the "apprehensions of the greatest personages" of the past and the future.[16]

Less than a dozen years later, Penn seized the opportunity to do more than write in defense of the Quakers. He became the instrument for providing them with a great refuge where liberty of conscience was built into the very frame of government. When Penn in 1682 published his first set of laws for the newly founded Pennsylvania, Section 35 read as follows:

> That all persons living in this province who confess and acknowledge the one almighty and eternal God to be the creator, upholder, and ruler of the world, and that hold themselves obliged in conscience to live peaceably and justly in civil society, shall in no ways be molested or prejudiced for their religious persuasion or practice in matters of faith and worship, nor shall they be compelled at any time to frequent or maintain any religious worship, place, or ministry whatever.[17]

We may note the Jeffersonian parallels in the latter portion of this legislation, while the earlier phrases affirm a kind of belief that even the deist could accept. Penn clearly moved beyond Jefferson in his concern for religious practice and religious worship. At the same time, the freedom not to worship is explicit, although provision was made in these early laws for people to abstain "from their common daily labor" on "the Lord's Day."[18]

Penn, of course, was neither Jeffersonian nor deist. He, like Williams, would defend liberty of conscience because religion is too precious a commodity to be bought and sold, traded to the highest bidder, or surrendered to the strongest sword. And his colony, it soon became clear, was to be a refuge not for Quakers alone, but for all those of tender conscience. Before a century of such unusual freedom had passed, Pennsylvania found within its borders an unbelievable hodgepodge of religious groups: Catholics, Protestants, and Jews hardly began to exhaust a list that included Anglicans, Baptists, Presbyterians, Methodists, Lutherans, Moravians, Mennonites, Brethren, Schwenkfelders, and more. Even more unbelievable than the amazing fact that such a mélange could live side by side without killing one another was the even more surprising fact that Pennsylvania actually prospered. Although it had been founded much later than such colonies as Connecticut and Virginia, which enjoyed and preserved their establishments, Pennsylvania grew stronger and richer – so it seemed – by the hour. William Penn spoke eloquently on the subject of liberty of conscience, but the prosperity of his colony spoke more eloquently and persuasively to that point. Was it just possible that society and economy could flourish without an establishment of religion? Of course, it was possible and plausible: Behold Pennsylvania! One must not suggest that this colony had no problems, that diversity led to perfect harmony, that Quaker pacifism was not both resisted and resented, that Anglican missionaries could readily adjust to so wild a swarm of fanatics, that denominations themselves did not further quarrel and divide. But, despite all, *Pennsylvania prospered*. Rhode Island might be able to demonstrate what liberty of conscience meant for the individual; Pennsylvania demonstrated what it meant for society.

One of the problems that Christian love seemed unable to solve had to do with Pennsylvania's neighbor to the south. A half-century earlier, another English king had given land to Lord Baltimore. The resulting colony of Maryland found itself beseiged by many problems, the dispute with Pennsylvania being only a rather late arrival in that doleful sequence. The first problem facing Baltimore, and one that he needed no one to tell him about, was that he was a Catholic in a vigilantly Protestant realm. He was founding an English colony in an Atlantic world where Protestant Virginia lay immediately to his south, and Puritan New England, somewhat more remotely to his north. Maryland might well be suspected of encouraging Roman Catholic Spain "or some other forraigne enemy to suppresse the Protestants in those parts, or perhaps grow strong enough to doe it of themselves."[19] By politics if not by principle, Lord Baltimore recognized that Maryland could not be a Catholic "refuge" in the way that Pennsylvania was early a Quaker one. Land could not be sold first to English Catholics, nor could control of the government be boldly Catholic. From the beginning, Catholic and Protestant must learn to live together peaceably, to be good neighbors, good citizens, good laborers. Even on the first ships sailing to the Chesapeake, this modus vivendi must be fixed. Thus Baltimore instructed that all acts of Roman Catholic religion aboard ship "be done as privately as may be" and that all Roman Catholics "be silent upon all occasions of discourse concerning matters of religion."[20] A religious minority, especially a politically suspect religious minority, must not give offense to a powerful state and a powerful church.

Baltimore's problems were wider than that, to be sure, and every act of charity seemed to be answered by intrigue or rebellion against him. As early as the 1640s, William Claiborne wrested control from Baltimore's hands and expelled any Jesuit unlucky enough to be located. Back in control by 1646, Baltimore invited more Protestants to settle in Maryland, thinking thereby to allay suspicion and encourage a prosperous growth. In 1649, he supported the passage of the Act of Toleration, which was designed to settle the ever-threatening religious war between Protestant and Catholic. That act provided that "no persons professing to believe in Jesus Christ should be molested in respect of their religion, or in the free exercise thereof, or be compelled to the belief or exercise of any other religion, against their consent."[21] Except for its Christological tone, this act echoed language that would become far more familiar in the second half of the eighteenth century. Its line of direct influence, however, was broken by persisting and enlarging difficulties in Baltimore's effective proprietorship: England's Civil War; Pennsylvania's encroachment; the Glorious Revolution, which exchanged the controversial Catholicism of James II for the more politic Protestantism of William III. After Maryland was declared a royal colony in 1691, the Anglican forces lost little time in making this once-Catholic colony their very own. Parishes were laid out, vestries appointed, commissaries (Thomas Bray) invited, and soon missionaries sent forth. While Roman Catholicism remained an underground force in Maryland for the rest of the colonial period, the colony did not present any continuing testimony to or manifestation of those liberties peculiar to conscience.

By the time Anglicanism asserted itself in Maryland, England had asserted its own measure of religious toleration. The Toleration Act of 1689 preserved the privileges and unique status of the Church of England, but brought an end to the long and unhappy history of the bloodiest forms of religious persecution. Its effect in the colonies was quite uneven, with some authorities arguing that the provisions did not even apply and other authorities only seeing to it that they were not applied.

In fact, the development of religious liberty, or even religious toleration, in America, moved quite unsteadily through the first half of the eighteenth century. Congregationalism maintained its position in New England, while Anglicanism – as we have just noted – strengthened its hold, not only in Maryland but in all the Middle Colonies as well.

By the mid-eighteenth century, the forces of establishment appeared even stronger than before. Rhode Island and Pennsylvania were pockets of liberty, but the strong voices of Williams and Penn had long been stilled. Then an eruption of popular piety stirred religious passions throughout all the colonies and within a great many of the churches. Establishment seemed threatened not by legislation or regicide, but by that Spirit that blows where it will, breaking out of all the approved containers. No establishment, foreign or domestic, was strong enough to say, "Only here, and not there." Having one's credentials approved did not mean nearly so much as having one's heart warmed. Being the pastor of a major parish was not nearly so important as being a preacher to the whole waiting world. To some, it seemed like the Cromwellian madness all over again, with zealots and fanatics and enthusiasts ready to turn society and the political order upside down.

Because of the effort of established churches to staunch this Pietist surge, the initial effect of the Great Awakening on religious liberty was negative. Connecticut, for example, passed laws in 1742 that virtually nullified earlier timid steps toward toleration. Congregationalists who withdrew from the Standing Order to create Separatist churches no longer benefited from earlier acts of toleration, and when such schismatic Congregationalists chose to call themselves Baptists, those earlier acts were repealed altogether. The defenders of establishment argued that they were simply trying to preserve society and promote peace. Well, yes, one Separatist responded: They are for peace "upon the same terms that the Pope is for peace, for he wants to rule over all Christians throughout the whole world." If these high and mighty leaders prevail in Connecticut or elsewhere in New England, then "separates and Baptists would have no more liberties here than the protestants have in France or Rome."[22]

Others, moved to question more than mere motivation, reflected on the whole nature of the church–state relationship. A leading Separatist, Solomon Paine, decided by 1752 that the whole notion of alliance was theologically wrong:

> The cause of a just separation of the saints from their fellow men in their worship, is not that there are some hypocrites in the visible church of Christ, nor that some fall into scandalous sins in the Church, nor because the minister is flat, formal, or even

saith he is a minister of Christ, and is not, and doth lie; but it is
their being yoked together, or incorporated into a corrupt constitution, under the government of another supreme head than
believers, which will not purge out any of the corrupt fruit, but
naturally bears it and nourishes it, and denies the power of godliness, both in the government and gracious effects of it.[23]

Here is language far closer to that of Roger Williams than to that of
Thomas Jefferson, but closer in time to the latter than to the former. For
Pietists awakened by the revival or for churches brought into existence
by this Awakening, for New Lights and New Side and all New Born,
what does Christ have to do with Satan? Come out, and be separate.[24]
Thus saith not John Locke, but the Lord. Also, and this is important for
the whole Revolutionary period, thus saith not the learned and the mighty,
but the foolish and the lowly.

The Congregational establishment held as far as the laws were concerned; that establishment slipped as far as the shifting sentiments were
concerned. Anglicanism also maintained its external structure intact in
all the turbulence of revivalism and unchecked emotion. By holding itself aloof from the movement, however, the Church of England isolated
itself more and more from its potential public. It took refuge in its liturgy, depended on its patronage, and grew ever more insistent on having
its episcopacy in full working order in America. The main effect of the
Awakening on Anglicanism was to make it appear increasingly "flat,
formal" (to quote Paine) and correspondingly remote from the concerns
of masses of Americans. Anglican ministers reported to their superiors
in London that in all the furies of this revivalism, "the Church . . . stood
steady in that Storm."[25] So it did, but the storm covered – and carried –
much of the land.

Anglicanism suffered even more, of course, as Revolutionary passions
grew. As the rhetoric against England's Parliament and king increased in
volume and scorn, some of those harsh words fell on the Church of
England. Missionaries of the Society for the Propagation of the Gospel
were regularly Tory. When Thomas Bradbury Chandler wrote in 1767
that "Episcopacy and Monarchy are, in their Frame and Constitution,
best suited to each other" and that "Episcopacy can never thrive in a
Republican Government, nor Republican Principles in an Episcopal
Church,"[26] he alienated all potential patriots. Somehow, Chandler convinced himself that this line of argument made a logic-tight case for sending bishops to America. No bishops ever came, but a revolution did, and
the effect on Anglicanism was swift and devastating – particularly in
New England and the Middle Colonies.

The Congregational establishment faced a different set of problems. Its loyalty was not in question; its good judgment and its charity were. And just as anti-England rhetoric spilled over onto that nation's church, so pro-liberty rhetoric spilled over onto a New England Way that seemed peculiarly, stubbornly resistant to the idea of "a full liberty in religious concernments," to quote the 1663 charter of neighboring Rhode Island. Not that no one was around to point out the apparent inconsistency. Isaac Backus, for one, thought it appropriate in 1774 to indicate that "taxation without representation" had its application in the religious no less than the political realm. To the Massachusetts legislature, he pointed out what to the dissenters seemed so obvious:

> That which had made the greatest noise, is a tax of three pence a pound on tea; but your law of last June laid a tax of the same sum every year upon the Baptists in each parish. . . . And only because the Baptists in Middleboro' have refused to pay that little tax, we hear that the first parish in said town have this fall voted to lay a greater tax upon us. All Americans are alarmed at the tea tax; though, if they please, they can avoid it by not buying tea; but we have no such liberty. We must either pay the little tax, or else your people appear even in this time of extremity, determined to lay a greater one upon us. But these lines are to let you know, that we are determined not to pay either of them; not only upon your principles of not being taxed where we are not represented, but also because we dare not render that homage to any earthly power, which I and many of my brethren are fully convinced belongs only to God.[27]

When earlier in 1774 Backus had made similar points to the Continental Congress gathered in Philadelphia, John Adams had thought the whole discussion trivial, since establishment in New England was such a "slender thing."[28] And so it seemed to many that establishment in New England was not really worth worrying about, was certainly not to be spoken of in the same breath with Anglican Establishment. That benign view, however, was not shared by the dissenters in New England, or even by John Adams in his old age. (In Virginia, Backus's fellow Baptist John Leland voiced similar sentiments against Anglicanism; Leland's language, however, reflected rather than anticipated Jeffersonian rhetoric.)

Connecticut did not abandon all establishment until 1818, and only then because the dissenters made common cause with the Jeffersonian Republicans. Anglicans, Baptists, and Quakers – unlikely allies in most circumstances – united on the issue of religious liberty to force a written constitution that would provide that "no person shall be compelled to join or support, nor by law be classed with, or associated with any congregation, church or religious association."[29] In far-off Monticello, Jefferson could not resist congratulating John Adams that "this den of priesthood is at length broken up, and that a protestant popedom is no longer to disgrace American history and character."[30] Even Adams at this juncture was prepared to speak of priestly "Bigotry and Intollerance" as he accepted the defeat of his own party with equanimity. Neither Jefferson nor Adams lived to see the break up of the priesthood in Massachusetts, but that came too, a half-dozen years after their deaths in 1826.

All this takes us far beyond the colonial period, to be sure, but it was necessary to enter the nineteenth century in order to demonstrate that Congregational establishment, no less than Anglican, suffered defeat at the hands of those who prized religious liberty so highly. Most of the dissenters who enlisted in that battle were conservative theologically; nonetheless, they became liberal politically if that were the only way to uproot institutions of such impressive power and such weighty traditions. It took deep religious conviction, not indifference and not calculating cynicism, to dig up those taproots of establishment. Those who dared not pay to any earthly power the homage that they were convinced belonged only to God fought for religious liberty on the grounds of conscience: private, inviolate, sacred conscience. Without the Jeffersonians, they may never have won a struggle that had begun long before the Jeffersonians appeared on the scene. And without the difficult, irascible, fanatical dissenters, the crusade waged so brilliantly by Jefferson and Madison would have been denied many of its more colorful members and much of its more passionate rhetoric.

NOTES

1   Thomas Hughes, S.J., *History of the Society of Jesus in North America,* vol. 1, *Documents* (New York, 1908), pt. 1, pp. 10–11.

2   Quoted in W. S. Perry, ed., *Historical Collections Relating to the American Colonial Church* (New York, reprinted 1969), 4: 11–12.

3   Quoted in Richard J. Hooker, ed., *The Carolina Backcountry on the Eve of the Revolution* (Chapel Hill, N.C., 1953), pp. 100–3.

4   Quoted in E. S. Gaustad, *A Religious History of America* (New York, 1974), p. 106.

5   Thomas Bradbury Chandler, *An Appeal to the Public, In Behalf of the Church of England in America . . .* (New York, 1767), pp. 110–11.

6   Quoted in J. W. Lydekker, *The Life and Letters of Charles Inglis* (London, 1936), pp. 158–60.

7   Thomas Barton, the society's missionary to Lancaster, Pennsylvania, quoted in Perry, *Historical Collections,* 2: 484–5.

8   Jonathan Mayhew, *Observations on the Charter and Conduct of the Society for the Propagation of the Gospel* (New York, reprinted 1972), pp. 51–6.

9   In 1750, the approximate numbers of churches in colonial America were as follows: Congregational, 465; Presbyterian, 233 (for a combined total of nearly 700 churches); Anglican, 289; Lutheran, 138; Baptist, 132; German Reformed, 90; Dutch Reformed, 79; Roman Catholic, 30. The number of Quaker meetings is not available, but it was roughly comparable with the number of Lutheran or Baptist churches (E. S. Gaustad, *Historical Atlas of Religion in America* [New York, 1976], Appendix B).

10 Quoted in David Lovejoy, *Religious Enthusiasm in the New World* (Cambridge, Mass., 1985), p. 53.

11 Quoted in Perry Miller, ed., *Roger Williams: His Contribution to the American Tradition* (New York, reprinted 1962), p. 111.

12 Ibid., p. 192.

13 Ibid., pp. 162–3.

14 Quoted in Gaustad, *Religious History,* pp. 66–7.

15 William Penn, *The Select Works of William Penn* (London, 1782), 3: 1–2.

16 Ibid., 3: 7–9.

17 Quoted in Jean R. Soderlund, ed., *William Penn and the Founding of Pennsylvania, 1680–1684* (Philadelphia, 1983), p. 132.

18 Ibid. Penn's legislation did provide for Sunday as a day of rest and worship, his humanitarian concern expressed in the manuscript draft in these words: "for the ease of man and beast from their common daily labor." But clearly, Penn was no free thinker of the libertine stripe, for he also stipulated, in Section 37, punishment for "all prizes, stage plays, cards, dice, May games, gamesters, masques, revels, bull-baitings, cock-fightings, bear-baitings, and the like, which excite the people to rudeness, cruelty, looseness, and irreligion" (p. 132).

19 Quoted in Hughes, *History of the Society of Jesus,* 1: pt. 1, pp. 10–11.

20 Quoted in Thomas O'Brien Hanley, S.J., *Their Rights & Liberties: The Beginnings of Religious and Political Freedom in Maryland* (Westminster, Md., 1959), p. 77.

21 Ibid., p. 115.

22 Reuben Fletcher, *The Lamentable State of New-England* (Boston, 1772), unpaged.

23 Quoted in S. L. Blake, *The Separates of Strict Congregationalists of New-England* (Boston, 1902), p. 58.

24 2 Corinthians 6:17.

25 Commissary Roger Price, quoted in H. W. Foote, *Annals of King's Chapel* (Boston, 1896), 1:509.

26 Chandler, *An Appeal to the Public,* pp. 110–11.

27 Quoted in Alvah Hovey, *A Memoir of the Life and Times of the Reverend Isaac Backus* (Boston, 1859), pp. 220–1.

28 Ibid., p. 210.
29 Connecticut constitution, quoted in R. J. Purcell, *Connecticut in Transition, 1775–1818* (Washington, D.C., 1918), p. 401.
30 Thomas Jefferson to John Adams, May 5, 1817, in *The Adams-Jefferson Letters: The Complete Correspondence Between Thomas Jefferson and Abigail and John Adams,* ed. Lester J. Cappon (Chapel Hill, N.C., 1959), 2:512.

3

Religious Freedom and the Desacralization of Politics: From the English Civil Wars to the Virginia Statute

J. G. A. POCOCK

I

Very far back in the history of Christianity lie the origins of what became known as the problem of church and state; this was well known to those who debated questions of this kind in the period I shall particularly speak of, and we cannot discuss what they said without considering the history that they knew, or thought they knew. In A.D. 324, Constantine became emperor and began to establish Christianity as the official religion of the Roman Empire, at which time – according to later legend – a voice from heaven cried out that poison had been poured into the veins of Christendom. The tale could well have been known to James Madison when he declared in his "Memorial" that by universal consent – or so he said – the Christian religion had been pure only in the ages before its establishment, which of course – although he did not say so – had also been the ages of persecution. It was about one hundred years after Constantine that Augustine, bishop of Hippo, wrote the classic of Christian political philosophy that is called *De Civitate Dei* and inaugurated the debate that was still going on, in changed terms and in changed circumstances, thirteen and three-quarter centuries later. The concerns of Hellenic and Latin men had been political before they were ecclesiastical.

The Christian Church must be set in opposition to the Greek city and the Jewish law, the two main modes of civil and religious organization during its prehistory. In the city, typified by Athens in one way and by Rome in another, it was premised that man is by nature political, that his highest nature is fulfilled in civic action and political decision. Athenian philosophy challenged this, declaring that contemplative knowledge stands even higher than action but that the relation between the two can never be terminated or resolved. Roman empire extended the practice of politics even beyond the activity of citizenship, creating the ideal of a race of rulers, magistrates, and warriors whose business was the protection and administration of the known world, in all its diversity, according to justice and law. In this world, the gods were the gods of the city where they were not the gods of philosophers: there was poetic theology, the multiple myths invented by man; political theology, the decisions of the city about which gods should be worshiped; and philosophical theology, the idea of the divine affirmed by the human intellect (which might itself be divine). To the philosopher – as Gibbon was to put it – all cultic religions were equally false; to the magistrate, equally useful. A philosopher might seek to transcend the city and its gods, to remain indifferent to them, or both.

In Israel, one god, ruler of all the world and recognizing no other, had communicated himself to a particular people in the Law, by which he organized and ruled them. He ruled directly by the Law, mediately by priests and kings, and, after his kingdom's mysterious collapse, prophetically by messengers who pronounced his word. The Christian contention was that the Word of God – which they said was also the Logos of Greek philosophy – not merely had been spoken, but also had become flesh in the body of the man Jesus, who, after his departure, had left his work behind him, both in a written gospel and in the structure or body of a Church, which not merely conveyed his message but also was the vehicle of his presence as Word, and so the mystical continuation of his body. The Church was both a body of men and the Body of Christ; it communicated his word both as made flesh in the sacraments and as a signified message, no longer a body of law for the Jews but a redeeming presence valid in and for all the peoples of a mystical Israel. There was a human association that was not a city of men, but a presence of Christ in men and a communion of men with Christ, active in this world to redeem men from the Fall, which had been a loss of communion with God in eternity.

This was what Augustine called the *civitas Dei,* significantly using the Latin word for "city" to repudiate the Greek meaning, which the word had borne until then. He denied that man is a political being whose nature is fulfilled in ruling himself in society or in exercising knowledge with the philosophers. The end of human life lies not in self-rule but in a redemption of the self that the self cannot achieve. Political association, the work of the unredeemed self, had been initiated by the fratricides Cain and Romulus; it typically displays only the lust for domination and, at its best, can bring social order (limited in time and space) but not communion with God. The earthly city can never be the city of God; no one has ever separated church and state with greater finality than Augustine.[1]

But this was not in fact the final word. From the time of Constantine, the empire could not be ejected from the Church or subjected to it, and there were important theological questions to complicate the issue. It may be said that the fundamental problem underlying it was that of justice: a cardinal virtue by general consent, the architectonic virtue according to readers of Plato's *Republic*. Could it be said that justice, although it might not be a sufficient, was not a necessary means of salvation; and if it formed part of the process of redemption, did not Christ manifest himself in the mechanisms of justice? It could still be maintained that the Church was the means of that manifestation, the *civitas Dei* persisting in the interstices of the *civitas terrena* and exerting the influence of the Spirit on the practice of politics; but there were those who replied that this was to make Christ too indirectly incarnate in the structure of this world, of which he was the judge, that the Second Person of the Three-in-One took part in rule as well as redemption, and that the magistrate was in his way (as wielder of the sword) as fully a representation of Christ as was the priest as administrator of the sacraments. To Dante in the early fourteenth century, the emperor was a direct and immediate manifestation or personation of Christ;[2] to Henry VIII of England two hundred years later, the king, although not a priest, was Christ's vicar, the executive of his judgments, in a way that the pope could not be.[3] The politics of incarnation were no light matter; the relation of justice to redemption, of the sword to the sacraments, was no easy question. To understand the Virginia Statute, we have to reach a point where these problems could appear frivolous, sinister, or absurd; this had to be achieved before they could be relegated to the sphere of private judgment, private opinion, and private liberty, when those who took them seriously had to acknowledge that they were no part of the public business. What I have called the desacralization of politics was the renewal of its separation from salvation, an operation in some ways Augustinian and in some ways not.

The next step in a story that I am summarizing with blasphemous brevity was taken at the Protestant Reformation. We may start from that point in its various programs that is known as the priesthood of all believers. If the just were saved by faith alone, if grace was the reward of faith and faith the vehicle of grace, then redemption came by way of experience, and experience was immediate and could not be deputized to a mediator. This necessarily called in question the status of the sacraments – in which bread and wine become flesh and blood, and the Incarnation becomes immediate to the worshiper. To Zwingli, the *est* in *Hoc est corpus meum* meant *significant;* to Luther, it meant *est.* But the experience of faith was increasingly distinct from that of communication, whatever was held to occur when the sacraments were administered and whether the minister was held to be performing a sacred or simply a social act. Communication in fact was strengthened in its modern meaning: instead of an act of communion, in which the bread enters the worshiper's mouth and becomes mystical Flesh, it was an act of information, in which the Word enters the worshiper's ear and becomes faith in the Spirit. There are a great many senses in which the Reformation was the revolt of the Word of God against the Body of Christ, compelling revision and, in some cases (although not all), diminution or abandonment of the creed that the Word had become Flesh.

Complicated politics ensued.[4] In most medieval ecclesiologies, the Church, claiming that it alone was the vehicle of incarnation, had claimed sole exercise of Christ's continuing authority to command as king or judge in the affairs of this world. But it was inherent in Augustine's original dualism of cities that the authority to command existed in nations that had never heard of Christ, Moses, or Abraham and, although it could not redeem, was rooted in the nature of unredeemed man: whether only in that of fallen man or in that of unfallen man as well was a question emphasized by Aristotle's teaching that authority is natural. The partisans of the *imperium* could therefore challenge the Church with Christ's saying that his kingdom is not of this world and deny that churchmen could exert magisterial authority. But they had to decide whether they meant that the kingdom of this world is God's kingdom in some other sense or that it is not; whether it is natural or artificial; whether it exists in all human societies, irrespective of Christ's presence among them; whether it forms part of the work of redemption or not; whether it is a necessary consequence of human sinfulness, or a mere bundle of convenient devices; in the last analysis, whether it claims an authority derivable from God or is prepared to do without it. The more the kings and magistrates of Protestant Christendom denied the authority of the Church, the more deeply they needed authority immediately from God. They found it in claiming that the preaching of the Word required administration, decision, and judgment; that these things were the province of magistracy; and that God, in sending his Word into the world, had sent magistrates with *imperium* to administer and decide concerning it. What occurred in the consecration of the elements, or had occurred at the Incarnation of Christ, was a matter for judgment.

To this, some Protestant clergies replied that the Word had been entrusted by God to apostles and ministers and that although they did not claim any secular *imperium,* authority over the Word and the congregations who met to hear it and receive the assurance of grace was theirs *jure divino*. It came to be a central question in England, Scotland, and some American colonies whether such *jure divino* clergies could be admitted or whether they required license from the magistrate (king, Parliament, governor, assembly), whose no less divine right to judge in this world extended over them and made theirs *jure humano* rather than *divino*. In England, the matter had been predetermined insofar as the Church of England was a church by law established. This – it seems arguable – was the central issue of Protestant religious politics. Paine, Jefferson, and Priestley, as we know, could see no difference between divine right in the clergy and in the magistracy, and thought both the product of monkish superstition; but I question how well Paine and Jefferson understood the history of the Reformation. Priestley is another matter, and an examination of his writings on the subject might well have been on the agenda of this conference.

But at this point – especially at a point where Priestley's name has been mentioned – it is necessary to return to the Protestant Reformation, which founded the priesthood of all believers on the Word rather than on the Flesh, on the preaching of the Word as a means to the action of grace and salvation by faith alone. Faith, it was said, comes by hearing; the Word awakens faith and opens it to the assurance of grace. But this meant that the communication of the Word is with the Spirit, or, in other terminology, that the Word is the vehicle by which the Spirit of God (the Third Person of the Trinity) communicates with the soul of the believer. Individuals may study the Word and receive the Spirit by its means, but the Word is preached to congregations of believers, who thus become congregations in and even of the Spirit. But the Spirit bloweth where it listeth; it is harder to bring under magisterial control than is the Flesh or even the Word, and when it has taken hold of an individual or a congregation, it may become the light by which they read the Word and interpret it. We hear next that the letter killeth, but the Spirit maketh alive; there is an antinomian tendency that avers that although the Spirit comes by means of the Word, it ceases to be determined by it and can put it aside or even negate it.[5]

This is a moment of great and terrifying importance. The minister and the magistrate can claim authority over the preaching of the Word, but not over the movements of the Spirit; they have good reason to set themselves against the antinomian and enclose the Spirit within the Word (or even the Flesh), whence it came; even the doctrine that the Word is a system of signs shared among social beings who communicate by its means may tell on the side of magisterial authority. The antinomian congregation, claiming to communicate by means of the Spirit, will repudiate ministerial or magisterial authority over it; but the congregation must now decide what the Spirit authorizes it to do with respect to that authority and its *imperium*. The congregation may simply claim exemption from it in the name of the Spirit; but the members are themselves social, political, historical, and, indeed, material beings, and does the Spirit enjoin them to nothing with respect to the Flesh organized according to these forms? They face a choice between the quietism that says that Christ's kingdom is not of this world, and the millennialism (let us call it) that says that Christ's kingdom – often now termed the Spirit's – is yet to come, that there will be a time when the affairs of this world are taken up into the Spirit and organized as it requires. (The social experience and aspirations of the congregation are extremely likely to affect its ideas of how this will be.) There are, of course, innumerable mixtures and gradations between the quietist and millennialist extremes; but if we suppose a magistrate observing a congregation hesitant between the two, there can be no doubt which he would prefer it to adopt. He might even take its claim to exemption from his authority under the protection of his *imperium,* and inform the congregation that he renounces all authority over it so long as its members consent to act as private and not public beings; their kingdom is not of this world. There remain two questions: on what grounds might or should the congregation accept this relegation to privacy, and what would be its understanding of the Spirit when it is expelled from the world? What would be the magistrate's understanding of his own authority when he has so decisively separated it from that of the Spirit? Neither question can receive simple or will receive unconfused answers.

II

The first English Civil War, to the considerable extent that it was a war of religion, was a consequence of the English Reformation. This had been in the first instance an act of state, imperial rather than Protestant in character, in which the king had annexed all magistracy and jurisdiction over the Church in his kingdom, without claiming for himself any sacerdotal character. To claim this was not to separate church from state or to subject church to state; the Church was ruled by judges as well as by priests, and the king as supreme head and judge of the Church within his realm was Christ's representative in that capacity. Henry was by no means unlike Constantine, equal to the apostles and exercising an episcopal jurisdiction without being a bishop or claiming a bishop's power to consecrate; in governing both Church and realm, however, bishops were his officers. We are not intolerably far, here, from understanding Thomas Paine's later claim that monarchy was the popery of politics. Henry could say that he was not a pope because he knew he was not a priest, but the question had now to be asked: what was a priest in Henry's realm, where he retained a power to consecrate and ordain but exercised no jurisdiction except that which the king gave him? What was the authority to consecrate if it was derived from no authority to judge in either pope or king? The English Reformation coinciding with the Protestant, it followed that many English priests dealt with this dilemma by redefining themselves as Protestant ministers, whose authority was less to consecrate elements than to preach the Word while exercising jurisdiction as lesser magistrates under the king. This did not mean that magistracy ceased to be inherent in the Church; only that it was inherent in the Church as ruled and defined by the supreme headship of the king.[6]

Other consequences followed. In order to delimit the sacerdotal and magisterial function in Church government, it came to be widely argued that certain things were *adiaphora,* matters of indifference, not necessary to salvation, and that over these the magistrate, which was to say the king, retained jurisdiction. The idea that there are points in religion over which worshipers may dispute and disagree without imperiling their salvation is so central to our ideas of religious freedom and tolerance that we must positively compel ourselves to remember that the *adiaphora* were defined not in order to exempt them from magisterial authority, but to establish royal authority by extending it over them. They were questions of public order and discipline, and therefore subject to the magistrate. At the same time, however, the definition of some things as *adiaphora* logically entailed the definition of those other things that are necessary to salvation; and in a Protestant universe, these could not simply be restricted to the consecration of the elements that maintain the presence of the Flesh in the world. The Word was to bring faith and the assurance of grace; and the Word conveyed doctrines, commands, prophecies, and covenants, some of which were assuredly necessary to salvation if salvation meant anything at all. Where the *adiaphora* left off, the magistrate's jurisdiction might cease; what then took its place? The authority of the clergy preaching the Word? of the congregation seeking the Spirit? of the individual seeking the assurance of salvation? And who was to determine the boundaries between things necessary and not necessary to salvation? It might be held that just as only a judge can disqualify himself, so only the magistrate could determine where his *jurisdictio* and *imperium* reached their limits. And there were enough texts of Scripture proclaiming that the powers that be were ordained by God, that they are to be obeyed not for wrath's but for conscience's sake, that they who resist receive to themselves damnation, and that rebellion is as the sin of witchcraft, to leave it highly probable that obedience in things not necessary to salvation was necessary to salvation itself: you might not be saved by obeying the king, but you might very well be damned for disobeying him. We have to remind ourselves how very deeply and widely such convictions were held.

There also ensued an intensified hatred of priests and of priests of the Roman Church especially. They were already detested by Protestants for intruding themselves and the sacraments of which they said they held the monopoly between the preaching of the Word and the Spirit in the believer; the magistrate as judge in Israel was expected to expel them from this usurpation. They were now further detested for claiming, as ministrants of the Body of Christ, to intrude on the magistrate's judicial power and depose him from it, as Pope Gregory VII had claimed to depose Emperor Henry IV and Pope Sixtus V claimed to depose Queen Elizabeth I. The assertion that the Flesh could thus intrude on the Word – of which the magistrate became the guardian – was taken as evidence of the falsity of the pope's claim to guarantee Christ's presence and exercise the power of the keys. The pope was an antichrist, falsely proclaiming the presence of a Christ who would return only when his Word was fulfilled; the doctrine of transubstantiation was Peter's ultimate denial of his master. It therefore came to appear – and this is particularly evident in England – that the authority of the prince, as supreme governor of the Church and sovereign in all things not necessary to salvation, was the ultimate guarantor of the freedom of the Word and the Spirit from antichristian usurpation. This – in King James I's phrase "the true law of free monarchies" — made the supremacy of the magistrate the species of religious liberty about which the English and Scots cared most deeply at the time of the first American settlements. It also gave the prince's rule apocalyptic significance; as Godly Prince, he had a role to play in the prophesied warfare between the Dragon and the Spirit, and to lessen his authority, even in the name of religion, might be to take Antichrist's part in the last days that might always be at hand.[7]

The first Civil War, then, had the character of a war of religion for two sets of reasons.[8] The activity of William Laud and the bishops of his persuasion convinced some Englishmen that priests were once again seeking to legislate for the Church along lines not consonant with the supremacy of the Word, and therefore held a view of their own authority not consonant with the judicial supremacy of the king as head of the Church and as Godly Prince. To this antichristian prelacy, the king himself had calamitously become a convert; from the Godly Prince, he was on the way to becoming the Man of Blood. Militants like John Milton therefore envisaged a final Reformation that would set the Word free from all restrictions on its power, but left unclear the character of the magistrate who would carry this out. There could be a series of substitutions within the framework of Godly Rule: an apostate prince might be deposed by a godly Parliament; an apostate Parliament, by a godly army or people; and an apostate army or people might backslide – as ultimately they did – and choose them a captain back to Egypt. But none of this defined the nature of magistracy or its relation to clergy. There was a Word that must be heard in the Spirit; there were clergy who claimed to be the ministers of the Word, loudly declared themselves to be nothing else than that, and proclaimed their readiness to obey the just judge or godly magistrate when he should be known. But if – as seemed to be the case – he was not yet known, must he not be identified by his readiness to further the Word? And who should be the judges of that? If the ministers, then were they not asserting control over how the Word should reach the Spirit and offending against the priesthood of all believers: new presbyters, yet but old priests writ large? If, however, the only recourse was to the whole body of all who held magistracy – from the king and the peerage down to the lords of manors, the freemen of boroughs, and the fathers of families – must they not be judges of themselves, and must not the evident ungodliness of most of them be preferred to the priesthood that would be usurped by any of the godly who might put themselves forward in that role and, by that very act, prove the falsity of their claim to godliness? The dilemma of Reformation became insoluble and intolerable. Hobbes's *Leviathan* is one attempt to escape from it, and a great part of what we call toleration and freedom of religion is another.

While all this was going on – and, indeed, at the very outset of the Civil War and providing another set of reasons that made it a war of religion – there appeared congregations and sects willing to put forward, in various forms, the antinomian claim that the presence of the Spirit among them emancipated them in one sense or another not only from the priests of the Flesh, but also from the ministers of the Word and the magistrates of judicial order. Some claimed that the Spirit authorized them to interpret the Word and the law, others that it abolished both the Word and the law and set them free to act only as it moved them; there is an uncontrollable variety of positions of this sort, and we have to abbreviate it. Many of these sectarians had never exercised magistracy or expected to; they were the mechanic preachers, women prophets, and unintelligible Welshmen whose prevalence as early as 1642 convinced many godly gentry that even the rule of bishops was preferable to this. There was more than class antagonism at work here; what the magisterial classes already feared, and were to fear much more, was the Spirit set free from the Word and the law, drastically criticizing, reinterpreting, and negating all the structures of religion and society. We are often warned – and in many ways rightly – against overestimating the importance of these people in Civil War England; there were not very many of them, and what they did was of less importance than what they said and wrote. They left behind an explosion of fascinating literature and a vivid, if distorted, memory in the minds of the magisterial classes;[9] and we cannot hope to understand the Virginia Statute for Religious Freedom without taking account of them. Some of the princples that the statute lays down are directly indebted to the radical sects for their existence; others, paradoxically, are indebted to the reaction against the sects, although this fact is somewhat obscured by the political and religious circumstances – including the sectarian revival – obtaining in Revolutionary Virginia. We are, therefore, not merely at a turning point in our story, but at a crossroad whose signs are by no means easy to read.

Sects like those of the English interregnum were the first to assert that the magistrate should refrain from interfering in matters of religion, because the operations of belief in human hearts are beyond his competence and cannot be restrained or directed by his coercive power. By this, they meant a number of things that were not necessarily compatible with one another, and words like "toleration" and "religious freedom" do not necessarily provide the umbrella under which all of these can be grouped.[10] They did indeed mean, and plainly assert, that belief must be spontaneous and in that sense free, and cannot be enforced by the sword; but that does not answer the question of what they understood belief to be. Suppose that the author of such a statement meant that the Spirit is immediately present and acting in the hearts of the congregation; when he asserted the Spirit's freedom, he in fact meant that the Spirit's authority is so absolute and mysterious that the magistrate's authority cannot, without blasphemy, be set over it. Must the Spirit not then direct the magistrate in the exercise of his authority? If so, what would the brethren of the free Spirit expect the magistrate to do in the event of some other sect claiming that the Spirit is moving it to incompatible or hostile acts? "Every sect sayeth O give me liberty," Oliver Cromwell is supposed to have observed, "but give it him, and to his power he will not grant it to any other." This is not quite fair; there were sectarians who held that the magistrate should not repress even manifest error, but whether they were asserting a principle of freedom or a tactical preference is another question. Without according error any right to exist, they may have decided against making the magistrate the judge of truth and error; the sword, as the English knew very well by this time, was a double-edged weapon.

But to exile the magistrate from the realm of the Spirit could not be done without consequences.

A magistrate forbidden in the name of the Spirit to coerce belief might find it easiest to suppose that belief is not the action of the Spirit at all. This might move him to reassert his authority over actions that he chose to consider merely human, or it might free him from the intolerable burden of having to decide what was acted by the Spirit and what was not. In times of religious division and diversity, skepticism may reinforce authority by delimiting it as well as by extending it. Thomas Hobbes – notorious for having argued that should a sultan enjoin Muslim public worship, it might be the Christian subject's duty to obey – observed elsewhere in *Leviathan* that Christians in England were reverting to the condition mentioned in the Epistle, where "some follow Paul, some Cephas, and some Apollos," and piously added that this might be according to the purposes "not of them that plant and water, but of God himself that giveth the increase."[11] From anyone but Hobbes, we should take this as an expression of religious liberalism; but we know that Hobbes did not believe in the Spirit, we are not sure that he believed in God, and we see clearly that it was Leviathan's sovereignty that he was laboring to establish. Paul, Cephas, and Apollos must be equally subject to the magistrate, who will not interfere with them so long as they claim no rights against him; and Hobbes tells us that England stands at the end of a historical process in which popes, bishops, presbyters, and congregations have successively failed to establish spiritual monopolies of the interpretation of the Word. Leviathan is now the final judge in such matters, even should he be a sultan;[12] how often he will see fit to exercise his judgment is entirely up to him. Paul, Cephas, and Apollos afford him embarrassment, but also opportunity.

Sects that cry out in the name of the Spirit – they existed in 1649 and 1785, and still exist two hundred years later – face a mirror image of the magistrate's choice regarding sovereignty. They must decide whether they want legislation in the name of the Spirit, or only to be exempt from legislation in the same name; it is akin to the choice between millennialism and quietism, which was mentioned earlier. If they decide that legislation and the Spirit have nothing to do with each other, they must decide in what name legislation is carried on and is to be obeyed. The Spirit may pervade and revolutionize politics or may, by withdrawing, secularize and desacralize them; and here a peculiar importance attaches to some changes in the concept of Spirit itself that occurred among the antinomian sects. Some of them came to hold that there was no Spirit other than that which operated within them, from which it could follow that the Spirit does not exist apart from the human faculties in which it is expressed and the material creation on which these faculties are focused. There arose a theist materialism or atheist spiritualism, in which God was the world and the world, God; in which reason was Spirit and Spirit, reason. To Gerrard Winstanley the Digger, God was "the great Spirit Reason" and could not be known or said to exist apart from what reason could say about the material universe; we debate endlessly whether Winstanley was mystic or atheist.[13] This was very far-out thinking, as far out as the seventeenth century could go; but it was a way of thinking already ancient in folk unbelief, and it is still met with today. What is important about it for our purposes is that it exhibits the Spirit secularizing and desacralizing itself and preparing the way for that all-important change in which religious freedom becomes freedom of religion and, in ceasing to be the freedom of the Spirit, becomes the freedom of reason and opinion.

We find a comparable development among intellectuals belonging to the propertied and magisterial classes. They took up both the Protestant hatred of priests interfering with the operations of faith and the Anglican hatred of priests interfering with the exercise of civil authority, and added a further hatred of priests interfering with the operations of property. A landed clergy, they asserted, prevents the re-creation of a classical citizenry, which bears its own arms and owns the land on which such arms are maintained; a celibate clergy hinders the earth from being peopled and encumbers it with unproductive drones who must be maintained by the industry of others.[14] Whether the goal be ancient virtue or modern productivity, James Harrington's Oceana or Francis Bacon's Great Instauration, the prime necessity is the abolition of all that separates the priest from the citizen, the reabsorption of the clergy by the laity and the sacerdotium by whatever sort of imperium prevails in the society envisaged. The first move in attaining this end is the assertion of the primacy of the Spirit, which restores the priesthood of all believers; but the priesthood of the believer must next be absorbed by his citizenship (whether virtuous or productive), and it follows that the Spirit must be wholly and exclusively expressed in the Flesh. Seventeenth-century materialism, where it existed, was arrived at by the way of Incarnation; but there must be no Body of Christ distinct from the fabric of society, and we begin to move – against a great deal of resistance – toward the point where God and the world are identical. Religion must be civil; it must be the religion of society itself. To some, this doctrine was known as "the religion of nature"; to others, as "the religion of old Rome." It could be a force either ancient or modern.

These late moves in the abortive English revolution – which was still a profound transformation of the role of religion in English society – bring us to the point where "religious freedom" could begin to mean what it meant to Jefferson, Madison, and other Virginians in 1785. There were sects claiming exemption from magisterial authority, and uncertain whether to claim it for themselves, in the name of the Spirit; there were magistrates looking for ways to assert authority and finding themselves helped as well as hindered by the separation of the Spirit from the state; and there were movements afoot that aimed at the total absorption (which need not mean the annihilation) of the Spirit by social practice and social science. Looking back, we are inclined to see a sense in which the Enlightenment had already begun, although nobody knew it yet. This was how matters stood (let us say) when the revolutionary experiment collapsed in England, and the governing classes set grimly about the restoration of magistracy in all its forms over a confessionally divided society.

III

Restoration politics in England present the spectacle of a ruling nobility and gentry more Anglican, with important exceptions, than their king. Charles II was restored mainly at the instigation of presbyterians, a term that in England meant little more than a coalition of conservatives aiming at parliamentary control over congregational and regimental independents. But these followed a profound and unexpected backlash effect, in which the country gentry declared in favor of a rigorous Church Establishment aimed at the repression of all forms of social indiscipline. This meant the restoration of the Church of the royal supremacy; Church and Crown were to reinforce each other's supremacy at all points. And it meant, even in Scotland, a restoration of episcopacy in the form understood by James VI and I. The English ruling classes had lost none of their Erastian hatred of priests claiming to interfere in government *jure divino*. The Virginian solution – an episcopal church without a bishop, controlled by the county and parish gentry – reveals, one suspects, what would have contented many gentlemen in England; but in England, governed immediately by the authority of the Crown, bishops had to be accepted ("no bishop, no king"). They were now careful to avoid the tactical mistakes of the Laudian clergy, from whose ranks many of them had come. A second unexpected development occurred when significant groups of presbyterians and independents – both ministers and their lay followers and patrons – accepted ejection from the Church on St. Bartholomew's Day 1662, and joined with Quakers and other sectarians who managed to survive the persecutions of the decade to constitute the so-called Dissenting interest. They were enough to destabilize Restoration politics. There followed an era of jockeying for position between the monarchy and certain magnate politicians, competing for the patronage of Dissent, and of intense and important debate over the principles on which Dissent was to be included in or excluded from the civil order. From this there emerged by the end of the century the regime of Toleration, of which the Virginia Statute for Religious Freedom was, if properly considered, a rejection.

The paradox of the matter was that the Church of England, however ardently it desired to subject itself wholly to its supreme head, could never quite trust him: Charles I, Anne, and George III are the only sovereigns of the age of Anglican supremacy who were both born in the Church and wholly committed to it. The parliamentary gentry had imposed a severe and repressive Anglicanism for class reasons of its own; but the restored Stuarts – whether because of their personal leanings toward a Gallican type of Catholicism, or in response to the schism of 1662 – held the Anglican interest, dominant though they knew it to be, too narrow a power base to secure their own rule, and from 1660 to 1688 experimented at intervals with a policy of Indulgence, which would make the Crown the protector of the Catholic and Dissenting minorities. Indulgence was therefore a separation of church and state, although not of state and religion. The Crown, clinging to its *jure divino* status, declared the Established Church of which it was head an insufficient although a necessary basis for its own authority; its posture was *politique*. But the Anglican gentry remained in control of Parliament, and the fact that Indulgence had to be imposed by prerogative permitted a revival of the constitutional issues of Charles I's reign before the Civil Wars. Although the basic confrontation was that between Anglicanism and Dissent, the further fact that Indulgence extended the royal protection to Catholics permitted revival of the fear that the Crown was about to sell out to priestly enemies of its own authority. We must remind ourselves that the Anglican gentry who resisted the policy of Indulgence were, again for class reasons of their own, convinced and even fanatical supporters of the absolute and sacred authority of the Crown. What the history of England would have been like if Charles II, James II, or James Edward the Old Pretender had been or had become committed members of the Anglican Church we cannot say; but it would not have been Whig.

Given the fact of the Dissenting schism, there were three political possibilities. One was persecution, the use of coercion by state and church to compel the Dissenters to return to the established discipline. The second was comprehension, the achievement of the same aim by agreement and concession. The third was Indulgence, the policy preferred by the kings. None of these corresponds at all closely to Toleration, as it became a principle of the Whig regime in the eighteenth century; or to tolerance, as a recommended attitude in the face of religious diversity; or to religious freedom and the separation of church and state, as they came to be established in Virginia and the United States of America. Of the three, Indulgence comes closest to Toleration, as it was practiced in the eighteenth century; there was to be a national church, with certain recognized exceptions protected by a special policy of the state. But after the Anglican gentry in Parliament imposed the Test Act on Charles II and made communion in the Established Church a requisite for holding Crown or corporation office, Indulgence became largely a means of making exceptions to this principle; and it was James II's policy of promoting Catholics to high office that brought down what might otherwise have been a workable solution.[15] The Toleration Act, which followed the fall of James II, was a parliamentary preemption of a limited Indulgence: it was a statute instead of an exercise of prerogative; it retained and reinforced the Test Act; and it offered Dissenters freedom of worship in exchange for exclusion from civil office. Persecution and comprehension disappeared from the scene, and it was not the issue of religious toleration, but of religious indifference to civil rights and political indifference to religious belief, that was asserted in the Virginia Statute for Religious Freedom and the United States Bill of Rights.

The king in all these political changes faced a difficult problem in self-definition. He could not head a regime of prerogative Indulgence or parliamentary Toleration without intimating that it was insufficient for him to be supreme head of the Church of England; still less when he found himself at the head of other realms where that Church was not established. William III was head of an episcopal church in England, but in Scotland, a presbyterian regime was busy persecuting episcopacy when it did not tolerate it; Queen Anne, that good daughter of the Church, found the Union with Scotland in 1707 a bitter pill to swallow. But if the king was not at one and the same time and in one and the same sense a civil and a religious magistrate, what was he? To proclaim himself a civil sovereign whose authority had roots independent of the relations of his subjects to God was very close in that age to proclaiming himself a Hobbesian Leviathan, and Hobbism was feared less because it led to despotism than because it might lead to atheism or, by a back door, to the pantheism of some radical sects. Yet the gentry and clergy bent on maintaining the Anglican supremacy had no desire to proclaim the king either a godly prince or a vicar of Christ. The former threatened a revival of Puritanism; the latter, a return to Rome; and some of the most rigorous High Churchmen found it difficult to answer the charge that they were Hobbists in disguise. As for some of those who were to emerge, as did

Shaftesbury and Locke, as the champions of a parliamentary toleration, they were moved less by a regard for freedom than by a hatred of clerical interference with civil government, and were not indifferent to the possibility that the royal prerogative might be exercised on their side. They were responsive in their own way to the Hobbism latent in theories of Indulgence and Toleration.

The crucial move toward an attitude on these matters that we should call liberal – there was as yet no equivalent to our definition of the term – was made by those who then, as now, were termed Latitudinarians, although this word, too, is not easy to apply with precision. Whether clerics or laymen, they saw the Anglican settlement to which they adhered as threatened on the one side by a revival of the claim that the Church is a spiritual body divorced from secular society, descending directly from Christ and communicated by his sacraments, and on the other side by renewed assertions that the Spirit is immediately active in the congregations or sects of worshipers. The former led to what was termed "priestcraft," a manipulative monopoly of the means of Incarnation; the latter, to what was termed "enthusiasm," an alleged ubiquity of the unmediated Spirit. A Machiavellian, a Hobbist, or an atheist sovereignty might emerge to exploit the confusion between the two. The Latitudinarians, accordingly, set about reintegrating the divine with the world in which it operated, aiming at denial of the extremes on either hand. Some of them – although the identification of Latitudinarians with Cambridge Platonists does not stand up well to close scrutiny – found in Platonism a means of asserting the immanence of the divine in a world rationally understood; but there came a reaction (in which persecuting High Churchmen were especially prominent) that declared Plato, with his ideas and real essences, his allegories and mysticism, the spiritual father of both priestcraft and enthusiasm at the same time – a point to which we must return in order to understand the religious thought of Thomas Jefferson. There was a tendency among Latitudinarians – to tell the story in the simplest of terms – to move from Plato to Newton, from the immanence of divine reason in the world to the evidence of laws through which the world is ruled by a God who cannot possibly be confounded with his own creation.[16]

Their aim was to establish a rational and sociable religion, which would offer no grounds for priests to rule the world in the name of a special authority or for prophets to illuminate and transform it in the name of a special freedom. It would be a religion of practical morality rather than theological, ecclesiological, or political speculation – one practiced by holy living and holy dying in this world, not by erecting principles on which to rule or rebel against it. To accept the practice and usage of the reasonable social world was to accept the world's authorities, including the authority of its magistrates; but it was the aim of moderate religion to avoid rigorous and disputatious definitions, even of authority itself, in the belief that it would be more effectively asserted when asserted in a moderate form. In questions of doctrine and discipline, the Latitudinarian impulse again was to avoid dispute and approach dissentience in an eirenic and even an ecumenical spirit. The literature of theology tended to become a historical literature, in which disputes were narrated and explored rather than pursued. There arose a willingness to treat profound questions of theology as matters on which reasonable men might disagree, which were perhaps too profound for the human mind to resolve – a tolerance and moderation that, however admirable we find them, we must remember were arrived at for reasons rather conservative than liberal, and arose from a determination that the clergy should not drive themselves by dispute into making either priestly or prophetic claims that would prove fatal to their authority as social functionaries. In many ways, these Anglicans were reverting to adiaphorism; but instead of elevating the magistrate to the status of God's judge and instrument, and so preparing the way for an antinomian reaction, they were declining to define his office with rigor, thus sharing the Whiggish tendency to lodge authority in manners before magistracy, practice before politics. A magistrate, however, who was willing to practice moderation had little to fear for his authority and was well placed to enjoin dissenting sects to accept Toleration and exclusion from civil office when it was judged proper, on civil or ecclesiastical grounds, that such offices be reserved for members of the national church.

If there was no national church, the magistrate could have no sacred office; but there could be no national church if the church were a mere association of reasonable worshipers holding the same doctrines. This is one of a number of points at which we discover John Locke, once considered the accredited reigning philosopher of the Whig and Latitudinarian order, holding positions that were a little too radical for that order to approve. It was probably as the author of the *Essay Concerning Human Understanding* and (when these became known to be his) the *Letters on Toleration* that Locke enjoyed his greatest prestige in the eighteenth century; the *Treatise on Government* (also unacknowledged in his lifetime) may have ridden on the back of his renown as a philosopher. At every point in his writings, we can find Locke's inveterate anticlericalism carrying him to the brink of doctrines that Church and Parliament would be obliged to disown. He was certain that the being of God can be known and rationally demonstrated, as he was sure that it had been revealed that Jesus was the Christ and Messiah; but in reducing the necessities of

Christian belief to these two propositions, he came close to reducing all religious experience to an experience of knowing, an operation of the rational mind. He therefore held the utmost contempt for priests who intruded themselves on the mind's operations – where they had little function and no authority – and for the distinctions, definitions, and dogmas that they sought to impose on the mind and that, when they were not nonsense, could be no more than matters of opinion. The mind must indeed form opinions. It proceeded by making judgments concerning the evidence presented to it by the senses and by experience; but where these judgments were not demonstrable (as many were not), they could be no more than probable, habitual, or warranted by authority. The varieties of religious experience (to use William James's later phrase) issued in a variety of religious opinions; the variety of religious opinions could be accounted for only by the variety of religious experience; and experience was nothing other than the reception of diverse information, on which the mind acted to form a diversity of judgments.[17]

We have reached a moment of profound change in the definition of religion itself, one that is altogether crucial to our understanding of the opening words of Jefferson's preamble to the Virginia Statute of Religious Freedom and, to that extent, of the statute itself. Hitherto, religion had been about the operations of God in the world, the operations of the Word in becoming Flesh or in becoming the vehicle of the Spirit. It had been about Incarnation and inspiration, and belief had been defined as the product of the experience of one or other of these operations. Where freedom to hold diverse beliefs had been denied (as it generally had), it had been on the grounds that the nature of God's operations in these respects had been made known; where the same freedom had been affirmed (as was beginning to happen), it had been on the grounds that the uniqueness and mystery of God's operations, and the responses to them of the Spirit in the individual worshiper, were beyond the magistrate's competence and must be left to proceed spontaneously. Freedom of religion had been the freedom to experience God; this had left unsolved many problems of definition and so of authority. But the effect of many changes taking place at the end of the seventeenth century – among which the appearance of Lockean philosophy is rather prominent – was to redefine religion as the holding of opinions, religious experience as the formation of opinions, and religious freedom as the freedom to hold, form, and profess opinions concerning the operations, the attributes, and even the existence of God – a great victory for the intellectualization of experience. Without this victory, it is doubtful if religious experience could ever have been defined in such a way as to present a radical claim to freedom; but the price paid was that it had to be redefined as the formation and holding of opinions concerning one's own religious experience, and the opinions tended to substitute themselves for the experience and even the religion. There was freedom of belief and freedom of experience on a scale never claimed or legislated before; but the belief and the experience were now only matters of opinion.

IV

In the opening words of Jefferson's preamble to the Virginia Statute of Religious Freedom, the General Assembly of Virginia is made to profess itself "well aware that the opinions and belief of men depend not on their own will, but follow involuntarily the evidence proposed to their minds"; and only after this outspoken (but, in the event, not printed) profession of determinism, to proceed to the certainly more often quoted words "that Almighty God hath created the mind free, and manifested his supreme will that free it shall remain by making it altogether insusceptible of restraint"[18] – the freedom consisting, we must suppose, of freedom to follow the involuntary dictates of the evidence that the Almighty has willed that the mind shall encounter. The problem of free will and determinism is an ancient one and was being discussed during Jefferson's lifetime by his correspondent Joseph Priestley;[19] we should not suppose that means do not exist of rendering the first two statements of the statute philosophically reconcilable. But it is apparent that we are dealing here with Jefferson the future *idéologue,* the reader of Destutt de Tracy who would try to make the science of ideology, the science of how the mind (or was it the brain?) generates ideas and opinions, one of the principal divisions of the curriculum of the University of Virginia. Perhaps some authority on the history of this university will tell us what became of this part of Jefferson's proposals; I do not think it was of lasting effect. The fundamental premise of the Virginia Statute, at all events, is that religion is a system of opinions and that opinions are formed in the mind. The rest of the preamble is the rhetoric of this premise.

But it would be vain and unwelcome to expound this premise to those who believed they had experienced, or were seeking to experience, the immediately pentecostal action of the Spirit: radical sects in Commonwealth London, Baptist revivalists in Revolutionary Virginia,[20] or born-again Christians in the twentieth-century United States – such as that distinguished resident of Lynchburg, the Reverend Jerry Falwell, whom I seriously suggest ought to be with us today, since the historical study of the statute is incomplete if we do not take account of his variety of religious experience. To all these, it would appear that to define their spiritual experience as opinion – and opinion involuntarily formed by the evidence proposed to their minds – was to miss the point and miss it deliberately, to deny that the Spirit was acting on and in them. And so indeed it was, and was intended to be. We entirely fail to understand the relations of religion and philosophy in the eighteenth century if we do not comprehend that the view of religion I have been exploring was directed against both the Flesh and the Spirit, against both dogmatic priesthoods and the revolutionary spiritualism of the sects, against both superstition and enthusiasm, and that it was only the historical accidents of the 1770s and 1780s that permitted Jefferson and Madison to define the Virginia Statute of Religious Freedom as directed against priesthood and superstitions only.

At the end of the seventeenth century, reasonable religion among conservative Protestant elites, such as the English Latitudinarians or the Scottish Moderates a half-century later, had been intended, in ways that make it hard to distinguish from the rational deism that appeared alongside it, to protect the established clerisies against the authority of Rome, the anarchy of the sects, or the overreaction of anticlerical erastianism to either of them.[21] It had therefore developed a view of religion as so far bound up with the culture and discipline of society as to preclude the transforming action of God in either the sacraments of the Church or the prophesyings of the congregation. This had not prevented the recurrent appearance of enthusiastic sects: the Moravians and the Methodists, the Great Awakening and the Virginia revivals. But it had established among the cultivated classes an identification of Christ's gospel with the normal discipline of human society so complete as to incur the reproach of "Socinianism," as was (rather inaccurately) termed any theology that tended to make Christ a rational being rationally understood, to deny his divinity or his co-substantiality with his Father, or to deny that he had brought any message beyond rational theology, philosophy, and morality (with obedience to law and authority entailed in the last). The Church was not the body of such a Christ, but an association of worshipers sharing this rational view of him; it might reinforce the normal authority by which the magistrate enforced social discipline, or it might have neither art nor part in a magistracy that owed the Church nothing for its existence. Such had been the view of Bishop Hoadly of Bangor, who (although no Socinian) had horrified his brethren and delighted the anticlerical faction among the Whigs with his denial that the Church possessed corporate authority of any kind whatever. But if there was no *civitas Dei* on a pilgrimage through this world, then the *civitas terrena* could equally claim no share in the processes of redemption, and it was doubtful if these could be located anywhere. Such a religion might look to a future state of rewards and punishments, but could scarcely claim to be the vehicle of a redemptive communion with God. Sects therefore arose that offered to discharge this role.

Such were the more obviously "Socinian" effects of a religion of civility that tended to reduce Christianity to a civil religion. But the history of what was termed "Socinianism" did not end there. If there was nothing especially new about Christ's teaching – if Christianity was "reasonable" (Locke), "not mysterious" (Toland), "as old as the creation" (Tindal) – he must have taught the current version of a natural religion as old as mankind; and ingenious archaeologists of the mind were ready to trace this religion back to the Druids or the Chaldeans, the Egyptians or the Chinese. They were also prepared to expound this religion as having been libertine and Spinozistic, hermetic and pantheistic, based on that identity between the Creator and his Creation that had attracted the radicals of the English interregnum and continues to find exponents to this day.[22] The Masonic lodges, to which not a few Revolutionary Americans belonged, contained many adherents of this "religion of nature"; and when Jefferson denied that Christianity formed any part of the ancient common law of England, which was as ancient as the Saxons,[23] it is permissible to ask what religion he thought the Saxons had practiced. However, anything Spinozistic or pantheistic could be and was condemned as threatening a revival of enthusiasm, of the belief that the Spirit is equally incarnate in all men (and even women, added Ann Lee and Joanna Southcott); and a Voltairean deism or Humean skepticism acted at this point to reinforce the caution of the moderate clerics in condemning superstition and enthusiasm alike. The belief that the Spirit was incarnate in a few sacred objects or persons reinforced the authority of priests; the belief that it was incarnate in anybody and everybody ensured the anarchy of enthusiasm; the mutation of one belief into the other constantly occurred. David Hume permitted himself to believe that there might be happy periods in which enthusiasm, having destroyed priestcraft, would burn itself out and give place to the perception that all beliefs were merely opinions; but he did not believe that such periods would last very long. The human mind, for all Hume could see, was inveterately religious and alternated between superstition and enthusiasm.[24]

If Jefferson had not hated Hume so much, as the ideologist of the Whig regime in Great Britain, he might have found much to attract him in Hume's ideas about the history of religion. I do not see much evidence that Jefferson believed in a Spinozistic religion of nature, and unlike both the neo-Stoics and the neo-Epicureans of the age, he seems to have retained a belief in personal immortality. Hume, of course, did not; but the notion that religion progressed from polytheism to scientific enlightenment – which could be learned from Hume, whatever his doubts about the finality of the progress – would have appealed to Jefferson, as did the doctrine that both priestcraft and enthusiasm were perpetuated by the philosophers of antiquity (especially Plato). And when Jefferson laid down that the way to deal with religious dispute was to take no notice of it, he was repeating in the name of religious freedom the advice that libertine philosopers had always been giving to the secular magistrate – magistracy being now, in Jefferson's view, diffused through the whole body of the people. The possibility of repressive tolerance has at least appeared: "I defend your right to say what you like," he is telling the believer, "but I shall take no notice of it and give you no answer." Silence is his weapon in the confusion of tongues; what happens if the speaker requires an answer is a new problem in the politics of speech. Or perhaps not; Constantine may be said to have encountered it at the Council of Nicaea.

As practiced in Whig England (and in another way in Scotland), moderate religion had been part of the ideology of a regime founded equally on the Toleration Act and the Test Act. It had affirmed the separation of Dissenting sects from a national clergy and magistracy, while protecting both from having to become, or to answer to, either the priests of the Incarnate Word or the prophets of the Gift of Tongues. What it encountered in the 1770s and 1780s, both in England and in Virginia, was a limited (and in Virginia, a successful) counterrevolution on the part of those who were not contented with toleration at the hands of a state from which they were partly excluded and who demanded a disestablishment of religion and a "separation of church and state" not merely on the grounds that the claim to civil rights was autonomous and absolute, but also in the name of a conception of the Christian religion unlike any with which the debate of the Restoration period had had to reckon seriously. It is of much significance that this initiative was taken less by representatives of the Old Dissent than by exponents of Unitarianism and beliefs akin to it, for those who did not believe that Jesus was a Person of the Trinity who had taken on flesh for the redemption of mankind did not have to concern themselves with the modes of his continuing presence in this world.

When Edmund Burke delivered and published his *Speech on Conciliation with America,* he gave, among the reasons for considering America a distinctive political culture that should receive distinctive treatment, the existence in the colonies of what he called "the dissidence of dissent, the protestantism of the Protestant religion," and characterized as a religion of free enquiry, whose proponents "agreed in very little except the principles of liberty." They held, in short, that religion consists of inquiry into the attributes of God, not of beliefs concerning them, and that this inquiry cannot be expected to reach finality in this world, if in the next. They had gone beyond the principle expressed in the preamble to the Virginia Statute, that religious opinion should be free and the subject of free enquiry, to the principle that free inquiry into belief is of the nature of belief and of the nature of religion itself. Burke's most intelligent critic, Josiah Tucker, the Dean of Gloucester, described them as "the modern new-light men," who protested against everything and would protest against themselves and their own opinions if they could find nothing else to protest against – a splenetic but not an unfair characterization. Tucker added that persons of this persuasion were not confined to the colonies; they were to be found in England among the followers of Richard Price and Joseph Priestley, who were then agitating for the repeal of the Test Act, and he suspected Burke of forwarding a design to keep the colonies within the empire until the number of such new believers was great enough to take it over.[25]

Burke and Tucker had, in their different ways, perceived that what they had to do with was not a postreligious phenomenon or a simple assertion that all religion lies outside the competence of the state, but a highly specific assertion that the nature of religion consists of free inquiry into the constitution of the universe. They were not dealing with Spinozistic pantheists, but it is arguable that they were dealing with their descendants. Joseph Priestley's laboratory at Northumberland, Pennsylvania, was in fact a temple to the Unitarian view of how God operates in his universe, and John Adams in old age joined with Jefferson in denouncing Athanasians and speculating humorously on the probable origins of all religious metaphysics among the Hindus.[26] They would all have understood without difficulty that passage in Jefferson's autobiography that reads,

> Where the preamble declares that coercion is a departure from the plan of the holy author of our religion, an amendment was proposed, by inserting the word(s) "Jesus Christ," so that it should read "a departure from the plan of Jesus Christ, the holy author of our religion." The insertion was rejected by a great majority, in proof that they meant to comprehend, within the mantle of its protection, the Jew and the Gentile, the Christian and Mahometan, the Hindoo and the infidel of every denomination.[27]

If this really happened, I much doubt that the General Assembly was concerned about the freedom of Jews, Muslims, and Hindus to worship in Virginia or thought that their freedom would be worse off if placed under Jesus's protection. It seems far more likely that Unitarians, Socinians, and other kinds of deist and humanist had the votes. Unitarianism in the strict New England sense had not yet appeared in Virginia, but advanced Episcopalian clergy and laity were moving in very similar directions, and Jefferson in later years would look forward (vainly) to a time when all educated youth would adopt it.

V

Jesus Christ being now taken away by vote of the General Assembly of Virginia (if what Jefferson recalled be true), as in former times purgatory had been taken away by act of the Parliament of England – does anyone know what the leaders of revivalism in Virginia thought of this vote if they heard of it? – we must consider what to say about the Virginia Statute for Religious Freedom in its historical context. It is a product of the Protestant Enlightenment, which was itself occasioned very largely by the very Protestant determination to maintain the rights of the civil magistrate and civil society; and there was in Protestantism a very strong tendency toward self-secularization and even de-Christianization. On the radical, or enthusiastic, side, the Spirit could substitute itself for Christ and then convert itself into the powers latent in humanity. On the magisterial, or "Socinian," side, Christianity could be transformed into a purely civil and reasonable religion as old as mankind. It is the magisterial tendency that is evident in Jefferson's preamble declaring religious beliefs to be opinions, and in his often-expressed conviction that Jesus was a teacher of deism and that they who thought so were better Christians than were all the churches that had proclaimed him a divine being. This tendency could develop out of an otherwise orthodox reasonable religion, which had been taught by Anglican Latitudinarian clergy and other members of Protestant elites, engaged in resisting priesthood on the one hand and sectarianism on the other; they had been aware of the "Socinian" danger latent in their doctrines, but had not always been able to check it. If religion is no more than opinion, the magistrate could afford to tolerate it; if he could not be trusted to do so, his authority must be absorbed into that of a liberal society in which the obligation to respect opinion could be made absolute. The Virginia Statute for Religious Freedom, incidentally, is not the end of this process. Since, as Jefferson never tired of saying, the earth belongs to the living, statutes can always be revoked; the separation of church and state had to be written into the Bill of Rights and the Constitution, in order to place it as far out of reach of the sovereignty of the living as possible. The liberalization of magistracy is an unending battle.

The paradox of the statute is that the drafting of this highly "enlightened" and "Socinian" measure coincided with the appearance of a popular religious revival in parts of Virginia. The conventional assumption among historians seems to be that the statute was indebted to the revival and allied with it, that the revival challenged the Anglican supremacy, and that the Henry–Nicholas proposal to give public funds to all Christian denominations alike, which the statute defeated, was a disguised attempt to preserve that supremacy. I must leave it to specialists in Virginia history to tell us whether this reading is correct. But the premise that religious convictions are opinions involuntarily formed in the mind, on which Jefferson's preamble bases the statute as a whole, is not, never can be, and never has been intended to be satisfactory to the pentecostal understanding of religious revival, in which Jesus and the Holy Ghost are held to be immediately, imminently, and experientially present to and in the congregation. Since pentecostal religion is built into the structure of American society and is a powerful force in the present day, it is highly important that its freedom from state interference is legislated in a historic document that formally declares it to be much less than it believes itself to be; the liberation of religion entailed a minimization of religion. If our neighbor from Lynchburg were present at this conference, and if he holds (as they say he does) that there exists a "secular humanist" ideology bent on denying the necessity of any specific religion, he is, of course, perfectly correct in this belief; but he might be obliged to recognize that "secular humanism" is active and vocal in the Virginia Statute for Religious Freedom itself. Freedom of religion and freedom from religion had by the time of the statute's framing become close partners, and have remained so.

The doctrine that belief is only opinion, and opinion only *idéologie* in a Lockean and Destuttian sense, was formulated wherever there were Protestant elites anxious to moderate and control – if necessary by tolerating them – those who held that Christ is really present in either the sacraments or the congregation. The literature of this doctrine shows it to have been consistently opposed to enthusiasm as well as to sacerdotalism. It is therefore a question why Jefferson consistently gave it an antisacerdotal cast, to the point where he seems to say little of its companion tendency. I must leave it to Jeffersonian specialists to tell us what he thought of popular religious enthusiasm – I should be surprised to learn that he liked it, and if he welcomed it, he may have done so in a spirit more Humean than he cared to admit – and whether we are to view the matter in terms of political tactics; was it because Jefferson was allied with the sects against the establishment that he attacked his opponents as sacerdotal and said little of his allies as enthusiastic?[28] This would raise the larger question of the politics of the statute: why did a gentry-dominated Assembly choose to unmake its religious establishment at a time of revolution and revival, and was there a design of replacing a sacerdotal ascendancy with a secular and "Socinian" one, equally efficacious in moderating the sects? These are only speculative questions, and I do not know if they are well posed.

Our neighbor from Lynchburg might further observe that "secular humanism," at least at the end of the eighteenth century, was significantly religious in character. Josiah Tucker, that neglected genius, held that the American Revolution was religious in origin, a phenomenon of the later history of Protestantism; from the Puritan error that dominion was founded in grace, the colonists had moved to the Lockean error that moral personality was a sufficient foundation for a claim to civil rights. He specifically associated this with "the protestantism of the Protestant religion," the Unitarian religion of free inquiry, which saw God as immanent in his universe and denied Jesus any central role in maintaining his presence. The man from Lynchburg might deny that this is Christian, but should not deny that it is a religion and an enthusiastic one at that; perhaps we have here another reason for Jefferson's employment of only the sacerdotal horn of the dilemma on which Hume had tried to impale religion. He would be in good company, of many generations' standing, if he further pointed out that this is a religion liable to proceed through pantheism (all things are God) to atheism (there is no separate God); the reproach goes back to the Renaissance, and should oblige him to admit that even atheism can have a religious origin. Deism and Unitarianism are very different in character, but both share in the process whereby freedom of religion was attained through defining religion as something less than its adherents might affirm it to be. The Virginia Statute is not neutral as to religion; it defines it, declaring it to be something – opinion or free inquiry – and denying it to be something else – a presence of Christ as anything more than a historic figure about whom opinions may be held. Our neighbor from Lynchburg is without doubt a good Christian, a good American, and an upholder of the separation of church and state. He must therefore find acceptable, as the cost of religious freedom, a legislative declaration that religion is something less than he believes it to be; I should like to know his estimate of these costs. Whatever they may be, paying them brought to his forebears religious freedom earlier, and on a larger scale, than can be said of the inhabitants of most other Christian or post-Christian communities. Being myself a subject of another such community, I am aware that the American is not the only way of attaining religious freedom, although it possesses advantages of its own.

The story I have been tracing is a political one, the history of the rivalry between Christ and the magistrate, the latter of whom has never been at ease with the institutionalized affirmations of the former's presence. He therefore seeks to deinstitutionalize that presence and render it less immediate, paying as much as he must and as little as he can of the price of relinquishing any role of his own in Christ's redemptive mission; he never quite ceases, even in Virginia, to legislate what that mission and presence shall be, and how they may be maintained in ways consonant with his authority. When organized religion, in fear of its own priests and sects, joins enlightened philosophy in affirming the primacy of civil society and civil reason, it enhances the magistrate's role as representative of both; and when the functions of magistracy are taken over by liberal political society as a whole – which is what happened at the Revolution – the role of magistracy is diffused but not diminished. In America, the relative weakness of established churches spells the importance of pentecostal sects, and religious freedom becomes a matter of arranging the freedom of the sect from the establishment and the freedom of the magistrate (or the liberal state) from either. The Virginia Statute successfully legislates both freedoms; the magistracy is set free from religious imperatives by giving up authority over religion. But at the same time, it describes religion as consisting of free inquiry and the formation of opinions. To describe is not to impose or to give exclusive recognition to the form described; but it is to describe religion in the form to which it is easiest to accord freedom, and it necessarily privileges the view that makes religion consist of freedom. The statute denies nothing, and may accord much, to the pentecostal sects, which affirm the reality of Christ's presence; but at the same time, it says nothing about them, and the view of religion stated in the preamble is not theirs. It may, not impossibly, have the intention of neutralizing them, of guaranteeing them freedom and taking no further interest in their doings. Either the relation between *imperium* and pentecost is not stated at all, or the *imperium* knows the pentecost only as one opinion among others.

It should seem, then, that the statute goes a little way, by a noncoercive route, toward establishing a kind of Unitarian universalism – the religion of free inquiry – not as the official religion of American society, but as that most easily recognized by that society's magistracy and values, and toward regarding the pentecostal sects as a kind of loyal opposition. Organized religions arrive from overseas, with their priesthoods and rabbinates and so forth, and begin to undergo pressures that, if not resisted (they often are), will cause them to be reborn as liberal and undogmatic sects in the late-Protestant image. Pentecostal sects emerge from the provinces and may prove more recalcitrant, partly because they lie deeper in the American grain, being born of the reaction against free inquiry and "secular humanism," partly because the pentecostal wind has not ceased blowing and has been blowing particularly hard in the past few years. But when the pentecostal sects talk of remaking liberal society in Christ's image, the statute and its progeny are there to tell them that this is only bluster; their kingdom is not of this world. The secular magistrate retains his position as the best guarantor of a free society, and has not ceased trying to remake religion according to his own specifications.

Postscript

After attending the conference at which this paper was presented and reflecting on the discussions that there took place, certain points stand out in the writer's mind. The first is the wide gap between the view of Jefferson's preamble here presented and the view, often expressed, that would derive the Virginia Statute's philosophy of religious freedom from such giants of the American past as Roger Williams. This went on until Professor Rhys Isaac arose in his wrath to denounce the imposition of New England categories on the autochthonous history of Virginia. However that may be, it seems clear to the present writer that the freedom of the Spirit is one thing and the freedom of opinion is another, and that although there are ways of seeing the latter as a historical mutation of the former, there are just as many of seeing it as a strategic means of reducing and minimizing the power of the Spirit to disturb the civil order. And here might be found the historical irony of the statute: that its immediate beneficiaries, the Baptists and revivalists, welcomed it enthusiastically (I choose the word with care), in the name of a freedom of the Spirit that its preamble dismisses from serious discussion. The irony was made almost visible on the last evening of the conference, at a reception memorably held on the north terrace at Monticello. The late-afternoon sun shone down on the western face of the building, and a perfect half-moon hung in the blue sky above. Nothing more Newtonian could be imagined, and the domed chamber to which we had been admitted seemed some temple of Sarastro. It was a long way from any camp meeting in the hills.

The preamble to the statute speaks clearly in the voice of the Enlightenment, which held less and less that there was anything that could usefully be said about religion or to its votaries. The doctrine that all is opinion leads by stages to Professor Richard Rorty's somber conclusion that in the liberal society, we should say as little as possible that cannot be tested by the experience of others. Yet the statute and its sequels enduringly legitimate the sectarianisms of America and set the voice of pentecostalism free to affirm that some have had experiences of the Spirit as yet unshared by others. This paper repeatedly and ironically asks why the Reverend Jerry Falwell was not invited from Lynchburg to join the celebration at Charlottesville; it is a way of pointing out that no representative of evangelicalism or fundamentalism was present and that neither the preamble to the statute nor the premises underlying every paper at the conference offered reason to believe that dialogue with such a representative would have been possible. As a friend, although not a citizen, of the Republic, it disturbs me when the beneficiaries of its freedom are presumed incapable of speaking to one another. I wonder what would have happened if the evangelical voice had been heard.

The statute appears to have set religion free (a great gain), while condemning it to unspecificity and, in the end, to undiscussability (surely something of a loss). Discussion, of course, is free; but on the premises of the preamble, what is there to discuss? Rorty's view of the priority of democracy over philosophy seems to accord priority to those for whom the universe has been disenchanted, while according liberty but not dialogue to those for whom the *entzauberung* has not occurred. What happens if the latter form a majority? Their perceptions have been relegated to a private sphere. The critique of liberalism (in which this writer does not usually engage) seems to have something to say. And the statute seems to presuppose – although it cannot ordain or enjoin – that there will always be religion, whose defining characteristic shall be its unspecificity. Burke's "dissidence of dissent . . . agreeing in nothing but the principles of liberty" points directly to the too much derided dictum attributed to President Eisenhower: "Our country is founded on a fundamental religious faith, and I don't care what it is." There does seem to be a sense in which the Virginia Statute has imprinted precisely that character on American religion.

NOTES

1 Herbert Deane, *The Social and Political Ideas of St. Augustine* (New York and London, 1963); Peter Brown, *Augustine of Hippo* (London, 1967); R. A. Markus, *Saeculum: History and Society in the Theology of St. Augustine* (Cambridge, 1970).

2 Charles Till Davis, *Dante and the Idea of Rome* (Oxford, 1957).

3 G. R. Elton, *Reform and Reformation: England, 1509–1558* (Cambridge, Mass., 1977), chap. 8, "The Royal Supremacy."

4 Quentin Skinner, *The Foundation of Modern Political Thought* (Cambridge, 1978), vol. 2 *The Age of Reformation*.

5 G. H. Williams, *The Radical Reformation* (Philadelphia, 1962).

6 A. G. Dickens, *The English Reformation* (New York and London, 1964).

7   William M. Lamont, *Marginal Prynne, 1600–1669* (London, 1963), *Godly Rule: Politics and Religion, 1603–1660* (London, 1969), and *Richard Baxter and the Millennium* (London and Totowa, N.J., 1979).

8   Anthony Fletcher, *The Outbreak of the English Civil War* (London, 1982).

9   Christopher Hill, *The World Turned Upside Down* (Harmondsworth, Eng., 1972).

10 See, nevertheless, W. K. Jordan, *The Development of Religious Toleration in England* (Cambridge, Mass., 1936).

11 *Leviathan*, bk. IV, p. 47.

12 One wonders whether Hobbes ever heard of the apostasy of Sabbatai Zevi and what he thought of it.

13 Hill, *World Turned Upside Down;* Christopher Hill, ed., *Winstanley: The Law of Freedom and Other Writings* (Harmondsworth, Eng., 1973; Cambridge, 1983).

14 I owe much on this subject to Mark Goldie, of Churchill College, Cambridge.

15 J. R. Western, *Monarchy and Revolution: The English State in the 1680s* (London, 1972); J. R. Jones, *The Revolution of 1688 in England* (New York, 1972).

16 Rosalie Colie, *Light and Enlightenment: Cambridge Platonists and Dutch Arminians* (Cambridge, 1957); Margaret C. Jacob, *The Newtonians and the English Revolution, 1689–1780* (Ithaca, N.Y., 1976).

17 Maurice Cranston, *John Locke: A Biography* (London, 1957); John Dunn, *The Political Thought of John Locke* (Cambridge, 1969); Geraint Parry, *John Locke* (London, 1978); Neal Wood, *The Politics of Locke's Philosophy* (Berkeley and Los Angeles, 1983).

18 Thomas Jefferson, *Writings,* ed. Merrill D. Peterson (New York and Cambridge, 1984), p. 346. The first passage quoted is missing from the text in the *Statutes at Large* distributed at the conference. I do not know the legislative history of the statute well enough to say when or how it disappeared.

19 Jack G. Fruchtman, *The Apocalytic Politics of Richard Price and Joseph Priestley: A Study in Late-Eighteenth-Century English Republican Millennialism,* Transactions of the American Philosophical Society, vol. 73, no. 4, 1983.

20 Rhys Isaac, *The Transformation of Virginia, 1740–1790* (Chapel Hill, N.C., 1982).

21 J. G. A. Pocock, "Clergy and Commerce: The Conservative Enlightenment in England," in *L'Eta dei Lumi: Studi Storici nel Settecento Europeo in Onore di Franco Venturi,* ed. R. Ajello et al. (Naples, 1985).

22 Paolo Rossi *The Dark Abyss of Time: The History of the World and the History of Nations from Hooke to Vico,* trans. Lydia G. Cochrane (Chicago, 1985); Margaret C. Jacob, *The Radical Reformation: Pantheists, Freemasons and Republicans* (London, 1981).

23 Jefferson, *Writings,* pp. 1494–5.

24 David Hume, *The Natural History of Religion,* and "Of Superstition and Enthusiasm," in *Essays Moral, Political and Literary,* ed. Eugene F. Miller (Indianapolis: Liberty Press, 1981).

25 Josiah Tucker, *A Letter to the Right Honourable Edmund Burke* (Gloucester,

Eng., 1775) and *A Treatise Concerning Civil Government* (London, 1781); J. G. A. Pocock, "Josiah Tucker on Burke, Locke and Price: A study in the Varieties of Eighteenth-Century Conservatism," in Pocock, ed., *Virtue, Commerce and History, Chiefly in the Eighteenth Century* (Cambridge, 1985).

26 Lester J. Cappon, ed., *The Adams–Jefferson Letters: The Complete Correspondence Between Thomas Jefferson and Abigail and John Adams* (Chapel Hill, N.C., 1959), 2, passim.

27 Jefferson, *Writings*, p. 40. I do not know to what extent the records of the Assembly confirm this account.

28 The thesis that Plato had been the founder of both priestcraft and enthusiasm was authoritatively set forth in Jakob Brucker, *Historia Critica Philosophiae* (Leipzig, 1740). Jefferson owned and often cited a one-volume English epitome of this work by William Enfield, a Warrington Academy minister; but his frequent denunciations of Plato treat him as only the founder of priestcraft. I am indebted to Professor Anton Donoso for bringing Enfield to my attention.

Rembrandt Peale's portrait of Thomas Jefferson, painted from life in 1800, on the eve of his presidency. Courtesy of The White House.

4

The Political Theology of Thomas Jefferson

THOMAS E. BUCKLEY, S.J.

"God Forbid!" that Thomas Jefferson should become president of the United States, wrote "a Layman" in 1800. The Virginia politician not only was no Christian, but also "denies the truth, and avows the pernicious folly of all religion." The presidential election that year brought national politics its first heavy dose of religious controversy as Federalist writers in pamphlets, newspapers, and broadsides attacked Vice President Jefferson for being at least a deist and, more likely, an "infidel" and propagator of "atheistical principles."[1] Critics reiterated the same arguments: Jefferson avoided church services, rejected the Scriptures, profaned the Sabbath, thought one religion as good as another and not much of any of them, and wanted a government blind to moral considerations.[2]

Conservative clergy led the assault. James Abercrombie, an Episcopalian minister in Philadelphia, was typical when he urged his confreres to join "our great and common cause" in keeping "an acknowledged *unbeliever*" from the presidency of "a Christian community."[3] Rallying to the call, parsons in New York, Boston, and elsewhere attacked Jefferson for the antireligious polemic they uncovered in his writings. In search of ammunition, they most frequently cited the *Notes on Virginia*. "It does me no injury for my neighbour to say there are twenty gods, or no god," Jefferson had written in defense of religious liberty. "It neither picks my pocket nor breaks my leg."[4] Then and forever after, his critics expressed horror at such "indifference" to doctrinal truth.[5] Assailing another famous Jefferson work, churchmen argued that under pretext of eliminating religious establishments, the Virginia Statute for Religious Freedom had been designed to destroy religion; and they pointed to the current moral atmosphere in Virginia as proof of that intention.[6] Jefferson's proposals for public education also alarmed them. If the wishes of this

American Voltaire were fulfilled, schoolchildren would shortly be reading Greek, Roman, and American history, rather than the Bible.

The Virginia politician's views on religious freedom and on education as well as his authorship of the *Notes on Virginia* had been known for many years and criticized before.[7] But not until 1800 did they assume national proportions and become a major campaign topic. Well aware of the Republican challenge to their political dominance, Federalist apologists argued that someone who advocated freedom from religion more than religious liberty could not be trusted at the helm of a Christian nation. Jefferson's election threatened to "destroy religion, introduce immorality, and loosen all the bonds of society."[8]

Jefferson would never forget the enmity of northern clergy – "political pimps," a supporter termed them – but his friends were not impotent; by autumn, the Republican press had seized the offensive. Rejecting the allegations of atheism, these apologists asserted Jefferson's Christianity and cited his benefactions to clergy, his membership in the Episcopal Church, and even his personal collection of Bibles. Most important, they repeatedly appealed to his writings: the Declaration of Independence as a statement of belief in God, the witness of his *Notes on Virginia* to "all the glorious attributes of the Deity, his infinite justice, goodness and wisdom," and, above, all the Virginia Statute for Religious Freedom.[9] John Beckley, Republican Party leader from Virginia and clerk of the House of Representatives, refuted the critics:

> Read, ye fanatics, bigots, and religious hypocrites, of whatsoever clime or country ye be – and you, base calumniators, whose efforts to traduce are the involuntary tribute of envy to a character more pure and perfect than your own, read, learn, and practise the RELIGION OF JEFFERSON as displayed in the sublime truths and inspired language of HIS ever memorable "Act for establishing religious freedom."[10]

Did Jefferson express a public religion in the Statute for Religious Freedom, as Beckley claimed, or was it "irreligion," as his critics charged? Americans disagreed in 1786 and in 1800. They disagree today.[11] His writings on the rights of conscience have generated an enormous volume of literature, much of it controversial. In the development of American political thought and public policy, Jefferson is recognized as the preeminent spokesman for religious liberty and the separation of church and state.[12] Certainly of all that he held most dear, freedom – particularly of belief, conscience, and thought – was the signal value in life. As he wrote to Benjamin Rush in the heat of the 1800 election: "I have sworn on the altar of god eternal hostility against every form of tyranny over the mind of man."[13] Separation was the way to achieve that freedom: separation first from the tyranny of Great Britain, or from any control by civil · government; and then from religious dogmatism or slavish obedience to the ecclesiastical order, the church.

The complexity of his achievement has not been fully appreciated, perhaps because of the paradoxical way in which he made his contribution. Jefferson repeatedly insisted that his religion was private, but drafted public documents with strong religious overtones. He thought theology of little or no academic value, yet issued profound theological statements. Some contemporaries considered his views the height of irreligion, but others found them deeply religious as well as political. He argued for separation of church and state based on the nature of religion itself, and founded a public policy for the United States on a theology. Those who opposed his views did so in the name of preserving religion, but it was his consistent approach to keep civil government away from religion in order to preserve religion truly. In the last quarter of the eighteenth century, he offered America and then the world a political theology, one of religious liberation.

Jefferson's whole stance toward freedom of religious belief and church–state relations was located within the overarching framework of theology in the sense in which Bernard Lonergan used that term as that which mediates between religion and culture.[14] He presented his theology, or, as Beckley termed it, "the religion of Jefferson," not as an alternative to the creeds and faiths of the various churches or religious groups in America, or in terms of his personal relationship with his God – although that certainly influenced his public statements and writing – but as a way for Americans to interpret their collective experience, their relationship with God and with one another in terms of religious faith.[15] At the core of this theology, he talked about God and man and the nature of belief. From this theological foundation, he developed his thoughts on religious freedom and separation of church and state. In this context, it is striking how Jefferson's case for liberty of belief and expression anticipates statements from contemporary Christian bodies, such as the World Council of Churches and the Second Vatican Council.[16]

In the laws and documents he drafted, Jefferson enunciated a civic faith clearly related to and dependent on a transcendent God that most Americans understood and accepted. His initial contribution came in a series of Revolutionary testaments written between 1774 and 1777. Then, a quarter of a century later, his presidential statements refined his thoughts for the young republic. Despite the gap between these two periods, Jefferson's fundamental faith in Virginia and the United States did not change with the passing years. All three of the achievements he wished engraved on his tombstone were works or dreams of his young manhood.

His formulation of an American faith profoundly influenced what Americans thought they were doing as a people as well as government policy making in the area of religious freedom and church–state relations. The expression of this belief system was not Jefferson's task alone. George Washington, Benjamin Franklin, John Adams, George Mason, James Madison, and other lesser known figures contributed to it in different ways, particularly in the public press. But in his memorable statements, Jefferson spoke for them as well as all Americans; and particularly in the Statute for Religious Freedom, he defined terms for the American debate on the issues of religion in society and church–state relations then and ever since. Calling it "the religion of Jefferson" was a novel idea in 1800. Although later generations did not use the term, they adopted his "religion" to a degree that neither he nor Beckley could have imagined.

By the middle of May 1776, Jefferson was in Philadelphia, arriving there about the time the Virginia Convention resolved that the Continental Congress should "declare the United Colonies free and independent states, absolved from all allegiance to, or dependence upon, the crown or parliament of Great Britain."[17] On behalf of the Virginia delegation, Richard Henry Lee offered the resolution of independence on June 7; and shortly afterward, Jefferson began work on his most famous contribution to the American testament. The significance of the Declaration of Independence can scarcely be overestimated. In justifying the separation of the American colonies from Great Britain, Jefferson offered an eloquent statement of the natural-law philosophy of the origins of government. The ideas were not original, as Jefferson himself later acknowledged; his task was to invest them with the proper tone and spirit demanded by the occasion.[18]

In doing so, his first draft enunciated the key tenets of the American faith. The appeal was to "the laws of nature & of nature's god. . . . that all men are created equal & independent, that from that equal creation they derive rights inherent & inalienable, among which are the preservation of life, & liberty, & the pursuit of happiness."[19] Jefferson espoused the divine institution of a universal moral order inherent in creation and known through reason as the source of natural rights antecedent to civil government. The term "laws of nature" pertains particularly to the political order within the scope of natural-law theory. Government originates by human consent, the result of men banding together to protect their natural rights. When these rights are abused, thereby defining the presence of tyranny, men are entitled to change the existing government.

Hence the bill of particulars against George III and the assertion of American independence.[20]

This was not the first time Jefferson publicly expressed himself on the existence of God, the origin of natural rights, and the rights of separation. Two years earlier, in draft resolutions proposed for the Virginia Convention of 1774, he had presented similar views, which some friends later published as *A Summary View of the Rights of British America*. The rights he claimed for Virginians came from "the laws of nature," not from the king. "The god who gave us life, gave us liberty at the same time," the young Albemarle County burgess had written. "The hand of force may destroy, but cannot disjoin them."[21]

The rhetoric was appropriate to his reconstruction of history. At the outset, Jefferson compared the first settlers of Virginia with their Saxon forebears, drawing a parallel between the natural rights of Saxons and of Virginians. Just as centuries before, in moving from northern Europe to Britain, the Saxons had exercised "a right, which nature has given to all men" to leave their place of origin and emigrate to another land to establish a society "under such laws and regulations as to them shall seem most likely to promote public happiness," so their descendents had come to America. In Britain, the Saxons had been free men living under their own laws without control or force from their "mother country," until the Normans came and destroyed the ancient constitution. Virginians had repeated the Saxon experience:

> America was conquered, and her settlements made and firmly established, at the expence of individuals and not of the British public. Their own blood was spilt in acquiring lands for their settlement, their own fortunes expended in making that settlement effectual. For themselves they fought, for themselves they conquered, and for themselves alone they have the right to hold.

Virginia had been the settlers' achievement, as Britain had been that of the Saxons. As the latter had fought over the years to regain their liberties against Norman impositions and the usurpations of kings, so Jefferson's generation continued that struggle.[22]

As a delegate to the Continental Congress in 1775, Jefferson was appointed to help draft what became the Declaration of the Causes and Necessity for Taking Up Arms. This statement also begins with a rendition of history: "our forefathers . . . left their native land to seek on these shores a residence for civil & religious freedom. At the expence of their blood, to the ruin of their fortunes, with the relinquishment of every thing quiet & comfortable in life, they effected settlements in the inhospitable wilds of America." His rendition of history was not entirely accurate, but what Jefferson was attempting to provide in this declaration and in the *Summary View* was not fact, but a collective experience that would not only justify the events of 1775, but also give Americans a shared past. He offered what Robert Bellah has termed a "myth of origin," a sense of rootedness, of owning a common heritage.[23] After recounting in summary form the injustices and injuries committed by Parliament, General Thomas Gage, and the British army at Boston, Jefferson concluded: "We do then most solemnly, before god and the world declare . . . we will use . . . all those powers which our creator hath given us, to preserve that liberty which he committed to us in sacred deposit, & to protect from every hostile hand our lives & our properties." He closed with an appeal for the "assistance of Almighty god to conduct us happily thro' this great conflict."[24]

Thus Jefferson articulated for his fellow Americans a set of shared beliefs fundamental to the development of a national faith. First, a sense of common beginnings rooted in historical events as distant as the time of the Saxons and oriented toward the achievement of liberty; second, an insistence on natural rights derived from a law of nature implanted by a creator in his handiwork and recognized as self-evident by reason; and finally, the acknowledgment of dependence on a divine Providence overseeing the American experiment. The Declaration of Independence repeats these themes.[25]

Jefferson summarized his ideas in the images he proposed for the Great Seal of the United States. John Adams described the plan in a letter to his wife. A religious metaphor dominated one side: "The Children of Israel in the Wilderness, led by a Cloud by day, and a Pillar of Fire by night." Jefferson identified the American people as the new Israelites being led out of slavery to freedom by God, represented as cloud and fire in the Old Testament theophany. America was their Israel, the promised land. On the other side of the seal were "Hengist and Horsa, the Saxon Chiefs, from whom We claim the Honor of being descended, and whose Political Principles and Form of Government We have assumed."[26] There you have it. The biblical story was placed alongside a particular reading of history. Two myths intersected to explain the American experience and to provide elements for a common American faith: an emphasis on the quest for civil and religious liberty guided by divine Providence.

Jefferson's contribution to America's identity in these early documents of the Revolution is beyond debate, but while expressing his fundamental political thought, the documents do not exhaust his political philosophy.[27] While composing the Declaration of Independence in June 1776, the Virginian had an opportunity to pen something more concrete than theories of origins and rights – a frame of government for his native state. Forced by congressional duties to remain in Philadelphia, he nevertheless drew up his own version and posted it to his confederates in Williamsburg.[28] Jefferson's proposed constitution consisted of four sections with a preamble justifying separation in terms of George III's misdeeds. The first three sections elaborated the functions of executive, legislative, and judicial branches of government. The final one listed "Rights Private and Public," and for the first time, Jefferson expressed publicly his position on religious liberty: "All persons shall have full and free liberty of religious opinion; nor shall any be compelled to frequent or maintain any religious service or institution."[29] Although the convention did not accept his schema, it demonstrates that the rights defended in the Virginia Statute for Religious Freedom were included in his Declaration of Independence. For Jefferson, separation from Britain provided the occasion to establish "the rights of conscience" given by God but denied by the state.[30] Another decade would pass before Virginia acknowledged his formulation and many more years before his concepts entered the American creed.

Bernard Bailyn has argued that the extension of the values contained in the Declaration of Independence to religious freedom was part of the "Contagion of Liberty." But the disease took time to spread among Jefferson's countrymen.[31] For Jefferson, the values of republicanism and, particularly, his devotion to equality and individual rights necessarily connected the ideas presented in the Declaration of Independence with those expressed in the religious-freedom statement of his proposed constitution for Virginia, in the speeches he gave that autumn on the right of religious freedom and the need for disestablishment, and in the Statute for Religious Freedom, which was drafted the next year. The rights of the Revolution demanded expression in the realm of conscience and practice. But in this respect, as one of his first biographers pointed out, he found himself ahead of his generation.[32]

To appreciate Jefferson's contribution to the American concept of religious freedom as well as the difficulties he faced in promoting it, one must understand the position of those who disagreed with him in 1776. The formulation of the religious-liberty statement in the Declaration of Rights illustrates the differences between Jefferson and the majority of lawmakers in Virginia. His statement on religious liberty was not included in the constitution because the state convention had already approved a separate Declaration of Rights. The last article guarantees religious toleration, which young James Madison substantially modified by exchanging the word "toleration" for the phrase "free exercise of religion." The final version reads:

> That religion, or the duty which we owe to our CREATOR,
> and the manner of discharging it, can be directed only by reason

and conviction, not by force or violence; and therefore, all men are equally entitled to the free exercise of religion, according to the dictates of conscience; and that it is the mutual duty of all to practise Christian forbearance, love, and charity, towards each other.[33]

Government – that is, "force or violence" – is not to coerce individual conscience or practice. The right of religious freedom is acknowledged, but as a correlative to the prior "duty" of religion and its exercise.[34] From its leaders' perspective, the commonwealth permitted freedom of belief for the sake of religion, not atheism; and the religious-liberty article concludes by making Christian virtues normative for human relationships. Virginia's founding fathers recalled all too well the recent pitched battles between the Establishment and dissenting religious groups. The Separate Baptists, in particular, had challenged their authority, straining social and political structures. Hopefully, freedom of conscience and practice, together with a strong dose of "Christian forbearance, love, and charity," would restore peace.[35] Thus Virginia's leaders had not done what Jefferson and Madison wished and disestablished the Church of England; in fact, they had explicitly rejected that option. Then and afterward, conservative leaders denied that the wording of the Declaration of Rights had intended that eventuality. Their program in 1776 was to maintain the religious status quo while granting only minimal concessions necessary to conciliate the dissenters and ensure their support in the Revolution. In years to come, they would slowly expand the circle of rights granted to non-establishment groups by suppressing certain vestries, broadening the marriage laws, and passing similar measures in order to cope with the realities of ecclesiastical pluralism in Virginia life. But there were limits to what these "nursing fathers" to the church would consider.

The survival of their religious community was not the only concern. If these civil servants disestablished Anglicanism, they would deprive themselves of authority, for the Church of England in Virginia had never been a separate organization, separately administered. Those who ruled the state, ruled the Church. From the beginning of the colonial period, public taxation and property grants had supported the Church, and the civil government had controlled it. Nominally episcopal in policy, it was actually congregational in practical management. Although from time to time, a commissary was sent out from London with supervisory powers, the Virginia clergy remained firmly under the gentry's thumb in parish vestries and the House of Burgesses. Whenever the reverend gentlemen challenged this arrangement – for example, at the time of the Parson's

Cause – they lost. The lay leaders of state and church in the Virginia Convention made it clear to Madison that arrangements would stay that way. Although, according to Edmund Randolph, the bulk of Virginia's ruling class "dreaded nothing so much as a schism among the people," they thought that an official policy along the lines of a liberal toleration would be sufficient to quiet the disgruntled and hold society together.[36] At the same time, the Established Church served as a prop to the social order. After all, it was *their* church; it belonged to them more than to the clergy or the common folk. These Virginia gentlemen were separatists, not revolutionaries.[37] They desired freedom from Great Britain for the sake of maintaining life as it had always been. From this perspective, the Church was important to maintain virtue and public morality, vital qualities in a republic. Disagreeing about means, not ends, Jefferson thought those qualities were not inimical to a society that guaranteed complete religious freedom. His friends in Williamsburg did not concur. They refused to disestablish a bulwark of their prestige and a major instrument for their social and political control of the state.[38]

Jefferson and Madison were not satisfied. Although working separately in Philadelphia and Williamsburg, they were as one in their conviction that freedom of religious belief and worship is a natural right that should be guaranteed in Virginia's fundamental law and that the privileged position of the state church maintained by public taxation violated that natural right and ought to be terminated.[39] The convention's work was therefore insufficient, and in the fall session of the Assembly, Jefferson was on hand to lead the struggle for disestablishment. He had resigned his position in the Continental Congress and returned to Monticello in September. The next month, he was at Williamsburg, once more a legislator from Albemarle County in the newly established House of Delegates, the real power center in the new state government. Almost immediately, he began working for the abolition of artificial privileges and vested interests inconsistent with republican ideals; among these, he counted a religious establishment. Jefferson had allies. Not only was Madison an able, although quiet, lieutenant in the House, but outside the door, vociferous dissenters were demanding relief from Church taxation and the fulfillment of the promise of complete religious freedom held out by the Declaration of Rights.

The previous August, newly elected Governor Patrick Henry, responding to a gracious letter from a Baptist Association, had praised the "catholic spirit prevailing in our country" and rejoiced that "religious distinctions which formerly produced some heats are now forgotten."[40] His optimism proved premature, as he soon discovered that autumn. The opposing forces met head on. Separate Baptists and Presbyterians insisted on "EQUAL LIBERTY," and Establishment supporters struck back with forceful arguments for retaining the church–state alliance.[41] The Episcopal Church, as it had begun to style itself after independence, had powerful supporters in the legislature. Jefferson himself afterward remembered: "Our great opponents were [Edmund] Pendleton and Robert Carter Nicholas, honest men, but zealous churchmen." The strength of the opposition inside the Assembly, a majority of whom were Church members, would give Jefferson what he later termed "the severest contests" of his political career.[42]

Jefferson determined to confront the opposition. Drafting a series of resolutions supporting legislation for religious freedom and disestablishment, he pulled together from various sources an extensive list of arguments to bolster his case. These notes, which formed the basis for one or more speeches delivered in the Assembly that fall, are proof positive that the thoughts embodied in the Bill for Establishing Religious Freedom, although not enacted into law for another decade, were already fully developed in 1776.[43] Indeed, the wording of these notes is at times almost identical with that of the bill, which was drafted the next year. The Declaration of Independence and the Virginia Statute for Religious Freedom, therefore, belong to the same period in his life. There is yet a third entry. Both the debate notes and the statute bear a marked resemblance to another product of Jefferson's pen. Several years later, while serving as American minister to France, he published his *Notes on Virginia*. This book provided a further opportunity to present his views on religious liberty in his native state. We can take these three texts together, as essentially expressing his convictions on religious freedom. They develop Jefferson's public theology of the relationship of God to the human person and the nature of belief, and in so doing, elaborate fundamental ideas about God and man.

To a certain degree, Jefferson's views on the rights of conscience, on church–state relations, and on the limitations of civil authority came from a variety of American, British, and Continental sources. His historical studies persuaded him that religious liberty was among the ancient rights of the Saxons and that Christianity was not part of the common law.[44] His dependence on John Locke is easily charted, since some of his debate notes were copied from his précis of Locke's *Letter Concerning Toleration*.[45] Like the ideas contained in the Declaration of Independence, arguments for religious toleration and liberty of conscience were "in the air" in America. Jefferson may well have read William Livingston's *Independent Reflector*, and he was certainly familiar with the arguments over an American episcopacy and the extension of the English Toleration Act that had intermittently filled the pages of the *Virginia Gazette* during the past dozen years.[46] Yet in the theological foundation he laid for religious freedom and its universal implications, he surpassed the thought of his generation.

The work of previous ages was his first concern, for Jefferson thought and wrote from a historical perspective. In his prepared remarks for the legislative debates of 1776 as well as in his query on religion in Virginia in the *Notes,* he began his case against the Anglican Establishment by explaining the legal history and judicial status of religion in the commonwealth. Having researched his subject extensively, he listed with characteristic thoroughness all the statutes of Great Britain and Virginia that restricted religious belief and practice, noting down in particular, the punishments available to the civil arm for dealing with such crimes as apostasy, heresy, recusancy, popery, and blasphemy. An impressive summation. Edmund Randolph later described the speech in the Assembly: "the severest persecutions in England were ransacked for colors in which to paint the burdens and scourges of freedom in religion; and antiquated laws in England, against the exercise of which the people would even there have recoiled, were summoned up as so many demons hovering over every scrupulous conscience not bending to the church."[47] Years passed, and we can glimpse the emotional depth of Jefferson's concern from the passionate tone in his *Notes on Virginia,* in which he condemned the "religious slavery" that Virginians continued to accept. In the early 1780s, he anguished over his limited success in obtaining freedom of belief and worried for the future of people's rights once the Revolution was over. A "zealot" might come to power and begin a persecution; or society become corrupt and virtue lost as other interests, particularly a zest for "making money," came to obsess Americans. "From the conclusion of this war," he predicted with uncharacteristic pessimism, "we shall be going down hill."[48]

However dramatic his legislative presentation may have been in 1776, the Albemarle delegate made an important point. He wanted the legislature to appreciate not the actual toleration in Virginia – the bulk of these old laws were unenforced – but the contemporary legal status of religious freedom. The laws, he argued, should reflect the liberality of the Revolutionary age. Now at the outset of the republic was the appropriate time to clean up the statutes, particularly those dealing with religion. Virginians had a right to live with the security of good laws, rather than simply depend on the climate of opinion. Opinions can change.

Jefferson then turned to his most fundamental reason for supporting disestablishment of the state church: the nature of religious belief as an *"unalienable right."* He ranked religious freedom among the most important of natural rights. This was not self-evident to the legislators, however, and Jefferson would labor mightily to convince them. These were essentially the same men who had sat in the convention the previous spring and summer.[49] While embracing the Declaration of Independence, with its essentially Lockean political philosophy, many of his liberty-minded auditors could not accept Jefferson's perspective that natural rights included complete freedom of religious belief and practice, required the disestablishment of the state church, and mandated the equality of all religious groups.[50]

In attempting to persuade his fellow legislators to these views, the young delegate began from the premise that in forming society, men surrendered only those rights necessary for civil government. All others they retained, especially the rights of conscience. "If [there] is [any] *unalienable right,"* he wrote in his debate notes," [it] is religious." The reason is that "God requires every act [to be done] according to *belief."* Founded as it is on a divine imperative, the core of Jefferson's argument is a theological statement: God requires belief. This is God's choice as creator. There is a correlative responsibility for man. In his prepared remarks for the Assembly, Jefferson wrote that in the exercise of "religious rights," each person is "answerable to God." He repeated this practically verbatim in the *Notes on Virginia:* "We are answerable for them to our God." Religious belief is the human response to a divine command. Thus for Jefferson, the most fundamental right an individual possesses is that of conscience – the right to one's belief and its expression.[51]

The Virginia Statute for Religious Freedom makes a further statement concerning divine activity: "Almighty God hath created the mind free." Belief must be based, therefore, on the evidence submitted to human reason. For the exercise of conscience to be honest and therefore acceptable to God, it must rest on what the human mind accepts as true. "That belief [is] founded on [the] evidence offered to his mind: as things appear to himself, not to another." Other minds may be more brilliant, but each individual can operate with only the reason God has given him. Any kind of coercion destroys the proper exercise of conscience and violates the divine imperative. The next year, he wrote it again, more tersely, in the opening words to his proposed Bill for Establishing Religious Freedom: *"Well aware that the opinions and belief of men depend not on their own will, but follow involuntarily the evidence proposed to their minds."* Senate amendments would cut that phrase out of the text, together with the statement that God chose *"to extend [religion] by its influence on reason alone"* before the statute was finally approved. The legislature would acknowledge God's creative action in making the mind free, but not the logical consequence.[52]

In the statute, the *Notes on Virginia,* and these sections of the debate speeches, Jefferson presented a theology of God's relationship with man. The God described here is not deistical, remote from human beings or unconcerned with their affairs. Rather, Jefferson posited a creator who is personally involved and expects an individual response expressed in sincere belief. Man is held to account, in Jefferson's view. Perhaps his most eloquent statement of divine activity and human accountability comes from his observations on slavery in the *Notes on Virginia*. After pointing out that the "liberties" of the United States are "the gift of God," he exclaimed, "They are not to be violated but with his wrath? Indeed I tremble for my country when I reflect that God is just: that his justice cannot sleep for ever: . . . The Almighty has no attribute which can take side with us in such a contest."[53]

Elsewhere, Jefferson described this relationship between God and man in terms of morality and credited the existence of a "moral sense" as its basis. Jefferson regarded morality as essentially instinctive. Years later in a letter, he offered the clearest explanation of his position. What he termed the "moral principle" comes from the "Creator." "Nature hath implanted in our breasts a love of others, a sense of duty to them, a moral instinct in short, . . . impelling us to virtuous actions, and warning us against those which are vicious." Instead of "truth," beauty, "self-love," or even love of God, Jefferson considered this "moral sense" to be the foundation of morality. Counseling his daughter, he urged her to follow conscience, that "faithful internal Monitor," as a guide in knowing right from wrong.[54]

The same principle applies in public life and to nations as well as individuals. When President Washington asked him as Secretary of State for his opinion of America's treaty obligations toward France after that country's revolution, Jefferson began his response with a disquisition on "the moral law of our nature." To this, "man has been subjected by his creator," and the "evidence" of the existence of this law is one's "conscience" or "feelings." Jefferson argued that what applies to individuals also applies to nations, and he continued: "for the reality of these principles I appeal to the true fountains of evidence[,] the head and heart of every rational and honest man[;] it is there nature has written her moral laws, and where every man may read them for himself."[55] Morality is not the product of unaided instinct, therefore, but of reason and instinct working together. This combination reveals to human beings not only their obligations and responsibilities, but also the law of their nature and those natural rights given by their creator.[56]

A corollary to conscience as a natural right is the exclusion of civil government from the area of religious thought. A person cannot surrender to someone else, even the civil magistrate, responsibility for his own conscience; for that, each person is answerable only to God. Jefferson made the same point in his *Notes* while betraying his frustration over the legislature's recalcitrance in refusing to revoke Virginia statutes limiting religious freedom: "The error seems not sufficiently eradicated, that the operations of the mind, as well as the acts of the body, are subject to the coercion of the laws. But our rulers can have authority over such natural rights only as we have submitted to them." However, the Senate excised that limitation on its power and also removed from the statute the statement that *"the opinions of men are not the object of civil government, nor under its jurisdiction."*

Jefferson attempted to differentiate between the sphere of activity appropriate to civil government and that reserved to the individual. Distinguishing between belief and action in his *Notes on Virginia,* he pointed out: "The legitimate powers of government extend to such acts only as are injurious to others. But it does me no injury for my neighbour to say there are twenty gods, or no god. It neither picks my pocket nor breaks my leg." The lawyer in Jefferson insisted that a distinction be drawn between belief and action; the state can move against an individual only when his external activity violates law. To restrict "opinion or tendency of opinion" is an injury against freedom of religious belief. The statute repeats this view: " to suffer the civil magistrate to intrude his powers into the field of opinion and to restrain the profession or propagation of principles on supposition of their ill tendency is a dangerous fallacy, which at once destroys all religious liberty." Officials are tempted to make their views normative for society when they should make no move until an "overt" offense takes place.[57] Jefferson was keenly aware of the fallibility of all human authority, whether civil or ecclesiastical. In his arguments before the Assembly, he pointed out that magistrates are human instruments, capable of corruption. Wherever they had uniformity, hypocrisy or atheism had resulted.

In recognizing the affinity between civil and religious liberty and the need to limit governmental authority, Jefferson resembles no one so much as his English contemporary the Dissenting clergyman Richard Price. Price had been active in England on behalf of greater religious freedom in the early 1770s, and he was extremely sympathetic to the American movement toward independence. In the spring of 1776, he published his *Observations on the Nature of Civil Liberty* in London, and it was quickly reprinted in Philadelphia that summer. Jefferson, in fact, was sending copies of it to Virginia and must have read it himself. Price was arguing for the Americans' right to independence when he wrote:

> As no people can lawfully surrender their *Religious* Liberty, by giving up their right of judging for themselves in religion, or by

allowing any human beings to prescribe to them what faith they shall embrace, or what mode of worship they shall practise; so neither can any civil societies lawfully surrender their *Civil* Liberty, by giving up to any extraneous jurisdiction their power of legislating for themselves and disposing their property. Such a cession, being inconsistent with the unalienable right of human nature, would either not bind at all; or bind only the individuals who made it.

Neither the individual in religious matters nor the community in civil matters can turn over authority to a person or group external to itself without giving up its freedom. For Price as for Jefferson, the rights of *"private judgment"* were all important. The state has no jurisdiction over matters of religion or conscience, but can regulate and punish only external acts against the peace and tranquillity of society. After the passage of Jefferson's statute ten years later, Price published it in London with a laudatory preface.[58]

But Jefferson went beyond Price, Locke, and other advocates of conscience rights in developing the reasoning behind religious freedom and in wishing it extended to all. In addition to his theological argument from the nature of God's relationship with man, he saw the religious pluralism resulting from complete freedom as a positive good, and he praised the diversity of places such as Pennsylvania and New York.[59] What Robert Carter Nicholas fussed over as the "Babel of Religions" did not bother Jefferson.[60] The Virginia legislator advocated pluralism for numerous reasons, not least of which was his supreme confidence in the power of uncoerced reason to discover truth. In the 1776 debates, Jefferson stated that uniformity is neither desirable nor attainable. A state religion suppresses "free enquiry," the only sure path to improvement and human progress. Replacing government as teacher and enforcer, Jefferson would set up truth, reason, and open discussion. Freedom of investigation destroys error, he argued. In one of his abstracts from Locke, Jefferson wrote: "[tr]uth will do well enough if left to shift for herself . . . she has no need of force to procure entrance into the minds of men, error indeed has often prevailed by the assistance of power or force." His statute echoes this viewpoint: "truth is great and will prevail if left to herself." All that was needed was to permit "free argument and debate; errors ceasing to be dangerous when it is permitted freely to contradict them." Only "error . . . needs the support of government," he wrote in his *Notes on Virginia*. "Truth can stand by itself."[61]

The functions he assigned to the churches and clergy in society also made him regard religious pluralism as a positive benefit for America. He was convinced that for all important purposes, religion is reducible to morality, and that the morality taught by all religious groups or churches is essentially the same. He expressed this position on the Assembly floor in 1776 when he argued that the special status of the Established Church was unnecessary for the welfare of society, since "[the] teachers [of] every sect inculcate [the] same moral principles." Speaking of places where religious pluralism was practiced, the *Notes on Virginia* reflect the same attitude: "Religion is well supported; of various kinds, indeed, but all good enough; sufficient to preserve peace and order." Jefferson thought that the clergy exists to provide moral teaching, and a major presupposition of the statute was that each individual selects a church based on the moral instruction and example of its ministry. To require a person to contribute "to support this or that teacher of his own religious persuasion, is depriving him of the comfortable liberty of giving his contribution to the particular pastor whose morals he would make his pattern, and whose powers he feels most persuasive to righteousness."[62] Although he attended church services from time to time and contributed to the support of the minister in his local parish, Jefferson did not have a developed ecclesiology. Outwardly, he styled himself an Episcopalian; inwardly, he sympathized most with the Unitarians, but thought he formed "a sect by himself."[63] The church as institution or community had little to offer Jefferson. Monticello, his friends, and his library were all he needed for true communion.[64]

In part, this was due to his narrow view of theology. He dismissed it as not worth studying because he thought it outside rational analysis. Jefferson considered theological statements, whether made by church councils, creeds, or individuals, to be simply "opinion," based not on reason, but on revelations unacceptable to a thoughtful man. Churches define themselves on the basis of these differences, but they do not affect the public sphere. Whether you are Calvinist or Arminian, Trinitarian or Unitarian, pray in church or shout under the trees, sprinkle children over the font or dip adults in the creek, it does not touch your life as a citizen. In the Jeffersonian scheme of things, the religious dimension of personal belief was private, absolutely. He repeated it in a multitude of ways. The statute's line is famous: "Our civil rights have no dependence on our religious opinions, any more than our opinions in physics or geometry."[65] He advised others not to waste time in theological study, eliminated it (with the help of his friend, the future Bishop Madison) from the curriculum of the College of William and Mary when he was the state governor, and tried to keep it out of the University of Virginia.[66]

If theology was irrelevant, its clerical practitioners were suspect, particularly if they were Presbyterians, Jesuits, or Episcopalians with Tory or Federalist proclivities.[67] He thought that the ministry had violated "the pure and holy doctrines of their master" and placed them in the same class with "soothsayers and necromancers."[68] The origin of this intense dislike for the clergy is unclear. Jefferson had grown up in Virginia in anticlerical times, and his sentiments may have come from his early studies with an Establishment minister or his college days at William and Mary, with its partially clerical faculty.[69] But before the Revolution, he counted among his friends several members of the Anglican Establishment in Virginia, and after the tithes were ended, he gave his own parish clergyman a healthy contribution and a strong letter of recommendation.[70]

Perhaps he trusted the person, but not the institution. In the Revolutionary period, he criticized the lack of American patriotism displayed by the bulk of the Anglican ministers, and later commented on the "fangs" of the Episcopalians.[71] Certainly, he feared the influence of the clergy and for many years favored their exclusion from the state legislature.[72] The election campaign of 1800 increased Jefferson's animosity, particularly toward northern Episcopalians and Congregationalists, whom he considered enemies of religious freedom;[73] and when John Holt Rice united Presbyterian and other religious sentiment against Jefferson's choice of Thomas Cooper as a professor at the University of Virginia, the university's father could hardly contain his anger.[74] Truth could stand by itself, he thought, if the clergy were not so powerful.[75] Religious pluralism helped keep them divided.

Pluralism included nonbelievers. Jefferson went beyond Locke that autumn of 1776 in insisting that religious liberty is the right of everyone. In his *Letter Concerning Toleration,* the English philosopher had argued that toleration cannot be extended to atheists, to those whose religion involves allegiance to a foreign power (that is, Roman Catholics), and to those whose religious faith does not permit them to extend to others the toleration they demand for themselves. "It was a great thing," Jefferson wrote, that Locke had gone "so far . . . but where he stopped short, we may go on." He tried to do so in a bill proposed by Edmund Pendleton to facilitate the naturalization process of *"Foreign Protestants."* Both in committee and on the floor, Jefferson spoke for broadening the license to include Jews, Catholics, and other non-Protestants; and the bill was changed to read just "foreigners," and then "persons." But it failed to pass the legislature.[76]

The concern of the majority of the Assembly, at least ostensibly, was for the protection and preservation of religion as they understood it. In his closing arguments for complete religious freedom and disestablishment, Jefferson argued that true religion would not suffer from such a policy. In this respect, he subscribed to the anti-Establishment position of the dissenters when he pointed out that Christianity had not needed state support for the first three hundred years of its existence, that decline had set in after civil government had begun to favor it, and that the "gates of hell" would not prevail in a disestablished Virginia.[77] Voluntary support for the clergy would only increase their quality and their zeal. Jefferson's debate notes conclude with a discussion of the problems and evils of forced contributions to the Church. He called his fellow legislators to be consistent with their work of the previous summer. The "Declaration of Rights is *freedom of religion,*" he pointed out. Compelling people to support a religion other than their own makes them cooperate in "heresy." In the statute, he called that practice "sinful and tyrannical."[78]

The unpersuaded Assembly did little that fall of 1776 except to repeal the British statutes and exempt dissenters from Church taxes.[79] Despite the limited gains, Jefferson prepared to press the issue. His new position on the Committee of Revisors established by the legislature to bring Virginia's laws into conformity with republican spirit and principles provided a splendid opportunity. The result was the Bill for Establishing Religious Freedom, which he drafted early in 1777. The revisors presented their complete work to the Assembly two years later, but it never passed as a unit. Instead, bills were brought up individually or in a group. The greatest single period of activity came in the 1785 session, when Madison submitted 118 bills, including Number 82, the Bill for Establishing Religious Freedom. Despite Senate conservatives anxious to cut out phrases, sentences, and even the entire preamble if possible, the bill finally passed both houses and became law in January 1786.[80]

The statute contains everything for which Jefferson had been working since the Revolution began. Although considered "ungrammatical" and "somewhat defaced" by amendments,[81] the lengthy preamble asserts the freedom of the human mind, the separate spheres of religious and civil rights, the error of compulsory religion or church taxes, the fallacy of allowing government officials to meddle in religious matters, and the all-sufficiency of truth. The enabling clause briefly states that all are free to believe, to express their belief, and to worship as they choose without in any way affecting "their civil capacities." The final paragraph is pure Jefferson: "the rights hereby asserted are of the natural rights of mankind." Since these rights were being expressed only in statutory law, future legislatures might change them; but if they diminished them, they would be violating "natural right." In the corpus of Jefferson's work, there is no equal in terms of binding future generations.

Madison professed himself well satisfied with the results – he ought to have been, for he had generaled an exhausting political campaign – and

Jefferson reported from Paris, probably with some exaggeration, that the statute "has been received with infinite approbation in Europe and propagated with enthusiasm." He busied himself sending copies to the European courts and saw to its publication in the next edition of the *Encyclopédie*.[82] His delight was well merited. From the beginning of the Revolution, the Virginia legislator had made the assurance of freedom of thought for every individual a principal objective of his political career. In that respect, the bill as law represented the most progressive statement yet enacted in the United States, and it would profoundly influence the formulation of the First Amendment and its later interpretations.[83]

There is more. The Virginia Statute offers the preeminent statement of the American faith as Jefferson defined it: a belief in God-given natural rights, the most important being freedom of thought and its expression; and the precedence of this right over any claims of civil government to control or influence it. But the statute is not neutral toward religion. The opening lines refer to "Almighty God" in terms of creation, and the next appeal is to "the plan of the holy author of our religion," who did not use "coercions" to spread it. Thus the statute presupposes a belief in God. This is not to say that Jefferson did not intend freedom of conscience for the nonbeliever, but only that he expressed himself in terms acceptable to what was then a Christian society.[84] Also critical are the implications for the churches in the United States. If the individual is free, so is the church. As voluntary societies of individuals exercising natural rights, the churches are outside the purview of the state. Finally, the statute espouses a fundamental optimism that reason and free discussion will ultimately yield truth. All of this can be said to be a part of the American creed, the way we think about ourselves and structure our society and politics.

As he argued from an essentially theological position to freedom of religion and separation of church and state, so Jefferson, once in a position of executive leadership, did not remove religion from public discourse. While a major purpose of his administration was "to strengthen . . . religious freedom," he did not desire a "government without religion." That charge, he later confided to an ally, was a "lie" fostered by his enemies.[85] While Jefferson maintained a discreet silence throughout the 1800 election campaign, his supporters published repeated refutations of the charge of irreligion. Pointing to everything Jefferson had written, but especially to the Statute for Religious Freedom, they stated his belief in a God of goodness, justice, and wisdom whose "revealed will" is demonstrated in nature and its laws. One enthusiastic Jeffersonian went so far as to say that the statute proved that its author believed in divine inspiration and the "God-Head of Christ." That was excessive. But one of the most interesting comments of the campaign came from "A Republican" in the Philadelphia *Aurora*, arguing that both the statute and the *Notes* proved Jefferson's belief in Christianity. He had said that "reason and enquiry" would eventually yield the truth and that Christianity had prevailed under the Roman government when it had only reason and inquiry to support it. Thus Jefferson must consider Christianity to be the true religion.[86]

The new president was keenly aware of the Federalists' animosity and their reluctance to yield power. The charge of atheism stung him.[87] He began his inaugural address, therefore, by emphasizing the rights of minorities and the need for conciliation among political groups. He then presented the existing system of religious pluralism in the United States as the model for the political pluralism that should exist. Just as the nation had banished "religious intolerance," Jefferson proposed it now eliminate "political intolerance." He continued: "Every difference of opinion is not a difference of principle. We have been called by different names brethren of the same principle. We are all Republicans, we are all Federalists." He made religion in America the paradigm for politics. Replace "opinion" with "theology" and "principle" with "virtue," and Jefferson's political and religious programs for the nation were identical.[88]

Amid all the hostility from northern clergymen the previous fall and winter, one sympathetic minister had written to Jefferson applauding his stand on religious freedom and urging him to make "a public avowal of your belief in the christian religion," since such a statement "would be a signal triumph to religion."[89] In the inaugural address, the president now obliged him and incorporated several favorite themes. Speaking of the "blessings" of America, he included "a benign religion, professed, indeed, and practiced in various forms, yet all of them inculcating honesty, truth, temperance, gratitude, and the love of man; acknowledging and adoring an overruling Providence, which by all its dispensations proves that it delights in the happiness of man here and his greater happiness hereafter." After a brief renewal of commitment to religious freedom along with other First Amendment rights, Jefferson closed with an appeal for the support of "that Infinite Power which rules the destinies of the universe."[90]

His points were well taken. At least one serious Christian thought that the address "united the people" and reported to a correspondent in London: "Our new President is said to [be] unfriendly to religion. His inaugural speech contradicts that insinuation . . . he believes in the divine mission of our Saviour, in the resurrection of the body by his power, and in a future state of rewards and punishments."[91] Jefferson had not actually said all that, but the implications of the civic faith he presented were sufficient to satisfy Benjamin Rush.

Despite continuing attacks on his personal religion, conciliation marked his presidency. Repeatedly expressing his sense of the national faith, Jefferson called on Americans to be grateful "to Him" for keeping them out of Europe's war and thankful for "his bounty" and the blessings of "religion at home." "Kind Providence," he told his fellow citizens, saved the United States from the rest of the world's problems, and "Heaven" was preserving "our beloved country" for the years yet to come of "prosperity and happiness." Even to the chiefs of various Indian tribes, the president urged an acceptance of "the will of the Great Spirit to which we must all submit."[92] Jefferson did not display religious indifference in the executive office. He expressed a public faith in God with which his fellow Americans could identify. Twenty years earlier, he had written Edmund Randolph that his "humble and earnest prayer to Almighty god" was for a good government and a strong union.[93] Now as president, he called on all the resources at his command, including a common religion that he had helped formulate, to solidify that union and make that government a more effective instrument in bonding the American people together.

He voiced it again in his second inaugural address, returning to biblical imagery to describe the nation's relationship with God:

> I shall need, too, the favor of that Being in whose hands we are, who led our fathers, as Israel of old, from their native land and planted them in a country flowing with all the necessaries and comforts of life; who has covered our infancy with His Providence and our riper years with His wisdom and power, and to whose goodness I ask you to join in supplications with me.

He invited to prayer but did not mandate it. The distinction was an important one for him. Explaining his policy, Jefferson pointed out that the Constitution locates the "free exercise" of religion "independent of the powers of the General Government. I have therefore undertaken on no occasion to prescribe the religious exercises suited to it, but have left them, as the Constitution found them, under the direction and discipline of the church or state authorities acknowledged by the several religious societies."[94] Acknowledging God and inviting his fellow citizens to prayer did not contradict Jefferson's policy of separating church and state, perhaps because his theology also separated religious belief from both these institutions.

Separation did not mean hostility to the churches, much less to religion. The "wall" motif did not prevent Jefferson's administration from overtly supporting Christianity among the Indians. For example, the War Department provided assistance for a Presbyterian school among the Cherokee;[95] and Jefferson himself – albeit with a caution from Secretary of State Madison, who feared someone might sniff out "a principle, not according with the exemption of Religion from Civil power" – approved a treaty with the Kaskaskia tribe that granted one hundred dollars annually for seven years for "the support of a priest" who would minister to the Indians and teach school. The treaty also committed the government to allocate three hundred dollars to help build the church.[96] Freedom of religion, not separation, was Jefferson's absolute.

He is rightly famous as the father of the American doctrine of church–state separation, but he should also be counted as one who helped establish and promote a theological vision of America's place within salvation history. As president, he consolidated elements of a national faith that he had articulated a quarter of a century before. What John Beckley termed "the RELIGION OF JEFFERSON," Sidney Mead titled the "religion of the Republic," and Robert Bellah called "American civil religion."[97] Far from being a twentieth–century–style secularist or advocating a national polity indifferent to religion, Jefferson publicly expressed what became the American faith – a complex of ideas, values, and symbols related to and dependent on a transcendent reality we call God. This civil religion interpreted the historical experience of the American people, validated their republican political arrangements, and shaped the political culture that united the citizens of the new republic.

His death cemented it. Occurring on July 4, 1826, fifty years after the signing of the Declaration of Independence and on the same day as John Adams's death, it caused a sensation throughout the nation. Daniel Webster spoke of their lives as "gifts of Providence"; their deaths proved God's predilection for America. Jefferson's legacy to his countrymen was an "entire religious liberty." In the view of another panegyric, he had broken "the shackles of civil and religious bondage." It was left to William Wirt, in glowing nineteenth-century prose, to summarize the gift of the Virginia Statute, "one of the most morally sublime of human productions." For sixty-five pages of text, Wirt described these "Apostles of *human liberty*" and "sainted Patriots" and wondered over the manifest "voice of Heaven" that sanctified the "Jubilee" day, "by a double apotheosis."[98]

The timing of Jefferson's death strengthened the civil faith for which he bears so much responsibility. He who was so intensely private about religion, provided a public religion for the nation. Like Molière's Jourdain, who had spoken prose for forty years without knowing it, Jefferson had been doing theology. From the beginning of the republic, this Enlightenment figure offered a theological explanation of the nation's origin, defining it in terms of the search for freedom to fulfill the relationship between God and man inherent in creation. The free exercise of natural rights, particularly that of conscience, responded to a divine imperative. Jefferson's work was to express that right and then so hedge it round that government might never tamper with it, that religious liberty might be absolute. In his emphases on freedom of belief and worship and on separation of church and state, Jefferson set the terms of the debate for the nature and place of religion in our society. It has not yet ended.

NOTES

A number of scholars from various disciplines read preliminary versions of this paper. In particular, I wish to thank Michael J. Buckley, S.J., John R. Connolly, James N. Hanick, Angus B. Hawkins, and Michael Genovese for their comments and suggestions.

1 [Asbury Dickins], *The Claims of Thomas Jefferson to the Presidency, Examined at the Bar of Christianity. By a Layman* (Philadelphia, 1800), pp. 8, 9; "The Jeffersoniad," *Columbian Centinel* (Boston), July 5, 1800; "Caius," *Federal Gazette and Baltimore Daily Advertiser*, August 4, 1800.

2 In addition to those noted above, some of the more prominent examples of Federalist propaganda include [William Linn], *Serious Considerations on the Election of a President: Addressed to the Citizens of the United States* (New York, 1800), a pamphlet that was widely serialized in the press; [John M. Mason], *The Voice of Warning to Christians, on the Ensuing Election of a President of the United States* (New York, 1800); "The Jeffersoniad," *Columbian Centinel*, June 25, July 9, August 20, 1800; a series of articles by "Burleigh," *Connecticut Courant* (Hartford), July 7–October 6, 1800; and "A Letter to a Friend," *Connecticut Courant*, August 18, 1800.

There are several useful articles on religion in the campaign: Charles O. Lerche, Jr., "Jefferson and the Election of 1800: A Case Study in the Political Smear," *William and Mary Quarterly*, 3d ser., 5 (1948):467–91; Charles F. O'Brien, "The Religious Issue in the Presidential Campaign of 1800," *Essex Institute Historical Collections* 107 (1971): 82–93; Fred C. Luebke, "The Origins of Thomas Jefferson's Anticlericalism," *Church History* 32 (1963): 344–56; and Constance Bartlett Schulz, "Of Bigotry in Politics and Religion," *Virginia Magazine of History and Biography* 91 (1983): 73–91.

3 James Abercrombie, Sermon published in Gazette of U.S. and Daily Advertiser (Philadelphia), August 30, 1800.

4 Thomas Jefferson, *Notes on the State of Virginia*, ed. William Peden (Chapel Hill, N.C., 1955), p. 159.

5 [Thomas Green Fessenden], *Democracy Unveiled; or, Tyranny Stripped of the Garb of Patriotism, by Christopher Caustic* (Boston, 1805), p. 102. A more

typical example of the religious polemic is [Clement C. Moore], *Observations Upon Certain Passages in Mr. Jefferson's "Notes on Virginia," Which Appear to Have a Tendency to Subvert Religion, and Establish a False Philosophy* (New York, 1804).

6 They delighted in citing the gloomy message to his flock of his old friend, Episcopal Bishop James Madison, president of the College of William and Mary and cousin to the other James Madison (*An Address to the Members of the Protestant Episcopal Church, in Virginia* [Richmond, 1799]).

7 John Swanwick, *Considerations on a Act of the Legislature of Virginia, Entitled an Act for the Establishment of Religious Freedom* (Philadelphia, 1786); [William Loughton Smith], *The Pretensions of Thomas Jefferson to the Presidency Examined; and the Charges Against John Adams Refuted* ([Philadelphia], 1796).

8 [Linn], "Serious Considerations," *Connecticut Courant*, September 8, 1800.

9 *American Mercury* (Hartford, Conn.), October 2, 1800; [Samuel Knox], *A Vindication of the Religion of Mr. Jefferson, and a Statement of His Services in the Cause of Religious Liberty* (Baltimore, n.d.), p. 17.

10 John Beckley, *Address to the People of the United States; with an Epitome and Vindication of the Public Life and Character of Thomas Jefferson* (Philadelphia, 1800), p. 77. See also Gloria Jahoda, "John Beckley: Jefferson's Campaign Manager," *Bulletin of the New York Public Library* 64 (1960): 247–60.

11 For a sympathetic interpretation of Jefferson's public religion, see Sidney E. Mead, *The Old Religion in the Brave New World: Reflections on the Relation Between Christendom and the Republic* (Berkeley, 1977), pp. 81–104; William B. Huntley, "Jefferson's Public and Private Religion," *South Atlantic Quarterly* 79 (1980): 286–301; and Harold Leonard Hellenbrand, "The Unfinished Revolution: Education and Community in the Thought of Thomas Jefferson" (Ph.D. diss., Stanford University, 1980), pp. 214–24. Critical appraisals may be found in David Little, "The Origins of Perplexity: Civil Religion and Moral Belief in the Thought of Thomas Jefferson," in *American Civil Religion*, ed. Russell E. Richey and Donald G. Jones (New York, 1974), pp. 185–210, and "Thomas Jefferson's Religious Views and Their Influence on the Supreme Court's Interpretation of the First Amendment," *Catholic University Law Review* 26 (1976): 57–72. Walter Berns, "Religion and the Founding Principle," in *The Moral Foundations of the American Republic*, ed. Robert H. Horwitz (Charlottesville, Va., 1979), pp. 157–82, argues that Jefferson did not have a public religion.

12 More important studies generally complimentary to Jefferson, include Dumas Malone, *Jefferson and His Time* (Boston, 1948–81), 1: 274–80; Merrill D. Peterson, *Thomas Jefferson and the New Nation: A Biography* (New York, 1970), pp. 133–45; Willibald M. Ploechl, "Thomas Jefferson, Author of the Statute of Virginia for Religious Freedom," *The Jurist* 3 (1943): 3–51; Henry Wilder Foote, *Thomas Jefferson: Champion of Religious Freedom* (Boston, 1947); Sidney E. Mead, *The Lively Experiment* (New York, 1963), pp. 55–71; Elwyn A. Smith, *Religious Liberty in the United States: The Development of Church–State Thought Since the Revolutionary Era* (Philadelphia, 1972), pp. 28–67; and

Cushing Strout, *The New Heavens and New Earth: Political Religion in America* (New York, 1975), pp. 77–90.

13 Jefferson to Rush, September 23, 1800, *Jefferson's Extracts from the Gospels: "The Philosophy of Jesus" and "The Life and Morals of Jesus"*, in *The Papers of Thomas Jefferson*, 2d ser., ed. Dickinson W. Adams, (Princeton, N.J., 1983), p. 320.

14 Bernard J. F. Lonergan, S.J., *Method in Theology* (New York, 1972), p. xi.

15 An excellent treatment of Jefferson's personal religion and the complex evolution of his thoughts on Christianity may be found in Eugene R. Sheridan, introduction to Adams, *Jefferson's Extracts from the Gospels*, pp. 3–42. See also Malone, *Jefferson and His Time*, 4: 190–205; Sanford Kessler, "Jefferson's Rational Religion," in *The Constitutional Polity: Essays on the Founding Principles of American Politics*, ed. Sidney A. Pearson, Jr. (Washington, D.C., 1983), pp. 58–73; and Charles B. Sanford, *The Religious Life of Thomas Jefferson* (Charlottesville, Va., 1984).

The distinction between public and private religion has been carefully developed by Sidney E. Mead, "The Post-Protestant Concept and America's Two Religions," in *The Nation with the Soul of a Church* (New York, 1975), pp. 11–28.

16 A summary of the modern Christian argument for religious freedom may be found in James E. Wood, Jr., "Theological and Historical Foundations of Religious Liberty," *Journal of Church and State* 15 (1973): 241–58.

17 Julian P. Boyd, ed., *The Papers of Thomas Jefferson* (Princeton, N.J., 1950–), 1: 291. For his arrival in Philadelphia, see Jefferson to John Page, May 17, 1776, ibid., 1: 293.

18 Jefferson to Henry Lee, May 8, 1825, *The Works of Thomas Jefferson*, ed. Paul Leicester Ford (New York, 1904–5), 10: 343.

19 Boyd, *Papers of Jefferson*, 1: 423.

20 For the Declaration's emphasis on natural law and natural rights, see Carl L. Becker, *The Declaration of Independence: A Study in the History of Political Ideas* (New York, 1942), pp. 24–79, and Paul K. Conkin, *Self-Evident Truths: Being a Discourse on the Origins & Development of the First Principles of American Government – Popular Sovereignty, Natural Rights, and Balance & Separation of Powers* (Bloomington, Ind., 1974). pp. 75–118. For a very different perspective, see Morton White, *The Philosophy of the American Revolution* (New York, 1978). Useful discussions on natural rights may also be found in Leo Strauss, *Natural Right and History* (Chicago, 1953), and John Finnis, *Natural Law and Natural Rights* (Oxford, 1980). For Enlightenment thought on the relationship of God and nature, see Ernst Cassirer, *The Philosophy of the Enlightenment*, trans. Fritz C. A. Koelln and James P. Pettegrove (Boston, 1951), pp. 56–8.

21 Boyd, *Papers of Jefferson*, 1: 134, 135.

22 Ibid., 1: 121, 122. For an analysis of this work in terms of natural rights, see Adrienne Koch, *The Philosophy of Thomas Jefferson* (New York, 1943), pp. 135–6. Jefferson's reverence for the ancient Saxon liberties of his forebears

is emphasized in Gilbert Chinard, *The Commonplace Book of Thomas Jefferson* (Baltimore, 1926), pp. 57–9. See also Lynton K. Caldwell, "The Jurisprudence of Thomas Jefferson," *Indiana Law Journal* 18 (1943): 193–213, and H. Trevor Colbourn, "Thomas Jefferson's Use of the Past," *William and Mary Quarterly*, 3d ser., 15 (1958): 56–70.

23   Boyd, *Papers of Jefferson*, 1: 193; Robert N. Bellah, *The Broken Covenant: American Civil Religion in Time of Trial* (New York, 1975), pp. 2–30. In his *Notes on Virginia* Jefferson would take a different position on the colonial foundations, emphasizing the religious persecution in Virginia and referring to the execution of Quakers in New England (p. 157).

24   Boyd, *Papers of Jefferson*, 1: 202, 203.

25   The final draft of the Declaration of Independence, as amended, added an appeal "to the Supreme Judge of the world for the rectitude of our intentions," and stated "a firm reliance on the protection of divine Providence" (ibid., 1: 432). Jefferson would not have disagreed with these sentiments, as his other writing makes clear.

26   Adams to Abigail Adams, August 14, 1776, *Adams Family Correspondence*, ed. L. H. Butterfield (Cambridge, Mass., 1963), 2: 96.

27   Jefferson to William Fleming, July 1, 1776, *Papers of Jefferson*, ed. Boyd, 1: 412; Malone, *Jefferson and His Time*, 1: 173.

28   Jefferson to Thomas Nelson, May 16, 1776, *Papers of Jefferson* ed. Boyd, 1: 292.

29   Ibid., 1:363. The same statement is found in all three drafts, although he dropped from the final version the rejection of "seditious preaching or conversation against the authority of the civil government" (ibid., 1: 353).

30   Ford, *Works of Jefferson*, 1: 78.

31   Bernard Bailyn, *The Ideological Origins of the American Revolution* (Cambridge, Mass., 1967), pp. 245, 268–71.

32   George Tucker, *The Life of Thomas Jefferson* (Philadelphia, 1837), 1: 102.

33   William T. Hutchinson, Robert A. Rutland et al., eds., *The Papers of James Madison* (Chicago, 1962–00), 1: 175. For Madison's role at the convention, see Thomas E. Buckley, S.J., *Church and State in Revolutionary Virginia, 1776–1787* (Charlottesville, Va., 1977), pp. 17–20.

34   The convention did not expressly state that religious freedom is a natural right, although in his *Notes on Virginia,* Jefferson would claim it had done so. He and other foes of the Establishment preferred that interpretation, but it was not the intention of the 1776 convention (p. 158). In the final draft of the Virginia Declaration of Rights, the first article was changed from the statement "That all men are born equally free and independent, and have certain inherent natural rights, . . ." to "That all men are by nature equally free and independent, and have certain inherent rights, . . ." The preservation of slavery was a major factor in the change of wording (Robert A. Rutland, ed., *The Papers of George Mason* [Chapel Hill, N.C., 1970], 1: 283, 287–91).

35   For an interesting analysis of the Virginia Declaration of Rights, see Will-

moore Kendall and George W. Carey, *The Basic Symbols of the American Political Tradition* (Baton Rouge, La., 1970), pp. 61–74.

36 Edmund Randolph, *History of Virginia*, ed. Arthur H. Shaffer (Charlottesville, V., 1970), p. 263.

37 David John Mays, *Edmund Pendleton, 1721–1803: A Biography* (Cambridge, Mass., 1952), 2: 132.

38 George MacLaren Brydon, *Virginia's Mother Church and the Political Conditions Under Which It Grew* (Richmond and Philadelphia, 1947–52), 1: 98–102; 2: 334–5; Arthur Pierce Middleton, "The Colonial Virginia Parish," *Historical Magazine of the Protestant Episcopal Church* 40 (1975): 133–41. An excellent treatment of dissenters and the problems of gentry control may be found in Rhys Isaac, "Religion and Authority: Problems of the Anglican Establishment in Virginia in the Era of the Great Awakening and the Parsons' Cause," *William and Mary Quarterly*, 3d ser., 30 (1973): 3–33, and *The Transformation of Virginia, 1740–1790* (Chapel Hill, N.C., 1982), pp. 143–240.

39 For Madison's position that "freedom of conscience" is "a *natural and absolute right*," see Douglass Adair, ed., "James Madison's Autobiography," *William and Mary Quarterly*, 3d ser., 2 (1945): 199.

40 Henry to Baptist Association meeting in Louisa County, August 13, 1776, in *The Virginia Gazette* (Dixon and Hunter), August 24, 1776.

41 Religious Petitions, 1554–1802, Presented to the General Assembly of Virginia, October 16, 1776, Virginia State Library, Richmond (hereafter VSL) (microfilm); Buckley, *Church and State*, pp. 21–37, covers the various petitions and legislative history of this session.

42 Ford, *Works of Jefferson*, 1: 62.

43 Boyd, *Papers of Jefferson*, 1: 530–58. An expanded version of the first portion of his debate notes may be found in Bernhard Fabian, "Jefferson's *Notes on Virginia*: The Genesis of Query XVII, *The different religions received into that State?*," *William and Mary Quarterly*, 3d ser., 12 (1955): 124–38.

44 Chinard, *Commonplace Book of Jefferson*, pp. 57–9, 351–5, 359–62.

45 Jefferson, *Notes on Virginia*, p. 159; John Locke, *A Letter Concerning Toleration*, ed. Patrick Romanell (Indianapolis, 1955), pp. 17–19; Boyd, *Papers of Jefferson*, 1: 545. A useful textual study is S. Gerald Sandler, "Lockean Ideas in Thomas Jefferson's Bill for Establishing Religious Freedom," *Journal of the History of Ideas* 21 (1960): 110–16. See also Sanford Kessler, "Locke's Influence on Jefferson's 'Bill for establishing Religious Freedom,' " *Journal of Church and State* 25 (1983): 231–52.

46 Some of Jefferson's arguments are strikingly similar to those used by Livingston in a two-part series entitled "The Absurdity of the Civil Magistrate's Interfering in Matters of Religion" (1753). This may be because Livingston also drew on Locke; see Milton M. Klein, ed., *The Independent Reflector* (Cambridge, Mass., 1963), pp. 306–18. Carl Bridenbaugh, *Mitre and Sceptre: Transatlantic Faiths, Ideas, Personalities, and Politics, 1689–1775* (New York, 1962), mainly deals with the opposition to bishops in New England, but Virginia receives brief treatment (pp. 316–32). See also Arthur L. Cross,

The Anglican Episcopate and the American Colonies (New York, 1902), pp. 226–40, and Brydon, *Virginia's Mother Church*, 2: 347–59.

47   Boyd, *Papers of Jefferson*, 1:535–6; Jefferson, *Notes on Virginia*, pp. 157–9; Randolph, *History of Virginia*, p. 264.

48   Jefferson, *Notes on Virginia*, pp. 159, 161. Jefferson's fears were not unique. There was a general anxiety as the Revolution progressed that Americans lacked the requisite virtue for a republic. This sentiment motivated those who wished a general assessment in 1784 and 1785.

49   The Virginia Convention of 1776, which approved the Declaration of Rights and the state constitution, had not been specially elected for that purpose. Instead, the legislature constituted itself as the convention. This was one of the reasons Jefferson was dissatisfied with its work and repeatedly urged a new constitution for the state ("Jefferson's Proposed Revision of the Virginia Constitution," *Papers of Jefferson*, ed. Boyd, 6: 278–317).

50   Conklin, *Self-Evident Truths*, p. 99.

51   Boyd, *Papers of Jefferson*, 1: 537. Quotations are from Fabian, "Jefferson's *Notes on Virginia*," p. 129. Jefferson, *Notes on Virginia*, p. 159.

52   Boyd, *Papers of Jefferson*, 2: 545; Fabian, "Jefferson's *Notes on Virginia*," p. 129. The upper house of the legislature was a purely revisory body; its task was to amend or reject what the House of Delegates had proposed for its consideration (Jackson Turner Main, *The Upper House in Revolutionary America, 1763–1788* [Madison, Wis., 1967], pp. 128–31).

53   Jefferson, *Notes on Virginia*, p. 163.

54   Jefferson to Thomas Law, June 13, 1814, *Jefferson's Extracts from the Gospels*, ed. Adams, pp. 355, 356–7. The concept of a "moral sense" had been developed by those who had expanded on John Locke's ideas, particularly Jean Jacques Burlamaqui and Henry Home, Lord Kames. Writing to Law, Jefferson praised Kames, whose book he had read a half-century before as "one of the ablest of our advocates" (ibid., p. 358). Jefferson to Martha Jefferson, December 11, 1783, *Papers of Jefferson*, ed. Boyd, 6: 381.

55   "Thomas Jefferson's Opinion on the Right of the U.S. to Renounce their Treaties with France," April 28, 1793, Papers of Thomas Jefferson, Library of Congress, ser. 1, reel 18.

56   A helpful discussion of this may be found in White, *Philosophy of the American Revolution*, pp. 113–27, and in Koch, *Philosophy of Jefferson*, pp. 17–18, 135–6, 143. A different outlook on Jefferson is provided by John P. Diggins, who argues that Jefferson was confused about the sources of morality and unsure about "the meaning of moral conduct" ("Slavery, Race, and Equality: Jefferson and the Pathos of the Enlightenment," *American Quarterly* 28 [1976]: 206–28).

57   Jefferson, *Notes on Virginia*, p. 159; Boyd, *Papers of Jefferson*, 1: 537; 2: 546.

58   Richard Price, *Observations on the Nature of Civil Liberty, the Principles of Government, and the Justice and Policy of the War with America* (London, 1776), pp. 3, 4, 25; Richard Henry Lee to Jefferson, July 21, 1776, and Jefferson to Lee, July 29, 1776, *Papers of Jefferson*, ed. Boyd, 1: 471, 477; D. O. Thomas, *The*

Honest Mind: The Thought and Work of Richard Price (Oxford, 1977), pp. 174–86. Price also took liberties in rewriting sections of the statute before publishing it (Boyd, *Papers of Jefferson*, 2: 552–3).

59 Jefferson, *Notes on Virginia*, pp. 160–1. Although in commending those two states, Jefferson skipped over the religious test then being used in Pennsylvania and ignored the fact that the five lower counties of New York had had an establishment during most of the colonial period.

60 *Virginia Gazette* (Purdie and Dixon), June 3, 1773.

61 Fabian, "Jefferson's *Notes on Virginia*," p. 129; Boyd, *Papers of Jefferson*, 1: 537, 547–8; 2: 546; Jefferson, *Notes on Virginia*, p. 160.

62 Boyd, *Papers of Jefferson*, 1: 538; 2: 545; Jefferson, *Notes on Virginia*, p. 161.

63 For his Episcopalian connection, see Jefferson to Henry Ingle, November 6, 1807, declining to continue as a member of Washington Parish because the new church building was too far from the executive mansion (Worthington Chauncey Ford, ed., *Thomas Jefferson Correspondence Printed from the Originals in the Collection of William K. Bixby* [Boston, 1916], pp. 148–9, and Jefferson to [Benjamin Holt Rice], August 10, 1823: "I have been from my infancy a member of the Episcopalian church, and to that I owe and make my contributions," Pierpont Morgan Library, New York (xerox, VHS).

On Unitarianism, Jefferson to Benjamin Waterhouse, June 26, 1822: "I trust that there is not a *young man* now living in the US. who will not die a Unitarian" (Adams, *Jefferson's Extracts from the Gospels*, p. 406). Jefferson to Ezra Stiles Ely, June 25, 1819, ibid., p. 386.

64 While manifesting great concern for the freedom of the individual, he did not involve himself in the church's liberation. He had copied from Locke the statement that the church is a *"voluntary* society" of people who come together to worship God as they choose, but Jefferson was more concerned for the person than for the group or collectivity. His draft constitution in 1776 left the church firmly under the thumb of the secular power. It treated ecclesiastical law in the same way as the civil law of chancery, common law, or marine law, by requiring a jury trial; and just as with any public responsiblity, church offices obtained by bribe were rendered illegitimate, and all church officials, like civil ones, were required to make "an oath of fidelity" to the state government. Thus Jefferson lumped church officials with civil, judicial, and military figures as officers of the state (Boyd, *Papers of Jefferson*, 1: 352, 354, 545). It might be argued that these were Revolutionary times, and he was concerned about seditious preachers. Clearly, he ranked the potential influence of the clergy above that of tavern- or innkeepers, from whom he required no oaths.

65 This is interesting in terms of the conscientious objectors present in Virginia at that time. Quakers, Mennonites, and others wanted freedom on conscience grounds. Belief did affect their lives as citizens.

66 Buckley, *Church and State*, pp. 61–3; Jefferson to Thomas Cooper, October 7, 1814, *The Writings of Thomas Jefferson*, ed. Andrew A. Lipscomb and Albert Ellery Bergh (Washington, D.C., 1903) 14: 200.

67 Jefferson thought that the restoration of the Jesuit Order had been "a retrograde step from light to darkness" and equated "Jesuitism" with "bigotry" (Jefferson to John Adams, August 1, 1816, *The Adams–Jefferson Letters: The complete Correspondence Between Thomas Jefferson and Abigail and John Adams,* ed. Lester J. Cappon [Chapel Hill, N.C., 1959], 2: 484).

68 He wrote this to a former Episcopalian minister: Jefferson to Charles Clay, January 29, 1815, *Jefferson's Extracts from the Gospels,* ed. Adams, p. 363.

69 Malone, *Jefferson and His Time,* 1: 50–3.

70 Examples of Jefferson's clerical friendships may be found in Jefferson to William Preston, August 18, 1768; James Ogilvie to Jefferson, March 28, 1770; Jefferson to Ogilvie, February 20, 1771; Ogilvie to Jefferson, April 26, 1771; "Subscription to Support a Clergyman in Charlottesville," [February 1777]; and "Testimonial for Charles Clay," [August 15, 1779], *Papers of Jefferson,* ed Boyd, 1: 23, 38, 62–4, 67–8; 2:6–7; 3: 67.

71 "Testimonial for Charles Clay," [August 15, 1779]; Jefferson to James Madison, December 8, 1784, ibid., 3: 67; 7: 558. Yet he maintained a cordial relationship with Bishop James Madison until the latter's death in 1812.

72 Jefferson to Chastellux, September 2, 1785, ibid., 8: 470. The Virginia legislature excluded clergymen, as did most new state constitutions (*Journals of the House of Delegates of Virginia* [Richmond, 1827–8], November 1, 1777, p. 9; Gordon Wood, *The Creation of the American Republic, 1776–1787* [Chapel Hill, N.C., 1969], p. 158); that practice has only recently been ruled unconstitutional by the Supreme Court (*McDaniel* v. *Paty* 435 U.S. 618 [1978]).

73 Jefferson to the Attorney General (Levi Lincoln), January 1, 1802, *Works of Jefferson,* ed. Ford, 8: 129.

74 David E. Swift, "Thomas Jefferson, John Holt Rice and Education in Virginia, 1815–1825," *Journal of Presbyterian History* 49 (1971): 32–58.

75 He did not believe that ministers had "the right of discussing public affairs *in the pulpit*" (Jefferson to P. H. Wendover [endorsed as "not sent"], March 13, 1815, *Writings of Jefferson,* ed. Lipscomb and Bergh, 14: 280).

76 Locke, *Letter Concerning Toleration,* pp. 50–2; Boyd, *Papers of Jefferson,* 1: 548, 558–9.

77 George F. Sensabaugh, "Jefferson's Use of Milton in the Ecclesiastical Controversies of 1776," *American Literature* 26 (1955): 552–9.

78 Boyd, *Papers of Jefferson,* 1: 539, 2: 545; Fabian, "Jefferson's *Notes on Virginia,*" p. 131.

79 Episcopalians had their taxes suspended each year until 1779, when the legislature finally ended Church taxation indefinitely. For this legislative process and the continued control of Church affairs by the Assembly, see Buckley, *Church and State,* pp. 32–7 and passim.

80 Boyd explains the work of the revisors and gives the full text of the statute (*Papers of Jefferson,* 2: 305–324, 545–53).

81 William Nelson, Jr., to William Short, April 8, 1786, William Short Papers, Library of Congress; Madison to Jefferson, January 22, 1786, *Papers of Jefferson,* ed. Boyd, 9: 196.

82 Jefferson to George Wythe, August 13, 1786; Jefferson to Madison, December 16, 1786, *Papers of Jefferson,* ed. Boyd, 10: 244, 603–4.

83 Marvin K. Singleton, "Colonial Virginia as First Amendment Matrix: Henry, Madison, and Assessment Establishment," *Journal of Church and State* 8 (1966): 344–64; Robert Allen Rutland, *The Birth of the Bill of Rights, 1776–1791* (Chapel Hill, N.C., 1955). Leading Supreme Court cases referring to the statute include *Reynolds* v. *United States,* 98 U.S. 145 (1878); *Everson* v. *Board of Education,* 330 U.S. 1 (1947); *McCollum* v. *Board of Education,* 333 U.S. 203 (1948); and *Engel* v. *Vitale,* 370 U.S. 421 (1962). A helpful survey is Richard E. Morgan, *The Supreme Court and Religion* (New York, 1972). See also Strout, *New Heavens and New Earth,* pp. 285–313.

For another perspective on Jefferson's work and the meaning of the First Amendment, see Edwin S. Corwin, "The Supreme Court as National School," *Law and Contemporary Problems* 14 (1949): 3–22, and Mark DeWolfe Howe, *The Garden and the Wilderness: Religion and Government in American Constitutional History* (Chicago, 1965).

84 The phrase "holy author of our religion" is ambiguous and could have been understood as a reference to Jesus Christ. Much later both Jefferson and Madison, although in slightly different versions, denied this intention and made the point that an amendment to insert the words "Jesus Christ" after this phrase had been rejected. For a discussion of this, see Buckley, *Church and State,* pp. 157–8, especially n. 45.

85 Jefferson to John Bacon, April 30, 1802; Jefferson to DeWitt Clinton, May 27, 1807, *Works of Jefferson,* ed. Ford, 8: 229; 9: 63.

86 [Knox], *Vindication of the Religion of Mr. Jefferson,* p. 18; [DeWitt Clinton], *A Vindication of Thomas Jefferson; Against the Charges Contained in A Pamphlet Entitled, "Serious Considerations," Etc. By Grotius* (New York, 1800), p. 37; "On the Election of President of the United States," *Aurora,* November 14, 1800.

87 Jefferson to James Monroe, Eppington, May 26, 1800, Jefferson Papers, University of Virginia, Charlottesville, ser. III, reel 4 (abstract of letter, microfilm).

88 U.S. Congress, comp., *A Compilation of the Messages and Papers of the Presidents* (New York, 1897), 1: 310.

89 William Arthur to Jefferson, Pequee, January 8, 1801, Papers of Thomas Jefferson, Coolidge Collection, Massachusetts Historical Society, Boston, reel 5 (microfilm).

90 Thomas Jefferson, First Inaugural Address, in March 4, 1801, U.S. Congress, *Messages and Papers of the Presidents,* 1: 311, 312.

91 Benj[ami]n Rush to Granville Sharp, Philadelphia, March 31, 1801, in John A. Woods, ed., "Correspondence of Benjamin Rush and Granville Sharp, 1773–1809," *Journal of American Studies* 1 (1967): 34.

92 Thomas Jefferson, First Annual Message, December 8, 1801; Second Annual Message, December 15, 1802; Third Annual Message, October 17, 1803; Second Inaugural Address, March 4, 1805; Fifth Annual Message, December

3, 1805; Eighth Annual Message, November 8, 1808, in U.S. Congress, *Messages and Papers of the Presidents,* 1: 314, 330, 349, 370, 371, 444. Jefferson to Chiefs of Indian Tribes, April 11, 1806, Jefferson Papers, University of Virginia, Charlottesville, ser. III, reel 4 (transcript of letter, microfilm). On Jefferson's presidential style, see Robert M. Johnstone, Jr., *Jefferson and the Presidency: Leadership in the Young Republic* (Ithaca, N.Y., 1978).

93   Boyd, *Papers of Jefferson,* 6:249.

94   Jefferson, Second Inaugural Address, U.S. Congress, *Messages and Papers of the Presidents,* 2: 367–8, 370. A fuller elaboration of this policy may be found in a letter that Jefferson wrote to a northern clergyman, Samuel Miller, January 23, 1808 (Ford, *Works of Jefferson,* 9:174–6). Miller was an unabashed Republican, and he and Jefferson had corresponded before (see, for example, Miller to Jefferson, New York, March 4, 1800, Jefferson Papers, Henry E. Huntington Library, San Marino, California, box 2).

95   Dorothy C. Bass, "Gideon Blackburn's Mission to the Cherokees: Christianization and Civilization," *Journal of Presbyterian History* 52 (1974): 203–26; William G. McLoughlin, *Cherokees and Missionaries, 1789–1839* (New Haven, Conn., 1984).

96   [Madison to Jefferson], in Message to Congress of October 17, 1803 [dated received October 1, 1803], Papers of Thomas Jefferson, Library of Congress, ser. 1, reel 29; U.S. Government, comp., *A Compilation of All the Treaties Between the United States and the Indian Tribes Now in Force as Laws* (Washington, D.C., 1873), p. 425. Helpful studies include R. Pierce Beaver, *Church, State and the American Indian* (St. Louis, 1966), and Robert F. Berkhofer, Jr., *Salvation and the Savage, An Analysis of Protestant Missions and American Indian Response, 1787–1862* (New York, 1972).

97   Robert Bellah, "Civil Religion in America," in *American Civil Religion,* ed. Richey and Jones. Bellah further clarified his interpretation of civil religion in *The Broken Covenant* and "The Revolution and Civil Religion," in *Religion and the American Revolution,* ed. Jerald C. Brauer (Philadelphia, 1976). Mead evaluates civil religion in *The Nation with the Soul of a Church* and *The Old Religion in the Brave New World.* A helpful discussion of meanings, terms, and issues may be found in Martin E. Marty, *A Nation of Behavers* (Chicago, 1976), pp. 180–203, and Ellis M. West, "A Proposed Neutral Definition of Civil Religion," *Journal of Church and State,* 22 (1980): 23–40.

    Two important studies dealing with civil religion in this period are Catherine L. Albanese, *Sons of the Fathers: The Civil Religion of the American Revolution* (Philadelphia, 1976), and Nathan O. Hatch, *The Sacred Cause of Liberty: Republican Thought and the Millennium in Revolutionary New England* (New Haven, Conn., 1977), pp. 139–75.

98   Daniel Webster, *A Discourse in Commemoration of the Lives and Services of John Adams and Thomas Jefferson, Delivered in Faneuil Hall, Boston, August 2, 1826* (Boston, 1826), pp. 8, 38; William Johnson, *Eulogy on Thomas Jefferson, Delivered August 3, 1826, in the First Presbyterian Church, . . . Charleston* (Charleston, S.C., 1826), p. 31; William Wirt, *A Discourse on the Lives and*

Characters of Thomas Jefferson and John Adams, . . . Delivered . . . in the Hall of Representatives of the United States, on the Nineteenth October, 1826 (Washington, 1826), pp. 9, 44, 68, 69; Merrill D. Peterson, *The Jefferson Image in the American Mind* (New York, 1960), pp. 1–8.

Portrait by Charles Wilson Peale, c. 1792, of James Madison, who secured passage of the statute. Courtesy of the Thomas Gilcrease Institute
of American History and Art, Tulsa, Oklahoma.

5

James Madison, the Statute for Religious Freedom, and the Crisis of Republican Convictions

LANCE BANNING

The Virginia Statute for Religious Freedom was an early fruit of the most famous partnership in American political history. Thomas Jefferson prepared it, as part of the proposed revision of the code of laws that his Committee of Revisors reported to the General Assembly in 1779. James Madison secured its passage, six years later, in the wake of a petitioning campaign that demonstrated overwhelming disapproval of a bill providing for a general assessment for support of teachers of the Christian religion, which he had barely managed to postpone in the previous session. Defeat of the assessment and approval of the Bill for Establishing Religious Freedom marked a major turning point in the development of the American relationship of church and state. They were of critical importance, too, for the expression and development of Madison's political ideas. His great "Memorial and Remonstrance Against Religious Assessments," long accepted by historians and jurists as a classic explanation of the reasoning behind the statute (and even the First Amendment to the Constitution, which he introduced a few years later), may have been his clearest and most eloquent enunciation of the fundamental principles that guided both partners through much of their careers. The lessons that he learned from the Virginia struggle over church and state were probably the most important catalyst for the conclusions that became his most distinctive contribution to the Founding.

Madison's own faith is something of a puzzle, so strongly did he feel that religion is a profoundly private matter. Reared in the Established Church, he continued to prefer its services throughout his life, and yet he never entered full communion or identified himself as an Episcopalian. Although his father was a vestryman and Madison had been tutored by the local rector, climate, politics, and educational superiority outweighed denominational considerations when the three of them decided on a college, choosing Presbyterian but fiercely patriotic Princeton. There, he dressed in homespun, joined the Whigs in student battles with the rival Cliosophs, and stayed for an extra summer to read law and Hebrew with President John Witherspoon, whose antihierarchical opinions and defense of toleration touched his spirit in a way that two revivals evidently failed to do. When he returned from college, two years before an angry Parliament passed the Coercive Acts, Madison was deeply moralistic and determined to enroll his name in "the Annals of Heaven."[1] He knew the Bible, read divinity, condemned the enmity toward religion of the popular reviews, and wrote so favorably of those who testified their disapproval of temporal enjoyments "by becoming fervent advocates in the cause of Christ" that there is room to wonder if he gave at least a passing thought to entering the ministry himself.[2] How far he may have veered toward deism later in his life is open to conjecture, for religious topics simply disappear from his surviving papers after 1776. What we cannot doubt is what he wrote in a sketch of an autobiography: He was "under very early and strong impressions in favor of liberty both civil and religious."[3]

Civil and religious liberty were intimately linked in Madison's career and thinking. His earliest political involvement, in 1773, was prompted by the persecution of dissenters in neighboring Culpeper County. "Is an ecclesiastical establishment absolutely necessary to support civil society?" he asked a Pennsylvania classmate, through whom he purchased copies of the latest treatises on toleration.[4] Northern opposition to the Tea Act and other parliamentary encroachments suggested different conclusions, for "dependent states" at least.

> If the Church of England had been the established and general religion in all the Northern colonies as it has been among us here . . . , it is clear to me that slavery and subjection might and would have been gradually insinuated among us. Union of religious sentiments begets a surprising confidence [in rulers] and ecclesiastical establishments tend to great ignorance and corruption, all of which facilitate the execution of mischievous projects.[5]

A broad comparison of Pennsylvania with Virginia reinforced the lesson. Pennsylvania's "liberal, catholic, and equitable way of thinking as to the rights of conscience" encouraged immigration, commerce, virtue, industry, the arts, and a productive love of fame and knowledge. "Religious bondage shackles and debilitates the mind and unfits it for every noble enterprise, every expanded project."[6] "I have . . . nothing to brag of," Madison complained, as to the state and liberty of my country. Poverty and luxury prevail among all sorts: pride, ignorance, and knavery among the priesthood, and vice and wickedness among the laity. This is bad enough, but it is not the worst I have to tell you. That diabolical, Hell-conceived principle of persecution rages among some, and to their eternal infamy, the clergy can furnish their quota of imps for such business. This vexes me the most of anything whatever. There are . . . in the adjacent country not less than 5 or 6 well meaning men in close jail for publishing their religious sentiments, which in the main are very orthodox. I have neither patience to hear, talk, or think of anything relative to this matter, for I have squabbled and scolded, abused and ridiculed so long about it . . . that I am without common patience.[7]

As Orange County mobilized behind the recommendations of the Continental Congress, Madison found more to brag of. He joined his father on the committee of safety, practiced with a rifle, drilled with the local minute company, and boasted of his neighbors' marksmanship and vigilance against opponents of the Revolution, including local parsons whose appeal to conscience, he predicted, would be answered with a coat of tar and feathers if they stubbornly continued to resist the people's will.[8] The rights of conscience, nevertheless, still ranked among his first concerns. When feeble health compelled him to abandon thoughts of active military service, the gratitude of Baptist neighbors may have helped him win election to the state convention of 1776, which framed one of the earliest, most widely imitated Revolutionary constitutions. Here, despite his youth and modesty, he made his first important contribution to a lifelong battle for religious freedom, standing on a set of principles that placed him from the start among the most advanced reformers of his age.

When the Virginia constitution came to the convention from committee, George Mason's draft of a Declaration of Rights contained a generous, although basically conventional, protection for dissenters:

That religion, or the duty which we owe to our Creator, and the manner of discharging it, can be directed only by reason and conviction, not by force or violence; and therefore, that all men should enjoy the fullest toleration in the exercise of religion, according to the dictates of conscience, unpunished and unrestrained by the magistrate unless, under color of religion, any man disturb the peace, the happiness, or safety of society. And that it is the mutual duty of all to practice Christian forbearance, love, and charity towards each other.

Madison was not content. The language of the article, like the language of the preface to the Declaration of Rights, suggested the enormous influence of John Locke, whose famous *Letter on Toleration* grounded freedom of conscience on the nature of human understanding and the separate origins and purposes of church and state, yet listed several opinions that the magistrate should punish.[9] On his copy of the printed draft of the religious article, Madison prepared a change that pressed Locke's premises to logical conclusions from which Locke himself had shied. In place of Mason's "all men should enjoy the fullest toleration," Madison's amendment, which was introduced by Patrick Henry, would have said:

> all men are equally entitled to the full and free exercise of [their religion] according to the dictates of conscience; and therefore that no man or class of men ought, on account of religion, to be invested with peculiar emoluments or privileges; nor subjected to any penalties or disabilities unless, under color of religion, any man disturb the peace, the happiness, or safety of society.[10]

Someone asked if Henry really meant to disestablish the church. He denied it; the amendment failed; and Madison wrote a substitute, this time asking Edmund Pendleton to introduce it. The new proposal altered Mason's "all men should enjoy the fullest toleration . . . unpunished and unrestrained by the magistrate" to "all men are equally entitled to enjoy the free exercise of religion unless the preservation of equal liberty and the existence of the state are manifestly endangered."[11] As approved by the convention, Article XVI incorporated Madison's replacement of the reference to "toleration" with recognition of an equal right and simply dropped the clause referring to the state's authority to keep the peace.

Momentous implications were contained in what might seem a minor change of wording. However broadly it extends, Madison perceived, "toleration" is a privilege permitted by the state; and it implies a state authority to set a standard from which some degree of deviation, but perhaps no more, may be allowed. An equal right not just to hold, but freely to express and exercise the varied dictates of free conscience places differing opinions on entirely different grounds.[12] Although the failure of his first amendment left the question of Establishment unsettled, the logic of his second demanded fully equal treatment for competing faiths and urged withdrawal of the state from all of that separate sphere that Locke had carefully defined without consistently defending. In its final phrasing, Article XVI erected an ideal that no society had ever written into law and spurred the commonwealth at once toward its achievement. Dissenters seized on it immediately to call for equal treatment. Among

Virginia's legislative leaders, it identified the shy, young representative from Orange as one from whom extraordinary deeds might be expected.

Madison's mature position on religious freedom was probably complete in its essentials when he drafted these amendments. He seems from that point forward, with unwavering consistency, to have envisioned total freedom of opinion, absolute equality for various denominations, and an end to the prevailing intermixture of the logically distinctive spheres of politics and religion, this world and the next.[13] He probably agreed with the dissenters that, despite the failure of his first amendment, Article XVI implied a speedy disestablishment and revocation of a panoply of statutes punishing dissent, providing tax support for the Established Church, and licensing or regulating both dissenting preachers and the regular parishes and clergy. When the General Assembly met for its October session, Thomas Jefferson, who had been absent in the spring, assumed direction of a legislative drive to effect these reforms. Madison, who served on the Committee for Religion but was still too inexperienced for an assertive role, gave Jefferson his full support.[14]

The effort met with only limited success. While Madison and Jefferson, who called the fight the hardest of his life, already looked toward disestablishment, repeal of all restrictions on opinion, and a wholly voluntary system of support for all denominations, most delegates were not prepared for such a large departure from tradition. The Assembly did revoke all parliamentary statutes concerning religion. It did suspend collection of religious taxes, from which the dissenters now received exemption. But the state retained the power to license dissenting preachers and meetings as well as to supervise the Established Church, whose parishes continued to perform several civil functions. Although the gains were great, many fundamental issues continued unresolved.

Jefferson's Bill for Establishing Religious Freedom, number 82 of the revisors' code, was introduced to the Assembly in 1779, as was a bill providing for a general assessment for support of the Christian religion. Neither was enacted. Except for the repeal of the law providing salaries for the Established clergy, another measure of 1779, the legislature passed no major bills relating to religion for the duration of the war.[15] Jefferson's ability to press his program of reforms was nearly ended by his election as governor and subsequent appointment to a ministry abroad. Madison was not a member of the General Assembly from 1777 through 1783, although he was acquiring the maturity and stature to finish what his older colleague had begun.

Defeated in his bid for reelection in the spring of 1777 – he refused to offer the customary treats to voters – Madison was quickly chosen by the legislature as a member of the Council of State, where he served with

Governors Henry and Jefferson. Two year later, in December 1779, the legislature sent him on to Congress. Here, he rapidly acquired a national reputation, first as and effective spokesman for Virginia's interests, and then as a leading advocate for federal reforms. He was instrumental in the management of Virginia's western cession, which prepared the way for ratification of the Articles of Confederation and creation of a national domain. He introduced the compromise that resulted in the congressional recommendations of April 18, 1783, which called on the states to approve an amendment to the Articles granting Congress power to impose a 5 percent duty on foreign imports, to complete the western cessions, and to levy other taxes sufficient to provide for the continental debt. He also wrote the eloquent accompanying address, which characterized these measures as vital to the nation's needs and to the international reputation of "the cause of liberty."[16]

By the time his term in Congress ended, in November 1783, Madison was fully qualified to take a leading role within his state. He and Jefferson had spent a good share of the year together, boarding at the same establishment for several weeks during the winter while Jefferson waited to learn whether he should sail for Europe to take up his duties as a peace commissioner, and for several more during the fall, when Jefferson went north again to take a seat in Congress. As their conversations swept the spectrum of state and federal needs, their old acquaintance ripened into the remarkable alliance and deep personal friendship of their later years. Each determined to pursue appropriate items of a shared agenda. When they parted at Annapolis in late November, Madison intended to reenter the Assembly in the spring to seek the state's support for necessary federal changes and to push for legislative action on several reforms that Jefferson had much at heart, including the revision of the state constitution and consideration of the stalled revision of the laws.[17]

Virginians who expected the returning congressman to be a vigorous new force in the Assembly were quickly proved right. Early in the session, Patrick Henry met with Madison and Joseph Jones and offered to support them on the floor if they would sketch a plan to strengthen Congress.[18] With Henry's powerful assistance, Madison secured approval of a federal power to retaliate against the British navigation laws, along with several other measures signifying a determination to comply with congressional recommendations. He could not prevent a declaration that Virginia's full compliance with the Treaty of Paris, which required removal of impediments to British creditors, would be contingent on prior reparations for British violations of the treaty. But as chairman of the Committee on Commerce, he was responsible for resolutions leading to the Mount Vernon Conference and for a bill restricting foreign traders to specific ports. On May 29, he also moved successfully for printing the proposed revision of the laws, an early step toward legislative action.[19]

For all these great successes, Madison was not entirely pleased with the spring session. Richard Henry Lee's support had persuaded him to join in an attempt to move for the calling of a convention to revise the state constitution. But Lee and Henry were traditional opponents, and the former governor's ferocious disapproval crushed the move and carried a resolution intended to bar its revival. Later, Madison and Lee were checked again when they attempted to defeat a resolution postponing the collection of the tax for 1784, without which the Assembly could not fulfill its earlier resolution to meet its congressional requisitions. Madison was thoroughly disgusted with the postponement of the tax, the sorry condition of state accounts, and bills so poorly drafted that they threatened to reduce the legislature to contempt. He also noted with distaste that several petitions had appeared requesting an assessment for religion and that friends of the Established Church had "introduced a notable project for reestablishing their independence of the laity" in the form of an incorporation bill. "Extraordinary" as this project was, he wrote, it would lie over for the fall, "preserved from a dishonorable death by the talents of Mr. Henry."[20]

Madison was fully as successful in the fall Assembly session as he had been in the spring. Still seeking full compliance with the Treaty of Paris, he drafted an important law prohibiting further confiscation of Loyalist property, and only a last-minute accident prevented the enrollment of an act providing for installment payments of British debts. As chairman of the Committee for Courts of Justice as well as the Committee on Commerce, he successfully introduced an assize bill, establishing a system of circuit courts. Working closely with George Washington, he led a major legislative thrust to speed internal improvements.[21]

Once again, however, Madison was scarcely able to enjoy his triumphs. Long and tedious, the session was preoccupied from the beginning with religious issues. Outvoted in the House of Delegates and heavily afflicted by a sudden (temporary) turn in Presbyterian opinion, he felt compelled to sacrifice his opposition to the Bill for Episcopal Incorporation as part of what must certainly have seemed an arduous and close attempt to postpone the final passage of a measure that could have pressed Virginia's – and perhaps America's – relationship of church and state into a mold profoundly different from his and Jefferson's desires: A Bill Establishing a Provision for Teachers of the Christian Religion.[22]

The House of Delegates had found a quorum on October 29. Several petitions requesting a religious tax had been submitted. The Bill for Episcopal Incorporation lay over from the spring. Although the Presbyterians and Baptists protested several features of the latter bill and continued to object to special treatment for the old Establishment, neither group repeated its traditional support for an entirely voluntary system of church finance. The silence of the dissenters, the continuing decline of the Episcopalians, and mounting fears of immorality and inattention to the public good, which members of the Revolutionary generation generally identified as mortal dangers to republics, all made the moment right for yet another effort to support the Christian churches. In the eighteenth century, almost no one doubted that good conduct rested on religion, and a general assessment that would free a citizen to designate which church would get his taxes seemed to many a fair and liberal way to secure the morality without which no republic could endure.[23]

Making many of these points, Patrick Henry quickly moved for an assessment act, and over Madison's objections, by a vote of 47 to 32, the Committee of the Whole approved the preparation of a bill. Madison was not immediately alarmed. When Henry was elected governor and left the House, Madison hoped that no bill would issue from the select committee, which Henry had chaired, or that a bill would be defeated in the absence of the orator's support.[24] By the beginning of December, though, when the assessment bill appeared, he knew the threat was real. On November 12, the House of Delegates had received its annual petition from the Hanover Presbytery. In a remarkable reversal of its previous positions – "shameful" was the word that Madison selected – the Presbytery dropped its opposition to a general tax, providing that the act was fair to all denominations. With this important portion of the clergy "as ready to set up an establishment which is to take them in as they were to pull down that which shut them out," with the overwhelming weight of an increasing number of petitions favoring an assessment act, and with the pro-assessment forces willing to revise the marriage law and the incorporation bill in order to satisfy the main objections of dissenters, the prospect for successful legislation was growing day by day.[25]

While the assessment bill lay on the table, the House turned its attention to the new Episcopal incorporation bill, which carried on December 22 by a vote of 47 to 38. Although he still believed the bill to be "exceptionable" in several features, Madison decided to abandon his objections and voted for it. Some such act, he wrote, was necessary to permit the church to hold and manage property, and the final version seemed as harmless as current circumstances would permit.[26] Moreover, the defeat of the incorporation bill, he reasoned, might redouble its supporters' "eagerness" for the "much greater evil" of the general assessment, to which the House immediately proceeded.[27]

To Madison's dismay, support for the assessment showed few signs of cooling. The bill passed its preliminary readings by a vote of 44 to 42, and opponents had no options left except to argue that a measure so important should be printed for the public's consideration before its final passage. In support of this appeal for a delay, Madison prepared one of the most elaborate speeches of his long career. Sometime during the debates, in fact, he drafted outlines for at least two major speeches.[28]

If he followed the surviving outlines, the shorter speech observed that the assessment bill required the courts to determine what was Christian, and asked how they would do so. Which Bible would they use – "Hebrew, Septuagint, or Vulgate?" Which translation? How would they decide which books were canonical and which apocryphal when Catholics, Lutherans, and other Protestants disagreed? How should they interpret Scripture? What doctrines would the courts admit as Christian? "What clue" could guide them through "this labyrinth"?

The longer speech placed state support in a broader context. The tendency of the assessment bill, it opened, was to establish Christianity as a state religion, and religion was "not within [the] purview of civil authority." The fundamental issue, Madison insisted, was not whether religion was necessary, but whether an establishment was necessary for religion. Man was naturally religious, he maintained, but history suggested that establishments "corrupted" the religious impulse. Contemporary Pennsylvania, other middle states, and early Christianity all showed that religion could thrive without state support, which would discourage immigration and might even lead Virginia's own dissenters to seek a freer climate. Henry warned that immorality had led to the collapse of several mighty states. Most such states had had established churches, Madison observed. So did most of the New England states, which were as troubled as Virginia. Rising immorality was not a consequence of the absence of a state-supported church, but a result of wartime dislocations and "bad laws." The proper cures were peace, a better administration of justice, education, the personal example of leaders, laws that would "cherish virtue," and an end to the hope for a general assessment instead of voluntary support for religious bodies. The assessment bill, he finished, would "dishonor Christianity." The "progress of religious liberty" was inconsistent with the resurrection of a state religion.

Madison was seldom a "forensic" member of a legislative body (in his own disdainful phrase), but he could be uncommonly effective when he was. He was undoubtedly an able parliamentary tactician. On Christmas Eve, eight other delegates who had supported the Episcopal Incorporation Act joined him in voting to postpone the final reading of the assessment bill until November 1785.[29] The vote was 45 to 38, almost exactly a reversal of the numbers that had carried the incorporation.

Madison's appeals and legislative strategy were not, of course, the only influence on this outcome. By itself, postponement of the final reading of the bill did not ensure defeat of the assessment. Yet Madison had plainly served as legislative leader of his side, and his defense of freedom left a memorable impression on its other friends. Two of them, the brothers George and Wilson Cary Nicholas, with Madison's speeches fresh in mind, turned naturally to him for leadership of an attempt to muster public opposition to the bill. They urged him to prepare a form for a petition, which could be circulated through Virginia's counties in the months between Assembly sessions as an instrument for shaping and expressing general opinion.[30] The product, the anonymous "Memorial and Remonstrance Against Religious Assessments," would become a cornerstone in the American tradition of religious liberty.[31]

Madison's "Memorial" was more eclectic than inventive, an effort reminiscent of Jefferson's attempt, when drafting the Declaration of Independence, to set forth the general understandings of the age. Drawing on the body of his knowledge rather than on a few specific sources and recalling all the arguments that moved his own emotions, Madison attempted to arouse the intellects and feelings of many different segments of Virginia's varied public: evangelicals and skeptics, Baptist ministers as well as the enlightened members of the vestries, all who shared or could be taught to share his own abiding love of freedom. The comprehensive reach of the appeal, together with its unfeigned fervor and the author's skillful interweaving of its several themes, explain its lasting impact.[32]

Like Jefferson again, if Madison was specially indebted to a single source, that source was Locke.[33] As he had done before, however, he carried Locke's contractual philosophy to rigorous extremes, allowing none of the departures that Locke himself had made from his original insistence on the separate spheres of church and state. Beginning from the point where Locke had started and quoting Article XVI of the Declaration of Rights, he called religious liberty "unalienable" in its essential nature. Because opinion, by its nature, cannot be coerced, it is the right of every man to hold and exercise his own convictions. Moreover,

> what is here a right towards men is a duty towards the Creator.
> It is the duty of every man to render to the Creator such homage
> and such only as he believes to be acceptable to Him. This duty
> is precedent, both in order of time and in degree of obligation,
> to the claims of civil society. Before any man can be considered
> as a member of civil society, he must be considered as a subject
> of the Governor of the Universe: And . . . every man who be-

comes a member of any particular civil society [does] it with a saving of his allegiance to the Universal Sovereign.

"In matters of religion," Madison insisted, "no man's right is abridged by the institution of civil society, and . . . religion is wholly exempt from its cognizance."[34]

But if society itself has no legitimate authority to intervene in the sphere of conscience, "still less" can any such authority devolve on the "legislative body."

> The latter are but the creatures and vicegerents of the former. Their jurisdiction is both derivative and limited: it is limited with regard to the coordinate departments, more necessarily is it limited with regard to the constituents. The preservation of a free government requires not merely that the metes and bounds which separate each department of power be invariably maintained, but more especially that neither of them be suffered to overleap the great barrier which defends the rights of the people. The rulers who are guilty of such an encroachment exceed the commission from which they derive their authority, and are tyrants. The people who submit to it are governed by laws made neither by themselves nor by an authority derived from them, and are slaves.[35]

Having hinted at the deep regard for fundamental charters that had guided him throughout the 1780s – the profound respect for fundamental law that would become the starting point for his and Jefferson's strict construction of the federal Constitution – Madison implied that no one should be tempted to conceive of the assessment as only an inconsequential violation of pure doctrine, a valid compromise between the rights of conscience and the needs of the state. The proper time to "take alarm" for liberty, he cautioned, is at the first experiments of power, as the Revolutionary patriarchs had done (and as he and Jefferson would do themselves when confronted with the plan for a national bank).[36]

> The free men of America did not wait till usurped power had strengthened itself by exercise and entangled the question in precedents. They saw all the consequences in the principle, and they avoided the consequences by denying the principle. . . . Who does not see that the same authority which can establish Christianity, in exclusion of all other religions, may establish with the same ease any particular sect of Christians in exclusion of all other sects? that the same authority which can force a citizen to contribute three pence only of his property . . . may force

him to conform to any . . . establishment in all cases whatsoever?[37]

Equal rights are yet another test of the validity of every republican law. Quoting once again from Mason's Declaration, Madison reminded legislators that "all men are to be considered as entering into society on equal conditions, as relinquishing no more, and therefore retaining no less, one than another, of their natural rights." Like Jefferson, therefore, and unlike Locke, he forcefully maintained that there can be no logical exceptions to the rule:

> Whilst we assert for ourselves a freedom to embrace, to profess, and to observe the religion which we believe to be of divine origin, we cannot deny an equal freedom to those whose minds have not yet yielded to the evidence which has convinced us. If this freedom be abused, it is an offence against God, not against man: To God, therefore, not to man, must an account of it be rendered.

Any breach of this first principle, even one that would afford an equal preference to every Christian, must imply either that the civil authority is competent to judge religious truth or that the state may legitimately "employ religion as an engine of civil policy. The first is an arrogant pretension falsified by the contradictory opinions of rulers in all ages; . . . the second an unhallowed perversion of the means of salvation."[38]

What logic teaches, experience confirms; and Madison could transit neatly to a series of historical and practical objections to the bill. He argued first, as he had done in the Assembly, that Christianity did not require state aid, "for it is known that this religion both existed and flourished, not only without the support of human laws, but in spite of every opposition from them, and not only during the period of miraculous aid, but long after it had been left to its own evidence and the ordinary care of Providence." State support had several consequences, the "Memorial" suggested, quite opposite from those its advocates intended. It weakened Christians' confidence in the intrinsic excellence of their religion and encouraged nonbelievers to suspect that its supporters were "too conscious of its fallacies to trust it to its own merits." Instead of bolstering the purity and power of the faith, ecclesiastical establishments had always had the opposite effect. What were the fruits of nearly fifteen centuries of state support? "More or less, in all places, pride and indolence in the clergy, ignorance and servility in the laity, in both, superstition, bigotry, and persecution." Every Christian teacher knew that Christianity was purest and had achieved "its greatest lustre" in the "ages prior to its incorporation with civil policy," when its ministers "depended on the voluntary rewards of their flocks."[39]

If Christianity required no help from government, but prospered best without it, neither did the needs of government demand establishments or general assessments:

> What influence in fact have ecclesiastical establishments had on civil society? In some instances they have been seen to erect a spiritual tyranny on the ruins of the civil authority; in many instances they have been seen upholding the thrones of political tyranny; in no instance have they been seen the guardians of the liberties of the people. . . . A just government . . . will be best supported by protecting every citizen in the enjoyment of his religion with the same equal hand which protects his person and his property, by neither invading the equal rights of any sect, nor suffering any sect to invade those of another.

"What a melancholy mark" the general assessment would appear, Madison warned, of "sudden degeneracy" from the policy of "offering an asylum to the persecuted and oppressed of every nation and religion."

> It degrades from the equal rank of citizens all those whose opinions in religion do not bend to those of the legislative authority. Distant as it may be in its present form from the Inquisition, it differs from it only in degree. The one is the first step, the other the last in the career of intolerance.

The foreign sufferer could only see a general assessment "as a beacon on our coast, warning him to seek some other haven." The bill would add another motive to the many presently existing for further emigration from the state. It would destroy the harmony and moderation that had prevailed among the different sects while the laws forbore to "intermeddle" with religion. "Torrents of blood have been spilt in the old world by vain attempts of the secular arm to extinguish religious discord by proscribing all difference in religious opinion." Such differences were best assuaged, and Christianity was most generally diffused, "by levelling as far as possible every [artificial] obstacle to the victorious progress of truth," not by "ignoble and unchristian" efforts to defend the faith from error.[40]

Returning once again to the words of the Virginia constitution, words that he himself had written, Madison completed the "Memorial" by powerfully restating its main theme. "The equal right of every citizen to the free exercise of his religion," he concluded, "is held by the same tenure with all our other rights."

> Either then, we must say that the will of the legislature is the only measure of their authority and that, in the plenitude of this authority, they may sweep away all our fundamental rights, or that they are bound to leave this particular right untouched and sacred. Either we must say that they may control the freedom of the press, may abolish the trial by jury, may swallow up the executive and judiciary powers of the state, nay that they may despoil us of our very right of suffrage and erect themselves into an independent and hereditary assembly, or we must say that they have no authority to enact into law the bill under consideration.[41]

Nowhere else in any of his writings was Madison more eloquent or more explicit in explaining the consistent core of fundamental principle that guided him through all the turns of his career. In its brief but clear elucidation of the origins of governmental power, its insistence on inherent, equal rights that individuals do not surrender when they enter a society, its fear of even slight transgressions of the chartered bounds of power, and even its concern with rulers who might free themselves entirely from dependence on the people, the "Memorial" is indispensable for understanding why the future "father of the Constitution" would also be the future captain of the Jeffersonian resistance, the author of the Virginia Resolutions of 1798.[42] In its sincere regard for both the purity of faith and the protection of the state from bigots, the petition nicely balances Christian and republican preoccupations. In its insistence on the total separation of these spheres, it linked the youth of 1776 to the distinguished elder statesman who worried in retirement that he might have missed an implication of the principle before the War of 1812 when he had given in to Congress and issued a presidential proclamation for a day of prayer.[43] In its conviction that the truth requires no artificial aids and its assumption that religious freedom is the litmus test of freedom of the intellect in all its forms, the powerful "Memorial" is one with Jefferson's great bill, which it would soon explain and help to pass.

Completed by the end of June, the anonymous "Memorial" was circulated widely by George Nicholas through the central Piedmont and the Shenandoah Valley and by George Mason through the Northern Neck.[44] By the time of the petition's appearance, as Madison had hoped, opinion was already shifting noticeably against the general assessment. Lay and clerical Episcopalians were increasingly at odds over governance and doctrine. In August, Presbyterians assembled in a general convention and overwhelmingly agreed on a long petition disapproving the assessment, condemning several features of the Incorporation Act, and calling for the first time for approval of the Bill for Establishing Religious Freedom. The General Committee of the Baptists also roundly and specifically condemned the tax.[45] During its 1785 session, the General Assembly received more than one hundred religious petitions, only eleven of which supported the assessment. Among the ninety that condemned the measure, signed by nearly eleven thousand Virginians, thirteen were copies of Madison's "Memorial."[46] So plainly did the people speak that no one tried to resurrect the general assessment, and Madison seized the occasion to win enactment of the Virginia Statute for Religious Freedom.

Chairman of the Committee for Courts of Justice, as before, Madison decided early in the session to force the laggard House of Delegates to action on the much-postponed revision of the laws, which had been printed at his instigation in 1784. On October 31, he introduced more than one hundred bills, virtually the whole of the revision except for portions that had been enacted in previous years.[47] It was a huge commitment for the busy House and for its legislative leader, yet the Delegates agreed to set aside three days per week until the work was finished. Holding faithfully to the agreement, they labored systematically through the revision, amending and enacting thirty-five proposals. But with the opposition steadily increasing and supporters growing tired, progress stalled completely on the Bill on Crimes and Punishments, number 64 of the revisors' code. The session had already stretched into December, and it was clear that there was insufficient time and patience to complete the task. From the remainder of the code, therefore, Madison extracted number 82, the Bill for Establishing Religious Freedom. Despite significant, "warm" opposition on the floor, it passed the Delegates on December 17 essentially unchanged. Opponents in the Senate carried an amendment, which was defeated in the lower house, that would have devastated Jefferson and robbed the bill of much of its importance by striking his impressive preamble and substituting Article XVI of the Declaration of Rights. The Delegates immediately refused the change. Tedious maneuvering continued nearly to adjournment of the session, but Madison's tenacity and legislative skills were equal to the challenge. The statute was signed by Speaker Harrison on January 19, 1786, with its preamble fundamentally unmarred.[48]

Although he never bragged about his legislative feats and did not change his custom of reporting the Assembly's actions in a style that never mentioned his own role, Madison did not disguise his exaltation. Sending news of victory to Jefferson in France, he explained that a dispute between the houses had "defaced the composition" of the act. Delegates who favored Jefferson's original language had "thought better to agree" with minor Senate changes in the preamble "than to run further risks, especially as it was getting late in the session and the House was growing thin." But the enacting clauses of the bill, he said, had passed unchanged, "and I flatter myself have in this country extinguished forever the ambitious hope of making laws for the human mind."[49] Passage of the statute was a proud achievement. It was also an important moment in the continuing development of Madison's political ideas.

To many of his legislative colleagues, Madison had never seemed more formidable than in the 1785 Assembly. "Can you suppose it possible that Madison should shine with more than usual splendor this assembly?" one delegate inquired. "It is, sir, not only possible but a fact. He has astonished mankind and has by means perfectly constitutional become almost a dictator upon all subjects."[50] With Patrick Henry governor again and Richard Henry Lee in Congress, Madison had no competitor for domination of the House of Delegates and played a leading role on nearly every major issue.[51]

From Madison's own perspective, nevertheless, the session "afforded less ground for applause" than any he had yet attended.[52] He was relieved to find that one presession worry did not develop into an immediate danger. "Not a word has passed in the House as to a paper emission," he told Monroe.[53] Yet he continued to detect a threat. "A considerable itch for paper money" was apparent, he reported at the session's end, and "the partizans of the measure . . . flatter themselves, and I fear upon too good ground, that it will be among the measures of the next."[54] Even his success with the revision of the laws was tempered in his mind by the reflection that "it might have been finished at one session with great ease if the time spent on motions to put it off and other dilatory tactics had been employed on its merits."[55] It is clear that Madison's determination to hold impatient colleagues to this work cost him considerable good will and influence as the session lengthened. Their resentment may have been responsible in part for a series of defeats that left him powerfully disheartened.[56]

As always, federal measures were high on Madison's agenda. He had traveled to New York and Philadelphia before the session started and come back even more impressed with the necessity of strengthening the Confederation, which he increasingly believed might soon collapse entirely if Congress continued to be unable to confront the nation's commercial problems.[57] Appointed to a committee to prepare a resolution authorizing the Virginia delegates to move in Congress for a federal power to regulate the country's trade, he probably prepared its resolutions of November 14 and made at least one major speech in their support.[58] But in the end, the Delegates were willing to confide this power only under conditions so restrictive that he felt obliged to vote against it.[59] He was checked, in fact, in every effort to support the dignity and needs of Congress. On December 19, he introduced another bill to reopen the courts and provide for installment payments of the British debts. This, too, was so disfigured by amendments that he preferred to let it die.[60] And while the Delegates turned back a move to remit the year's tax entirely – a "narrow escape," said Madison, from a "severe attack" on public credit – this was accomplished only by a compromise that once again postponed collection. "The wisdom of seven sessions," he complained, "will be unable to repair the mischiefs of this single act," which would make it impossible to pay "a shilling" to Congress.[61]

Uniformly disappointed on federal issues, Madison was hardly more successful on domestic matters. While no one raised the cry for paper money, his Port and Assize acts of 1784 were both subjected to serious attack. Supplemental legislation needed to initiate the plan for circuit courts was defeated by a vote of 63 to 49, and operation of the Assize Act had to be suspended to prevent its repeal.[62] The Port Act, too, was nearly overturned, and he anticipated its repeal at the next session. "It would have been repealed at this," he wrote, "if its adversaries had known their strength in time and exerted it with judgment."[63] From all these points of view – and despite the passage of the Bill for Establishing Religious Freedom – the 1785 Assembly seemed to Madison the nadir of his legislative service. The setbacks, threats, and disappointments suffered in its course bore no small part of the responsibility for what can fairly be described as the most important intellectual crisis of his life.[64]

"True it is," Madison's "Memorial" had said, "that no other rule exists by which any question which may divide a society can be ultimately determined but the will of the majority; but it is also true that the majority may trespass on the rights of the minority."[65] True it also seemed to be – and never more apparently than in the 1785 Assembly – that the demands of the majority were not invariably consistent with justice, honor, and the public good. With every legislative session, Madison had felt increasingly revolted and dishonored by poorly drafted, fluctuating laws. Since his return from Congress, he had struggled unsuccessfully for constitutional revision, won partial victories or none at all on federal issues, and crafted several urgent state reforms, only to see them gutted in succeeding sessions. By the spring of 1786, as his attention turned increasingly toward the Annapolis Convention and the possibility of sweeping federal reform, his discontents were equaled only by his fears. For every year had also seen a new and always rising tide of measures, passed or threatened, that offered to protect the people from depressed conditions by preventing creditors from pressing their legitimate claims or by depriving the state and federal governments of the means to keep their contracts and perform their necessary duties.

Virginia managed to avoid the most objectionable measures of the postwar years: paper money, property confiscations, and laws preventing citizens from suing for recovery of debts.[66] To Madison, however, the escape seemed narrow and increasingly in doubt. Nor was it any consolation to a man of continental vision that the malady seemed national in scope. Throughout America, he was beginning to conclude, the "multiplicity," the "mutability," and the "injustice" of state laws were calling into question "the fundamental principle of republican government, that the majority who rule in such governments are the safest guardians both of public good and of private rights."[67] The framers of the early Revolutionary constitutions, he had begun to think, had assumed that "a provision for the rights of persons," for republican self-government, would "include of itself" protection for the rights of property and other liberties that individuals had not surrendered to the state.[68] But, every day, experience produced new proofs that this assumption was mistaken. "What we once thought the calumny of the enemies of republican government," he would tell the Constitutional Convention, "is undoubtably true": The rule of the majority does not provide an automatic guarantee of private rights or public good.[69]

It was not just the debilities of the Confederation, Madison informed his colleagues, that had brought them to the Constitutional Convention. "Interferences" with "private rights" and rising discontent with the injustices and defects of legislation in the states were everywhere endangering the popular commitment to the Revolutionary order. "Debtors have defrauded their creditors. The landed interest has borne hard on the mercantile interest. The holders of one species of property have thrown a disproportion of taxes on the holders of another species." Even in societies without hereditary ranks, he argued, there are differences of interest or opinion between the "rich and poor, debtors and creditors, the landed, the manufacturing, the commercial interests, the inhabitants of this district or that district, the followers of this political leader or that political leader, the disciples of this religious sect or that religious sect." Wherever "a majority are united by a common interest or passion," Madison concluded, "the rights of the minority are in danger." It was therefore not enough for the Constitutional Convention to propose reforms that would permit the union to fulfill its proper ends. If it could not prepare a system that would also remedy these other "evils," "republican liberty" would not endure.[70]

Much of the American elite shared Madison's alarm with the "abuses of republican liberty practised in the states." Many, maybe most, defined the problem as a classic crisis of relationships between the many and the few, creditors and debtors, rich and poor: a crisis generated by what Elbridge Gerry called "an excess of democracy."[71] Madison's distinctive contribution was to understand these discontents in slightly different terms, to see the crisis of republican convictions as inseparably entangled with the crisis of the union, and to argue that both problems could be solved *without* departing from the fundamental maxims of the Revolution. The proper remedy, he said, was to "enlarge the sphere" of republican government

> and thereby divide the community into so great a number of interests and parties that, in the first place, a majority will not be likely at the same moment to have a common interest separate from that of the whole or of the minority, and in the second place, that in case they should have such an interest, they may not be apt to unite in the pursuit of it.

This, he argued, was "the only defense against the inconveniences of democracy consistent with the democratic form of government."[72] It might, at once, "perpetuate the union and redeem the honor of the republican name."[73]

Of all the thoughts and works that won James Madison his prompt and lasting recognition as first among the Framers, none was more important than this vision of the large republic as a wholly democratic remedy for democratic ills. A remarkable reversal of the standard eighteenth-century wisdom, the concept that the public good and private rights might both be rendered more secure in an enlarged republic was the major premise of the arguments by which the great Virginian led the Constitutional Convention to a thorough reconsideration of the proper structure of a liberal republic. Linked with the idea that a majority can be a faction – "a number of citizens . . . who are united and actuated by some common impulse of passion, or of interest, adverse to the rights of other citizens, or to the permanent and aggregate interests of the community" – the case for an extension of the sphere of republican government became the centerpiece of his defense of the completed Constitution.[74]

Of all the influences that led him to this thought, none was more important than Virginia's recent struggle over church and state. The movement for a general assessment elicited his earliest explicit recognition that the rights of the minority can be endangered by majority control and form a natural boundary beyond which the majority ought not to go.[75] More obviously still, the failure of the general assessment, followed by the relatively easy passage of the Statute for Religious Freedom, was almost certainly the single most important catalyst for his conclusion that a multiplicity of interests – and thus a large, diverse republic – is the most effective democratic safeguard for the rights of all.

Madison was deeply dedicated to the Revolutionary principle that governments derive their just authority from popular consent and must remain responsive to people's will. He was dedicated, too, to "justice," by which he meant equality before the law and scrupulous respect by government for natural law and natural rights. However obvious it seems to us that the desire to reconcile these two commitments is the fundamental paradox of every liberal democracy, early revolutionary thinkers did not necessarily anticipate a conflict. In 1776, as Madison suggested, most patriots believed that governments derived entirely from the body of the people would necessarily pursue the people's interests and defend the people's rights. Bills of rights were not intended to protect some citizens from others, but to defend the whole society from the ambitions of its rulers. Theory and experience combined to make it difficult to understand how the majority, the greater number of the equals who composed the whole society, could will an act that would be inconsistent with the common good, which was their own. Only long experience with a disturbing train of measures could compel committed democrats to reexamine these assumptions, for the thought that the demands of the majority might be repeatedly at odds with justice and the long-term public good could force consistent thinkers to conclude that they might have to choose between the two commitments, neither one of which could be relinquished.[76]

For Madison, as has been shown, the troubling legislative measures and repeated disappointments of the postwar years precipitated just this sort of crisis. The national breadth and steadily accumulating evidence of mounting discontent with vicious legislation prompted sharp alarm for the survival of the Revolution. In all of Madison's experience, however, the threat of the assessment may have been more critical than any other single influence in persuading him that declarations of inherent rights and written constitutions are feeble barriers to rulers who can fairly claim to speak for the majority itself. More clearly still, other issues, it would seem, presented him with such compelling proof that his convictions could not tolerate a democratic version of the rule that might makes right.[77]

In all his personal experience, moreover, Madison had never been involved in a dispute that made it more apparent that the body of the people do not naturally divide into two polar pairs, such as the many and the few, but into a plurality of groups whose multiplex variety can pose a stubborn obstacle to the success of any partial interest. On this insight, which was strongly reinforced by his awareness of the pluralistic nature of divisions in the Confederation Congress, he was able to erect a new conception of the character of democratic factions. And in the outcome of the struggle over the assessment, he began to see how the apparent conflict of democracy and civil rights might be resolved.

The evidence is plain; the implications are more than incidentally important to understanding Madison's assumptions and intensions. All his famous presentations of the case for an extension of the republican sphere list differing opinions about religion as a "latent cause" of faction, often as the first of several potential sources of majority oppression.[78] Among the clearest indications that he did not see political divisions in strictly economic terms, this emphasis on differences among religious sects should warn us, too, that Madison did not define the public good as nothing more than the result of bargaining among competing interests. Neither did he hope that the enlarged republic would defeat the will of the majority by freeing representatives from their constituents' desires.[79] On several occasions, he was quite explicit in suggesting that the struggle for religious freedom, not the clash of different economic interests, was the fundamental prototype for his solution of the democratic riddle, the model he had most in mind when he envisioned how the great republic would "control the violence of faction."[80]

The best example may have come when he explained to Jefferson why he was not initially inclined to worry that the recently completed Constitution did not include a bill of rights.

> Repeated violations of these parchment barriers have been committed by overbearing majorities in every state. In Virginia I have seen the bill of rights violated in every instance where it has been opposed to a popular current. Notwithstanding the explicit provision contained in that instrument for the rights of conscience, it is well known that a religious establishment would have taken place in that state if the legislative majority had found, as they expected, a majority of the people in favor of the measure; and I am persuaded that if a majority of the people were now of one sect, the measure would still take place and on narrower ground than was then proposed, notwithstanding the additional obstacle which the law has since created. Wherever the real power in a government lies, there is the danger of oppression. In our governments the real power lies in the majority of

the community, and the invasion of private rights is *chiefly* to be apprehended, not from acts of government contrary to the sense of its constituents, but from acts in which the government is the mere instrument of the majority number of the constituents.[81]

The rights of conscience, Madison had warned in the "Memorial," are "held by the same tenure with all our other rights." The power that could threaten liberty of conscience could endanger all the rest. The forces that protected it, it followed, might protect them all. In every free society,

> the security for civil rights must be the same as for religious rights. It consists in the one case in the multiplicity of interests and, in the other, in the multiplicity of sects. The degree of security in both cases will depend on the number of interests and sects, and this may be presumed to depend on the extent of country and number of people comprehended under the same government.[82]

Had the Presbyterians and the Episcopalians managed to cement their tentative alliance, Madison had seen, nothing could have stopped the general assessment.[83] Jealousies between the sects had done what no appeal to principle could have accomplished. And differences among the many more denominations of a vastly larger, federal republic would offer multiplied protection.

If Madison had died in 1786, we would remember him today for his achievements in the Continental Congress and his vital part in the enactment of the Statute for Religious Freedom. As Madison went on, instead, to even larger deeds, his magnificent "Memorial" assumed a rightful place beside his friend's great statute among the documentary foundations of the libertarian tradition. Meanwhile, his involvement in Virginia's battle over church and state became a crucial building block in the creation of the great republic. There are thus more ways than one in which this battle left a lasting imprint on the Founding.

NOTES

1 Madison to William Bradford, November 9, 1772, *The Papers of James Madison*, ed. William T. Hutchinson, William M. E. Rachal, and Robert A. Rutland, 14 vols. (Chicago and Charlottesville, Va., 1962–), 1: 75. Hereafter cited as *PJM*. I have modernized spelling and punctuation and expanded abbreviations throughout the essay.

2 Ibid., 1: 96., see also 1: 51–60, 101.

3 Douglas Adair, ed., "James Madison's Autobiography," *William and Mary*

Quarterly, 3d ser., 2 (1945): 198. See also Irving Brant, *James Madison,* 6 vols. (Indianapolis, 1941–61), 1: 114–115, 118, chap. 5 passim; Ralph Ketcham, *James Madison: A Biography* (New York, 1971), pp. 37–43, 49–50; and, especially, "James Madison and Religion – A New Hypothesis," *Journal of the Presbyterian Historical Society* 38 (1960): 65–90. Brant believed that Madison, who always distrusted enthusiasm, moved from a rational Christianity toward more unorthodox opinions as he aged. I agree with Ketcham that the evidence permits no firm conclusions about the nature of Madison's convictions after he entered public life.

4 Madison to Bradford, December 1, 1773, *PJM,* 1: 101. Madison was particularly interested in acquiring Joseph Priestley's *Essay on the First Principles of Government; and on the Nature of Political, Civil, and Religious Liberty;* Josiah Tucker's *Apology for the Present Church of England* . . . ; and Philip Furneaux's *Essay on Toleration* (Ibid., 1: 101, 160, and notes).

5 Madison to Bradford, January 24, 1774, ibid., 1: 105.

6 Madison to Bradford, April 1, 1774, ibid., 1: 112–13.

7 Madison to Bradford, January 24, 1774, ibid., 1: 106.

8 Madison to Bradford, July 28, 1775, ibid., 1: 161 and above.

9 John Locke, *Epistola de Tolerantia/A Letter on Toleration,* ed. Raymond Klibanskey and J. W. Gough (Oxford, 1968). Locke's list of four opinions not entitled to toleration were aimed primarily against atheists and Catholics, but extended to any "doctrines incompatible with human society" or to any church that refused to teach the principle of toleration (pp. 131–5). Madison was certainly familiar with the *Letter,* which was a favorite text of Witherspoon (see James H. Nichols, "John Witherspoon on Church and State," *Journal of Presbyterian History* 42 [1964]; 166–74).

10 Madison's amendments are in *PJM,* 1: 173–75. For the proceedings in convention, I have followed Brant, *James Madison,* 1: chap. 12; Thomas E. Buckley, S.J., *Church and State in Revolutionary Virginia, 1776–1787* (Charlottesville, Va., 1977), pp. 15–19; and the editorial note in *PJM,* 1: 170–71.

11 Locke rejected toleration for sects opposed to equal liberty. Madison's phrase sought stricter limits on state action. He may have been influenced in writing his second amendment by Priestley, who pointed to the inconsistency between Locke's premises and conclusions and urged the magistrate to interfere only in case of "manifest and urgent necessity" (*The Theological and Miscellaneous Works of Joseph Priestley,* ed. J. T. Rutt, 25 vols. [New York 1771; 1823; 1972], 22: 33).

12 It has often been suggested that Madison would certainly have seen the liberal provision for religious freedom in Jefferson's draft of a constitution for Virginia, which arrived in time to influence the drafting committee. Jefferson's phrasing would also have guaranteed freedom, as opposed to toleration. Yet it did not look unambiguously toward disestablishment, nor did it place the rights of conscience on as fair a ground as Madison's second amendment. "All persons shall have full and free liberty of religious opinion," Jefferson wrote, "nor shall any be compelled to frequent or maintain

any religious institution" (Julian P. Boyd, ed., *The Papers of Thomas Jefferson* [Princeton, N.J., 1950–00], 1: 363). Madison would certainly have recognized that Locke defended freedom of religious *opinion* and went on to justify restrictions on the grounds that *conduct* is a legitimate concern of the civil authority. Free "exercise," a term already present in the committee's draft, afforded broader protection, while Madison's remarkable phrasing of the exception – "unless the preservation of equal liberty and the *existence* of the state are manifestly endangered" – clearly seems a carefully considered response to Locke's support for civil action whenever religious beliefs appear to threaten the moral foundation of political society. In the matter of religion, as in so much else, Madison's relationship to Jefferson was one of mutual influence and respect.

13 "He never once narrowed his objective and never ceased to think of the dangers that lurked in small deviations" from the principle of separation (Irving Brant, "Madison: On the Separation of Church and State," *William and Mary Quarterly*, 3d ser., 8 [1951]: 24). Despite some minor errors and dubious assertions, this fine article, along with Ketcham's work, renders it redundant to attempt another summary review of Madison's position on church and state. The current essay therefore focuses on the interaction of Madison's views about religious and political liberty.

14 For the fall Assembly session, see Buckley, *Church and State*, pp. 21–36; *Papers of Jefferson*, 1: 525–58; Brant, *James Madison*, 1: 296–304; and the editorial note in *PJM*, 1: 186.

15 Buckley, *Church and State*, chap. 2. The 1779 bill creating a Christian establishment is reprinted in Appendix I.

16 I have offered a fresh interpretation of the years in Congress in "James Madison and the Nationalists, 1780–1783," *William and Mary Quarterly*, 3d ser., 40 (1983): 227–55.

17 See especially *PJM*, 7: 401–3, 418–19.

18 William Short to Thomas Jefferson, May 14, 1784, *Papers of Jefferson*, 7:257.

19 An excellent discussion of this session is in Brant, *James Madison*, chap. 20; see also *PJM*, 8, for May and June 1784.

20 Madison reported on the session at length in a letter to Jefferson of July 3, 1784, from which the quotations are taken (*PJM*, 8: 92–5). For the terms and background of the Bill for Episcopal Incorporation, see Buckley, *Church and State*, pp. 81–8. Madison told his father that the bill was "wholly inadmissable" in this original version (*PJM*, 8:217), but the letter to Jefferson shows that he was most disturbed by the degree to which it would have freed the clergy from lay supervision. The corporation would have been composed of the body of the clergy, whose convocation would determine creeds and rites and possess sole power to remove incumbent ministers. Madison does not appear to have objected in 1784 to giving the Episcopalians title to their present holdings, although the dissenters repeatedly opposed this transfer of state title to a single denomination, but he and Jefferson both saw dangers in a church's unrestrained capacity to increase its holdings.

Madison's fullest condemnation of the latter power can be found in Elizabeth Fleet, ed., "Detached Memoranda," *William and Mary Quarterly*, 3d ser., 3 (1946): 556–8.

21 I have depended primarily on Madison's postsession report to Jefferson, January 9, 1785 (*PJM*, 8: 222–33), together with legislative drafts and other correspondence printed in ibid., 8: 122– 217. Brant's discussion of the fall session is not as clear or full as the spring session. (*James Madison*, 2: 343–60, 365–6).

22 The text of this bill, too, is conveniently available in Buckley, *Church and State*, Appendix 1. This book offers a fine discussion of the implications of Virginia's actions as well as an excellent history of the path to the Virginia settlement. Also helpful for placing Virginia's struggle over a general assessment in the national context is William G. McLoughlin, "The Role of Religion in the Revolution: Liberty of Conscience and Cultural Cohesion in the New Nation," in *Essays on the American Revolution*, ed. Stephen G. Kurtz and James H. Hutson (Chapel Hill, N.C., 1973), pp. 197–255.

23 The preface to the bill of 1784 summarized this view in rather eloquent fashion: "Whereas the general diffusion of Christian knowledge hath a natural tendency to correct the morals of men, restrain their vices, and preserve the peace of society, which cannot be effected without a competent provision for learned teachers, . . . and it is judged that such provision may be made by the legislature, without counteracting the liberal principle heretofore adopted and intended to be preserved by abolishing all distinctions of preeminence among the different societies or communities of Christians; "Be it therefore enacted . . ."

24 Madison to James Monroe, November 27, 1784, *PJM*, 8:157–8; see also 8:172, 175.

25 Both quotations are from a letter to Monroe of April 12, 1785 (*PJM*, 8:261), but they seem a fair expression of Madison's reaction from the first. For the background of the petition and Presbyterian lobbying in the Assembly, see Buckley, *Church and State*, pp. 92–9. The Presbyterian clergy was by no means united on this change of course, and several Shenandoah Valley congregations petitioned against both the assessment and the incorporation bills before the session ended.

26 Madison to Jefferson, January 9, 1785, *PJM*, 8:228–9. It is not clear which features of the bill Madison still found objectionable. Partly in response to the objections that Madison shared with the dissenters, the revised bill was very different from the one drafted in the spring. Rather than incorporating the clergy alone, it made each parish vestry and clergyman a corporate body with control over parish property, which could not exceed the value of eight hundred pounds per year. A convention composed of the clergyman and one layman from each parish became the governing body of the church, which could not appoint or remove a minister without vestry approval. Thus both the clerical independence and the indefinite power to acquire property, which had been the strongest of Madison's objections in the spring,

were removed. Indeed, Madison reported that the legislature had actually intended a convention composed of the clergyman and *two* laymen from each parish, but that an unnoticed error had crept into the bill, which he hoped would prove "a standing lesson to [the laity] of the danger of referring religious matters to the legislature" (Madison to James Madison, Sr., January 6, 1785, ibid., 8:217; see also Buckley, *Church and State,* pp. 106–7).

27 *PJM,* 8:229.

28 Ibid., 8:197–9. The editors tentatively date both outlines December 23–24, but it seems likely from internal evidence that the longer speech, as Brant and Buckley thought, was actually delivered during the November debates preceding preparation of the bill, which turned out to be considerably more liberal than the bill of 1779. The bill of 1784 offered support for "teachers" of the Christian religion, authorized exceptions to the rule that revenues would be used to support ministers and church buildings in favor of the Mennonites and Quakers, and provided that the taxes of individuals declaring no religious preference would be used to support "seminaries of learning." In these provisions and in the absence of any discrimination against Catholics, the bill was an advance over the laws of any other state. As will be seen, however, Madison still saw it as "obnoxious on account of its dishonorable principle and dangerous tendency" (ibid., 8:229).

29 Buckley, *Church and State,* 109–110, which includes a map of the vote.

30 George Nicholas to Madison, May 22, 1785, *PJM,* 8:264–5. After 1784, the Assembly met only in the fall.

31 Ibid., 8:298–306. One author calculates that Madison's opinions, expressed most fully in this classic, have been cited in at least forty federal and fifty-five state cases concerning church and state since 1878 (Donald L. Drakeman, "Religion and the Republic: James Madison and the First Amendment," *Journal of Church and State* 25 [1983]: 427–45).

32 Madison was not a man of ready, violent emotions, yet religious freedom was a subject on which he was quickly and repeatedly aroused. See his letter to Monroe of May 29, 1785, written at about the time as the "Memorial": "It gives me great pleasure to observe" that Congress has expunged the clause in the land-sales bill that would have set aside portions of land for support of the majority's religion. "How a regulation so unjust in itself, so foreign to the authority of Congress, so hurtful to the sale of public land, and smelling so strongly of an antiquated bigotry could have received the countenance of a committee is truly matter of astonishment" *(PJM,* 8:286).

33 All authorities suggest the debt to Locke, on whom, of course, successive generations of English Protestant Dissenters had built a more and more complete defense of total toleration. The "Memorial" is also fairly and traditionally considered an elaboration of the principles of Jefferson's bill, which also showed Locke's influence. A good, recent discussion of the Virginians' similarities and differences from Locke is Sanford Kessler, "Locke's Influence on Jefferson's 'Bill for Establishing Religious Freedom,' " *Journal of Church and State* 25 (1983): 231–52.

34 *PJM*, 8:299.

35 Ibid., 8:299–300.

36 Madison has usually been seen as a late convert to strict construction. I have disputed this interpretation in "James Madison and the Nationalists" and in "The Hamiltonian Madison: A Reconsideration," *Virginia Magazine of History and Biography* 112 (1984): 3–28.

37 *PJM*, 8:300. Madison returned time after time in later writings to the example of Revolutionary resistance to first encroachments. A sensitivity to the power of precedent to alter a constitution over time was another distinguishing characteristic of his thought. Both the Virginia Resolutions and the "Letters of Helvidius" made this danger a major theme.

38 Ibid., 8:300–1.

39 Ibid., 8:301.

40 Ibid., 8:301–3.

41 Ibid., 8:304.

42 Banning, "James Madison and the Nationalists" and "The Hamiltonian Madison" develop the argument that the Madison of the 1780s was far more consistent with the Madison of the 1790s than prevailing views suggest.

43 Madison, "Detached Memoranda," pp. 560–2.

44 The editorial note in *PJM*, 8:295–8, dates completion of the "Memorial" around June 20, 1785, and discusses the reasons why Madison hid his authorship from all but a few. The most obvious reason for his wish for anonymity, however, appears to have been overlooked. The "Memorial" was supposed to impress the legislature as an unsolicited expression of popular opinion.

45 For an excellent discussion of developments between the sessions, see Buckley, *Church and State,* chap. 4.

46 Ibid., pp. 144–152, and the editorial note in *PJM*, 8:297–8. Madison's "Memorial" obtained approximately seventeen hundred signatures. Although decidedly most influential in the long term, it was by no means the most widely subscribed at the time. Twenty-nine petitions, signed by nearly five thousand people, followed a different, antideistic draft, whose authorship is still anonymous but may have been the work of the Baptists. Twenty-one followed the Presbyterian memorial of August 25. There can be no doubt, as Madison was well aware, that overwhelming opposition from the dissenters was principally responsible for crushing the assessment.

47 *Papers of Jefferson,* 2:305–665, includes all 126 bills of the revision, which had been initiated by Jefferson in 1776, together with a lengthy headnote on its preparation, contents, and legislative history.

48 The finished bill, with the deletions in italics and helpful editorial notes, is in ibid., 2: 545–53. The best account of its passage is in Buckley, *Church and State,* pp. 157–63. In the House of Delegates, the move to substitute Article XVI for Jefferson's preamble was defeated on December 16, by a vote of 36 to 66. After the failure of a motion to postpone the final reading, it carried

the house the following day, by a vote of 74 to 20. The Delegates reinstated Jefferson's preamble by a margin of 56 to 35.

49 Madison to Jefferson, January 22, 1786, *PJM*, 8:474.

50 Archibald Stuart to John Breckenridge, December 7, 1785, quoted in ibid., 8:446, n. 3.

51 Again, I have relied primarily on the end-of-session report to Jefferson, progress reports to Washington and Monroe, drafts of legislation, and editorial notes in ibid., 8:389–484.

52 Madison to Monroe, January 22, 1786, ibid., 8:483.

53 Madison to Monroe, December 9, 1785, ibid., 8:437.

54 Madison to Jefferson, January 22, 1786, ibid., 8:477.

55 Ibid., 473.

56 Archibald Stuart, who had been astonished with Madison's influence early in the session, later wrote that the House "was upon the whole the most stupid, navish, and designing Assembly that ever sat, . . . and as . . . proof of this I need urge no other argument . . . but that Madison after the first three weeks lost all weight in the House, and the general observation was that those who had a favorite scheme ought to get Madison to oppose it, by which means it would certainly be carried" (Stuart to Breckenridge, January 26, 1786, ibid., 8:446, n. 3).

57 The most important document is the letter to Monroe of August 7, 1785 (ibid., 8:333–6). To me, this letter is the first firm indication that Madison was beginning to consider a thorough reconstruction of the federal system.

58 Ibid., 8:409–10, 413–14, 431–2.

59 Madison to George Washington, ibid., 8:438–9; Madison to Jefferson, ibid., 8:476–7. On the last day of the session, as a less desirable alternative, Madison supported (and may have been responsible for reviving) a successful resolution for a commercial convention; but he had no great hopes for the Annapolis Convention at this time (ibid., 8:483).

60 Ibid., 8:447–9, 465–6, 477.

61 Madison to Washington, December 9, 1785, ibid., 8:439–40; Madison to Jefferson, January 22, 1786, ibid., 8:478.

62 Madison to Jefferson, ibid., 8:475. Opposed by much of the bench and bar, the Assize Act never went into effect.

63 Ibid., 8:477. This bill was Madison's main effort at the level of state action to break the British strangle hold on commerce, which he considered dangerous to the very foundations of American republicanism. For its emasculation and eventual repeal by particularistic interests, see Drew R. McCoy, "The Virginia Port Bill of 1784," *Virginia Magazine of History and Biography* 83 (1975): 288–303.

64 It might be noted that, by contrast, the 1786 session would be more successful than the 1785 session. Although he felt unable to reagitate the question of British debts, Madison was reelected to the Confederation Congress and secured several resolutions that he desired in preparation for the Constitutional Convention. A proposal for installment payment of all debts was

checked, and paper money and a move to retire securities at their depreciated values were decisively repudiated. Even so – and just as he received the news of Shays's Rebellion – the treasury continued empty, and Congress again went unsupplied.

65 *PJM,* 8:299.
66 For Madison's hostility to paper money, see his letter to Jefferson of August 12, 1786, and his speech in the House of Delegates of November 1, 1786, (ibid., 9:94–5, 156–60).
67 "Vices of the Political System of the United States," ibid., 9:353–4.
68 "Observations on Jefferson's Draft of a Constitution for Virginia" (1788), ibid., 9:287–8.
69 Quoted in Rufus King's notes on the debates in Max Farrand, ed., *The Records of the Federal Convention of 1787,* 4 vols. (New Haven, Conn., 1837), 1:108.
70 Madison's notes of his speech of June 6, 1787, ibid., 1:134–6.
71 Ibid., 1:48.
72 Madison's speech of June 6, 1787, ibid., 1:134–6; see also his speech of June 26, 1787, ibid., 1:421–3.
73 Madison to Edmund Pendleton, February 24, 1787, *PJM,* 9:295.
74 *The Federalist,* ed. Jacob E. Cooke (Cleveland, 1961), No. 10, p. 57.
75 *PJM,* 8:299.
76 The indispensable authority for the development of American thought during these years is Gordon S. Wood, *The Creation of the American Republic, 1776–1787* (Chapel Hill, N.C., 1969), especially pp. 271–3.
77 I think it critical to realize that Madison implicitly identified himself with those who had mistakenly dismissed the warning that majorities are not safe guardians of private rights. And note the indication that he found the thought a novel and disturbing one in a passage in a letter to Monroe of October 5, 1786:

> There is no maxim in my opinion which is more liable to be misapplied and which therefore more needs elucidation than the current one that the interest of the majority is the political standard of right and wrong. Taking the word "interest" as synonymous with "ultimate happiness," in which sense it is qualified with every necessary moral ingredient, the proposition is no doubt true. But taking it in the popular sense, as referring to immediate augmentation of property and wealth, nothing can be more false. In the latter sense it would be the interest of the majority in every community to despoil and enslave the minority. . . . In fact it is only reestablishing under another name and a more specious form, force as a measure of right (*PJM,* 9:141).

78 "Vices of the Political System" ibid., 9:355–6; speech of June 6, 1787, *Records of the Federal Convention,* 1:135; *Federalist,* No. 10, p. 58; Madison to Jefferson, October 24, 1787, *PJM,* 10: 214.
79 I have discussed misreadings of *Federalist,* No. 10, in "The Hamiltonian

Madison" and in "The Practicable Sphere of a Republic: James Madison, the Constitutional Convention, and the Emergence of Revolutionary Federalism," in *Beyond Confederation: Origins of the Constitution and American National Identity*, ed. Richard Beeman et al. (Chapel Hill, N.C., 1987), pp. 162–87. The latter essay explores at greater length the thinking that produced the Virginia Plan.

80   *Federalist*, No. 10, p. 56.
81   Madison to Jefferson, October 17, 1788, *PJM* 11:297–8.
82   *Federalist*, No. 51, pp. 351–2. The phrasing is anticipated in Madison's letter to Jefferson dated October 24, 1787 (*PJM*, 10:214).
83   Madison to Jefferson, August 20, 1785, *PJM*, 8:345.

6

"The Rage of Malice of the Old Serpent Devil": The Dissenters and the Making and Remaking of the Virginia Statute for Religious Freedom

RHYS ISAAC

The Act for Establishing Religious Freedom remade Virginia. In its universal language, indeed, it was remaking America and the world.

The act was the issue of a long confrontation between popular evangelical dissenters and traditional gentry authoritarians. It was conceived in the experience of bitter conflict and was brought forth as law only when it became clear that without it, the politicization of religious differences would destroy the otherwise unchallenged political domination of the proud Virginia gentry.

The act was made out of the struggle of the dissenters. It was remade in the continuation of that struggle. Like any living instrument, it has been continually made and remade in the remembering of it from that day to this. The act is the charter of the new Virginia that the popular evangelical revolution brought into being, and its life has been the development of the traditions that have sustained that new Virginia.

The struggle out of which the act was made had been about command over words of authority, the preaching of the Word. The act itself was a potent form of utterance; and the continuity of the remembering of the act has been through the telling and retelling of the making of the act. Preaching, potent utterance, telling, and retelling – all forms of the word – represent more than their mere content. They constitute ways of knowing; ultimately, they reveal ways of being.

The act itself, the dissenters' petitions that carried it onto the statute books, and the remembering of the struggle that has been the life of the act ever since are all richly revealing of the Virginia that was then emerging – and so of the complex of ways that were to be part of the heritage of the South, of the United States, and of the world.

Mill Creek (or Mauck's) Meeting House, erected near the Shenandoah by Baptists, illustrating the stark contrast between popular evangelical sects and the Anglican liturgical church. Courtesy of the Harold Wickliffe Rose Papers, Yale University Library.

Early Struggles

Jefferson's Statute for Religious Freedom – like all his great compositions – has the quality of calm philosophic assurance: "Almighty God hath created the mind free"; and "finally . . . truth is great and will prevail." The obverse of that calm is the turbulence and violence of the region, the country, the continent, and the age in which Jefferson lived.

Albemarle County is adjacent to Orange County; both adjoin or lie close to the eastern Piedmont and upper-tidewater counties of Spotsylvania, Culpeper, and Caroline. Thomas Jefferson and James Madison, therefore, lived on the edge of the region where Virginia first seemed likely to be plunged into religious persecution, arbitrariness, and violence. The process began locally in a small way, when on May 26, 1768, a number of Baptist converts were presented by the grand jury in Orange County for having absented themselves from their parish church on Sundays. Conflict took a more startling turn a week later, when five of the Baptist preachers were seized by the sheriff of Spotsylvania County and roughly dragged before county justices, "who stood in the meeting house yard and who bound them in the penalty of one thousand pounds to appear in court." There, two days later, they were arraigned as disturbers of the peace, and then committed to prison when they refused to give bond not to preach again in the county for a year and a day. They were held for four weeks before their case was carried to Williamsburg, where the acting governor received advice from the attorney general that the prisoners had a right to apply to the General Court for a license under the English Act of Toleration, and should be released pending such appeal.[1]

It is reported that the evangelists' discharge was "a kind of triumph" for them, but the uncertainties of law and jurisdiction that had been exposed evidently raised concern among the colony's leaders. Their sense of the need to regulate the situation appeared at the next session of the legislature – Thomas Jefferson's first as a burgess. The Speaker then established a standing Committee of Religion, and the House promptly ordered it to bring in a Virginia bill of the same title as the English act – "for Exempting his Majesty's Protestant Dissenters from the Penalties of certain Laws."[2]

Imperial disputes caused the Assembly to be cut short; no bills were passed. The House, at the next Assembly, again called for a bill – this time "for granting Toleration to his Majesty's Subjects, being Protestant Dissenters," but nothing came of this initiative either. Meanwhile, in Jefferson and Madison's region, harassment, arrests, imprisonments, and assaults continued, aggravated by the uncertain state of the law.[3]

The rate at which the Separate Baptists were making converts and were meeting with violent opposition reached crisis pitch in 1771. In May of that year, in Caroline County, occurred the most shocking episode of all, when a minister, mounted on horseback and aided by a sheriff and some others, interrupted a preacher's hymn singing, ran a horsewhip into his mouth, and dragged him away from his open-air meeting to be whipped in a nearby field. Again, the event was a triumph for the persecuted, since the evangelist, when released, simply "went back singing praise to God, mounted the stage and preached with a great deal of liberty."[4]

In those times of patriot stirring, the idea of preaching with liberty – very much the aspiration of the popular evangelists – was a resonant one. Gospel witness of this kind was creating a great stir. An almost apocalyptic atmosphere is evident in the scattered records. The most vivid report of the horsewhipping episode – cited as an instance of "the rage of malice of the old serpent devil" – was written down close to Monticello, in Louisa County, along with a note that in the same evening's talking and sharing of experience, Brother Lovil informed the company "that the Blessed Jesus was riding victorious on the White Horse of the Gospel in many parts of the world unknown to us."[5]

The sense of the rising power of religion and of coming change that this little fragment suggests was about to be as unmistakably demonstrated in the vicinity of Jefferson and Madison's residences as the ugly mood of traditionalists in authority already had been. The company that stopped over in Louisa, sharing news and prophecy, had met there only because they were on their way to the first great General Association meeting of the Separate Baptists of Virginia, held at Blue Run Church in Orange County. The defiant mood of the evangelists was clear in the deliberations of the meeting. There was strong support for a motion to censure "every one that had obtained license" to preach from the civil authorities. Those preachers were under attack because they had let themselves "be restricted from the general license given them by King Jesus." The surge of popular support for the evangelical movement was equally clear. Probably the four or five thousand souls who gathered for the public preaching on the Sunday set aside for that purpose formed the biggest mass gathering ever assembled in Virginia to that date.[6]

In the face of such pressure, it was further alarming that the legal authorities had become publicly divided as to whether there existed a sound basis for Virginia courts to continue to deal with the cases of preachers being brought before them. They had hitherto proceeded along customary lines, unsupported by any colonial statute. In the spring of 1772, the House of Burgesses responded to this growing crisis by renewing its attempts to enact a law that might be a more certain basis both for liberty and for control. The rapid rise and uncompromising style of the New Light Separate Baptists brought on Virginia's first full-scale debate on religious liberty.[7]

The burgesses had no certain body of law from which to commence. Did the great English statute, the Act of Toleration of 1689, apply? It was recognized to be an essential part of the eighteenth-century's much-vaunted British constitution. If it did not apply, then the colony was still under a fearsome code of Elizabethan penal statutes dating from before 1607. But the extension of Parliament's laws to the colonies was even then being challenged, and – still more perplexing – Virginia lacked two of the principal agencies entrusted with the administration of licensing under the Toleration Act, since there were neither bishops nor courts of quarter session in the colony.[8]

Improvisation had so far solved the problem, glossing over institutional deficiencies. The governor had assumed the bishop's role in organizing the doctrinal subscriptions from the dissenting candidates that were a prerequisite for licensing; the General Court had taken to itself the statutory authority of the court of quarter sessions to issue the licenses. But in a period when legal sophistication was advancing in the colony, improvisation was increasingly uncomfortable and could be sustained only if there was general consensus among those in authority.[9]

By the beginning of 1772, however, it was public knowledge that there was no consensus. An authoritative "Address to the Anabaptist Preachers Imprisoned in Caroline County" (published in the *Virginia Gazette* on February 20, 1772, but dated and sent five months earlier) had admitted the disagreement among the lawyers even while it warned the itinerants that they could expect to feel the full rigor of the law. An earlier comment on the imprisonments, signed "Timoleon," had declared that since all proceedings against the preachers were unwarranted in law, the magistrates had become "tyrants."[10]

Alarm was certain to increase if the crisis was not resolved; the only acceptable resolution could come from the General Assembly in the form of a colonial statute that would end the local uncertainties. The attempt merely aggravated the problem. In the spring session of 1772, the House of Burgesses was unable to reach an assured agreement on how to strike a balance between the regulation felt necessary to uphold traditional authority and the rights to be allowed to dissenters. A bill was steered through the House that seems to have been designed to seek consensus by adopting the English Toleration Act as its pattern; but a fearful majority, feeling that the original gave too much liberty, introduced modifications banning night meetings and prohibiting proselytizing among slaves without the master's permission.[11]

The form of the English act, and these amendments to it, both signal clearly the way the conflict was, at base, a conflict over control of the Word – who should preach it to whom, and in what circumstances. Only approved persons licensed by authority were to preach, and only in regulated places, at regulated times. The institution of slavery made this problem more acute because of the large number of individuals it sustained who were deemed dependents, although their choices could not be controlled primarily by close familial relationships. Thus the issue of religious freedom, like that of other freedoms in Virginia, could not be separated in theory or practice from the fact of slavery. One of the main reasons why the Baptists (and later the Methodists) met with such hostility and repression was their insistence on carrying the gospel to all nations, gathering black and white, slave and free, wherever and whenever they could, for the preaching of the Word.[12]

Probably there was contention among the burgesses over the terms of the bill; certainly, a debate over the fundamentals occurred in the little college town of Williamsburg, where the Assembly met. The chairman of the House Committee of Religion asserted that the proposed bill allowed the dissenters "as complete a Toleration as they can desire," while others, ignoring the special problems posed by meetings involving slaves, advanced an Enlightenment modernist position that the great English act, the explicit model for the burgesses' draft measure, had long since been overtaken by subsequent "Revolutions of Opinions." In this situation, the House – uncertain whether its measure would satisfy dissenters, traditionalists, and libertarians – resolved to have the engrossed bill printed and circulated for public consideration, instead of sending it on in the usual way to become law immediately.[13]

Away from Williamsburg while he settled down to married life and began building his own great house, Thomas Jefferson could only follow at a distance as the confrontations produced by resistance to the rapid rise of the Baptists called forth the first loud and clear Virginia pronouncements in favor of unrestricted freedom of religion. The championship of this cause was assumed by two liberal young professors at the College of William and Mary. The Reverend Professor Samuel Henley preached a forthright sermon, "The Distinct Claims of Government and Religion," to the General Assembly itself on March 1, 1772, even as the House was engaged in preparing its bill. Four days later, the Reverend Professor Thomas Gwatkin, writing under the True-Whig pseudonym, "Hoadleianus," offered specific proposals for updating the Act of Toleration by substituting a deistic formula for the required subscription to dogmatic articles of faith. In August of the same year, the professors' most talented pupil, the future college president and first bishop of Virginia, James Madison, addressed his fellow students on this burning issue of the day. Having been "born to be free," they should make their stand against those of their fathers' generation who, as justices, had already arrested and imprisoned preachers and who now sought legislative confirmation for their repressive practices. He warned his fellow students against submitting to such elders: "Crouch not to . . . Bigot-Rage."[14]

Many of the fundamentals of Thomas Jefferson's later philosophic liberal program were clearly articulated in this extraordinary round of public polemic in Williamsburg in 1772. Samuel Henley was already declaring the work of his intellectual associates as a project "to strike off the shackles from the human mind." Together, he and his protégés celebrated "these modern ages of free enquiry," when "Knowledge" was becoming more and more "susceptible of daily improvement." (Later, when the first outspoken champion of dissenters and the course of religious freedom in Virginia had been driven by the Revolution back to England, Thomas Jefferson wrote him a letter that survives as proof that they had been friends; but in the years of his first legislative contest, Jefferson was not engaged, and his response cannot be known.)[15]

By contrast, the views of the other of the two great Virginia statesmen associated with the passing of the Statute for Religious Freedom were soon made very clear. Another James Madison (future president of the United States and a distant cousin of the student protégé of the Williamsburg professors) surveyed the scene after his return from his studies at the College of New Jersey in Princeton. By January 1774, he felt compelled to admit to a student comrade that he saw "nothing to brag of as to the State of Liberty" in Virginia, where "that diabolical Hell conceived principle of persecution rages." That same spring, he saw little prospect of the legislature ending its two-year deadlock on the issue, since the same "incredible and extravagant stories" about "the monstrous Effects of the Enthusiasm prevalent among the Sectaries" was likely to check any positive measures in the same way that they had during the previous sessions.[16]

James Madison was able to play a decisive role in the next important debate on religious freedom in Virginia. With the drafting of the Declaration of Rights by the Virginia Convention of 1776, the unresolved dilemma of 1772 was resolved. George Mason's draft called for the "fullest toleration," and that formulation was, in turn, overtaken and replaced by an even more sweeping one. The convention adopted James Madison's amendment, guaranteeing the "free exercise of religion." It is very important to note, however, that all three of the libertarians in this debate – Jefferson, Madison, and Mason – envisaged explicit reservations to the granting of freedom. At the base of earlier objections and, indeed, of the repressive proposals in 1772 was a fear of the consequences of allowing preachers to go among the slaves. Clearly, that fear still haunted these constitution makers in 1776.[17]

Article XVI of the Virginia Declaration of Rights, adopted in June 1776, guaranteed to "all men . . . the free exercise of religion." At a stroke, all the former legal claims to regulate the activities of preachers and the assembly of people for worship were eliminated – although slaves would continue to be subject to nonreligious restrictions on their movements. The Revolution had transformed the situation. Roles were now reversed. The dissenters, armed with the guarantees that were the basis of the compact on which the new commonwealth was believed to rest, were on the offensive; the old Establishment, for all the influential friends it still had, was on the defensive. When the convention reassembled in the fall as the first House of Delegates, it had to contend with a number of militant petitions. In particular, there was a very learned legal-philosophic one from the Presbyterian clergy; and a mass-supported Scriptural one (the "Ten-Thousand Name Petition") from the Baptists. Aware of the new situation, perhaps taught by the voice of the people claiming their rights and stirred by it to dream more daringly of a moral republic made *de novo,* Thomas Jefferson now shed the Establishmentarian-tolerationist assumptions that had certainly remained with him from his Virginia gentry upbringing as late as May 1776. Now, in November, he took a lead in the Assembly and embarked on a determined, initially unsuccessful, and so prolonged struggle for complete freedom of conscience – the unqualified withdrawal of the state from those aspects of life that were defined as "religion."[18]

The Petitions of 1785

In the fall of 1776, Thomas Jefferson joined in a struggle for religious freedom in the wake of a flood of petitions; nine years later, there was another great surge of petitions. The legislature, meanwhile, had slowly given ground: It had first suspended, and then terminated, the payment of taxes for the support of the Establishment clergy, but had doggedly maintained as much as it could of the old institutional fabric. At the time of the suspension of clerical salary payments, the Assembly had mooted a "general assessment" – a scheme whereby citizens would be compelled to assign a proportion of their state tax to whatever religious denomination they chose to support. Action on this proposal had, however, been postponed until the views of the people should be known. After the end of the war, the struggle had taken a new turn with an attempt by Establishmentarians now to fight back. They pressed to have a general assessment enacted. Their proposed measure – A Bill for Establishing a Provision for the Teachers of the Christian Religion – provoked a great conflict and called forth an unprecedented influx of petitions to the Assembly. (Some eighty papers came in against the assessment, with about eleven thousand signatures; and eleven papers for the bill, with only one thousand signatures.) In the new political climate of massively mobilized dissenter demand, the Christian teachers' bill was overwhelmed; Thomas Jefferson's Bill for Establishing Religious Freedom, which had been rejected in 1779, was triumphantly enacted.[19]

George Nicholas, having been through "a considerable part of the country" in the election time of the spring of 1785, declared that such was the opposition to a religious assessment that "it would be impossible to carry such laws into execution and the attempt would bring about a revolution." Madison, at home in the Piedmont, summed up the situation as "a fermentation below the Mountains and a violent one beyond them."[20]

Nicholas and Madison were direct observers and participants. Our history of the eighteenth century now is only what the documents tell us. No doubt, a vigorous tax revolt was a very important part of the commotions that Nicholas and Madison were watching; but our documents tell little of that, and we can only speculate on its proportional contribution to the antiassessment campaign. We know little also about the kind of politicking that went on. Only the ultimate results are clear, suggesting that the turnaround of the Assembly's attitude between December 1784 and October 1785 was effected more by changing the views of the delegates than by replacing them with new ones.[21]

A striking testimony to the moral as well as political suasion of popular consensus comes in two statements – retractions – sent to the House of Delegates from the southwestern region, where Baptists and Methodists had gathered many adherents, but where the gentry was particularly committed to the kinds of control promised by an establishment – even a plural establishment. There were delegates from this region who had an extraordinary record of repeatedly signing petitions in favor of revived Establishment, while they consistently recorded votes in the Assembly against such measures. Two groups of such persons were moved – perhaps as much by the moral fervor of the campaign as by the political pressures – to declare a change of heart. The memorialists from Dinwiddie County explained that, having seen the anti-Establishment petitioning, they were now "as decidedly opposed to a General assessment, as they were formerly in favour of it"; and those from Amherst County avowed that, having only supported the proposal as "One step at least towards Opening a Way for Obtaining a Supply of ministers who might be Instrumental . . . in Stoping the Prevailing Torrent of Iniquity," they were now aware that the assessment bill "has Distressed . . . many . . . in Different Parts of the State who have Advanced Reasons . . . against it of no Small Weight and Importance." Pressured and persuaded, the traditional Episcopal gentry leaders of Virginia abandoned the assessment and set up Jefferson's bill as an enduring declaration of the separation of church and state. They had received clear indications that a continuing mobilization of religion into politics might shatter their customary dominance at the polls.[22]

The documents most richly revealing of the persuasions and pressures that were brought to bear are the petitions that flooded into the Assembly, but they come to us accompanied by almost no reporting of how they circulated and whether or not they were presented with speeches at the courthouse. In short, there is no indication of the dramatics of the mobilization that the petitions represent – except for the objects themselves. As the strongest traces of all the agitation at church assemblies and on courthouse greens, the petitions must be studied not just as texts, assemblages of words enunciating ideas, but as the instruments and symbols of the contenders' actions.

First and foremost, they were artifacts – and artifacts of a special kind. In an age when oral culture was still vigorous and literacy was not strongly developed among the greater part of the population at large, there was a correspondingly great possibility of giving striking importance to a piece of writing by exhibiting it and circulating it in a public forum. Probably this potential was realized in some degree by the sheets of paper in quarto and foolscap format that constitute the bulk of the petitions. Within this range, there is a preponderance of larger rather than smaller sizes. The dramatic potential is most clearly seen to be realized in the considerable number of giant sheets – approaching one foot in width and over one foot in length – that were displayed and offered for signature despite the practical difficulties that such size made for circulation. All the major participants in the war of petitions produced some of their versions in large format – the great Baptist petitions from Henrico and Buckingham counties are strikingly handsome examples – but it was Madison's "Memorial and Remonstrance" that added to the dramaturgic importance of great physical size to the authoritative tone of its text in almost every presentation. Most of the manuscript versions are on the same scale as the printed broadside. A striking dramatic inversion of this form of grand presentation was produced in the Northern Neck region, where the "Memorial and Remonstrance" was a printed broadside; there, a version of the great Baptist petition was produced as a little handwritten book – save that the scribe did not use book format for the writing, but ran the lines of script across the fold, to take up the wider double spread. Being only four inches by six inches, it was easy to pass from hand to hand for signing in the blank pages in the back.[23]

Where, as in most cases, size was used to give importance, the forms of script generally reinforce the impressions of dignity, with scrolled headings and flourishes standing forth to the eye. Many petitions use variation of pen stroke to emphasize key words and mark the rhythms of the utterance. (The historian scanning this array of expressive forms may feel that the Quakers and Mennonites made the "witness" of their religious ways particularly present to the House in the fine ordering of the visual presentation in their petitions.)

Considering now the verbal messages that are associated with the striking artifact presentations, it appears that a particular kind of Christian commonwealth was taking shape in dissenter consciousness. Sharp definitions of the nature of the church and of the state emerged, so as to require their explicit formal separation. This was the basis of a broad anti-Establishment unity; but within that, there were at least two distinct outlooks and ways of expressing them, and behind these were two distinct cultures and the long lines of experiences that had created and sustained them.

The Presbyterians stood forth in this campaign as primarily a sectional and ethnic dissenting group. It was not from the converts of the Hanover Awakening of the 1740s and 1750s that the Assembly heard, but from the Scotch-Irish of the Shenandoah Valley and the southwest. It was their anger that produced what Madison referred to as an "explosion" beyond the mountains. These remonstrants were dissenters to the marrow, continuing a struggle extending back to Ulster – if not to Scotland. One of their petitions referred to Establishment as "the Principle which our Ancestors contested [un]to blood."[24]

In 1776, men of this temper had felt bold enough to threaten their own Virginia Assembly. They had warned "that the same motive, namely liberty that excited them to venture life and fortune in opposing Great Britain will still Determine them to bleed at every vein before they submit to any form of Government . . . subversive of their Religious Privileges that are a natural right, and nearer every Man of Principal than life itself." By 1785, the Scotch-Irish were sustaining a tradition of militancy that had become part of the epic of Virginia patriotism, celebrated in the the Fincastle Resolutions of '75 and the march of the "Shirtmen" to defend the tidewater region. They were also settling a score with the faction in their own church – a faction, centered on Hampton-Sydney College in the Piedmont, that had threatened to sell the past in 1784 by giving guarded approval to the legislature for a general assessment.[25]

The petitions from the Shenandoah Valley and Blue Ridge Scotch-Irish ring with references to the Revolutionary struggle and with the indignation these patriots felt at delays in the enactment of a full disestablishment. Their rights had been denied, they said, "before the wounds we received in our Country's Cause had ceased to bleed or the Arms with which we gained our Liberties began to rust."[26]

In keeping with this militant republican identity, the emphasis in the Presbyterian petitions is overwhelmingly constitutional and social-contractual. Their medium of expression is the language of natural religion. This can be clearly seen in the address of the Presbytery, dated October 28, 1784. That document refers to the "philosophic and liberal discernment, which prevails in America at present," and goes on to affirm didactically that "human legislation ought to have human affairs alone for concern," since "legislators in free States possess delegated authority [only] for the good of the community at large in its political or civil capacity." The leaders of the Presbyterians, then, were strongly articulating the fundamentals of Madison's "Memorial and Remonstrance" well before he immortalized them in that lapidary form, sometime in May 1785.[27]

The extraordinary great Convention of Presbyterian Ministers and Lay Representatives that met in August 1785 at Bethel Church in Augusta County inculcated the same lessons – perhaps consciously echoing the "Memorial" by this time. The first words of their address invoke the contract that made them "Citizens of this State, not by accident but choice," and then, after a recital of the expectations that had "inspired" them through all the Revolutionary struggles and the disappointments they had been forced to endure, they set forth their reasons for rejecting "absolutely" the assessment: "The end of Civil Government is limited to the Temporal liberty and property of Mankind and their protection in the free Exercise of Religion." Furthermore, "Religion and Morality" (it resumes in an epitome of the rational natural religion of the Declaration of Rights, Jefferson's bill, and Madison's "Memorial") "can be promoted only by the internal Conviction of the Mind, and its voluntary Choice." The address goes on to request the Assembly to remedy the initial shortcomings of the constitution of the commonwealth, "so far as it is possible for the Legislature to do it, by adopting the Bill in the revised Laws for establishing religious freedom."[28]

The Shenandoah Valley Presbyterians held that the convention's address expressed their views so forcefully that petitioners from many counties contented themselves with short endorsements of the Bethel statement. Other strongly Scotch-Irish counties, however, drafted petitions of their own, basing their protests also on the by-then conventional wisdom of the Lockean contract. They, too, expressed themselves in terms similar to the Presbyterian convention's address and Madison's "Memorial." In short, the Presbyterians realized and expressed their separation of church and state in the very conception and phrasing of their submissions to the legislature, confining themselves largely to rational, secular arguments and to the language of natural religion, rather than employing a rhetoric that invoked Scriptural revelation and the powers of divine grace.[29]

Another, more numerous and more generally circulated group of petitions make a sharp contrast; these present a case that rested primarily on the "Gospel" and the inspired nature of those sent forth to propagate it. Some twenty-eight counties sent in variants on two related formulas, subscribed altogether by nearly half of the eleven thousand Virginians who signed antiassessment petitions in 1785. There can be little doubt that these petitions originated with the Separate Baptists, and the text has already been referred to as the great Baptist petition in the discussion of size and format.[30]

The priority of emphasis in the great Baptist petitions (presented in some two dozen texts) is instantly signaled: "We do . . . earnestly declare against . . .[the assessment bill] as being contrary to the spirit of the Gospel and the Bill of Rights." This order is maintained in the development of its argument. First, it shows how the "divine Blessing" was sufficient to maintain the gospel "in the World for several Hundred Years" without state support and, indeed, "against all the powers of the Earth"; then argues that the "pious example" of stern magistrates and the manifestations of the power of "the Holy Ghost" within the ministers – "those whom divine grace hath called to that work" – will similarly revive religion, as Establishment could never do. Only after this sustained treatment of the power of the Spirit in the church, do these petitions turn to pragmatic demonstration, citing the superior religious and moral character of Pennsylvania, where there had never been an establishment, and going on to assert constitutional rights and to stress the grievances of non-Christians if they had to support Christianity in violation of the equality promised in the "Bill of Rights."[31]

This formula traveled widely. More than four thousand signatures were attached to its many and variously adapted copies. In the course of a year, however, it had become separated from its place of origin. In 1785, it circulated in southern and eastern Virginia within a triangle from the counties of Westmoreland to Henry to Princess Ann, an area that coincided largely with the Lower North and the Upper and Lower South District Associations of Separate Baptists; in 1784, the first recognizable text of it had drawn up and sent to the Assembly from Rockingham County, in the territory of the Upper North Association. This prototype text begins with an invocation of "the Great Mr Lock" (which evidently did not seem compelling to later adaptors, for they dropped it), and then moves on to an enumeration of the persecutions practiced in New England and to the blessings of liberty in Rhode Island – an appropriate topic for Separate Baptists. (In the later, widely circulated version, neighboring Pennsylvania was substituted for Rhode Island, so that this point in the argument was made with reference to a state better known to most Virginians.)[32]

The themes of the reworked and tautened long formula are certainly adumbrated in the earlier Rockingham petition's recital of the history of Christianity, which it declares to have been "propagated through the World for three hundred years . . . without and often against the use of secular force." The reference to a colony without establishment as a refutation of the necessity of such connection is a further parallel, but the relationship of the texts is most apparent in the conclusion, which very plainly foreshadows the content and the compelling rhythms of the version circulated in 1785. This form of an utterance – this great Baptist petition, written and rewritten by unnamed hands – gave voice to a new Virginia, indeed a new America, that was coming into being along with the new republic. The force of its expression and the number of signatures it accumulated should make it one of the most powerful documents of Virginia history, and the two-hundredth anniversary of its composition is an occasion to be marked along with that of the statute.[33]

Recast in more compelling rhythms and transferred to the lower and southside parts of Virginia, the great Baptist petition had a life of its own. Some twenty copies of it conformed to the pattern already outlined, but revealing variations on it were developed in many places. Commonly, the changes show pressures to increase the natural-rights, civil-contract arguments – often by inserting extracts from Jefferson's bill – but significantly, this was usually balanced by an insertion of strong religious rhetoric. At the level of the common folk, this great Baptist evangelical petition realized and expressed a sense of the separation of religious and secular authority by placing emphasis on the divine work that alone could cause a church to grow and on the inspired character of its ministers. The petition carried into the Assembly a powerful popular recollection of the decades of fearless apostolic witness that had been borne by the itinerant messengers of the gospel.[34]

In sum, then, the anti-Establishment petitions to the Assembly relay different messages and reveal distinct peoples in Virginia (most notably, the Scotch-Irish Presbyterians and the common-folk Baptists). The nature of their engagement in the struggle will now be further examined. What was at stake for these people in the struggle over the assessment bill?

As is always the case in great controversies, there was at stake for the contestants the kind of world in which they envisaged living. This can be seen most clearly in the confrontation between the Anglican Establishmentarians and the evangelical Baptists – a confrontation that had been sustained for more than two decades by 1785. Contrasting ideas of community, and the manner of religious observance in it, had divided them deeply all this time. The controversy of 1785 went to the heart of the matter. The Establishmentarians' assessment bill – the Christian teachers' bill, as they entitled it – aimed to restore, within a conceded new framework of religious pluralism, the ethos of the church "as by law established," under which they had grown up. A powerful set of symbols expressed for them a distinct kind of community. There was the grand church building, which was the largest enclosed space that most parishioners ever entered. Even more expressive were the internal furnishings that completed the statement – the high-walled pews and the three-tiered "desk" surmounted by pulpit and "tester," in which a hierarchy of clerk, reader, and parson officiated before a congregation made up of everyone in the district, seated in a way that plainly declared an order of rank and dignity in society.[35]

For the evangelical Baptists, church association was voluntary, and the customary settings were more varied and all very different from the Episcopalian. The buildings had been humble dwellings or tobacco houses in the early exciting days of carrying the Word into the Piedmont and tidewater regions of Virginia. More lately, the gathered congregations had set up many plain wooden meetinghouses. Yet much of the action – the most significant action – was out of doors, around a stump or simple stage where multitudes gathered for the great preachings and exhortings of the association meetings or the awakening of a revival. Images of such forms of gathering and of the kinds of social order they represented were among the most powerful messages communicated by the petitions.[36]

Associated with these starkly different images of settings were those of the contrasting symbolic figures who were expressly invoked in the petitions. The parson in the high pulpit was accorded the status and endowed with the attributes of a gentleman. He held commissioned rank, having been ordained by a bishop; he was learned, although probably not too erudite, in the manner of a squire. Being one of the "Men of Family and Education" (as a pro-assessment petition phrased it), the parson represented a whole social order and its decorum – he gave down "Public Instruction," delivering it in a "rational, solemn, and reverend Manner." The opposition to the negative image that was invoked by Establishmentarians, of ignorant, "mechanic," itinerant preachers, was most powerfully suggested by those petitioners who proclaimed that they "believe that the reputation of Religion will considerably depend on the literary as well as moral and religious Qualifications of its Teachers." This declaration was matched by many others in petitions supporting the assessment.

The dissenting Baptists reversed these preferences. The genteel parson, supported in a "liberal and plentiful Manner" (as the assessment supporters would have it), they perceived to be one of "the many hirelings whose Chief Motive and Design would be Temporal Interest" (as their great petition expresses it). That petition makes explicit the contrast with "Ministers . . . inwardly moved by the Holy Ghost . . . useful and Faithful Men . . ., whom Divine Grace hath called to that Work." Such were the men who, without the aid of polite learning, had "maintained" the gospel "against all the Powers of the Earth." Their successors had braved riot and imprisonment to carry the gospel through Virginia.[37]

Thus the petitions set up a confrontation between the old Virginia of the Anglican parish and the new Virginia of the gospel preacher. This was a crucial confrontation, contributing greatly to the process whereby the new overwhelmed the old. But the assemblage of petitions enables us to see other deeper lines of contrast that were being incised on new Virginia that the struggle of 1784 and 1785 was legitimating. The petitions on the side against the assessment, and so for the separation of church and state, represent a striking range of very distinctive modes of performance. They were so crafted as to operate very differently among the county menfolk for whom they were prepared and (in some instances) from whom they came. Deeper than style or phrasing, the dictions and relationships to medium of expression vary sharply among the petitions. The most striking and important divergence was between Madison's "Memorial and Remonstrance" and the great Baptist petition.[38]

Madison's "Memorial and Remonstrance" has remained famous because it explicates, in the mode of universal reasoning, the basis for denying either state or society the right to dictate to the individual in the matter of religion. In order to be effective, let alone authoritative – and authoritativeness was sought in every channel of the "Memorial's" communication – such a message had to be carried in the medium of a language that was Latinate and abstract. Evangelical sense of the power of the gospel was translated into philosophic history. The diction was distant from forms familiar even to the county gentry. If the "Memorial" owed anything at all to forms of speech, it was to the academic disputation and its successor, the debate, which Madison had mastered in Princeton at the College of New Jersey; but most of all, it came from the realms of silent discourse, the language of print that Madison so studiously pored over. It was an intricate, punctuated sequence, to be followed with the eye rather than the ear.[39]

From among the dissenter protests against the assessment bill, the Presbyterian petitions are closest in diction to the "Memorial and Remonstrance" and are, in that way, intermediate between it and the great Baptist petition. But there was in most Presbyterian pronouncements less distance between the language of the petitions and the words spoken aloud at the meetings from which the petitions came. Scotch-Irish congregations were accustomed to learned, hard-reasoned sermons. The strong insistence on natural rights enshrined in fundamental laws conveyed clearly the sense of identity of an embattled ethnic minority that had learned to resist by turning the weapons of the would-be oppressive world back on that world. The heroic republicanism that runs through the Presbyterian remonstrances echoes the martial addresses that for decades had stirred up these predominantly frontier folk from the time of the French and Indian War, through all the upheavals of the patriotic stuggle against continued British domination. These were a people led by a native gentry and a learned clergy that could more than hold their own with the old Virginians, and in a similar aggressive style.[40]

The Baptists, too, had proved that they could gain ground against the customary values of an older Episcopalian Virginia; but they had not done so by excelling in the proud assertive ways of those who stood opposed to them. The contrast between the Baptist evangelical and the Presbyterian ethnic mode of dissent – as well as between the popular evangelical and the gentry authoritative modes – can be clearly seen, or rather heard, in the great Baptist petition.

Of all the various petitions, it is this one that must be reconstituted as sound before its character, its effectiveness, and so its fuller meaning can be understood. It starts, of course, as a memorial to the Assembly in appropriate form, but from the minute it has declared the position taken – that the assessment bill is "contrary to the Spirit of the Gospel and the Bill of Rights" – the mode of address changes decisively. One can now hear the voice of the preacher or exhorter, giving his subject arrestingly, developing it with power, advancing another, and cumulating the whole in a punctuate, rhythmic fashion. "Certain it is. . . . Nor was it the better. . . . But it is said . . ." all build up to the rhetorical question (hardly an expected trope in a petition), "But what valuable Purpose . . .?" to the scornful dismissal – "That Religious Establishment and Government is linked . . . is something new" – to a compelling statement coupled to another question, and, at last, to the great climax that is pure oratorical demonstration and application, evidently inscribed by a preacher accustomed to persuade the secure of their need to be awakened:

> Finally if such tax is against the Spirit of the Gospel, if Christ . . . , if an Establishment . . . , If no more . . . , If it would not . . . , Nor . . . , or . . . , And if against the Bill of rights . . . your Petitioners . . . trust the Wisdom and uprightness of your Honourable House will leave them entirely free in Matters of Religion.[41]

Thus the great Baptist petition makes a striking contrast to Madison's "Memorial." The word as reason in print, controlled order; the word as preaching with liberty, effusive spirit. In these two distinctive documents, there was laid before the House two kinds of knowledge, side by side; each arose from a profoundly different way of being. Two Virginias were coming together after decades of bitter conflict. It had been primarily a struggle over the Word and the appropriation of the Word. The New Lights had defiantly practiced their belief that any man, however humble, if his neighbors recognized "a gift" in him, could preach, bringing home the Word of God. The upholders of the Established order had insisted that only a man qualified by higher learning – therefore, a gentleman – could perform this authoritative role. Now, in the "Memorial and Remonstrance," the printed reasoning of the gentry showed the rightness and necessity of giving freedom to the Word in the world. And in doing so, the lawmakers, who were masters of the words of printed reason – those who could articulate the world view of Jefferson and Madison – retained a mastery over Virginia and by the same process, America.

Dissenting Traditions

A statute in itself is a set of words on paper. Its actual power and meaning – its real existence – are in the place it holds in the minds of members of society. The making of a law, then, does not cease with the passing of a bill; the law merely enters another phase, and is made and remade in the tradition that is its life. So it has been with the great Virginia Statute for Religious Freedom.

Both the author and the sponsor of the statute in the legislature began to endow it with a particular, preferred meaning immediately on its enactment. James Madison, having worked so hard to get the bill adopted, wrote Jefferson that he hoped the legislature had now, "in this Country extinguished for ever the ambitious hope of making laws for the human mind." Jefferson, in turn, expressed similar views but with a wider – indeed, universal – sense of the extent of the reach of this portentous law:

> It is inserted in the new Encyclopedie. . . . In fact it is comfortable to see the standard of reason at length erected, after so many ages during which the human mind has been held in vassalage by kings, priests & nobles.

And so the act as the triumph of enlightenment was launched, and an image of Virginia as the domain of a rational gentry, projected.[42]

But there were other Virginias, other ways of appropriating the statute and remaking it as a part of different and diverse traditions.

The passing of the statute immediately reinforced the campaign to end the remaining legal advantages that the Episcopal Church enjoyed. The ad hoc measures that had brought about piecemeal disestablishment had now been replaced by a high-flown statement of principle. The new commonwealth was distanced even more explicitly from the old colony, and the claim of the Church to carry corporate identity and rights of property through from one to the other was undermined. The dissenters collectively – Presbyterians and Baptists both – were able, in the very next session, to secure the repeal of the Act for Incorporating the Protestant Episcopal Church.[43]

Within a decade – the Baptists proving particularly insistent – the dissenters were able to make good their claim that the possessions of the former Established Church were public property for common use and at the disposal of the local authorities. The occupation of the churches by the once-harried sectaries and the auction sales of the parsons' glebes – and even sometimes of the Church communion plate – proclaimed an unmistakable triumph and symbolic reversal that gave the new order proclaimed by the statute a very particular meaning.[44]

Perhaps that is why the statute was not much celebrated among Episcopalians, even though many of them had endorsed it willingly. Edmund Randolph's incomplete *History of Virginia* encompasses a denunciation of the deceptions by which, in his view, Church property had been despoiled, but it does not extend to commemorate Jefferson's triumph. Certainly, the great collector of episcopal legend, Bishop Meade, displayed a complex attitude. He was sure the seizure of the property was unlawful, although he declared it to have been a providential release for the Church – indeed, an essential prerequisite for its resurrection in a purified evangelical form in which it would be supported by only the contributions of the godly. His great compilations avoid all mention of the Statute for Religious Freedom; he clearly detested the uncompromising rationalism of both text and author.[45]

By contrast, the dissenters appropriated the act and remade it as the charter for the new place that they had begun to assume in Virginia. The Presbyterians, with their regional ethnic bases in the Shenandoah Valley and southwestern area and with a learned clergy and a native gentry of their own, moved easily and securely into the status of partners in the state. They already had two flourishing academies for instruction in classical learning, which had been incorporated as the Liberty Hall and Hampden-Sydney colleges in 1782 and 1783. Their sense of identity as dissenters was retained in association with their Scotch-Irish traditions. Both these readily combined with the militant republican patriotism eloquently expressed in the names of the colleges. In this ethos, the Statute for Religious Freedom was remade as a principal foundation of the reordered world in which Presbyterians, now a leading part of a new sociocultural establishment, took great pride. They were assured in a knowledge that their demands from the time of independence onward had been of decisive importance and that their extraordinary convention of lay and clerical delegates in Bethel, Augusta County, in 1785 not only had been of great moment in stopping the proposed revival of Establishment through the general assessment, but also had explicitly requested the final resolution of these protracted disputes by the adoption of Jefferson's bill.[46]

The statute, once enacted, was remade in the Presbyterians' knowledge of it, as part of the same tradition that was epitomized in their foundation narrative of the mission of the Reverend Samuel Davies to Virginia. This history of genteel piety, courageous persistence against a hostile worldliness, and a forthright patriotism that could not but win respect was a perfect expression of the polite evangelicalism that became the dominant tone of Virginia's elite through the nineteenth century and into the twentieth. William Henry Foote and Bishop William Meade were very close in their values and view of the past even as they narrated different parts of it. Meade, the churchman, commemorated the grandeur of a worldly Establishment that had to go down in ruins before it could be rebuilt in accordance with the gospel; while Foote, the descendant of the dissenters, told of the success in gaining recognition of a godly ministry and people. Foote celebrated the long struggle as "working out the system of things which has been the glory of Virginia." In a proud identification with the regime of his day, he rejoiced that "after an experiment of more than half a century the bill for religious freedom holds its place among the fundamental laws of the Virginia statute book." He declared that churches had flourished, and "professors of the gospel increased about ten-fold," while "even prisoners, slaves, and convicts enjoy freedom of conscience."[47]

With the Baptists, it has been different. Among them, the statute has been made and remade in memory as part of a tradition of identification with the poor and despised and an antagonistic relationship toward the Virginia that oppressed and persecuted them. Such a consciousness was there before the Revolution, as appears distinctly in the notes that Morgan Edwards made, based on the conversations he had in the course of his tour while surveying the situation of the Baptists in Virginia in 1770 and 1771. It comes through as a sense of stirring among the folk in the most expressive of the early Baptist church books – appropriately, the record of the Albemarle church, quite near to Jefferson's residence: "In as much as it hath pleased the Lord of his gre[at] mercy to allarm and awaken out of the learthygy of Sin the inhabitants of Virginia By Sundry of his Servants as imbassadoers . . . the people Called Battis(ts)."[48]

The identification with persecuted witnesses was immediate, deep, and enduring. It showed in the crowds that came to hear preaching through the bars of the prisons where defiant preachers were confined; it showed in the challenging attitude of the first General Association meeting in Orange County in 1771; it showed in the wording of the first great religious petition to be sent to the Virginia legislature, the Baptist-circulated "Ten-Thousand Name Petition" of the fall of 1776, praying that "every . . . yoke may be Broken and that the oppressed may go free"; and it has continued to be shown in every history that the Baptists have produced.[49]

The Baptists had been the first to petition for the adoption of Jefferson's bill. They did so in 1779 at the time of its initial circulation in the state. They evidently saw the thwarting of the churchmen's drive for a general assessment, and the consequent enactment of the Statute for Religious Freedom, as the great culmination – though not the conclusion – of their decades of struggle. A certain sense of arrival was no doubt expressed in the resolution of the Baptist General Committee in 1788, calling for the preparation of a "History of the Baptists in Virginia."[50]

There were delays and setbacks in the compilation and publication, but in 1810, when Robert Baylor Semple produced his volume, boldly entitled *The History of the Rise and Progress of the Baptists in Virginia*, it was a very clear statement of the Baptist identity as oppressed witnesses. The instant Semple introduced the Separate Baptist builders of his own present faith and order, he wrote that "they endured much persecution; but God prospered them and delivered them out of the hands of all their enemies." All the trials of the faithful messengers were recounted dramatically, and no doubt was left as to the triumph of their gospel, with God's protection, in the separation of the state from involvement with particular churches. Semple recorded the Baptists' formal approbation of the "bill drawn by the venerable Thomas Jefferson" and went on to observe that this outcome, this "inhibition of the general assessment," could "in a considerable degree be ascribed to the opposition made to it by the Baptists."[51]

Already there appear in Semple's *History* the marks of the assimilation process by which the Baptists were coming to be a part of the accepted fabric of the new Virginia society, and even to be associated with its authority structures as part of an informal establishment. (He noted the moderation of the unrefined sermon styles – the "Baptist whine" – together with the growing pressures for seminaries to train preachers and a steadily increasing acceptability of Baptists in polite society.) Nevertheless, the insistence on the identity of otherness to the fashionable world remained very strong. The force of Jefferson's statute in its declaration of the separateness of religion retained, then, a very particular significance for the Baptists.[52]

The Baptists' persecution identity persisted. In the next generation, when the tone of polite society was pious and severe, when Meade collected melancholy antiquarian links between a vanished worldly splendor and a sober, evangelical present, and when Foote chronicled the steady advance of the now prevailing genteel godliness in the form of Presbyterianism, the Baptists (represented by the Reverend James Barnett Taylor) still depicted their past – *Lives of Virginia Baptist Ministers* – as passionate revivalism and fearless witness in the face of a persecuting world.[53]

This tradition was so strong that as late as 1880, it supplied a powerful strain in the opening chapter of the historical section of the volume celebrating the centenary of the First Baptist Church in Richmond. One might expect a pious chronicle of civic Christianity, especially since there were no anti–New Light riots, arrests, and imprisonments in the new capital city in Henrico County. But no – the chapter is filled out with an extended listing of the mighty preachers, most of them tested in the fire of persecution, who might have played a part, although unrecorded, in the first days of the church. The special sense of distinctness and of a particular relationship to the act is even clearer when one makes a contrast with the *Memorials of Methodism in Virginia*, published at about the same time. In that work, a full chronicling of events for 1785 fails to include even a mention of the petition campaign against the assessment or of Jefferson's statute.[54]

The Baptist tradition of persecution narratives continued, finding powerful expression in the turn-of-the-century *Documentary History of the Struggle of Religious Liberty in Virginia*, by Charles F. James. A generation later came the results of Lewis Peyton Little's unremitting search through all the Baptist lore to that date, and through the order books of many counties, in order to document the great compilation that he published in 1938, which he significantly titled *Imprisoned Preachers and Religious Liberty in Virginia*. That this was not just the work of certain bookish Baptists, but part of a folk culture, can be seen from the entries that show how local congregations carefully mark the sites of the martyrs' persecution and preserve such relics as the lock and key of the Culpeper jail, where James Ireland was both incarcerated and subjected to mob harassment.[55]

That the tradition has lived on until closer to the present can be seen in Garnett Ryland's meticulous work *The Baptists of Virginia*, published in Richmond in 1955. This book, prepared by a member of a family associated through generations with Baptist history, introduces the themes of "intolerant laws in regard to religion" on its first page. But perhaps one can see also signs of accommodation, of assurance concerning the rightful and legitimate place that Baptists knew they had assumed in Virginia by this time. Certainly, the Great Revival of 1785 is summed up with the confident assertion that in its aftermath, and with the enactment of the Statute for Religious Freedom, the Baptist churches "became community churches and their members a cross-section of the population."[56]

Messages are marked as much by their silences as by their pronouncements. The past is made history by the ways it is remembered and told – and from what is not told. What is told, then, takes its larger meaning from who tells it and from the different stories others tell. While the erstwhile dissenters have made Virginia and the Statute for Religious Freedom in a certain image by commemorating continually the fearless witness of their founding evangelists, there have been quite other legends sustained by other Virginians.

The most easily identified of these other Virginias is the Old Dominion of the Cavaliers – a tradition of gallantry encompassing, through its many transformations, the great processes of nation building and state- or folk–defending from John Smith to Robert E. Lee. The most elusive is the heritage of the Afro-Virginians. The traditions of the slaves are an unseen and unheard part of the history surrounding the statute, not only because these were an oppressed and exploited people, but also because their consciousness of their past – of their origins and destiny – was not rendered into what we call "history" so much as into sacred song. Yet no account of the dissenting Virginia that made Jefferson's statute possible can be acceptable without at least registering the presence of these distinctive Christian witnesses; no account of the tellings and retellings in which both the struggle and the culminating statute have been commemorated should fail to point out that these Virginians had their own traditions.[57]

Accommodation: Rationalist and Gospel America

Thomas Jefferson's statute instituted the new, pluralistic Virginia in serenely deistic terms, and it was welcomed – indeed, had been keenly sought – by New Light exponents of the mystical regeneration of born-again Christians. There was a basis for this alignment beyond the circumstantial combination to overthrow designs for Establishment. Jefferson's system proclaimed individual judgment as sacred, sacred against the pressures of collective coercions; the evangelicals did the same for private conscience. Having created a private sanctuary in the mind, or heart, both could view the public domain as secular – a region where law and contract prevailed. It was, in time, to become apparent that the evangelicals' concept of law included the moral code they derived from Scripture. Thus – since it was not, to them, the way of salvation, and so part of "religion" – they were prepared, in the famous "Blue Laws," to enlist the state in enforcing on the community.

Over the new Virginia, a rationalist-individualist arch of republican authority was set up. Beneath this arch, richly communal forms of experimental religion were thriving and expanding. And since the principles of the Statute for Religious Freedom were widespread, its regime extended over the South and over the expanding American nation.

Yet it was not only the mysteries of religious experience that existed in a kind of contradiction with the philosophic deism of the statute. There had been other powerful presences in the petitions of 1785; another confrontation, in addition to that between Establishmentarians and dissenters, had been signified to the Assembly. In that same year, the Quakers and Methodists, following the dynamics of their own communities and stirred by the ferment of religious petitioning, circulated petitions for the freeing of the slaves. This initiative, in turn, elicited outraged, Scripture-based memorials vindicating slavery. These responses came from the same southwestern area that was so polarized between demands for established and demands for voluntary religion.[58]

It has not been usual to discuss Jefferson's statute in conjunction with the American paradox of slavery and freedom. Yet when it is viewed as part of a long social struggle for religious freedom in Virginia, both the statute's intimate connection with slavery and the nature of-the solution it propounded can be more clearly seen.

Religious freedom is, at base, an issue of social relationships. Repressive controls on the New Lights in Virginia had been a defense of certain kinds of traditional community against the claims of a religion of personal conversation. The parish church, where all were symbolically together in their due rank and order for the corporate worship of God, was seen to be threatened by break-away sectarianism. But the violence really came when the Baptist evangelists' campaigns of conversion cut into the little (and not so little) communities at the very base of society – the households, including the large plantations. Wives might be set in defiance of husbands, children divided from parents, and, most menacing of all, slaves set against masters. It seemed imperative to many to stop the mass gatherings for preaching and to enclose the sectaries within the safe bounds of licensed meetinghouses that could be put off-limits to slaves, unless they had their masters' permission.[59]

The Virginia colonial legislature's desperate attempt in 1772 to institute religious freedom – limited then to toleration – had come to grief over insistence on restrictions of this kind, which were unacceptable to evangelists and libertarians alike. In 1776, even the three great libertarians who attempted drafts of a constitution for the new commonwealth entered precautionary clauses guarding against social subversion through religious proselytizing among slaves. Petitions and pronouncements in the press all through the war years repeatedly sounded this alarm.

It is against the background of this slave owners' fear of subversion that the nature of Jefferson's resolution of the conflict can be best appreciated. The social struggle at the root of the religious strife was caused to vanish by a definition of religion as essentially in the mind – in "opinions," as Jefferson's first surviving legislative draft on the subject expressed it. Religion was no longer, as it had been for all preceding human history, a legitimate principle for determining social organization and obligation. The converse of this, however, was true to only a limited extent. Constraints on the body designed to coerce the mind in religion were expressly outlawed where they arose from "opinion," from a religious principle. But where coercion arose from *social* relationships, from the forms of civil society, the law was silent on them. Thus the statute of Virginia could promise freedom of religion in a slaveholding society. In this, it is a classic of Enlightenment liberalism – a model for the reorganization of a society that was to be made *of* independent, rational, individual decision makers, and *for* the property-owning adult males who could aspire to have these qualities recognized. As such, it was aptly reprinted in the *Encyclopédie* – sent forth to play its part in a remaking of the world. "Bourgeois liberty" may not be the best way to describe this system as it was taking shape in a farmers' republic, but this designation would draw attention to the restrictive aspects of the new freedom in its overall content.

To leave the evaluation at that would be to rest with the Enlightenment-intellectualist illusion. The statute did not make a new Virginia so much as register its existence. It was raised up by an emergent Virginia of New Light salvationists, black and white, a Virginia in which vibrant new forms of religious life demanded the religious revolution that preceded and accompanied the political revolution. Thomas Jefferson, James Madison, and their little cohort were blocked in every other fundamental reform they proposed. The new white and black popular cultures of evangelical experience and witness empowered the rationalists to frame the charter for their new order; in that way, they made a vital contribution to the expanding dual America of gospel religion and republican rationality.

NOTES

Parts of this paper were prepared while the writer was a visiting fellow at the Max-Planck-Institut für Geschichte in Göttingen. Thanks for the opportunity to work in this very stimulating environment are due to the director, Dr. Rudolf Vierhaus, and to Dr. Alf Lüdtke and Dr. Hans Medick, who kept the writer engaged in challenging discussions that were of the greatest value to him. Professor Kenneth Lockridge read a draft and offered prompt and compelling suggestions; so did Colleen Isaac.

1   Order Book, 1763–1769, Orange County, Virginia, cited in Lewis Peyton Little, *Imprisoned Preachers and Religious Liberty in Virginia: A Narrative Drawn Largely from the Official Records* . . . (Lynchburg, Va., 1938), pp. 91–2, 95.

2   [H. R. McIlwaine and] J. P. Kennedy, eds., *Journals of the House of Burgesses of Virginia, 1766–1769* (Richmond, 1906), pp. 190, 205.

3   Ibid., p. 252.

4   John Williams, Journal, May 10, 1771, MS, Virginia Baptist Historical Society, University of Richmond. See also Morgan Edwards, "Materials Toward a History of the Baptists in the Province of Virginia, 1772" MS, pp. 75–76, Furman University Library, Greenville, South Carolina.

5   Williams, Journal, May 19, 1771.

6   Ibid., May 12, 1771; Robert Baylor Semple, *History of the Rise and Progress of the Baptists in Virginia*, ed. George W. Beale (Richmond, 1894), p. 173.

7   J. P. Kennedy, ed., *Journals of the House of Burgesses of Virginia, 1770–1772* (Richmond, 1906), pp. 185–6.

8   "An Address to the Anabaptist Preachers Imprisoned in Caroline County, August 8, 1771," *Virginia Gazette* (Purdie and Dixon), February 20, 1772, was explicit about the problems of applying the English Act of Toleration.

9   For a fuller discussion of the initial legal perplexities of Virginia's colonial religious coercion and toleration laws and practices, see Rhys Isaac, "Religion and Authority: Problems of the Anglican Establishment in Virginia in the Era of the Great Awakening and the Parsons' Cause," *William and Mary Quarterly*, 3 ser., 30 (1973): 26–30. An earlier attempt to get a Virginia toleration act introduced is briefly discussed here. See also Rhys Isaac, *The Transformation of Virginia, 1740–1790* (Chapel Hill, N.C., 1982), pp. 150–3, 199–201.

10   "An Address to the Anabaptist Preachers"; "Timoleon" in *Virginia Gazette* (Purdie and Dixon), August 22, 1771.

11   Kennedy, ed., *Journals of the Burgesses, 1770–1772*, pp. 185–6. The bill was printed in the *Virginia Gazette* (Rind), March 26, 1772.

12   For a fuller discussion of the way alarm at the rise of dissent was linked to anxieties about slaves, see Isaac, *Transformation*, pp. 171–2, 220, 286.

13   Ibid., pp. 220, 221.

14   Dumas Malone, *The Life and Times of Thomas Jefferson: The Virginian* (Boston, 1948), p. 142; Samuel Henley, *The Distinct Claims of Government and Religion Considered in a Sermon Preached before the Honourable House of Burgesses, at Williamsburgh in Virginia, March 1, 1772* (Cambridge, 1772); "Hoadleianus" in *Virginia Gazette* (Rind), March 5, 1772, and Robert Carter Nicholas to "Hoadleianus" in ibid., June 10, 1773; James Madison, *An Oration, in*

Commemoration of the Founders of William and Mary College . . . (Williamsburg, Va., 1772), pp. 9–14.

15 Henley, *Distinct Claims*, p. iii; "Hoadleianus" to Robert Carter Nicholas in *Virginia Gazette* (Rindl), June 3, 1773; Madison, *An Oration*, p. 10; Thomas Jefferson to Samuel Henley, June 9, 1778, and March 3, 1785, *The Papers of Thomas Jefferson*, ed. Julian Boyd (Princeton, N.J., 1950–), 2:198–9; 8: 11–12.

16 James Madison to William Bradford, January 24, 1774, and April 1, 1774, *The Papers of James Madison*, ed. William T. Hutchinson and William M. E. Rachal (Chicago, 1962), 1:106, 112.

17 Robert A. Rutland, ed., *The Papers of George Mason, 1725–1792* (Chapel Hill, N.C., 1970), 1:284, 289–1. On the initial clauses directed against subversion of authority "under colour of religion," see ibid., 1:284; Hutchinson and Rachal, *Papers of Madison*, 1:174; and Boyd, *Papers of Jefferson*, 1:344. I have dealt briefly with the 1776 debate on Article XVI because, unlike the earlier 1772 debate, it has been very fully reviewed in the historiography. I have selected the slave owners' law-and-order concern for emphasis, because that has generally been overlooked. For recent discussion of these debates, see, in addition to the editorial commentaries in the *Papers* cited above, Thomas E. Buckley, *Church and State in Revolutionary Virginia, 1776–1787* (Charlottesville, Va., 1977), pp. 17–19.

18 For a fuller account of the developments from June to December 1776, see Buckley, *Church and State*, pp. 19–37. Buckley draws attention to the persisting establishmentarian assumptions in Jefferson's first constitutional draft (pp. 20–21).

19 For a brief but fuller summing up of the developments between 1776 and 1785 as this writer understands them, see Isaac, *Transformation*, pp. 275–85. For a yet fuller account see Buckley, *Church and State*, pp. 38–164. For the text of the bill as Jefferson published it, see Boyd, *Papers of Jefferson*, 2: illustration p. 305; for the amendments made during the enacting process, see ibid., 2:545–7.

20 George Nicholas to James Madison, April 22, 1785; Madison to Thomas Jefferson, April 27, 1785, in *The Papers of James Madison*, ed. Robert A. Rutland and William M. E. Rachal (Chicago, 1973), 8:264, 268.

21 For the absence of correlation between delegates' positions taken on the assessment question and their acceptance or rejection at the polls, see Buckley, *Church and State*, pp. 116–17.

22 Petitions from Dinwiddie County, November 28, and Amherst County, December 10, 1785, in Religious Petitions, 1774–1802, Presented to the General Assembly of Virginia, Virginia State Library, Richmond (microfilm); hereafter cited as V.R.P. (Note the dates are those endorsed on the petitions, indicating when they were received.) For a very illuminating discussion of the polarization in the southwestern region, see Richard R. Beeman, *The Evolution of the Southern Backcountry: A Case Study of Lunenburg County, Virginia, 1746–1832* (Philadelphia, 1984), pp. 140–56; see also Rich-

ard R. Beeman and Rhys Isaac, "Cultural Conflict and Social Change in the Revolutionary South: Lunenburg County, Virginia," *Journal of Southern History* 46 (1980): 525–50.

23   A tally was made of the 1785 religious petitions, measuring their sizes. Out of some ninety-two, twenty (22 percent) are smaller than quarto; eleven (12 percent) are quarto or small quarto; thirty-seven (40) percent are foolscap or large foolscap; and twenty-four (25 percent) are large or very large. The distribution of sizes of petitions is comparable within the Baptist and Presbyterian groups. The only set that is distinctive – so much so that this must be seen as a part of its strategy of authoritative assertion – was that made by the "Memorial and Remonstrance," all but one of which (Amherst, October 28, 1785) are in the large and several in the very large category. V.R.P.

24   Address of the Presbyterian Convention . . . , August 19, 1785, received November 2, 1785, V.R.P.

25   Petition from Albemarle, Amherst, and Buckingham counties, October 22, 1776; Presbytery of Hanover, November 12, 1784, V.R.P. On the heroic image of the "Shirtmen," see Isaac, *Transformation*, pp. 256–9; on the settling of scores within the Presbyterian camp, see Buckley, *Church and State*, pp. 93–4.

26   Petition from Rockbridge County, December 1, 1784; for a comparable heroic republican pronouncement in 1785, see Rockbridge, November 2, 1785, V.R.P.

27   Address of the Presbytery, October 28, 1784, V.R.P.

28   Miscellaneous Petition, November 2, 1785, V.R.P.

29   Petitions merely endorsing the proceedings of the Presbyterian convention came from the following counties: Augusta and Botetourt, November 12; Augusta and Rockbridge, November 12; Frederick and Berkeley, November 12; Prince Edward, November 12; Rockbridge, November 12; Frederick, November 15; and Berkeley, November 18, 1785, V.R.P. For petitions from Presbyterian areas that worked variations on Lockean themes, see Botetourt County, November 29; Rockbridge County, November 2; Washington County, December 12; and Bedford County, October 27, 1785, V.R.P.

30   The General Committee of the Association of Baptist Churches, as political watchdogs for the movement, had resolved in August 1785 "that it be recommended to those counties, which have not yet prepared petitions . . . to proceed thereon . . . ," (Semple, *History*, p. 96), and there follows a set of headings that corresponds fairly closely with those of the great popular petition. Only two of the extant Baptist church books reveal direct engagement in this work, responding in these cases to calls from their district associations (Mill Swamp Baptist Church, Isle of Wight County, Records, 1779–90, June 17, 1785, and Black Creek Baptist Church, Southampton County, Records, 1776–1804, May 10, 1785, University of Richmond). This, however, is not strong evidence against a Baptist attribution, since it was "the policy of the Baptists," as noted by Garnett Ryland, "to prepare and promote petitions signed by citizens generally" (Garnett Ryland, *The Bap-*

tists of Virginia, 1669–1926 [Richmond, 1955], p. 125). All the formula petitions came from regions of Baptist strength. That in itself is not conclusive, since the same eastern and southside region had seen the rapid growth of the Methodists. Nevertheless, the Baptist attribution must stand, since there is no record of Methodist organizational steps to circulate petitions on the assessment and no tradition of Methodist militancy on church–state issues.

31 The text here followed is petition from Buckingham County, October 27, 1785, V.R.P.

32 Petition from Rockingham County, November 18, 1784, V.R.P.

33 Ibid. The Rockingham petition culminates in the following insistent rhythm: "Now if . . . the power. . . . If Christianity was. . . . If leaving States. . . . And if it would Infringe our Bill of Rights." This should be compared with the conclusion of the great Baptist petition of 1785, quoted on p. 151 of this essay. Note the signature of the well-known Baptist, Silas Hart, prominent on this petition. See Ryland, *Baptists of Virginia*, p. 125n.

34 Significant variations on the formula include petitions from Caroline County, October 27; Amelia County, November 11; and Chesterfield County, November 14, 1785. Variants that incorporate extracts from Jefferson's bill include petitions from Nansemond County, October 27, and Westmoreland County, November 2, 1785, all V.R.P. That the Baptists launched popular petitions with strong evangelical-Scriptural resonances, while their leaders addressed the Assembly in the Latinate language of law and politics, can readily be seen by comparing any of these with either the General Committee's remonstrance, November 11, or that of the General Association, dated from Orange County on September 17, but with the Assembly Clerk's endorsement, "November, 1785," V.R.P.

35 For a fuller development of this argument, presented summarily here, see Isaac, *Transformation*, pp. 58–65, 123–4.

36 Ibid., pp. 163–72, 299–302, 314–17.

37 Petitions from Powhatan County, June 4, and Surry County, November 14, 1785, V.R.P. See Isaac, *Transformation*, pp. 285–93.

38 The text, and a valuable review of its relationship to the petition campaign of 1785, is given in Rutland and Rachal, *Papers of Madison*, 8:295–306.

39 On language and the media of speech and writing, see Walter Ong, *The Presence of the Word: Some Prolegomena for Cultural and Religious History* (New Haven, Conn., 1967), pp. 192–222. Suggestive also – although it does not address language and media as such – is Michel Foucault, *The Order of Things: An Archeaeology of the Human Sciences* (London, 1979 [originally published as *Les mots et les choses*, Paris, 1966]). On the oral "exercises" that Madison experienced in Princeton, see James McLachlan, "The *Choice of Hercules*: American Student Societies in the Early 19th Century," in *The University in Society*, ed. Lawrence Stone (Princeton, 1974), vol. 2, *Europe, Scotland and the United States from the 16th to the 20th Century*, pp. 460–1, 468–71.

40 For examples of the assertive, heroic republicanism of the Scotch-Irish coun-

ties, see petitions (or remonstrances) from Rockbridge County, December 1, 1784, November 2, 1785; Pittsylvania County, November 7; Botetourt County, November 29; Washington County, December 10, 1785, V.R.P.

41 The text followed here is in a petition from Goochland County, November 2, 1785, V.R.P.

42 Madison to Jefferson, January 22, 1786, *Papers of Madison*, ed. Rutland and Rachal, 8:474; Malone, *Jefferson*, 1: 279.

43 The story of the struggle through to its bitter end can be conveniently followed in H. J. Eckenrode, *Separation of Church and State in Virginia: A Study in the Development of the Revolution*, Special Report of the Department of Archives and History, Virginia State Library (Richmond, 1910), pp. 116–55. This work has been an invaluable outline of developments and guide to the documents for generations of scholars.

44 Ibid., pp. 147–51; for the bitter legend of the selling of church plate, see Bishop [William] Meade, *Old Churches, Ministers, and Families of Virginia* (Philadelphia, 1857; Baltimore, 1966), 1:301, 486; 2:162.

45 Edmund Randolph, *History of Virginia*, ed. Arthur H. Shaffer (Charlottesville, Va., 1970), pp. 263–4. Meade, *Old Churches*, 1:49–51.

46 William Henry Foote, *Sketches of Virginia, Historical and Biographical*, First Series (Philadelphia 1850; Richmond, 1966), pp. 404, 458.

47 Ibid., pp. 2, 348.

48 Edwards, "Materials," passim; Chestnut Grove Baptist Church, or Albemarle–Buck Mountain Baptist Church, Records, 1773–9, 1792–1811, University of Richmond, pp. 1–2.

49 Semple, *History*, pp. 33, 35; Williams, Journal, May 12, 1771; "Ten-Thousand Name Petition," October 16, 1776, V.R.P.

50 Semple, *History*, pp. 89, 103.

51 Ibid., pp. 17, 97.

52 Ibid., pp. 59–60.

53 James Barnett Taylor, *Lives of Virginia Baptist Ministers* (Richmond, 1837), passim.

54 *The First Century of the First Baptist Church of Richmond, Virginia, 1780–1880* (Richmond, 1880), pp. 55–65; William W. Bennett, *Memorials of Methodism in Virginia from Its Introduction into the State . . .* , 2d ed. (Richmond, 1871), pp. 219–32.

55 Charles F. James, *Documentary History of the Struggle of Religious Liberty in Virginia* (Lynchburg, Va., 1900). The author declared his task to be the countering of "a disposition to rob our Baptist fathers of the peculiar honor . . . of being the foremost . . . and unwavering champions of soul liberty" (p. 7). Little, *Imprisoned Preachers*, Frontispiece: pp. 184–91.

56 Ryland, *Baptists of Virginia*, p. 142.

57 On the form of Afro-American consciousness, religion, and knowledge, see Albert J. Raboteau, *Slave Religion: The "Invisible Institution" in the Antebellum South* (New York, 1978), and Lawrence W. Levine, *Black Culture and Black*

Consciousness: Afro-American Folk Thought from Slavery to Freedom (New York, 1977).

58 Petition from Frederick, Loudun, and Berkeley counties (Quaker), November 8, 1785, V.R.P. On the forthright protests these provoked, see Fredericka Teute Schmidt and Barbara Ripel Wilhelm, "Early Proslavery Petitions in Virginia," *William and Mary Quarterly*, 3d ser., 30 (1973): 133–46, and Beeman, *Evolution of Southern Backcountry*, pp. 219–21.

59 Rhys Isaac, "Evangelical Revolt: The Nature of the Baptist Challenge to the Traditional Order in Virginia, 1765 to 1775," *William and Mary Quarterly*, 3d ser., 31 (1974): 345–68. For the determination to restrict evangelists' access to slaves, see the "Bill for Extending the Benefit of the several Acts of Toleration to his Majesty's Protestant Subjects, in this Colony, dissenting from the Church of England," *Virginia Gazette* (Rind), March 26, 1772. On this whole subject, there is a strange silence in John Uno, *The History of the Virginia Baptists* (Richmond, 1886).

7

"Quota of Imps"

JOHN T. NOONAN, JR.

That diabolical hell-conceived principle of persecution rages among some and to their eternal infamy the Clergy can furnish their quota of Imps for such business. . . . Pray for Liberty of Conscience.

James Madison to William Bradford
January 24, 1774[1]

1. Criminal Prosecutions

The Perpetual Laws of the Commonwealth of Massachusetts from the Commencement of the Constitution in October 1780 to the last Wednesday in May 1789 included under Part IV, "Criminal Matters," a statute entitled An Act Against Blasphemy, which read in part:

That if any person shall wilfully blaspheme the holy name of God, by denying, cursing, or contumeliously reproaching God, his creation, government or final judging of the world, or by cursing, or reproaching Jesus Christ, or the Holy Ghost, or by cursing or contumeliously reproaching the holy word of God, that is the canonical scriptures, contained in the books of the Old and New Testaments, or by exposing them, or any part of them, to contempt and ridicule; which books are as follows [the books are named], every person so offending, shall be punished by imprisonment, not exceeding twelve months, by sitting in the pillory, by whipping, or by sitting on the gallows, with a rope about the neck, or binding to the good behaviour, at the discretion of the Supreme Judicial Court before whom the convictions may be, according to the aggravation of the offence.[2]

171

For the next sixty years, this statute was "repeatedly enforced." Under it, there were "many prosecutions and convictions."[3] The Revolutionary generation itself had made the law; many framers of the Massachusetts Constitution of 1780 were makers of the legislature which passed it. At the great constitutional convention of 1820, where religion was a major topic, no one suggested that there was anything wrong with the statute.[4] Only in 1833 was the legal argument made that the statute violated Article II of the Declaration of Rights of the Inhabitants of the Commonwealth of Massachusetts, which provided in part:

> And no subject shall be hurt, molested, or restrained in his person, liberty or estate, for worshipping GOD in the manner and season most agreeable to the dictates of his own conscience; or for his religious professions or sentiments; provided he doth not disturb the public peace, or obstruct others in their religious worship.[5]

Patently the Act Against Blasphemy incorporated a scriptural, Christian theology. Yet the act's compatibility with the rights secured by Article II seemed evident to three generations of Massachusetts men. In 1833 the prosecution of Abner Kneeland, the editor of the Boston *Investigator*, led the defendant to raise the issue. Kneeland was indicted for having in December 1832 published three things:

1. Hottentots cut off one testicle; a Frenchman believes in two; but "that same Frenchman . . . firmly believes that Jesus Christ was born without any testicles at all."
2. God is in "a curious and strange predicament" because of "the heterogeneous mass of contrariety he has to hear and answer every day."
3. "Universalists believe in a god which I do not. . . . Universalists believe in Christ, which I do not; but believe that the whole story concerning him is as much a fable and a fiction, as that of the god Prometheus. . . .
   "Universalists believe in miracles, which I do not; but believe that every pretension to them can either be accounted for by natural principles, or else is to be attributed to mere trick and imposture.
   "Universalists believe in the resurrection of the dead, in immortality and eternal life, which I do not, but believe that death is an eternal extinction of life to the individual who possesses it, and that no individual life is, ever was, or ever will be eternal."[6]

The first statement was construed at the time to refer not to Jesus as a eunuch, but to his conception without a human father.[7] The Suffolk County prosecutor, Samuel Parker, said he would not offend the jury by reading the passage aloud. They jurors could peruse it themselves: "it will produce a horrible disgust."[8] Kneeland himself did not care to dwell on the words, but argued learnedly that there was no scriptural evidence for the Virgin Birth, quoting and construing Matthew, Luke, and relevant parts of the Old Testament, such as Isaiah 7:14.[9] The trial in this aspect was as much a trial of the meaning of Scripture as the later famous trial in Tennessee involving Genesis and evolution. Kneeland did not object that the "horrible disgust" the jury might feel at a joke about the Virgin Birth or the other joke about prayer might influence its view of his denial of Universalist beliefs. What the members of the jury were asked to vote on was a man who not only laughed at the Lord's origin, but also explicitly denied that any one of them had immortal souls.

Kneeland tried to defend the charge of atheism by saying that he disbelieved only the god of the Universalists.[10] Pressed, he went on to appeal to Article II of the Declaration of Rights as guaranteeing his liberty to write as he had; his prosecution was unconstitutional.[11] Meeting this argument and anticipating the further claim that the Act Against Blasphemy itself violated Article II, Prosecutor Parker asserted that the Christian religion was "part and parcel of the Constitution itself."[12] The preamble to the Massachusetts Constitution acknowledged "the goodness of the great Legislature of the Universe." Article II itself, on which Kneeland relied, declared – before it came to the rights of conscience – "It is the right as well as the duty of all men in society, publically, and at stated seasons, to worship the SUPREME BEING, the great creator and preserver of the universe."[13] Article III explicitly provided for "the public worship of GOD." Article XVIII spoke of "frequent recurrence to the fundamental principles of the Constitution and a constant adherence to those of piety" as "absolutely necessary" to preserve "free government."[14] Part II of the constitution, "The Frame of Government," gave power to demand oaths, which the prosecutor interpreted as "appeals to God and his justice for the truth of what the witness says."[15] This part of the constitution required the governor, the lieutenant governor, the governor's council, and all members of the legislature to declare that they "believe the Christian religion."[16] The constitution conferred on Harvard College certain privileges and powers because it had qualified many persons "for public employments both in Church and State" and because the encouragement of arts and sciences "tends to the honor of GOD [and] the advantage of the Christian religion." For these reasons, too, the constitution itself made "the ministers of the congregational churches"

in six named towns the overseers of Harvard.[17] The prosecutor concluded, "The Constitution itself, the paramount law of the land, establishes the Christian religion, makes it a part of itself, maintains the positions I have stated – each and every one of them."[18] The prosecutor was
absolutely accurate in his enumeration of these provisions of the constitution of 1780, all of which were unchanged by the constitution of 1820.

Kneeland was tried before a jury in the Municipal Court of Boston in
1834 and found guilty. He appealed for another trial before a single justice of the Supreme Judicial Court, and after three juries had disagreed
was found guilty again in his fifth trial in May 1834.[19] His conviction
was upheld by the full bench in April 1838. Thereupon, in open court,
Kneeland claimed an appeal to the Supreme Court of the United States,
expressly invoking the First Amendment as protecting him as a citizen
of the United States.[20] Chief Justice Shaw briefly explained why this
appeal must be rejected, and Kneeland was sentenced to, and served,
sixty days in the common jail.[21]

Chief Justice Lemuel Shaw, speaking for four of the five justices, wrote
a cautious opinion. He construed the Act Against Blasphemy to make a
distinction between acts "denying God, his creation, government, and
final judging of the world" and acts "cursing or reproaching Jesus
Christ."[22] Shaw did not mention Kneeland's remarks on prayers or the
Virgin Birth. His statements about what the Universalists believed and
what he did not believe, Shaw indicated, had properly been found by the
jury to constitute denial of God and his activities. He harmonized the Act
Against Blasphemy with Article II of the Declaration of Rights by saying
that the statute did not prohibit the expression of honest doubt, but restrained "acts which have a tendency to disturb the public peace."[23] Shaw
did not demonstrate that any such tendency had in fact been shown beyond the unease any expression of skepticism might generate. Dissenting
"with great reluctance" in a court where dissents were rare, Justice Marcus Morton did not challenge Shaw's standard – "to disturb the good of
society" was Morton's phrase – but did not believe that Kneeland had
been shown to have broken the public peace.[24]

Shaw was a Unitarian, and Unitarianism was then the religion of many
of the ruling elite of Massachusetts.[25] It was a good deal more rationalistic than the Trinitarian Congregationalism from which it had emerged,
but it could not have reduced to a mere utilitarianism or a humanism
detached from Christianity. It was a scriptural religion. Unitarians were
"fervently biblical" and wrestled "with every verse of St. Paul."[26] An
Emerson could step out of "the Morgue" of Unitarianism and with legal
impunity translate Christianity into a set of lofty ideals and vague metaphors.[27] Kneeland's Voltairean skepticism was different; it was in fact

deeply disturbing to the peace of those who had balanced Scripture and modern thought and had made for themselves a mental universe they found intelligible and Christian.

Shaw's propositions were pale in comparison with Prosecutor Parker's claim that the constitution of Massachusetts "establishes the Christian religion." Dividing the Act Against Blasphemy in two and finding Kneeland's offense to be against the section relating to God, not "the Christian religion," Shaw appeared anxious not to proclaim a Christian establishment.[28] At the same time, he deliberately described Kneeland's words as "acts"; set out Kneeland's denial of miracles, the Resurrection, and Christ as part of the indictment that had been proved; and glossed over the large injection of Christian theology that colored his contemporaries' view of God's "creation, government, and final judging of the world."[29] Rhetorically, Shaw's opinion was not a ringing reassertion of Christianity as the established religion of the Commonwealth of Massachusetts. In practical effect, it endorsed the establishment of that religion as understood by Unitarians.

Writing two generations later, Oliver Wendell Holmes, Jr., in *The Common Law*, paid tribute to Shaw – he is one of the very few judges Holmes mentions at all and the only one he calls "great," quoting with approval Benjamin Curtis's view that he was "the greatest magistrate which this country has produced."[30] Holmes spoke generally, not of this case, but he added: "the strength of that great judge lay in an accurate appreciation of the requirements of the community whose officer he was. . . . [F]ew have lived who were his equals in their understanding of the grounds of public policy to which all laws must ultimately be referred."[31] Shaw, along with the Suffolk County prosecutor and all the judges who sat on Kneeland's case, knew that the governing elite of Massachusetts in 1838 would not accept the unconstitutionality of a statute protecting scriptural, Christian doctrine. At the very time Kneeland was prosecuted, Unitarians had lost the battle for financial establishment of their religion. They were not about to abandon all claims to state power. Shaw, better than Marcus Morton, knew that the elite wanted the statute enforced.

Religious Tests for Office

The constitution of 1780 had not only required the governor, lieutenant governor, and legislators to identify themselves as Christians; it had required them and all other officeholders (judicial, executive, or military), to take an oath, abjuring allegiance to the government of Great Britain and "every other foreign power whatever"; in particular, they had to swear that no foreign prince, person, or prelate "hath, or ought to have, any jurisdiction, superiority, preeminence, authority, dispensing or other power, in any matter, civil, ecclesiastical or spiritual within this Commonwealth."[32]

This oath, from its required abjuration of England, sometimes called "the loyalty oath," was also known as "the anti-papist oath." Article III of the constitution provided: "And every denomination of Christians, demeaning themselves peaceably and as good subjects of the Commonwealth, shall be equally under the protection of the law: And no subordination of any one sect or denominations to another shall ever be established by law."[33] This liberal provision was qualified by the oath. The oath was a survival from the colony, when Puritan sentiments and dislike of French Canada had joined in official distrust of Catholics. The 1780 convention, explaining its work to the people, put the matter plainly:

> Your Delegates did not conceive themselves to be vested with Power to set up one Denomination of Christians above one another; for Religion must at all times be a matter between GOD and individuals: But we have nevertheless, found ourselves obliged by a Solemn Test, to provide for the exclusion of those from Offices who will not disclaim those principles of Spiritual Jurisdiction which Roman Catholics in *some Countries* have held, and which are subversive of a free Government established by the People.[34]

The convention, in attributing a belief in papal jurisdiction to Catholics only "in some Countries," may sincerely have misinterpreted a Gallican current in the Catholic Church that severely limited the pope's authority. But it is hard to think of any Catholic of the time who would have held that the pope had neither jurisdiction nor authority, neither preeminence nor dispensing power, in any ecclesiastical or spiritual matter. The oath, taken at its face, barred all Catholics from any office in the government of Massachusetts. Doing so, it was entirely consistent with the theory of toleration provided by John Locke, which was the political gospel of the day. Locke excluded both atheists and Catholics from any toleration, because atheists denied the foundation of government and Catholics subordinated the state to the pope.[35] More tolerant than Locke as to personal beliefs, the constitution of 1780 was Lockean in its standards for office.

Locke did not think Catholics could be trusted to keep a promise.[36] The oath prescribed by the constitution showed an analogous distrust. The oath taker was to declare: "that no man or body of men, hath, or can have any right to absolve me from the obligation of this oath, dec-

laration, or affirmation; and that I do make this acknowledgement . . .
heartily and truly, according to the common meaning of and acceptation
of the foregoing words, without any equivocation, mental evasion, or
secret reservation whatsoever."[37] This declaration was aimed at what
was taken to be the Catholic doctrine on the use of mental reservation
and equivocation to conceal the truth from those the speaker reasonably
believed were not entitled to the truth. Eighteenth-century Catholic theology, expounded by such a moralist as Alfonso de' Liguori and unsym-
pathetically read, could be understood as defending such practices.[38] The
men of Massachusetts were determined not to be taken in by them, although if a Catholic could make the disclaimer of the pope's authority
with mental reservations, why could he not make the disclaimer of mental reservations themselves with another mental reservation?

The first Catholic priest to function on a regular basis in Boston was
Francis Matignon, a theologian educated at Paris and available to Boston
because of the dislocations caused by the French Revolution. He arrived
in 1792 and in 1795 became a citizen. When he did so, he took the oath
– with what reluctance or reservations or with what enthusiasm it is
impossible to say; he suffered no ecclesiastical penalty for his compliance.[39]

The oath was at all events a subordination of Catholics to other Christians and a public symbol of the inferiority of Catholics. In February
1820, when revision of the constitution of 1780 was contemplated, Samuel L. Knapp, a Protestant, sought its repeal. Knapp was a friend of Jean
Cheverus, the first Catholic bishop of Boston, and it is probable that his
argument was prepared in concern with Cheverus.[40] They made these
points:

1. Under the oath, no Catholic "is capable of holding any public
   office in this Commonwealth."
2. The oath is "absurd in view of the Federal Constitution."
3. Conscience, as Lord Mansfield had said, "is not controllable by
   human laws, nor amenable to human tribunals."
4. The oath is a species of persecution.[41]

On December 1, 1820, Bishop Cheverus himself wrote to a delegate
to the constitutional convention, pointing out that the nub of his objection was the oath's forced denial of the "spiritual" jurisdiction of the
pope.[42] The convention eliminated the oath, referring to it "as the oath
of abjuration," as though it applied exclusively to abjuration of the English Crown.[43] The voters approved, 17,552 to 9,244.[44] Two generations

after the Revolution, Catholics no longer had to choose between their consciences and their political rights in the Commonwealth.

The convention of 1820 also attacked the general oath required of the governor, lieutenant governor, and legislators that they "believed the Christian religion." Daniel Webster, on behalf of a select committee of the convention, said that a majority of the committee thought that the people had a right to demand the oath "as a qualification or condition for office." In the same way, the people had the right to prefer to elect one man over another "because he is a Christian." But the question was whether the oath was expedient. Ninety-nine percent of the inhabitants professed to believe in the Christian religion. Why mark the few who did not with "a sort of opprobrium"? To do so was not an injustice; it was an act of unkindness. Some persons, too, found what they were required to swear "too strong and intense." In conscience all they could give was "a general assent to the truth of the Christian religion." These scrupulous persons should not be penalized. Moreover, there was an anomaly in those subject to the oath. Judges were exempt. But "there can be no office in which the sense of religious responsibility is more necessary than in that of a judge." A judge "acts directly on individuals." A judge "should be under the fear of God and above all other fear." If judges did not have to declare themselves Christians, why should legislators?[45]

Debate followed in which James Prince, Esquire, of Boston supported Webster by quoting the injunction of Jesus, "Render unto Caesar the things that are Caesar's and unto God the things that are God's" (Matthew 22: 21), only to be checked by the Reverend Joseph Tuckerman, a Unitarian clergyman from Chelsea, who said of the oath, "We owe it to God, to Christ, and to our souls." Scripture, Tuckerman said, taught us "to *render* to God the things that are God's," not "*leave* to God the things that are God's." In his view, "the most beautiful feature" of the constitution of 1780 was that it "recognizes Christianity as the religion of the State."[46]

Samuel Hubbard, Esquire, of Boston, a Unitarian, dwelt on the undesirability of "a mahometan, or a deist, or a jew" holding office "over a Christian people." The Reverend Edmund Foster, a Trinitarian Congregationalist from Littleton, declared that nowhere on earth was there a land "where toleration was enjoyed at its fullest" more than in the Commonwealth of Massachusetts. Why change this happy state by dropping the oath? Henry Dearborn of Roxbury invoked Locke. It was not the business of religion to interfere in civil government. The Constitution of the United States excluded all tests for federal office. The convention went with Webster, Prince, and Dearborn. By a very narrow margin –

13,782 to 12,843 – the voters approved. The forty-year effort to test men's religious faith when they took office in Massachusetts was abandoned.[47]

Financing Worship

Oaths searched men's minds. Blasphemy prosecutions punished their expression. Both types of law may be fairly characterized as restraints on religious liberty, persecutory in their intent and operation. These laws were the outer guard of a religious establishment whose center was financial and pedagogic.

The Declaration of Rights of the Inhabitants not only asserted it to be the duty of all men publicly to worship the Supreme Being; it went on to explain this claim and to provide a government mechanism for enforcing it. Article III stated: "As the happiness of a people, and the good order and preservation of civil government, essentially depend upon piety, religion and morality; and as these cannot be generally diffused through a community, but by the institution of the public worship of GOD, and of public instruction in piety, religion, and morality; Therefore . . ."[48]

The didactic exposition of the connection between the public welfare and the public worship of God came from a drafting committee consisting of James Bowdoin, Samuel Adams, and John Adams. The person most responsible for the constitution of 1780 was John Adams. As Adams described his part: "I was by the Convention put upon the Committee – by the Committee upon the Subcommittee – and by the Subcommittee appointed to a Sub Sub Committee – so that I had the honor to be principal Engineer."[49] It reflected his lawyerly skills, his didacticism, his values. Duty and right he saw as strictly correlated.

Article III was to be the most bitterly fought provision in the Massachusetts Constitution.[50] But the fight was not over this preamble. Isaac Backus, the Baptist leader, was in "full concurrence" with it.[51] He did not think it entailed the consequence that was then drawn from it; for Article III went on – not in John Adams's words, but with his acquiescence – to say that the state should therefore tax to support religion. In Backus's view, imposition of this duty was to give "civil rulers power in religious matters."[52] At the Baptists' objection, Article III was recommitted for study.

After two weeks of consideration, the convention adopted an Article III little different in essentials from the original draft, but making these changes:

1. It was added that Christians were not to be subordinated to one another – a sop to the Baptists.

2. It was specified that the teachers supported should be "Protestant" – a floor amendment, added out of dislike of "Papists."[53]

3. The legislature, instead of being given power to act directly to raise money for God's worship, was given power to require "the several towns, parishes, precincts, and other bodies-politic, or religious societies, to make suitable provision, at their own expense, for the institution of the public worship of GOD, and for the support of public Protestant teachers of piety, religion, and morality in all cases where such provision should not be made voluntarily."

4. The "several towns, parishes, precincts, and other bodies-politic, or religious societies" were given "the exclusive right of electing their public teachers."

5. All monies paid by a taxpayer were to go to the support of the public teacher "of his own religious sect or denomination, provided there be any on whose instruction he attends"; otherwise, to the town in which the monies were raised.[54]

These provisions had the detail of a statute and the permanency of a constitution. They used "public teacher" as the equivalent of "ordained Protestant clergyman." They assumed "towns" and "parishes" were identical, except where, as had sometimes happened, towns were divided into more than one parish for the convenience of churchgoers.

Unlike the original draft, the new provisions appeared to let a variety of churches raise money to support their ministers; and if "religious societies" was understood to be used disjunctively from "towns" and "parishes," there was greater recognition of the non-Congregational churches, which were not identical with the towns. But from the standpoint of believers in a separation of church and state, the language was not an improvement on the original draft. The legislature was put in the position of enforcing taxation on behalf of religious worship and instruction. Any unbeliever who attended no minister's services was to have his taxes used to pay for the minister established in the town where the taxes were paid – the same provision had been in the original draft. Indeed, the constitution tacitly assumed that there were and would be no unbelievers. The mechanism of government was put at the service of the Protestant churches. The Baptist leaders urged the electorate to vote against Article III,[55] and individual towns like Needham rejected it as inconsistent with "the rights of Conscience." The electorate as a whole failed to provide the two-thirds majority for Article III that the convention's rules required for adoption.[56] Nonetheless, Article III was treated as part of the constitution of the commonwealth.

By a statute passed on June 28, 1786, the legislature confirmed the power of parish voters to vote money "for the settlement, maintenance, and support of ministers or publick teachers of religion; for the building or repairing of houses of publick worship, and all other necessary parish or precinct charges."[57] The assumption underlay the statute, as it did the constitution, that the voters of the parish were exercising a governmental function and that no distinction between town and parish needed to be made when the voters imposed a tax for the benefit of the town-established clergy.

Sometimes a religious society, when it was not identical with a town, applied to the legislature to be incorporated in order to have its tax rights made clear. For example, an act of June 18, 1791, permits certain named individuals to be incorporated as "the Protestant Episcopal Society of Great Barrington"; provides that taxes collected on nonresident proprietors' estates be equally divided between this society and the Congregationalist parish; and adds that the inhabitants of Great Barrington shall "have full liberty to join themselves with their families and estates, to either of the parishes in said town." The incorporating act, in short, gives incorporated Episcopalians a financial footing on a par with that of the Congregationalists who constitute the town.[58] Over 125 such acts were passed in the first 25 years of the commonwealth.[59] By means of them religious groups gained state recognition and power.

Litigation was necessary to establish the right of an unincorporated religious society to state support. In some parts of the state, the town taxed everyone not in a legislatively recognized society. In Harwich, for example, in 1796 a number of Baptists were jailed for not paying the tax to support the Congregational minister. Samuel Scudder, a Baptist, was imprisoned for not having paid the parish tax in Barnstable, and Ichabod and Lemuel Lombard, Baptists, had their cattle levied on and sold for failure to pay the Barnstable collector.[60] In 1783, John Murray, a Universalist minister, sued for taxes paid by members of his congregation; the town assessors of Gloucester had refused his request on the ground that his Independent Church was not a religious society. In court, the town, represented by Theophilus Parsons, argued that in denying divine retribution after death, Murray failed to qualify as a teacher of morality.[61] Reading Article III literally, the Supreme Judicial Court in 1786 held for Murray.[62] But the rights of suspect sects to tax money were carefully monitored. When Father Matignon sued the town of Newcastle in 1799 for the share of taxes paid by his communicants, the Supreme Judicial Court held that the restriction of teachers of piety to Protestants must be observed.[63] Matignon was told in open court by the justices: "Papists are only tolerated, and as long as their ministers behave well, we shall not disturb them. But let them expect no more than that."[64] When a declared Baptist attempted to avoid paying taxes to the regular Congregational parish, the Supreme Judicial Court said his claim was good only if he "had been dipped"; otherwise, his attendance at the Baptist services was "fraudulent in law, and only to avoid paying his taxes."[65] In 1800, the legislature required anyone asking his taxes to be applied to his own denomination to obtain a certificate from his minister that the taxpayer "frequently and usually, when able, attends with us in our stated Meetings for religious Worship."[66]

Theophilus Parsons – a felicitous name for the leader of a religious establishment – now Chief Justice, voiced the establishment's view of itself in two cases, famous in their age. In *Avery v. The Inhabitants of Tyringham,* the plaintiff, Joseph Avery, had been chosen minister of Tyringham at a legal town meeting in 1788 – the normal procedure where the town and the parish were one. In 1803, the town had dispensed with his services, relying on Article III's proviso that towns had the right to elect their public teachers. Speaking for the Supreme Judicial Court, Parsons held that the town could elect when there was a vacancy, but the minister could not be removed at will. The minister of a newly settled town was given a lot of land, besides the parsonage: this appropriation by the government was made on the assumption that the minister was being "settled" for life. The minister's function was to reprove vice "in public and private." He should not be restrained by the fear of being discharged. If there was dissatisfaction on the part of the town with its minister's deportment or doctrine, an ecclesiastical council could decide between them. The minister had tenure and, with it, a right to his salary of seventy pounds per annum.[67] A more thorough mixing of religion and the state could scarcely have been imagined than that described by Parsons: an agency of the state selected a person to conduct worship and teach religion; the state set aside property for his personal benefit; the Chief Justice of the state defined that person's duties; the rights of the town and its minister were subject to the determination of an ecclesiastical council. Subject only to disapproval by such an ecclesiastical body, the minister had a right for life to tax support.

In *Barnes v. First Parish in Falmouth,* Parsons made his own elaboration of the didactic portion of Article III of the Declaration of Rights. What were the motives, he asked, that had induced the people "to introduce into the constitution a religious establishment?" Laws could not enforce duties of "imperfect obligation," such as acts of kindness. Laws could not reach secret offenses. The life of man would be "wretched" if it depended only on the laws. Hence the people had "adopted and patronized a religion." They had chosen one whose divine authority was "admitted," which had been found to rest "on the basis of immortal truth." It was a religion, "as understood by Protestants," that tended to make every man better; and so this religion "was by the people established as a fundamental and essential part of their constitution."[68]

It was objected that it infringed your liberty of conscience to be made to pay a tax if you disapproved of any religion. The objection, Parsons replied, "seems to mistake a man's conscience for his money."[69] It was said to be intolerant to make a man pay for religious instruction he did not attend. But public religious instruction aimed to teach "a system of correct morals." Everyone benefited from the diffusion of this knowledge. It was contended that the Founder of Christianity had declared that his kingdom was not "of this world." But despite the saying, the Founder intended that man should be benefited by his religion "in his civil and political relations." An objector pressed that the moral commandments of Christianity were "so interwoven" with Christian faith that faith was taught with the morals; hence the state taught Christian doctrine. But, Parsons said, if this objection held, the state would be barred from teaching many branches of useful knowledge that "naturally tend to detect the arguments of infidelity." The people were, rather, to be applauded because they had "adopted a religion founded in truth; which in its tendency will protect our property here, and may secure to us an inheritance in another and a better country."[70]

Parsons spoke not only as a leading spirit of the convention of 1780, but also as the recognized "great man of his time." To his Republican enemies, he was "the Goliath of the Massachusetts Gentile-Army, a man as cunning as Lucifer and about half as good." To his admirers, he was "the Giant of the Law." He was also a convinced Christian believer in the Resurrection and a devout Unitarian.[71]

The Chief Justice's enthusiastic exposition of the truth and benefits of the religion established by the Massachusetts Constitution was a prelude to a technical and remarkably ungenerous holding that a "religious society" referred to in the constitution had to be a society incorporated by the legislature.[72] Consequently, Thomas Barnes, a Universalist minister of an unincorporated society, could not sue for his share of the taxes paid to the town by members of his congregation.

The practical effect of Parsons's holding was to require religious societies to incorporate. But many Baptists and other dissenters had scruples both as to recognizing the legislature's power over their churches and as to accepting from the state a power to share in taxes. Less than half the Baptist societies were incorporated; even fewer of the other dissenters' societies had applied for such legitimation by the state.[73] In the words of Governor Elbridge Gerry, the decision "produced a great excitement."[74] In the legislature, the dissenters presented a bill to override Parsons's decision. John Leland, a leading Baptist, once Madison's constituent and backer in Orange County, Virginia, declared that the Baptists did not want "the mischievous dagger" of civil power: governmental support of religion normally was "the first step in the case which leads in regular progression to inquisition."[75] The dissenters wanted only not to have to pay taxes to maintain a faith they did not believe in. Joseph W. Cannon, a Methodist from Nantucket, denounced the system outlined by Parsons as "an eternal disgrace to the state."[76] In response to such outrage, the legislature in 1811 passed An Act respecting Publick Worship and Religious Freedom, which put unincorporated religious societies on a par with incorporated ones. The Baptists, despite their disclaimers, were given power to participate in tax revenues.[77]

The constitutionality of the law was challenged in *Adams* v. *Howe* (1817). It was contended that the members of unincorporated societies could too easily avoid the duty established by the constitution to support the worship of God. According to the statute, a certificate by a committee of any religious society exempted a taxpayer from taxation for the support of public worship in "every other religious corporation whatsoever." In practice, this provision meant that if the holder of a certificate was not taxed by the town, his taxes were to be collected directly by his own religious society.[78] A dodge, according to the statute's critics, was for a taxpayer to make a deal with a religious teacher who asked only a trifling sum; paying this amount, the taxpayer got a certificate and was exempt from the tax levied to support the regular minister of the town. Manchester, for example, had "lost $10,000 by the law."[79] Chief Justice Isaac Parker agreed that "the indulgence granted by the legislature could destroy all decency and regularity of public worship." But the legislature had discretion to determine how the public worship of God should be supported.[80]

At the constitutional convention of 1820, Martin Phelps, a Baptist layman from Chester, proposed a new Article III, declaring that the discharging of religious duty to God "must be left to the reason and conscience of every man," but permitting religious societies "hitherto accustomed to support religious worship" by taxing their own members to continue to do so.[81] This almost complete disestablishment was too much for the convention, and Phelps withdrew his amendment. After much debate, an amendment was adopted that, like the original Article III, spoke of "the power and duty of the legislature" to require provision for the public worship of God, but like the 1811 statute put religious societies, incorporated or not, in an equal position to tax their members. The amendment was opposed with as great zeal by the defenders of establishment as if the 1811 statute were not in effect. Leverett Saltonstall of Salem, a Unitarian leader, declared: "Our religious establishments are part of our system of education. . . . I stand in the presence of our ancestors; they conjure us not to destroy what they planted with so much care, and under the influence of which we have so long-flourished; but to transmit to posterity what is only a trust-estate in us."[82] This appeal to the Pilgrims' and Puritans' past found the electorate responsive. The amendment was defeated by vote of the people, 19,597 to 11,065.[83] The disapproving majority were both now-entrenched Unitarians and country Trinitarians who agreed with Saltonstall and did not want the religious establishment, however impaired by the 1811 statute, further weakened by the principle of 1811 becoming part of the constitution itself.[84]

Meanwhile, shortly after the convention of 1820, a case had been decided that was to lead the Trinitarians themselves to wish for disestablishment. A dispute had broken out between two factions of Christians in Dedham. The parish – a body identical with the voters of the town – had elected a Unitarian as the town minister. The church – Trinitarians in good standing – refused to concur. The parish and a minority of the church members summoned an ecclesiastical council dominated by leading Unitarians; the council advised that the Unitarian be ordained. The parish ordained him. The church seceded from the parish and sued for possession of the money and documents of the First Church in Dedham.[85]

Chief Justice Parker traced the history of grants to the church in Dedham since the seventeenth century and held that the grants were to the church as a trustee and that the cestui que trust was the parish. The parish, he continued, was "the assembly of Christians in Dedham."[86] This assembly he equated with the inhabitants of the town. When the church had seceded from the parish, there had been "an extinction of the church" for all civil purposes. The parish, the beneficiary of the trust, could institute a new church or "engraft one upon the old stock if any should remain."[87] Article III recognized the right of each town to choose its own "public Protestant teacher of piety, religion, and morality," that is, its own "minister of the gospel."[88] The minority, who were "the church," could not rule "the great majority," who were the town. The majority would never consent to be taxed to support the minority's choice of a minister.[89] The great political principle of the Revolution, "No taxation without representation," was implicitly invoked to buttress the right of the majority to select the ministers whose wages they would have to pay.

Mark Howe presented *Baker* v. *Fales* (1820), Parker's historic decision, as an instance of "the disestablishment of established churches."[90] But *Baker* v. *Fales* was a victory for those who wanted change within the establishment; it was not disestablishment, except for the losers. It continued the union of church and state and in a sense emphasized it, as change often emphasizes features taken for granted. There was no denial of the power to tax for religion, but the power had to be exercised by the majority. The political machinery of town government was made the vehicle for a substantial shift in religious doctrine, from orthodox Trinitarianism to the Unitarianism that had infiltrated Boston and its environs.

Parker, a Unitarian himself, did not shrink from setting out the rule that would legitimate Unitarian takeovers. He pointed out that the defeated Trinitarians would not have to pay the Unitarian minister. Under the 1811 act, they could form a new religious society – surely this reference to a law the Trinitarians had fought was to put salt in their wounds.[91] Even more unctuous and galling was his final observation: "It is true, if there were any parish funds, they will lose the benefit of them by removal; but an inconvenience of this sort will never be felt when a case of conscience is in question."[92] Inconvenience of this sort, and feeling about it, were just what had led Deacon Eliphalet Baker to defend his suit.

Between 1820 and 1834, nearly one hundred Congregationalist parishes fell to the Unitarians – over one-quarter of the Congregationalist parishes in the commonwealth.[93] New legislation made easy the formation of religious societies that could issue tax exemptions.[94] Trinitarians, Baptists, and, above all, Universalists united in seeking an end to compulsory religious taxes. Only a rear guard of Unitarians defended the system to which they had fallen heir. Lemuel Shaw, Parker's successor as Chief Justice in 1830, reviewed all the legal arguments the Trinitarians had made and rejected them, asserting in the face of public opinion that *Baker* v. *Fales* was the law of the land – that is, Massachusetts.[95] If Shaw was here accurately appreciating the requirements of the community, it was the community of Unitarians among whom he was numbered. In 1834, by constitutional amendment, the system was substantially ended. The popular vote was 32,234 to 3,273 for dismantling the financial machinery that supported religious establishment.[96]

It is tempting to conclude that the end of tax support was the end of the establishment altogether. Howe described it as "disestablishment" and as a solution that "cut all churches free and clear from the state's authority."[97] But who owned the meetinghouses and other property that had belonged to the parishes? A church, unconnected with a parish, *Baker*

v. *Fales* had announced, "has no legal qualities." A secession of the church from the parish meant the "extinction of the church" for all legal purposes.[98] The statutes enacted in 1834 guaranteed that "all parishes" should "continue to have their existing rights."[99] The conclusion that seemed irresistible was that the inhabitants of the parish, the cestuis que trust for whom church property was held, could not only determine who their minister would be, but also determine who would use the meetinghouse. Nothing of the sort happened.

To quote a monograph on the question:

> When the church was disestablished in Massachusetts by constitutional amendment and appropriate legislation, the Congregationalists (Trinitarians) kept the church property that was still in their possession. They were not inconsistent in doing so, for they had always maintained that the church property belonged to the church members and not to the whole parish. On the other hand, the Unitarians also kept what church property had come into their possession. Since a part of the property was obtained through court decisions based on the assumption that the church property belonged to the town or parish and not to the church members, it seems the Unitarians must have changed their position. If the property belonged to the towns and parishes in 1820, how did it become Unitarian property in 1834? That question has never been satisfactorily answered.[100]

The question has not been "satisfactorily answered." But is not the answer clear? The Unitarians were endowed by the commonwealth with the property that had been that of the state-sponsored, state-financed parishes. In this respect, however, the Unitarians were no different from the Congregationalists, who "kept the church property that was still in their possession." That property, too, had been the parishes', not the churches'. To keep it may have been blessed by Congregationalist ecclesiology, but "possession" by a church conferred no legal rights, according to *Baker* v. *Fales*. If the Congregationalists kept the church property, they – just as much as the Unitarians – received an endowment by the commonwealth.

In the jargon of today's corporate world, the Unitarian and Congregationalist churches received "golden handshakes" on parting with tax support. They were on their own, but with handsome endowments. To say that the occasion of these gifts of land and buildings and funds was a "disestablishment" is to overlook the rich establishments that the state's patronage created as it said good-bye.[101]

The University at Cambridge

The center of the religious establishment was the institution that was almost coeval with the colony: Harvard College, whose special commemoration in the constitution of the Commonwealth because it had qualified many persons "for public employments both in Church and State," has already been remarked. The constitution in Part II, devoted to "The Frame of Government," had a special section entitled "The University at Cambridge, and Encouragement of Literature, etc." It confirmed the powers and privileges of Harvard College. It made the governor, lieutenant governor, council, and Senate the overseers of the college, along with the ministers of Cambridge, Watertown, Charlestown, Boston, Roxbury, and Dorchester. A further section of the constitution imposed on the legislature the duty "to cherish" the college.[102] No other religious educational institution was specified by name in the constitution. Harvard College was made an integral part of the commonwealth's "frame of government." The chief officials of the commonwealth were joined with the ministry of the adjoining towns as its supervisors. State and church together ruled an institution that was intended to produce statesmen and churchmen.

Harvard College in 1780 had no special unit called "a divinity school." The institution was only in aspiration a university. It took boys as young as fourteen, and its students were all adolescents. Instruction was by recitation from prescribed textbooks.[103] Divinity was part of the college curriculum, and divines were trained by instruction in the ordinary courses. The Unitarians captured the college in 1805 with the election of their candidate as Hollis Professor of Divinity. In alarmed reaction that Harvard was "gone," Trinitarians started their own theological school, Andover, in 1808. The presence of this school, in turn, led the Unitarians at Harvard to develop a separate department devoted to theological education that would faithfully express the Unitarian point of view. Harvard College President John Kirkland, the former minister of the New South Church, carried out this theological development.[104] The extent of toleration of other religious views at Harvard Divinity School was "the willingness of the Unitarian Congregationalists in charge of the Corporation and School to admit Trinitarian Congregationalists."[105]

At the Unitarians' behest, the legislature in 1810 altered the composition of the overseers, among other things adding fifteen laymen to be elected by the present overseers, raising the number of ministers to fifteen, and eliminating their restriction to named towns.[106] It was believed that the constitution could be circumvented if the incumbent governing boards of Harvard accepted the legislation. The legislation, like the constitution itself, specified that the ministers must be of "Congregational churches." The ruling Unitarians, who had taken over Congregational churches, had no hesitation in seeing their own ministers as "Congregational" within the meaning of the constitution. The college had been dedicated *Christo et Ecclesiae* – "to Christ and the Church." As late as 1820 to a devout Unitarian like Leverett Saltonstall, it was no empty phrase, but showed the care for religious instruction that had animated the commonwealth.[107]

In the convention of 1820, Joseph Richardson, a clergyman from Hingham, questioned whether the legislative alteration of the overseers was constitutional. How could an institution that was "partly the property of the State" be put out of the state's control?[108] More basically, Richardson attacked the special place of Congregational ministers in the constitution. It was "directly repugnant" to the Declaration of Rights to subordinate one denomination to another. But were not Episcopalians, Baptists, Methodists, Universalists, "and perhaps other denominations" subordinated to Congregationalists when only Congregationalist ministers could rule the college? He saw "this policy of preference and exclusion as verging too much to a national establishment of religion." The Congregational Church was made a "spoiled child of the State." In Richardson's view, the Congregationalists' privilege tended to "perpetuate a spirit of intolerance among different denominations of Christians" and so was inconsistent "with liberty, both civil and religious."[109] Richardson spoke as a Congregationalist minister, but as a Congregationalist Trinitarian who saw Harvard lost as long as Unitarian Congregationalists were its overseers, guaranteed their seats by a combination of the constitution and legislation.[110]

Richardson had declared that the state had fostered Harvard "with liberal munificence." Daniel Webster, for the convention's committee on "the Constitutional Rights and Privileges of Harvard College," gave some idea of this bounty. At the beginning, the colony government had endowed the college with four hundred pounds. In 1640, it gave the college the right to run a ferry over the Charles River, a right worth two hundred pounds annually by 1786. The colony regularly made annual grants and assisted in paying the salaries of the president and faculty; it also made a grant of lands in Maine eventually worth fifteen thousand dollars, and it built Massachusetts, Hollis, and Harvard Halls. In 1814, the legislature of the commonwealth granted the college ten thousand dollars for ten years to build University Hall and a Medical School building and to fund scholarships. These benefactions of the commonwealth were smaller than the two hundred thousand dollars that, by 1820, had been donated by individuals for scholarships. The recent subsidy of ten thousand dollars per annum, however, loomed large in comparison with the present annual income of the college of seventeen thousand dollars.[111] Harvard, not solely the state's child, had been and still was much indebted to the public for support.

Webster for the committee moved for an amendment to the constitution that would explicitly confirm the legislature's alteration of the overseers, with one change: the ministers need not be confined to "any particular denomination of Christians."[112] Joseph Story, a leading Unitarian, supported Webster. Richardson was still not content; the present Unitarian control would be undisturbed.[113] The convention adopted Webster's amendment, 227 to 14. With a heavy vote against it in the country, the people rejected it, 20,123 to 8,020.[114]

The old constitution, with its legislative gloss, stood. Neither the old constitution nor the proposed amendment separated the college from religion. In terms of either, only Christian clergymen could be clerical overseers. In terms of either, the purpose of the college, to advance the Christian religion, was the same. The whole quarrel was over what group of Christians should control.

In 1851, the ministerial overseers were eliminated from the constitution. But as late as 1855, Harvard's president, James Walker, could declare, "The College is preeminently a child of the Church." Only in 1865 was there a substantial separation of this child of the church from the Commonwealth of Massachusetts.[115]

Conclusion

Other manifestations of the religious establishment in Massachusetts could be set out: compulsory attendance at Sunday services, authorized by Article III of the Declaration of Rights, enforced by legislation of 1782, and abandoned only in 1833;[116] compulsory limits on work and recreation on the Lord's Day, enforced by statute;[117] restrictions of power to officiate at marriages to properly ordained ministers;[118] the use of the King James Version of the Bible in the public schools;[119] the use of Protestant textbooks in the public schools.[120] Enough, however, has been set out in detail to show that for generations after the Revolutionary constitution of Massachusetts and after the adoption of the federal Bill of Rights, a religious establishment reigned in the commonwealth. This state of affairs may be compared or contrasted with what other contributors to this volume have to say on Madison's Virginia. Here, I shall relate what happened in Massachusetts more directly to Madison himself.

First. The many controversies concerning the use of state power in

Massachusetts to aid this or that denomination of Christians were conducted peacefully. Force was used – to suppress contempt of Christianity, to collect taxes, to exclude unbelievers from office. But the laws themselves were enacted after elections. They were enacted in peace. In the long history of warfare over religion, the absence of brute physical fighting is noticeable. The constitution of Massachusetts, largely designed by Adams, made such peaceful battles possible; but the Constitution of the United States, designed by Madison, provided the larger context in which religious squabbles, intense and bitter as they often were, did not become civil war.

Second. The history of Massachusetts confirms Madison's sagacity when he wrote:

> Happily for the states, they enjoy the utmost freedom of religion. This freedom arises from that multiplicity of sects, which pervades America, and which is the best and only security for religious belief in any society. For where there is such a variety of sects, there cannot be a majority of any one sect to oppress and persecute the rest.[121]

The first sentence was palpable nonsense when Madison wrote in 1790, if it was understood to refer to the legal status of religious freedom in the several states. But Madison's thought was profoundly accurate if understood as prophecy, based on the fact that many denominations did exist. His reasoning paralleled the basis for political freedom that he masterfully set out in *The Federalist,* No. 10: Factions are built into democratic life, and a majority dominated by a faction will "vex and oppress" its opponents. But the power of factions is mitigated by representative government chosen from a broad territory. "Extend the sphere and you take in a greater variety of parties and interests; you make it less probable that a majority of the whole will have a common motive to invade the rights of other citizens."[122]

Exactly so in Massachusetts. The multiplicity of sects was the chief obstacle to religious establishment. The split of the Congregationalists into Trinitarians and Unitarians, the Universalist defection from the Unitarians, the increase of the Baptists, and the appearance of Catholics all led to changes promoting religious freedom, although not, in Madison's extravagant phrase, "the utmost freedom." When the anti-Catholic oath was made part of the constitution, there were not more than 600 Catholics in Massachusetts, including the Passamaquoddy Indians. In 1820, when the oath was repealed, there were 3,500 Catholics, and Bishop Cheverus, running as a delegate to the constitutional convention, could get 410 votes in Boston alone.[123] The legal change reflected the rise of the Catholic population. The Baptists in New England in 1770 numbered 530. By 1824, there were over 12,000, and there were as many Baptist churches as Trinitarian Congregationalist churches in Massachusetts.[124] The vote to end tax support came after this striking growth and the disenchantment of the Trinitarian Congregationalists at having been ousted by Unitarians. In such a fluid religious environment, one faction of Christians could not vex and oppress another faction indefinitely.

Third. Madison's large, liberal ideas, although far from being made law in Massachusetts, were not unnoticed or inactive. Samuel Knapp and Bishop Cheverus advanced the analogy of the federal Constitution when they attacked the anti-Catholic oath; Samuel Hubbard did the same, attacking the oath as to Christian belief; Kneeland invoked the First Amendment.[125] Madison's veto of the congressional statute incorporating an Episcopal church was cited by a Baptist critic of Theophilus Parsons's decision in *Barnes v. Falmouth:* Madison had recognized the truth of Christ's assertion, "My kingdom is not of this world."[126] In the Massachusetts legislature, supporting the bill to override Parsons, Josiah Cannon had moved, albeit unsuccessfully, "that 1000 copies of Mr. Madison's memorial against a 'General Assessment' to the Virginia Legislature in 1785 be printed for the members."[127] The whole temper of Richardson's remarks on the Congregational Church as the spoiled child of the state is Madisonian, as is John Leland's connection of financial support for the church and inquisition.[128] Isaac Backus, leading the Baptists in Massachusetts, found inspiration in Virginia "in which hath been the greatest revolution about baptisms and religious liberty, that I ever heard of in any government upon earth."[129] Madison lived in Massachusetts minds, even as his ideas failed to carry the day.

In Madison's words the agents of persecution have a theological character. They are imps, that is, devils – subaltern or puny devils, to be sure, but among the minor troops of Satan.[130] And his remedy was theological as well as political: "Pray for liberty of conscience."[131] For Madison, there was no substantial difference between outright persecution and establishment of a religion by the power of the state being used to demand oaths, levy taxes, and spend for instruction in religion. By Madison's measure, there were plenty of imps in Massachusetts: James Bowdoin and the two Adamses, Samuel and John; Theophilus Parsons; Isaac Parker; Samuel Parker; Daniel Webster; Joseph Story; Lemuel Shaw – to name only the most prominent of these subaltern satans. For them, freedom of religion and an established church were not contradictory concepts.

Our own measure today is Madison's: discrimination against any denomination does strike us as reprehensible. Persecution, we know, is perverse. But believers as we all are in religious freedom "to the utmost," perhaps we should stop before we embrace Madison's theological characterization of the champions of the establishment. We too may be part of an establishment. Our faults may be no more manifest to ourselves than were those to themselves of John Adams and the other imps who made Massachusetts.

NOTES

1 James Madison to William Bradford, January 24, 1774, *The Papers of James Madison*, ed. William T. Hutchinson and William M. E. Rachal (Chicago: University of Chicago Press, 1962), 1:104.

2 *The Perpetual Laws of the Commonwealth of Massachusetts from the Commencement of the Constitution in October 1780 to the Last Wednesday in May 1789* (Boston: Adams and Nourse, 1789), p. 194.

3 Chief Justice Lemuel Shaw, dictum, in *Commonwealth v. Kneeland*, 37 *Massachusetts Reports* 206 (1838), at 217.

4 Ibid.

5 A Constitution or Frame of Government for the Commonwealth of Massachusetts, Part I, "A Declaration of the Rights of the Inhabitants of the Commonwealth of Massachusetts," Article II, in *Perpetual Laws*, p. [9].

6 Abner Kneeland, *A Review of the Trial, Conviction and Final Imprisonment in the Common Jail of the County of Suffolk of Abner Kneeland for the Alleged Crime of Blasphemy* (Boston, 1838), in Leonard W. Levy, *Blasphemy in Massachusetts* (New York: Da Capo Press, 1973), pp. 473–4 (Hottentots), 478 (prayer), 480 (Kneeland's beliefs).

7 The editor of *American State Trials* mistakenly described the Virgin Birth of Jesus as "the Immaculate Conception," a phrase theologically reserved for Mary's own conception without sin ("The Trial of Abner Kneeland for Blasphemy, Boston Massachusetts, 1835," in *American State Trials*, ed. John D. Lawson [St. Louis: Thomas Law Book Company, 1921], p. 450).

8 Samuel Parker, address to the jury, January 24, 1834, in Levy, *Blasphemy in Massachusetts*, p. 207.

9 Kneeland, speech of Abner Kneeland, in ibid., pp. 317–19.

10 Ibid., pp. 322–9.

11 Ibid., pp. 335–6.

12 Parker, address to the jury, in ibid., p. 183.

13 Constitution, Part I, Article II, in *Perpetual Laws*, p. [9].

14 Ibid., Part I, Articles III and XVIII, pp. [10], [11–12].

15 Parker, address to the jury, in Levy, *Blasphemy in Massachusetts*, p. 183.

16 Constitution, Part II, Chapter VI, in *Perpetual Laws*, p. [25].

17 Ibid., Part II, Chapter V, p. [23].

18 Parker, speech to the jury, in Levy, *Blasphemy in Massachusetts*, p. 184.

19 Kneeland, *Review of the Trial*, in ibid., pp. 482–4.

20 Ibid., pp. 494–5.
21 Ibid., p. 505.
22 *Commonwealth* v. *Kneeland*, at 217.
23 Ibid., at 220–1.
24 Ibid., at 242.
25 Leonard Levy, *The Law of the Commonwealth and Chief Justice Shaw* (Cambridge, Mass.: Harvard University Press, 1957), p. 32.
    Shaw had no difficulty with the statute's obviously Trinitarian theology: Like any good Unitarian of the time, he saw no reason not to speak reverently of Jesus Christ and the Holy Ghost, although they were denied (*Commonwealth* v. *Kneeland*, at 214). Justice Morton said that he assumed that "we all" would contest as unconstitutional any legislation making it a crime merely to deny the divinity of Jesus or the Holy Ghost (ibid., at 238).
26 Sydney Ahlstrom, *A Religious History of the American People* (New Haven, Conn.: Yale University Press, 1972), p. 401.
27 Ralph Waldo Emerson to Margaret Fuller, April 22, 1841, *Letters*, ed. Ralph L. Rusk (New York: Columbia University Press, 1939), 2:395.
28 *Commonwealth* v. *Kneeland*, at 217.
29 Ibid., at 216 (recitation of Kneeland's denials), 217 (identification of the view of God's creation, government, and final judging of the world, as distinct from views "affecting the Christian religion").
30 Oliver Wendell Holmes, Jr., *The Common Law* (Boston: Little, Brown, 1881), p. 106.
31 Ibid.
32 Constitution, Part II, Chapter VI, in *Perpetual Laws*, p. [25].
33 Ibid., Part I, Article III, p. [10].
34 Massachusetts Constitutional Convention of 1780, An Address of the Convention . . . to their Constituents, *Journals* (Boston, 1832), pp. 220–1. Emphasis in original.
35 John Locke, *A Letter Concerning Toleration*, trans. William Popple, in Locke, *Works* (London: Longman, 1794), 9: 46–7.
36 Ibid., 9:45. In neither passage are Catholics named; every English reader knew who was meant.
37 Constitution, Part II, Chapter VI, in *Perpetual Laws*, p. [25].
38 Alfonso dé Ligouri taught that for just cause – for example, "to free oneself from importune and unjust interrogation" – it was not sinful to swear, using words capable of two meanings (Ligouri, *Theologia moralis*, 3: 151). So also it was lawful to swear with a "reservation which is not purely mental" – that is, with a qualification that could be perceived by others from the surrounding circumstances. So, for example, a criminal defendant, not bound to testify, could swear that he did not know of a crime, meaning "a crime as to which you can lawfully inquire." It was, however, always sinful to use "a purely mental restriction," which in no way could be perceived by others (ibid., 3:152). These nice distinctions, no doubt, were more irritating than helpful to hostile readers.

39 Robert H. Lord and John E. Sexton, *History of the Archdiocese of Boston* (Boston: Pilot, 1945), 1:479, 512.

40 Ibid., 1: 775.

41 Ibid., 1: 776. As late as 1810, as learned a man as Theophilus Parsons maintained that Article III of the Massachusetts Constitution was "intended to prevent any religious test, as a qualification for office. Therefore those Catholics, who renounce all obedience and subjection to the pope, as a foreign prince or prelate, may, notwithstanding their religious tenets, hold any civil office" (*Barnes* v. *First Parish in Falmouth, 6 Massachusetts Reports* 400 [1810], at 417).

42 Lord and Sexton, *History of the Archdiocese*, 1: 779.

43 Address of the Convention to the People of Massachusetts, Massachusetts Constitutional Convention of 1820, *Journal of Debates and Proceedings* (Boston, 1853), p. 630.

44 "Statement of the Votes for and Against the Articles of Amendment in the Several Counties," ibid., pp. 633–4.

45 Daniel Webster, speech, December 4, 1820, ibid., pp. 160–3. (The reports of speeches at the convention are said by the reporter to be abridgments, not verbatim transcripts.)

46 James Prince, speech, ibid., p. 164; Joseph Tuckerman, speech, ibid., pp. 169–71. On the religious beliefs of the delegates, I follow William G. McLoughlin, *New England Dissent, 1630–1833* (Cambridge, Mass.: Harvard University Press, 1971): for Tuckerman, see 2: 1168; for Hubbard and Foster, 2: 1158.

47 Samuel Hubbard, speech, Constitutional Convention of 1820, *Journal*, p. 175; Edmund Foster, speech, ibid., p. 175; Henry Dearborn, speech, ibid., p. 171.

48 Constitution, Part I, Article III, in *Perpetual Laws*, p. [10].

49 John Adams to Edmund Jennings, June 7, 1800, *Diary and Autobiography of John Adams*, ed. L. H. Butterfield (Cambridge, Mass.: Harvard University Press, 1961), 2: 401.

50 Ibid., 2: 31.

51 Isaac Backus, *A History of New England with Particular Reference to the Baptists* (Newton, Mass.: Backus Historical Society, 1871; New York: Arno Press and the New York Times, 1969), 2: 228.

52 Ibid., 2: 225.

53 Constitutional Convention of 1780, *Journals*, p. 46.

54 Constitution, Part I, Article III, in *Perpetual Laws*, p. [10].

55 Backus, *History*, 2: 227.

56 Ronald M. Peters, Jr., *The Massachusetts Constitution of 1780: A Social Compact* (Amherst: University of Massachusetts Press, 1978), p. 82.

57 *The Laws of the Commonwealth of Massachusetts* (Boston, 1807), 1: 327.

58 An Act Incorporating Certain Religious Societies in the Town of Great Barrington, in the County of Berkshire, *Private and Special Statutes of the Commonwealth of Massachusetts* (Boston, 1805), 1: 310–11.

59 Ibid., Index.
60 Backus, *History*, 2: 451.
61 John D. Cushing, "Notes on Disestablishment in Massachusetts, 1780–1833," *William and Mary Quarterly* 26 (1969): 173–5.
62 Ibid., p. 180. The case was followed on behalf of a Baptist minister in *Crossman v. Second Parish in Beverley* (1792), cited in Nathan Dane, *A General Abridgment and Digest of American Law* (Boston, 1823), 1: 188.
63 Lord, and Sexton, *History of the Archdiocese*, 1: 560–1.
64 Jean Cheverus to Bishop John Carroll, March 10, 1801, quoted in ibid., 1: 561.
65 Dane, *General Abridgment*, 1: 188.
66 *Laws of the Commonwealth*, 2: 932.
67 *Avery v. The Inhabitants of Tyringham*, 3 *Massachusetts Reports* (1807), at 160, 177–82.
68 *Barnes v. First Parish in Falmouth*, at 405–6.
69 Ibid., at 408.
70 Ibid., at 409–12.
71 Isaac Parker, Address to the grand jury of Suffolk County, November 23, 1813, 10 *Massachusetts Reports* 522 ("great man of his time"), 526 ("the Giant of the Law"), 520–31 (activity at convention of 1780), 536 (religious beliefs); Dr. Waterhouse to Thomas Jefferson, March 20, 1813, quoted in Samuel Eliot Morison, "The Great Rebellion in Harvard College, and the Resignation of President Kirkland," Colonial Society of Massachusetts, *Publications* 27 (1932): 59 ("Goliath").
72 *Barnes v. First Parish in Falmouth*, at 413.
73 McLoughlin, *New England Dissent*, 2: 1088.
74 Quoted in ibid., 2: 1098.
75 John Leland, in the Pittsfield *Sun*, June 6, 1811, quoted in ibid., 2: 1097.
76 Quoted in ibid., 2: 1100.
77 *Laws of Massachusetts from February 28, 1807, to December 14, 1816* (Boston, 1817), p. 227.
78 See the facts stated in *Adams v. Howe* 14 *Massachusetts Reports* 340 (1817).
79 Colonel David Colby, speech, January 6, 1821, Constitutional Convention of 1820, *Journal*, p. 559. The prevalence of the dodge is also confirmed by Asa T. Newhall of Lynnfield, speech, December 23, 1820, ibid., p. 394. Although these observations were made after the decision in *Adams v. Howe*, they refer to practices observed before the decision.
80 *Adams v. Howe*, at 344.
81 Martin Phelps, speech, December 20, 1820, Constitutional Convention of 1820, *Journal*, p. 346.
82 Leverett Saltonstall, speech, December 22, 1820, ibid., pp. 389–90. On his religion, see McLoughlin, *New England Dissent*, 2: 1153–4.
83 "Statement of the Votes," Constitutional Convention of 1820, *Journal*, pp. 633–4.

84 Compare the Suffolk County vote, 1,786 for and 908 opposed, with the Bristol County vote, 115 for and 2,015 opposed.
85 *Baker* v. *Fales*, 16 *Massachusetts Reports* 487 (1820), at 488–92.
86 Ibid., at 500.
87 Ibid., at 503.
88 Ibid., at 509.
89 Ibid., at 521.
90 Mark DeWolfe Howe, *Cases on Church and State in the United States* (Cambridge, Mass.: Harvard University Press, 1952), p. 40.
91 *Baker* v. *Fales*, at 521–2.
92 Ibid., at 522.
93 McLoughlin, *New England Dissent*, 2: 1196. For an estimate of Congregational parishes see 2: 1175.
94 Religious Liberties Act of 1824, *Laws of Massachusetts*, 9: 347.
95 *Stebbins* v. *Jennings*, 10 *Pickering's Reports* 172 (1830), at 192–3; McLoughlin, *New England Dissent*, 2: 1230–9.
96 Ibid., 2: 1259 (vote); Constitution of Massachusetts, Articles of Amendment 11.
97 Howe, *Cases,:* p. 54; Mark DeWolfe Howe, *The Garden and the Wilderness* (Chicago: University of Chicago Press, 1965), p. 41.
98 *Baker* v. *Fales*, at 503.
99 *Massachusetts Revised Statutes* (Boston, 1835) c. 20, Section 2.
100 Jacob C. Meyer, *Church and State in Massachusetts from 1740 to 1833* (Cleveland: Western Reserve University Press, 1930), p. 181.
101 "Every town is considered to be a parish, until a separate parish be found within it," the Supreme Judicial Court had said *per curiam* in 1807. But parishes were permitted to organize themselves as religious societies distinct from the towns and become the legal successors of the towns (see, for example, *First Congregational Society in Raynham* v. *Trustees of the Fund* 40 *Massachusetts Reports* 148 [1839]).
     Parishes were given the power to make by-laws regulating admission to membership. Nonmembers could not vote in the affairs of the parish (*Massachusetts Revised Statutes*, c. 20, Sections 3 and 4). By this legal device, the commonwealth assured that the religious denomination in control in 1834 could keep out members of whom the denomination disapproved.
102 Constitution, Part II, Chapter V, in *Perpetual Laws*, pp. [23], [24].
103 Morison, "The Great Rebellion," p. 66; Samuel Eliot Morison, "The History of Harvard College," in *The History and Traditions of Harvard College* (Cambridge, Mass.: Harvard Crimson, 1929), p. 25.
104 Conrad Wright, "The Early Period," in *The Harvard Divinity School*, ed. George Hunston Williams et al., (Boston: Beacon Press, 1954), pp. 21–7.
105 Williams in ibid., 9.
106 An act to amend the Constitution of the Board of Overseers of Harvard College, March 16, 1810, *Laws of the Commonwealth from February 28, 1807, to December 14, 1816*, pp. 164–6. The act was repealed on February 29, 1812

(ibid., p. 508); but the repealing act was itself repealed, and the Senate was added to the Board of Overseers (An Act to restore the Board of Overseers of Harvard College, and to make an addition thereto, February 28, 1814, ibid., pp. 541–2).

107 Saltonstall, speech, December 22, 1820, Constitutional Convention of 1820, *Journal*, p. 389.

108 Joseph Richardson, speech, November 24, 1820, ibid., p. 71.

109 Ibid., pp. 69–71.

110 On Richardson's religion, see McLoughlin, *New England Dissent*, 2: 1158.

111 Daniel Webster, *Report*, January 4, 1821, Constitutional Convention of 1820, *Journal*, pp. 527–31. The Baptists, despite their principles on church and state, were glad to have public support for what was referred to in the Massachusetts legislature as "The Baptist College," the Main Literary and Theological Institution (also known as Waterville College and later as Colby College). In 1813, the Baptist College received as public endowment the grant of a whole township of land in central Maine (McLoughlin, *New England Dissent*, 2: 1124). In 1818, the college unsuccessfully sought an annual subsidy of $3,000 from the legislature. After Maine became a separate state, a generous grant by the Maine legislature was readily accepted (ibid., 2: 1124–1216).

The Massachusetts legislature's refusal to issue a charter for Holy Cross College in 1849 was due to an unexpressed fear that a charter would legitimate an application for public support (Lord and Sexton, *History of the Archdiocese*, 2: 577–82).

112 Ibid., 2: 532.

113 Richardson, speech, January 5, 1821, Constitutional Convention of 1820, *Journal*, p. 543; Joseph Story, speech, January 5, 1821, ibid., pp. 544–5.

114 Constitutional Convention of 1820, *Journal*, pp. 551 (convention vote), 633–4 (popular vote). Suffolk County was for the change by a vote of 1,433 to 1,252; Bristol County, against it by a vote of 1,730 to 133.

115 Williams, *Harvard Divinity School*, pp. 9 (changes in overseers), 85 (President Walker quoted).

116 Constitution, Part I, Article III; An Act for making more effectual Provision for the Due Observation of the Lord's Day, October 22, 1702; Constitution of Massachusetts, Amendment, Article 11.

117 An Act for making more effectual Provision for the Due Observation of the Lord's Day, October 22, 1702. The act provided, among other things, that "no person shall recreate, disport, or unnecessarily walk or loiter, or assemble themselves in the streets, lanes, wharves, highways, common fields, pastures, or orchards of any town or place within this State." The penalty for disobedience was a fine of five shillings.

118 In 1707, John Murray, the Universalist minister in Gloucester, was found liable for a 50-pound fine for having performed a marriage and not being properly ordained (Cushing, "Notes on Disestablishment," pp. 174, 180–1).

119   The cause célèbre here came as late as 1859, when a teacher in the Eliot
      School, Boston, beat an eleven-year-old Catholic boy, Thomas J. Wall, for
      refusing on religious grounds to read the Lord's Prayer or the Ten Com-
      mandments in the King James Version. The teacher was prosecuted for
      battery and acquitted (*Commonwealth* v. *Cooke, 7 American Law Register* 417
      [1859]). An election in Boston, following the case, ended the compulsion
      there, but in other communities, compulsion was used on Catholics at least
      as late as 1865 (Lord and Sexton, *History of the Archdiocese,* 2: 601–5).

120   Ibid., 2: 313.

121   James Madison, "General Defense of the Constitution," speech, June 12,
      1788, *Papers of Madison,* 11: 130.

122   James Madison, "Number Ten," *The Federalist Papers,* ed. Roy P. Fairfield
      (Baltimore: Johns Hopkins University Press, 1981), p. 22.

123   Lord and Sexton, *History of the Archdiocese,* 1: 349 (Catholics in 1785), 1:
      715 (Catholics in 1820), 1: 779 (vote for Cheverus).

124   McLoughlin, *New England Dissent,* 2: 698 (Baptists in 1770), 2: 1113 (Bap-
      tists in 1824).

125   Kneeland, *Review of the Trial,* pp. 494–5; Lord and Sexton, *History of the
      Archdiocese,* 1: 776.

126   McLoughlin, *New England Dissent,* 2: 1092.

127   Ibid., 2: 1093.

128   Richardson, speech, November 24, 1820, Constitutional Convention of
      1820, *Journal,* p. 69; Leland, quoted in McLoughlin, *New England Dissent,*
      2: 1097.

129   Isaac Backus to John Rippon, August 19, 1791, excerpted in Backus, *The
      Diary of Isaac Backus,* ed. William G. McLoughlin (Providence: Brown
      University Press, 1979), 3: 1315.

130   Samuel Johnson, *A Dictionary of the English Language* (London, 1756). John-
      son illustrates with a line from John Milton, *Paradise Lost.*

131   Madison to Bradford, January 24, 1774, *Papers of James Madison,* 1: 104.

Thomas Sully's posthumous portrait of Patrick Henry, who opposed passage of the Virginia Statute. Courtesy of Colonial Williamsburg Foundation.

8

Jeffersonian Religious Liberty and American Pluralism

CUSHING STROUT

Opposite Thomas Jefferson's statue, in the dome of his Memorial, which overlooks Washington's Tidal Basin, these words are engraved:

> Almighty God hath created the mind free. All attempts to influence it by temporal punishments or burthens are a departure from the plan of the holy author of our religion. . . . No man shall be compelled to frequent or support any religious worship or ministry or shall otherwise suffer on account of his religious opinions or beliefs, but all men shall be free to profess and by argument to maintain, their opinions in matters of religion. I know but one code of morality for men whether acting singly or collectively.

The Jefferson Memorial does not indicate that these historic words come from the Virginia Statute for Religious Freedom, drafted by Jefferson and passed, after a long and bitter contest, in late December 1785. The excerpts do not reveal Jefferson's emphasis on the evils of "hypocrisy and meanness," produced by legal coercion; nor do they quote the crucial point that "our civil rights have no dependence on our religious opinions," any more than they do on "our opinions in physics and geometry." The Memorial words do not include either the favorite phrase of ardent supporters of separation between church and state – that it is "sinful and tyrannical" to compel a person to furnish money "for the propagation of opinions which he disbelieves," or even for the support of "this or that teacher of his own religious persuasion." Finally, the excerpts do not mention Jefferson's important corollary – that civil government may justifiably interfere "when principles break out into overt acts against peace and good order." To this extent, the Memorial phrases

201

have tamed the radical force of Jefferson's statute. But being short of its context, the wall's quotation eloquently illustrates the way in which Jefferson's legacy has been received.

The Virginia Statute for Religious Freedom, one of the great expressions of the Enlightenment in America as well as of Jefferson's mind, was a local, not a national, act. Yet many of its celebrants, in a historical vein, have found a national meaning in it as the spirit of American religious freedom, one defining a Jeffersonian "wall" of separation between church and state: "What happened first in Virginia happened in other places, soon or late," making Virginia "a model for the other states and for the new Federal Government," affirms a Protestant commentator, in tune with many historians and some justices of the Supreme Court of the United States.[1] Other historians and spokesmen for different religious traditions have found this view of our history too simple, too sectarian, or too responsive to an alien and doctrinaire secularism. The legacy of the statute commingles a questionable historical thesis with a historic affirmation of universal religious liberty. The celebrants make strange bedfellows because of the ideological diversity among those who claim to be Jefferson's heirs, whether they be Baptists, Presbyterians, freethinkers, Unitarians, Seventh-Day Adventists, or Jews – or even admirers of the German pastor and martyr to the Resistance, Dietrich Bonhoeffer, whose "religionless religion" one professor has celebrated as a bond between these two aristocratic democrats who treasured their religious privacy and the ethics of Jesus.[2]

The nationalization of Jefferson's statute has reflected a major change in the social and religious composition of the American people. Catholics, Jews, and agnostic or atheist "unbelievers" now play a much larger and more significant role in the United States than Jefferson could have imagined. He had envisioned that most Americans would become Unitarians, like himself; but particularly in his own region of the South, evangelical Protestantism would become increasingly dominant, while outside the South, massive immigration from southern and eastern Europe would bring a flood of Catholic and Jewish citizens. In these changed circumstances, the national application of Jefferson's ideas about the relation between religion and politics was bound to become controversial.

Jefferson's memory was linked to the idea of religious liberty not only by his own instructions for his monument at Monticello, but also by the very circumstances of the purchase of his house, which was falling into the decay of neglect when Uriah Phillips Levy bought it in 1836. This remarkable man, the stormy petrel of the navy, court-martialed six times and twice discharged from the service, was a proud Jew who admired

Jefferson most for his having done so much "to mold our Republic in a form in which a man's religion does not make him ineligible for political or governmental life."[3] Levy, in successfully defending himself in court for four days in 1855 against the prejudicial decision to strike him from the rolls of the navy, appealed to the First Amendment in defense of his right to the free exercise of his religion.

Jefferson made it clear in his *Autobiography* that the Virginia Statute was meant to include "within the mantle of its protection, the Jew and the Gentile, the Christian and Mahometan, the Hindoo, and infidel of every denomination."[4] Levy, like so many later commentators on American religious liberty, read the Constitution in the spirit of Jefferson's statute. In this sense, it is profoundly appropriate that the protector of Jefferson's beloved house on behalf of the republic was an admirer whose faith was much more of a minority position than was any held by those Protestants who had joined Jefferson and Madison in the struggle for disestablishment. Only a few of Jefferson's eulogists after his death made much of the Virginia Statute; and the North Carolinian Henry Potter, who believed that "we owe our religious freedom principally to Thomas Jefferson" and his "sacred document," did not mention that belief in Protestantism was a legal condition for holding public office in his state.[5] It would be forty-two years before those of Uriah Levy's faith could constitutionally serve there in public offices of trust.

It was not only Jews, but Catholics as well, who in many states would not, for a long time yet, feel that they were securely within the mantle of protection that Jefferson had defined in a universal way. When the Thomas Jefferson Memorial Foundation invited Al Smith to speak on July 4, 1928, at Monticello, he prudentially withdrew because of the slanders and threats issued by the Ku Klux Klan.[6] Almost a year later, Senator William E. Borah of Idaho cited Jefferson's mastery of religious freedom "in all its far-reaching effects upon a free people" to challenge an Alabama senator's effort to entangle the Senate with his campaign to make a polarity between "Romanism and Americanism."[7] When Jefferson was canonized in 1943 by fifty-five public figures in a symposium, it was labor leader William Green, child of a devout Baptist family, who made the strongest claim for the statute as "the first declaration for absolute religious liberty to be offered by a sovereign state in the history of the world."[8] Yet, ironically, five Baptist associations, totaling some 10 million members, joined in a public stand against the election of a Catholic president in 1960, a gross denial of Jefferson's point that political rights cannot be determined by religious beliefs.[9] A member of candidate Kennedy's ministerial audience in Houston was moved to ask: "Whose loyalty to the Constitution which separates Church and State and forbids

religious tests for public office was really open to question? His or ours?"[10]
Kennedy himself cited the harassment of Baptist preachers as background for Jefferson's statute.[11]

To come down now from this overview, we must look more
closely at the ideas in the statute and the history of their impact on
spokesmen for different religious groups in American culture, first in
Virginia, and then in the rest of the country. In the process, it will become evident that religious politics tend to generate what historians criticize as "the Whig interpretation of history," which seeks to find its spiritual ancestry in order to support its present posture.[12] The statute's words
inscribed on the Jefferson Memorial are shorn of any indicated context,
but while Jefferson meant them to represent "the natural rights of mankind," they also emerged from a specific struggle and an individual's
mind.

Jefferson's statute separates civil rights from religious opinions by legally prohibiting any connection between them. The civil rights of any
citizen are not diminished or enhanced by holding any religious opinions
or beliefs. To think otherwise is to forget that our opinions and beliefs
are the involuntary result of the impact of evidence on our minds. For
law to enforce any religious position would be to promote hypocrisy.
Morton White has pointed to a dilemma in this Jeffersonian formulation
of the case: If individuals have no power to believe except according to
what the evidence obliges them to believe, then there can be no duty to
believe. But if there is no duty to believe, how can there be any right to
believe?[13] Jefferson escaped from this dilemma by his assumption that
God had "created the mind free" and intends it to remain so. Jefferson's
friend Thomas Cooper, a scientist, widened the argument to include all
opinion and belief, drawing the logical conclusion that governments should
therefore "consider *action* and not *opinions* as the proper objects of their
control."[14]

Jefferson's bill makes the same distinction by justifying civil interference with religious opinions whenever they "break out into overt acts
against peace and good order."[15] It was this principle that enabled the
Virginia legislature to pass a law in 1788 stipulating bigamy and polygamy would be punishable by death, as noted much later by the Supreme
Court of the United States, which, quoting Jefferson, upheld the right
of Congress to make a law against bigamy and rejected the plea that
religious freedom protects the right of a Mormon to practice polygamy
under the doctrine of "plural marriage."[16] David Little has criticized the
"confusions created by a Jeffersonian approach to these questions" because "the sharp distinction between belief and action is mistaken." It

appeals, Little argues, only to those who, like Jefferson, minimize "the importance and relevance of the reasons behind our actions."[17] But Jefferson was not indifferent to the reasons that underlie actions; his distinction arose instead, from his view that the mind's formulation of its reasons for religious belief cannot be willed. Therefore, governments should control only actions, because they are voluntary. Antisocial actions cannot be justified by giving religious reasons. It was consistent with his outlook that his act went into effect along with a law penalizing Sabbath breakers.[18]

The Virginia Supreme Court of Appeals in 1946 reconciled the two by preventing a juvenile-court judge from imposing attendance at church for a year (as a penalty for throwing rocks) because it violated Jefferson's statute.[19] Certainly, the court correctly grasped Jefferson's point that trying to induce religious belief by such a penalty would contradict his basic principle. One hundred years earlier, the state's high court had also cited Jefferson's act, by then a part of the state constitution, in refusing to disqualify a witness in a homicide case because, although he believed in God, he did not believe in an afterlife of rewards or punishments. One can understand a prisoner's apprehension about a witness who believes that "offenses will meet their punishments here," but the court rightly made the point that the statute was meant to include all varieties of religious belief and that the law could not declare a witness incompetent by reason of his unorthodox religious belief.[20]

A few years later, in 1850, the state's high court, in a remarkable use of the Virginia Statute, heard a lawyer cite it on behalf of a minister, Jarvis C. Bacon, who was accused of having spoken against the right to own slaves. By that time, such speaking was forbidden by law. Yet the court allowed a motion for a new trial on the ground that any minister might spiritually seek to dissuade a Christian in his church from merchandising or owning slaves without thereby denying the secular legal right to slave property. The minister had only said that "to give him nothing for his labour, except once in a while a whipping or a few stripes," was thievery, and "a humane casuist" might find it worse than stealing corn, or even than committing murder or arson, if no "suitable comforts or necessaries" were given for his work, as slaveholders normally provided. In short, if casuistry made it possible legally to interpret the minister's remarks innocently, then "the spirit of the Constitution," with its commitment to "freedom of speech and of religious faith," encouraged the court to do so.[21]

Virginia's best tribute to the legacy of Jefferson, however, was in the battle over the proposal in 1926 for compulsory Bible reading in the public schools. Led by a memorial from Baptists, the strongest supporters of Jefferson's act in the 1780s, well over one hundred churches responded to the Baptists' plea for keeping the exercise voluntary, as it was in most of the schools. Citing the memorial of the Baptists as representing "the spirit in which the Virginia statute for religious liberty was enacted," the Richmond *News Leader* noted that the proposal would be resented by Catholics, Jews, and rationalists.[22] Sitting in the capitol building designed by Jefferson, a Senate committee defeated the bill by a margin of six votes.

The Reverend George W. McDaniel, the leader of the opposition, paid paradoxical tribute to Jefferson's act for its "quickening power" in multiplying Christians so that Baptists had become a majority. For him, separation between church and state was linked to separation of mind and conscience: "The one – education – deals primarily with the mind and is a proper function of the State; the other – the Bible – deals with the conscience, and that is inviolable." His religious position overlapped with Jefferson's philosophical one. For the Baptist, "religion is of such a personal, therefore sacred, nature that government must not touch it." Jefferson, for his philosophical reasons, would have agreed that "the Christian religion should not need any assistance from the State. Every time Christianity has united with the State, corruption has set in on both sides."[23] Even in 1785, Jefferson and Madison had badly needed the support of Baptists and Presbyterians to win the struggle for the act. Now that evangelical Christianity, in a fundamentalist form, had grown powerful throughout the South, it was not philosophers but Baptists who could lead the fight on behalf of the principles of Jefferson's act, and even they could win because most schools already had voluntary Bible exercises, as the Richmond *News Leader* pointed out. Methodists, fraternal orders, and patriotic societies supported the compulsory bill, as many of them did the drive to eliminate the teaching of evolution from the public schools, but the newspaper editorialists had a powerful appeal to history: "Virginia would have been shamed forever," and one of Jefferson's great achievements of "religious freedom would have become a hissing and a byword in this State."[24]

Outside Virginia, Jefferson's legacy of religious freedom was kept alive by Baptists and other small sects in places where there were legally privileged churches. Jefferson's closest ally, James Madison, had responded to Baptist pleas for a Bill of Rights to protect religious liberty in the new federal union, but his bold proposal for making the "religion" clauses of the First Amendment apply to the states was voted down in the First Congress. Whatever the clauses meant (and the vigorous controversy over that question continues), the battles for religious liberty would take place in the states; and if Congress could make no laws respecting an establishment of religion, that meant at least that it could not yet meddle with the establishments that existed in various states. Jefferson and Madison's victory in Virginia would spread beyond the borders of their state only if others carried their standard in other local struggles.

The exception indicating the rule is the Jacksonian Report on the Sunday-mail controversy. Richard M. Johnson's monument, raised by the Kentucky legislature, includes his authorship of the two Senate reports in which he denied any congressional authority to protect the Sabbath on the Jeffersonian ground that elected politicians are chosen by the citizens "to represent their *political* and not their *religious* views; to guard the rights of man, not to restrict the rights of conscience."[25] Johnson had friends in Jackson's cabinet as well as in the Post Office, particularly O. B. Brown, a Baptist minister who was chief clerk of the department and in whose Washington house Johnson was a long-term resident. Johnson's father had founded a Baptist church, and the son was active in promoting the work of Baptist missionaries among the Indians. Ironically, when he brought in a proposal for Congress to incorporate a theological seminary for training missionaries, his opponents regarded it as a violation of the "establishment" clause, forcing Johnson – not very credibly – to redefine its purpose as literary and not religious. The Senate amended his bill to make the institutions religiously pluralistic, and it later became George Washington University.[26] Johnson may seem to have been blind to inconsistency in his own position, but Jefferson himself had seen nothing wrong with using federal money or land to support religious groups engaged in missionary activity among the Indians, because he assumed that such aid was essential to civilizing them.[27] Indians, not being citizens, were a special case.

In the South outside Virginia, Jefferson's standard for religious liberty was raised against the exclusions of Protestant establishments, indifferent or hostile to the rights of Catholics and Jews. In Maryland, Thomas Kennedy, born a Scotsman in a Presbyterian family, wrote a poem celebrating Jefferson's Statute for Religious Freedom.[28] From 1819 to 1826, he fought stoutly to eliminate a Christian religious test for public office. Like other Pietists, Kennedy believed that religion is a matter solely between man and his Creator because "there is no law can reach the heart." In his view, Jews and Christians were "very nearly allied" in matters of religion, and his orations dilated more on the Scriptural forecast of a return of the saving remnant than on Jefferson's ideas.[29] In any case, there was the example of the Framers of the federal Constitution, who had responded affirmatively to Charles Pinckney's proposal to abolish any religious test for offices of public trust. Kennedy's opponents mounted a campaign that defeated him for reelection as delegate to the Assembly, but he bounced back into the ring, encouraged by support from newspapers all over the country; a substitute bill was finally passed that enabled Jews to hold public office without taking tests, although revised constitutions of the state distinguished between Jews and Christians in some respects until 1867, when the test was made a theistic one.[30]

In North Carolina, the struggle was also intense over the state's restriction of public office to Protestants. Some critics of the federal Constitution feared emigration from Europe of "Jews and pagans of every kind to come among us."[31] The Scotch-Irish Presbyterians in the state had secured for North Carolina in 1776 a constitutional ban against any legal preference for one denomination, but the constitution did restrict public office to Protestants and keep ministers out of the legislature. It was a considerable embarrassment that sixty years later William Gaston, a Catholic who had served in the state's House and Senate, was now an associate justice of the North Carolina Supreme Court, yet legally unfit for office, just as Jacob Henry, a Jew and a respected member of the legislature, had been in 1809. Henry's eloquent appeal to the spirit of the Bill of Rights had won him his seat,[32] but Gaston sought a general victory by taking his plea to the state's constitutional convention of 1836. His supporters appealed to Jefferson's statute, confident that "the glowing memory of his countrymen will linger around this Act, as the imperishable manifesto of the great rights of man."[33] But even more than twenty pages of such impassioned rhetoric could not win the elimination of all tests. Gaston was compelled to accept a compromise, by which he was cleared of any taint by a widening of the constitutional test from Protestant to Christian. Not until 1868 was the test widened further to include all believers in "Almighty God."[34]

Catholics in a Protestant state were receptive to the idea of separation between church and state. John England, the first bishop of Charleston, South Carolina, and a friend of Gaston's, spoke for two hours before the House of Congress on January 8, 1826, to disabuse Americans of their stereotypes about Catholics. "You have no power to interfere with my religious rights," he told them; "the tribunal of the church has no power to interfere with my civil rights." Indeed, he went so far as to reassure his listeners by saying that his church had no power to interfere with "our civil concerns," a self-denying ordinance that modern Catholics would find crippling because it would deprive the church of any role in public life.[35] South Carolina's constitution of 1778 had legally established Protestant Christianity and the Bible, but England was the beneficiary of Charles Pinckney's presiding in 1790 over the state's constitutional convention, which carried out disestablishment in the spirit of what Virginia had done four years earlier.

In New England, Baptists and Universalists would be the most vigorous proponents of complete disestablishment, and Jefferson's bill provided a model for them. It was printed in Massachusetts and Connecticut newspapers and was hailed by the Baptist leader Isaac Backus as exemplary.[36] One of Jefferson's supporters in the Virginia struggle, John Leland, continued the battle in Connecticut and Massachusetts. More radical than Backus, a more representative Baptist, Leland opposed chaplains in the legislature and joined with Jacksonians to endorse Sunday mail. He was like Jefferson, too, in extending the idea of religious liberty to include deists, Jews, Catholics, and Turks – all of whom were abhorrent to most Baptists.[37] Even so, it was the Baptists who compelled the Republicans to take a stand on disestablishment in Connecticut, but "the Republican Party was born, flourished and died in Massachusetts without ever advocating Jefferson's position on disestablishment," while it was the dissenting Calvinist Roger Williams whom Baptists after 1800 idealized most of all.[38] Elder John Leland, however, blended Jeffersonianism with his own unorthodox Baptist faith and sent the Virginian, on behalf of Berkshire Republicans, a mammoth cheese, the product of nine hundred cows, on the day in 1802 that Jefferson paid tribute to the Danbury Baptists in a letter that has become the *locus classicus* of the idea that Jefferson and Baptists had joined to endorse the First Amendment for "building a wall of separation between Church and State."[39] Thereafter, Connecticut Republicans asked Baptists to join them in Fourth of July celebrations.

Another Jeffersonian stalwart in the struggle for separation was Abraham Bishop, son of the mayor of New Haven and a polemicist against the Federalist and clerical "friends of order" in Connecticut. In his view, they had spoiled the post-Revolutionary hope that "this redeemed continent was to be the grand theatre of the millennial reign." Defenders of the Standing Order of Federalist–Congregationalists were "hypocrites, and have no righteousness of their own," because they thought they could inherit the "piety of our forefathers." It was an inevitable result of legally establishing religion: "Church and State always contaminate each other, so far as their union extends." Clerical politicians and political Christians were a resultant plague on the commonwealth, making for more hypocrites in New England "than in any other equal portion of the globe."[40] This hyperbolic judgment of his region, reflecting his passionate partisanship, was a political application of a major point in Jefferson's statute – that legal coercion in religious matters fosters hypocrisy.

By 1818 in Connecticut, the victory of the Jeffersonians in politics made possible the securing of a new constitutional right: No person could be compelled to join, support, or be legally classed with any religious association, and every denomination of Christians would have equal rights and privileges. In Massachusetts, the victory for disestablishing the Standing Order came fifteen years later, in 1833. But these legal forms of disestablishment, important as they were for Protestant groups considered marginal by heirs of Puritan establishments, could not prevent prejudices from developing against Jews and Catholics. Pietistic separationists were ardent supporters of voluntarism whenever taxes for religion were at issue, but "they did not object to the prevailing Puritan laws against profanity, blasphemy, gambling, theater-going, and desecration of the Sabbath, which they accepted as within the domain of the government in its preservation of a Christian society."[41] Unlike Jefferson and Madison, Pietists believed in a Christian society. Abraham Bishop, for all his Jeffersonianism, saw nothing strange in comparing Federalists with Jews, Catholics, and the British for failing to use reason, which always spoke for him in Republican accents.[42]

Jefferson lamented that all religious sects are intolerant when in power, as he wrote to the Jew Mordecai M. Noah in 1818, noting that "although we are free by law, we are not so in practice; public opinion erects itself into an inquisition, and exercises its office with as much fanaticism as fans the flames of an auto da fé."[43] Tocqueville saw in 1831 that "for the Americans the ideas of Christianity and liberty are so completely mingled that it is almost impossible to get them to conceive of the one without the other."[44] For Jefferson, the establishing of natural rights, not religion, was the essence of the republic, but this liberal secularity was contested in antebellum America by the belief that Protestantism was the religious basis of the Constitution and the nation, a faith to be preached in the public schools. This was the doctrine of Stephen Colwell, for example, a Presbyterian trustee of Princeton Theological Seminary and the University of Pennsylvania, a lawyer, and an iron manufacturer. He would summarize the provisions for religious liberty in America without reference to the Virginia Statute. He accepted the Catholic laity as American only because he thought they had "nothing in common" with the Catholic hierarchy's claims and principles.[45] Tocqueville did not include this Protestant Whiggism as a force that in time could become a part of that "tyranny of the majority" that democratic regimes engendered, but he came to America in 1831, too early to encounter the rabidly anti-Catholic Protestantism of the Know-Nothing Party, which in the 1850s had electoral victories in several states and had forty-eight members of Congress.

In Maine, a fifteen-year-old Irish-Catholic girl was expelled in 1854 from the public school because she refused to read the prescribed Protestant version of the Bible, although she was willing to read the Douay Version. Counsel for the plaintiff argued that the integration of immigrant children in the public schools is the best way "to instill into the children of emigrants our own notions of religious liberty."[46] One might think a Yankee court would be sympathetic to this nonlibertarian argument, but instead it perversely cited Jefferson, "than whom a more resolute champion of liberty never lived," to show that religious belief provides no indulgence "for any thing that is detrimental to society." The judge simply begged the question of what *was* detrimental and urged on the plaintiffs recognition of the need for "mutual charity and forbearance – of mutual concession and compromise," heedless that these were precisely the qualities in short supply on the Protestant, majority side.[47] Given the recent precedent in Boston of legal justification for racially segregated schools, cited by the defendants, the result in Maine is not surprising, especially since the Bill of Rights still applied only to the federal government.

Jefferson was consistent in advocating that no religious instruction or exercise in the public schools "shall be prescribed or practiced inconsistent with the tenets of any religious sect or denomination."[48] It was always his view that nothing important in religion is a matter of sectarian difference because for him religion is essentially ethics, not metaphysics or theology, and he had the Enlightenment's confidence that all religions would agree about morality, the concord itself being the best proof of God's being. The public-school movement of the 1850s, led by Horace Mann in Massachusetts, was similarly concerned with avoiding the strife of sects and inculcating a supposed common core of Christianity. Not surprisingly, a Unitarian led this Jeffersonian movement because it was Unitarianism, not Calvinism, that was sympathetic to the rationalistic and moralistic idea of religion.

Tolerance in this style was unaware of its own sectarianism. Jefferson's anticlerical animus was hottest against Presbyterians in Virginia, yet it was a Presbyterian minister, former chaplain at the University of Virginia, William H. Ruffner, who became superintendent of schools in 1870 as "the Horace Mann of the South." The issue would be joined in New York when Bishop John Hughes would see "common Christianity" as another name for deism, thus putting sectarianism in the schools. This argument against the public school was tied to the Catholic demand for public support of parochial schools. The Protestant response to Hughes was to refuse any aid to denominational schools and to secularize the public school even further to avoid any charge of its being sectarian in a Unitarian way.[49]

Dropping the use of the King James Bible in public-school exercises was much more controversial than initiating it. But the presence of Catholic and Jewish students indicated the need for reconsideration. In 1869, the issue came to a head in an Ohio case marked by wide-ranging philosophical and political forays. It concluded rather anticlimactically by the Ohio Supreme Court overruling the city court and upholding the power of the Cincinnati School Board to drop the practice of Bible reading and instruction in the public schools, if it saw fit, as a matter of its discretion – the same discretionary power that a Maine board had used to expell a Catholic girl for refusing to read the King James Bible. But the dissenting judge's opinion for the city's Superior Court cast a long shadow.

The Cincinnati School Board had hoped to consolidate Catholic and public schools, giving both access to the Common School Fund, but the Catholic archbishop withdrew his support. Plaintiffs claimed that the board's action would make the schools "deistical and infidel both in their purpose and tendency." An unusual array of legal talent debated the issues in court, after much community uproar had exposed the community's religious diversity. One remarkable lawyer for the board, Johann B. Stallo, was a German-born freethinker and science teacher who cited history to show that the Framers saw civil government as "a purely secular institution." His colleague, George Hoadly, cited the epitaph on Jefferson's tomb, referring to the Virginia Statute, and pleaded: "Freedom of the State! freedom of the soul! freedom of education! Just what we here contend for."[50]

Judge Alphonso Taft, father of William Howard Taft, made the modern argument by noting that both Catholics and Jews are injured in their religious feelings if the common schools are considered a Protestant preserve, a presumption at odds with the principle of separation between church and state. Taft formulated an idea that the Supreme Court in our time would make its own: "The government is neutral, and while protecting all, it prefers none, and it *disparages* none. The State, while it does not profess to be Christian, exercises a truly Christian charity toward all." Like Jefferson, Judge Taft would include within the state's "mantle of protection and encouragement Protestants, Roman Catholics, Jews and Rationalists alike," no one of whom, however numerous, "can boast of peculiar favor with the State." Judge Taft's dissent was supported by the state's highest court in a unanimous decision that found "the true Republican doctrine" in seeing religion as "lying outside the true and legitimate province of government." The judge boasted that his principles were "as old as Madison, and were his favorite opinions." The judge was right about the Madisonian concept of separation, but his own view was consonant as well with a laissez-faire attitude, characteristic of the business-oriented Republicanism of what came to be called the Gilded Age: "The great bulk of human affairs and human interests is left by any free government to individual enterprise and individual action."[51]

Jefferson's sense of his own religion was profoundly individualistic. If reason is the only oracle to guide religious opinion, as he told his nephew Peter Carr, "you are answerable not for the rightness but uprightness of the decision." This pregnant apothegm derived not only from Jefferson's emphasis on morality, but also from his acute awareness that his own religious opinions made him eccentric in the eyes of many Virginians and New Englanders. Actually, his common-sense Unitarianism had its own New England counterpart in John Adams, also a child of the Enlightenment, but to him it seemed much more individualistic than that: "I am of a sect by myself, as far as I know."[52]

The institutional ally of religious individualism was a wide separation between church and state as a matter of law. Jefferson's benign shadow often falls, therefore, on every defender of the individual's independent judgment in matters of religion. Among Protestants, there was an old prejudice that Jefferson had been an infidel, and his supporters had to point out that he was not a deist and not indifferent to whether or not people were atheists or polytheists. His point simply was that legal coercion of belief should be constitutionally forbidden.[53] Robert Baird, missionary agent of the American and Foreign Christian Union, expressed the common prejudice in 1856 when in his account, *Religion in America,* he claimed that Jefferson's statute made "the arch-infidel chuckle with satisfaction because by including non-Christians and infidels" in its protection, "it seemed to degrade Christianity" rather than merely having "embodied the principles of eternal justice." Baird portrayed Jefferson demonically as having done more than anyone else "to propagate irreligion in the most influential part of the community."[54]

Freethinkers, agnostics, and atheists claimed Jefferson as their own also by editing him to suit their tastes. At around the same time that the Jeffersonians were defending the action of the Cincinnati School Board, a more radical Unitarian than Jefferson had been was abandoning his faith in Christianity and turning instead, for "some American scripture" and an "American prophet," to Emerson: "The soul is its own Christ. Humanity is its own Messiah."[55] The idea was Emersonian; the words were those of Francis E. Abbott, pastor of a Unitarian church in Dover, New Hampshire, from 1864 to 1868, when he lost his faith in Christianity. For a while, he continued to share the meetinghouse with more orthodox Unitarians, who occupied it at a different time, but the minority eventually saw no reason why Abbott should any longer be entitled to occupy the church, since he was by his own insistence no longer a Christian. The presiding judge in this case agreed. He cited Jefferson's statute only to contrast it with the New Hampshire Constitution, which authorized provision for only "public Protestant teachers of piety, religion and morality." True, New Hampshire had once had a popular governor, William Plumer, who had given up the Baptist faith for skepticism, but that exception did not illustrate any rule. Abbott, the dissenting judge argued instead (for over 140 pages!), was religiously a Jeffersonian in all but name, so the term "Christian" in some "general sense" ought to include men like Plumer, Franklin, Jefferson, and Abbott.[56] But Dover's lapsed Unitarian was more honest than his defenders; he wanted his own church to be called an "independent society."

Abbott, as president of the National Liberal League, formed on July 4, 1876, would seek a constitutional amendment for "the total separation of Church and State," a "complete secularization of the government both national and state."[57] This extreme ideology of separationism was the mirror image of the ideology of the National Reform Association, which sought to make America officially Christian by amendment. Abbot's *Index* sponsored a petition of thirty-five thousand against the Christian amendment and got Senator Charles Sumner to introduce it. The two absolutes were doomed to be peripheral to the more moderate American center.

Jefferson's reputation among freethinkers is evident in Francis May Holland's *Liberty in the Nineteenth Century*, which lists significant historical events from a libertarian point of view. His list of dates is as parochial as those satirical prints of a Bostonian's skewed view of the United States. It begins with the Declaration of Independence and ends with the death of Robert Ingersoll. Jefferson is the only president whose election and inauguration are both cited. One might wonder why Grover Cleveland made Holland's list, but it was probably because William F. Vilas, Cleveland's postmaster general, was a student of the teachings of Jefferson and Madison on religious liberty and defended the "absolute independence of the church from the state and the state from the church, meaning by 'the church' every form or fashion of religious belief," as a doctrine, "which must be insisted upon continually as absolutely essential to the peace and concord of the country."[58] The other names making the list prominently feature New England abolitionists and literary men, along with obscure professors who were "dismissed for evolutionism" and other martyrs, who were punished for violating Sunday laws. For Holland, the opening of the American Museum of Natural History in New York on Sundays in 1892 was a major victory.[59]

It was not Jefferson, but Tom Paine who was the patron saint of the Boston Unitarianism that inspired the Free Religious Association, which opposed Sunday laws, Bible reading in the schools, and parochial schools; and it was not Virginia Republicanism, but Maine Republicanism that animated Senator James G. Blaine, dubbed "the plumed knight" by Robert G. Ingersoll, the most popular orator of the moderate freethinkers and himself a conservative Republican defender of protectionism and imperialism.[60] The link between Ingersoll's agnosticism and Blaine's conservatism was anti-Catholic feeling. Blaine made separation of church and state a national issue in 1876, when he submitted his own amendment calling for application of the First Amendment's "religion" clauses to the states (Madison's lost motion in the First Congress), prohibiting any public revenue to go to any school controlled by any religious or antireligious group, and permitting the reading of the Bible in any school. The voting was strictly partisan, as the proposal's Protestant cast indicates it would be, and the amendment failed in the Senate, despite President Grant's moral support, because Democrats, heirs of Jefferson, had become the party of the immigrants and opposed it.[61] Not surprisingly, the demagogic author of *Romanism a Menace to the Nation,* an ex-priest who called the parochial school "a curse to the Church and a menace to the Nation," urged support for President Grant's message that had inspired Blaine's amendment.[62]

The legendary Jeffersonian Democratic orator, William Jennings Bryan, contributed to an edition of his hero's works and celebrated the Statute for Religious Freedom in 1905 for expressing Jefferson's "sublime confidence in the triumph of truth" by free discussion.[63] Twenty years later, however, Bryan deserted Jeffersonian rationalism to take the stand at Dayton, Tennessee, on behalf of fundamentalism and a state law against the teaching of evolution in the public schools. David Dudley Malone, speaking for the American Civil Liberties Union, invoked Jefferson's idea of religious liberty to attack Bryan. Extending Jefferson's argument from religion to science, Malone asserted: "The truth always wins – and we are not afraid of it. The truth does not need the law. The truth does not need Mr. Bryan."[64] Bryan confessed that it was the greatest speech he had ever heard. (H. L. Mencken cynically said that it was the loudest.) Bryan's stand at Dayton seems completely at odds with his Jeffersonianism, but even twenty years earlier he had made Jefferson in his own image by praising him for having recognized that "our religion is a religion of the heart" and is "propagated from heart to heart" on the "basis of love."[65]

Unitarians had a better claim than Bryan to be Jefferson's modern heirs, and in the decade of the Dayton trial, they would like to have believed that Jefferson's statute was "written into the law of his State and into the soul of the Nation." But they saw instead that the "prevailing powers in Protestantism do not believe in religious freedom." The modernists in religion had been routed by the Baptist fundamentalists in seven states.

Lamenting this debacle, the editor of the Unitarian *Christian Register* felt that the principle of consent in Jefferson's Declaration of Independence had undermined the libertarianism of the great Statute for Religious Freedom by promoting majority rule in a country where "a cross section of any State would show that America has a Fundamentalist mind." In the apocalyptic tones of the jeremiad, the editor darkly proclaimed that "a virtual state church has thus arisen" in fundamentalist form, requiring "a new birth of freedom in the churches" for American deliverance.[66] The saving gospel would be Jefferson's moral reflections on Jesus. On April 13, 1947, Unitarians would celebrate at the Jefferson Memorial in Washington his "free religious faith," make hymns from his quotable writings, and read from his selections of Jesus's gospel – though the new birth of freedom could now be found in the old one, revitalized by victory in the war against fascism.[67]

Another religious liberal, Joseph Fort Newton, one of the leading clergymen in the country by 1939, took a more hopeful view even in 1927, assuming that Jefferson had led and won "the long fight for Religious Freedom, and later, in the First Amendment to the national Constitution." Jefferson's "outstanding achievement" was to see that "the absolute separation of Church and State" is "an unmixed blessing to both." For Newton, child of a Baptist family and ordained in its church, which he left for Universalism and, eventually, Episcopalianism, Jefferson pointed the way to "the religion of democracy – that is, the religion which traces and trusts the will of God revealed in the growing, unfolding life of the people."[68]

The most philosophically serious proponent of the religion of democracy was John Dewey. His edition of *The Living Thoughts of Thomas Jefferson* prints Jefferson's statute and many expressions of his religious opinions. Dewey saw that Jefferson's idea of natural equality was neither psychological nor legal: "It was intrinsically moral, as a consequence of the equal *moral* relation all human beings sustain to their Creator; – equality of moral claims and of moral responsibilities."[69] For Dewey, separation between church and state in America reflected the idea that "the state life, the vitality of the social whole, is of more importance than the flourishing of any segment or class." In this light, "the subordination of churches to the state" is the real meaning of separation, and he attacked the released-time programs as divisive because religion should express "the basic unities of life." The Hegelian background of Dewey's thought made him hostile to any "private possessions of spiritual insight and aspiration."[70] Religion would have to work itself out through science and democracy as forms of public life.

Another pragmatist, Horace M. Kallen, was also a modern celebrant

of Jefferson's statute and his "wall of separation between church and state."
In Kallen's view, "the team play of the diverse" is "the ideal of the
American way in religion."[71] Secularism affirms "an ethic of equal liberty and of union as collective guarantee of equal liberty," and in this
light, its basis is "the parity of all creeds, including such as doubt or deny
that it can be known that God is, or what God is."[72] Unfortunately,
Kallen's plea for equality contained a polemic that equated "red authoritarianism of the left" with "black authoritarianism of the right," a sym-
metry between Communism and Catholicism. He pricked with a pun
the Roman Catholic hierarchy in America, since 1895, for allegedly "an-
nuling the divorce of church and state." His only response to a Catholic
theorist's objection that Kallen's reading of the First Amendment " 'can-
onizes liberal Protestant ecclesiology in an extreme form and anathema-
tizes as un-American all dissenters' " was to dispose of it in a footnote as
"a disingenuous special plea" for "special privileges."[73]

This "you're another" mode of reply indicates how highly charged
disputes about church–state relations were coming to be, once the Supreme Court began in 1940 to apply the "religion" clauses of the First
Amendment to the states. Once they did, there would be no consensus
on what Jefferson's wall metaphor really meant. Vashti McCollum's case
was indicative: A Unitarian minister helped her file suit in 1945, assisted
by the American Civil Liberties Union; the Synagogue Council of America,
national (but not the local) Baptists, Seventh-Day Adventists, American
Unitarian Association, and Ethical Culture Society played the role of
amici curiae.[74] The American Humanist Association in 1958 might see
the "wall" as the true philosophy of the Founding Fathers, as would the
General Conference of American Rabbis and the United Synagogue of
America in 1962;[75] but many Protestant groups and Roman Catholic
spokesmen would find alien any ideal of freedom from religion.

It was this freedom that animated such plaintiffs as Vashti McCollum
and Madalyn Murray O'Hair, declared atheists, who protested released-
time programs, prayers, and Bible reading in the public schools and took
comfort in the Supreme Court's use of Jefferson's statute. McCollum, a
director of the American Humanist Association, is the daughter of a crusading, antireligious rationalist. Her own case, on behalf of her atheist
son in 1948, was based on the discrimination he suffered by being shunted
regularly to a separate room during Illinois's released-time program in
the public schools. Like most "scientific humanists," she sees the partic-
ularism of religion as a threat to a common identity, the theme of One
Woman's Flight: "There should be no Jews, no Catholics, no Protestants
in public schools. They're all American children."[76] The suggestion lurks
that some might be more American than others, however, when she has

Paul Blanshard, a crusading polemicist against Catholicism, write a postlude. Polarized with the Catholic bishops, who expressed collective disdain in 1948 for Jefferson's metaphor of "the wall of separation" as "the shibboleth of doctrinaire secularism," Blanshard lamented that "Protestant or Jewish parents hesitate to incur the bitter hostility of their Catholic neighbors," as McCollum had bravely done.[77]

Madalyn Murray O'Hair's campaign for freedom from religion is epitomized in her *Freedom Under Siege: The Impact of Organized Religion on Your Liberty and Your Pocketbook.* It recommends, among others, the books of Blanshard and Frank Swancara.[78] Swancara's *Thomas Jefferson versus Religious Oppression* and *The Separation of Religion and Government,* endorsed by the National Liberal League, print Jefferson's statute, while converting his hero into a deistical skeptic, "practically an atheist," like himself. Swancara had contemporary heroes to celebrate in Justices Black, Frankfurter, and Rutledge because their opinions for the Supreme Court provided a "Magna Carta of Freedom from Religion."[79] Ironically, Swancara cited some of Jefferson's clerical opponents, who saw his statute as "an alliance between civil authority and infidelity," to buttress his own view of Jefferson as a covert atheist who used deferential religious language in his statute to mollify an Assembly of professing Christians.[80] Rambling recitals of legal decisions and antireligious polemic, Swancara's books distort his hero. Jefferson's vigorous anticlericalism did not prevent him from having a Unitarian piety that even included, as he grew older, the hope (as he wrote John Adams) that after death we might "ascend in essence to an ecstatic meeting with the friends we have loved and lost and whom we shall still love and never lose again," and he believed the resurrection would be one that Jesus saw as material.[81]

Justice Frankfurter, in an address on Jefferson given in 1943, called him "an uncommon favorite of history" because his spirit had become separated from laws and particular policies "to establish sentiments of freedom as the enduring habits of a people."[82] On the Court itself, however, four years later, Jefferson's statute enjoyed an extraordinary second life as Justices Rutledge, Black, and Frankfurter read the meaning of the statute into the First Amendment's "religion" clauses. This abridged history gave meaning to what his metaphor of the wall meant, not just in Virginia, but by extension throughout American tradition. Given the development of this judicial ideology, it is not so surprising that an editor of Justice Brennan's judicial opinions could make the egregious error of citing Thomas Jefferson as having "drafted the First Amendment," something he could not have done unless the First Congress had met in Paris.[83]

This judicial version of history – not contested in *Everson v. Board of Education* (1947) – was best elaborated in Justice Rutledge's dissent from Justice Black's particular finding in this case. Jefferson and Madison were, in the Rutledge view, "irrefutable confirmation of the Amendment's sweeping content." Through Madison's work at Philadelphia, according to Rutledge, "all the great instruments of the Virginia struggle for religious liberty thus became warp and woof of our constitutional tradition, not simply by the course of history, but by the common unifying force of Madison's thought and sponsorship."[84] What is most remarkable about this version is that no attention is paid in it to the specific history of Madison's role in the congressional struggle over making the First Amendment, even though the language of the "establishment" clause is not his own. Rutledge simply moved Madison in one mysterious jump from his legislative victory in Virginia to the submission and ratification of the First Amendment.

Rutledge was not the first Court historian to abbreviate the history. Justice Murphy in the early 1940s had cited the preamble to Jefferson's statute about using temporal means in spiritual matters to produce "hypocrisy and meanness" and made a parallel between modern Jehovah's Witnesses and colonial dissidents, whose struggles had culminated in Jefferson's statute, the Northwest Ordinance, and the First Amendment.[85] Justice Black, speaking for the majority in *Everson*, also cited Jefferson's statute and earlier cases to show that the "religion" clauses of the First Amendment have "the same objective and were intended to provide the same protection against governmental intrusion on religious liberty as the Virginia Statute."[86]

Justice Frankfurter characteristically used to lecture the Court on the need for judicial self-restraint and deference to local legislatures, but on cases involving the "establishment" clause, he saw the need for "close judicial scrutiny" because a "great American principle" was at stake. He himself confessed that at an emotional level, something else was also at work: "As one who has no ties with any formal religion, perhaps the feelings that underlie religious forms for me run into intensification of my feelings about American citizenship."[87] He was passionately engaged to counter Black's decision by forming a caucus of "anti-Everson lads."[88]

Black had once joined the Klan, although in repudiating it in 1937, he had condemned "religious discord or antagonism" as a danger to "complete liberty of religious belief."[89] While he had a personally marked and indexed copy of Paul Blanshard's *American Freedom and Catholic Power,*[90] a polemic against the dangers of Catholic power to the "wall of separation," the practical upshot of his *Everson* decision was to sanction New Jersey's provision for reimbursing parents for transportation of Catholic parochial-school students as a matter falling within the state's power over health, safety, and welfare. Black, as the Court's strongest defender of free speech, wholeheartedly agreed with Jefferson's statute that it was "time enough" for government regulation of speech "when principles break out into overt acts against peace and good order."[91]

Despite its blurred history, Rutledge's vision of the Virginia Statute and the First Amendment as twins seemed to Black, Frankfurter, and Douglas what the last called "durable First Amendment philosophy," and the political writer Max Lerner wrote Rutledge to hail his dissent in the *Everson* case as "one of the great opinions of recent years, and it puts you in the company of the choice spirits in the great tradition of the Court."[92] The majority of law journals also endorsed the dissent, although a great scholar of constitutional law, E. S. Corwin, justly observed that the Supreme Court "has the right to make history, as it has often done in the past; but it has no right to *remake* it." Only Justice Stanley Reed on the Court challenged Rutledge's sweeping history, and Reed's narrow version – that the First Amendment means to prohibit only a national church and creed – became the favorite thesis of American Catholic commentators.[93]

Reinhold Niebuhr and John C. Bennett, colleagues at Union Theological Seminary in New York and editors of *Christianity and Crisis,* were critics of the Jeffersonian "wall" on historical and political grounds, hoping to alleviate religious tensions. In *Christians and the State,* Bennett carefully examined the different circumstances generating the statute and the First Amendment, without blurring them together, and concluded that auxiliary aids to parochial schools in matters of health, safety, and welfare could be justified by an American tradition in which "cooperation," rather than "separation," could sometimes be an appropriate term for the relation between churches and the government "where *both* have a stake in such cooperation," leaving an "area of experiment that is on this side of multiple establishment," a margin to permit compromises for the sake of making a civic "concession to a felt injustice that has a substantial basis," such as the Catholic complaint about the burden of paying for both public and parochial schools when conscience requires such a choice.[94]

Many Protestants and Jews did not share Bennett's view because they were committed to a principle of wide separation that both Jefferson and Madison had elaborated in the Virginia struggle. These religious voices therefore tended also to read the Virginians' principle of broad separation into the First Amendment, as "secularists," such as V. T. Thayer, have also done, fearing that auxiliary services will become "an entering wedge" for full support of parochial schools.[95] Between 1951 and 1974, separationists struggled "to break the accommodationist grip on so much of public policy in the country," breaking almost even in the lower courts, but winning six out of ten Supreme Court cases. Most of the plaintiffs were Protestants, nonbelievers, or Jews – in that order.[96]

Baptists are Jefferson's oldest supporters and have kept their eighteenth-century position green into modern times. The pastor of the First Church in Dallas spoke on May 16, 1920, to fifteen thousand people who were gathered in Washington on the east steps of the Capitol to hear about "Baptists and Religious Liberty." His theme was radically individualistic, denying the role of "sponsors, or deputies or proxies" in vital matters of faith: "Let the state and the church, let the institution, however dear, and the person, however near, stand aside, and let the individual soul make its own direct and immediate response to God."[97] Another Texas Baptist, Joseph Martin Dawson, who was much moved to discover that he was a cousin to the family memorialized at Jefferson's University of Virginia by Dawson Row, became the executive director of the Baptist Joint Committee on Public Affairs and a prime mover in creating Protestants and Other Americans United for Separation of Church and State, an active amicus curiae in church–state cases. Dawson opposed the majority conclusion in the *Everson* case, but supported the separationist view of history that it affirmed: "We had lost a battle, but won the war!"[98]

When Harvard President James B. Conant was under attack as a candidate for the ambassadorship to West Germany because he believed that a dual system of schools would be "harmful to our democratic traditions," Dawson testified on his behalf just as vigorously as he testified against President Truman's proposal to make General Mark Clark the ambassador to the Vatican.[99] Dawson gave the prayer at the unveiling in 1953 of the monument that commemorates the alleged meeting between John Leland and James Madison. Like them, Dawson rejected the idea of America being officially a Christian nation: "It was meant, not for Christians alone, but for Jews, Moslems, even unbelievers, also."[100] Himself a Mason, his Protestants and Other Americans United organization was financially launched by a gift from the Scottish Rite Masons, Southern Jurisdiction. They had been especially active during the 1920s in promoting a demand for a Department of Education as protection against the dangers they saw emanating from immigrants, radicals, and Catholics. Masons, like Baptists, polemically urged unity among Protestants to defend "the American school system, political liberty, and religious freedom as Rome is united to destroy them."[101]

Dawson wrote a book to honor the Baptist contribution to American religious freedom. In its perspective, Roger Williams and Thomas Jefferson had "united, inseparably, in a joint bequest of inestimable value to the unlimited future."[102] Dawson claimed Justices Black and Warren for the Baptists and thought that they were "probably mentally conditioned by their religious training," and he linked Justices Clark, Harlan, and Douglas as Presbyterians to their tradition because they were "doubtless disciples of freedom-loving John Witherspoon, one of the Founders."[103] The Catholic Justice William J. Brennan, Jr., was untypical, as were Al Smith and John Kennedy, in taking a Baptist-like position, rather than a Catholic one, on the First Amendment, as the Episcopalian Justice Potter Stewart had done. Dawson might even have added to his genealogy the Baptist father of Justice Rutledge, the fountainhead of separationist judicial history.

Dawson never considered the implications of his genealogy. If Baptist ideas are at the root of the First Amendment, how can it be a nonsectarian neutral rule for other denominations with quite different ideas? The rub would come particularly for Catholics, and it was no accident that the legal counsel for Dawson's Protestants and Other Americans was Paul Blanshard, a persistent and aggressive polemicist against the influence of Catholicism in America. In the Connecticut controversy over legislation to permit towns by referendum to use tax money for busing parochial-school pupils, for example, Blanshard's pamphlet, "The Bus Wedge," was sent to all the state legislators.[104]

The Baptist belief in Jefferson's metaphor of the wall as an interpretation of the First Amendment, the assumption that "the victory over establishment in Virginia reveals the principles behind the religious clause of the First Amendment,"[105] was never consistently applied in a rigorous form, especially by the laity. In national polls taken in 1964 and 1968, only 8 percent of all respondents opposed both prayer in public schools and financial aid to parochial schools. Baptists were more likely than other groups to accept prayer in the public schools.[106]

Presbyterian laity had been supporters of Jefferson's statute, even though at one point Madison had complained to Jefferson that its clergy seemed "as ready to set up an establishment which is to take them in as they were to pull down that which shut them out."[107] Eventually, however, the clerical leadership came to oppose the general assessment bill because of its partiality to the Episcopal Church, and an early-twentieth-century historian of the denomination's contribution took it for granted that Madison had put the principles of Jefferson's statute into the First Amendment. The historian appealed to George Bancroft's *History,* which simply asserts that the principles of Virginia had "triumphed throughout the country."[108]

In its statement of 1963, the United Presbyterian Church lived up to this Jeffersonian heritage by opposing devotional Bible reading and prayer in the public schools, creches on courthouse or school lawns, financial aid to parochial schools, and tax benefits for church business unrelated to religious purposes. Separation is "a first principle of our Constitution," but the recommendations wisely warned against using the debate over it as "a test of loyalty to democratic values." Separation is not to be confused with "a doctrine of Christian theology" or with church history, because "the concept obtains its meaning from the national experience of the United States of America." Jefferson's letter to the Danbury Baptists was the origin of the broad meaning of the First Amendment, "designed to prevent an immense variety of possible interconnections between government and churches," but blurring this position was Justice Douglas's historical point in the *Zorach* case that separation in America is not total.[109]

Senator Sam J. Ervin, Jr., of North Carolina was a modern Presbyterian and Jeffersonian in his view of separation. He found in the statute, "one of the greatest documents ever conceived by man," a key to the First Amendment, which he simply assumed had come from Madison's having "triumphed after much effort" in the conference committee on the amendment because he was "responsible for the phrasing of the First Amendment."[110] Ervin declared: "It is just as sinful and tyrannical now as it was in Thomas Jefferson's day to compel men to pay taxes for the direct or indirect dissemination of religious opinions they disbelieve."[111] He acted on his belief by offering amendments to the Higher Education Facilities Act of 1963 for grants and loans, in an effort to exclude church-controlled colleges and universities. Unsuccessful in the Senate, he joined with Americans for Public Schools and the Baptist Association of Virginia to enter an amicus curiae brief in *Flast* v. *Cohen* (1968) on behalf of federal taxpayers' having standing to sue on the basis of the "religion" clauses of the First Amendment to restrict the taxing and spending powers. Leo Pfeffer, lawyer for the American Jewish Congress, shared his argument time before the Supreme Court with Ervin. Successful in this important plea, Ervin was chosen to lead the fight against the Dirksen amendment's attempt to restore prayer in the public schools because his fellow senators knew that he was also a religious man from the Bible belt; only three southern senators from that region voted against Dirksen's amendment. As an ardent separationist, Ervin was honored in 1973 by fellow members of the Scottish Rite Masons.[112]

Another aspect of Jefferson's thought was alive in Dr. Luther A. Weigle's presidential address, "Religious Liberty," to the Federal Council of Churches of Christ in 1942, because it included the right "to disbelieve in God, to deny religion, and to act, speak, persuade, educate, and affiliate with others in ways appropriate to this disbelief or atheism."[113] Appropriately, Dr. Weigle cited Jefferson's statute. Yet this dean of the Yale Divinity School also wanted the public schools to express "the common religious faith of the American people,"[114] a position that would increasingly divide Protestants from Jews and Catholics, for whom this nineteenth-century solution to the problem would appear archaic and insensitive. In the famous *Schempp* case, in which Unitarians successfully protested against voluntary Bible reading and prayer in the public schools, Dr. Weigle spoke on behalf of the Bible as nonsectarian, although he insisted on both Testaments, particularly the New, which is not part of Jewish Holy Scripture.[115]

In this respect, Jefferson's "wall," oddly enough, was more congenial to an eschatological dissident sect, the Seventh-Day Adventists, who opposed parochial-school aid, released time, and religious ties in the public schools. Greatly influenced by Frank H. Yost's collaboration with Alvin W. Johnson in *Separation of Church and State in the United States,* which saw the meaning of the First Amendment in Jefferson's "wall," "Adventists considered the constitutional issues in the case best stated in the Rutledge dissent."[116] For them, Virginia's "historic struggle" against its Establishment was the key. Yost was a secretary of the Adventists' National Religious Liberty Association, organized in 1889 to oppose efforts of mainline Protestants to enforce Sunday closing laws in their campaign for a Christian America. Adventists, as a dissident minority awaiting the Second Coming, are suspicious of state religions and postmillennial reformers, although they supported Prohibition ardently.

American Jews have been beneficiaries of Jefferson's statute ever since the Jeffersonian Presbyterian Thomas Kennedy won the right of Jews to take public office in Maryland without any religious test. A Jewish historian of religious liberty hailed the statute near the turn of the century as "what we proudly cherish and proclaim as the American principle of absolute religious liberty."[117] As a tiny minority with much influence in middle-class life, the American Jews, one modern scholar has observed, find more emotional charge in church–state issues than in economic liberalism or civil liberties, which are also strong causes for them. Like Jefferson, Jews regard religion as a private matter insofar as they do not want a public identity as Jews, but as American citizens: "The Jew thus fights for separation of church and state in the name of a secular ideal, not a Jewish ideal." Enlightenment liberalism has a special meaning for Jews, whose civic rights are bound up with it. Appropriately, it was the Jewish-dominated Liberal Party in New York that led the campaign against the proposed new constitution of 1967, which would have eliminated the Blaine Amendment's stringent separationism.[118]

Jewish accounts of religious liberty in America are also prone to conflate Jefferson's statute with the First Amendment in order to achieve "that full freedom of religion which the Founding Fathers envisioned." In this foreshortened perspective, the First Amendment is seen as having been extended to the states in the Fourteenth Amendment, which actually did not happen with the "establishment" clause until 1947 in the *Everson* case. It is piety, not history, that leads such historians to say: "After the passage of Jefferson's measure, the long battle had been won not only for Virginia, but for the entire country." From this point of view, Joseph L. Blau identifies "secularism" with "the absolute separation of church and state," which is assumed to be necessary "if freedom of religion is to survive" – as though Virginia's standards had settled the issue. Yet with his right eye, Blau recognizes what he has not seen with his left eye: "the true history of the struggle for religious freedom is to be found after the principle of the wall of separation had been formulated."[119]

The most influential proponent of this Jewish version of religious liberty has been Leo Pfeffer, once active in the American Civil Liberties Union and currently a spokesman for the American Jewish Congress. Out of some fifty adversarial cases between 1951 and 1971 involving the "establishment" clause, Pfeffer was active in twenty of them at the trial stage and in fourteen at the appellate stage.[120] Pfeffer and Blau submitted briefs, arguing that the First Amendment justifies an atheist's refusal to take an oath for a notary license, and using terms that inspired Justice Black in the *Torasco* case to make an unhappy reference to "secular humanism" as a religion, a dubious definition that their opponents have used to charge the Court with having preferentially replaced one religion with another in the schools.[121] Pfeffer has also been a prolific writer on the constitutional history of religious liberty. In *God, Caesar, and the Constitution*, he characteristically saw Jefferson's statute as "the progenitor of the First Amendment's religious clauses," which implicitly reflect Madison's separation of religion and government. Having read Jefferson and Madison into the First Amendment, however, Pfeffer then conceded that it was "not clear and precise or self-defining," but dependent for its meaning on the Court "as a de facto continuing convention expanding or rewriting the Constitution as the need arises."[122]

From the standpoint of American Catholics, the tradition of separation was so entangled with rationalist or liberal Protestant views of the church that it made no place for believers in a hierarchical organization with a corporate idea of society. By the same token, if liberal individualism was alien to the Catholic Church, the traditional Catholic idea of separation as an inferior American expedient, in contrast to the ideal of a Catholic state in which error had no rights, was just as alien – not only to the Virginia Statute, but also to the First Amendment. Even so, American Catholics accepted the American situation, whatever its deviation from papal doctrine. In the 1920s, when many Protestants had no qualms about making Al Smith ineligible for the presidency or imposing Prohibition on a Catholic minority, it was a liberal Catholic, ironically, who pointed out that "to separate church and state one must become coldly analytical as Jefferson was," disconnecting government purposes from the purposes of "numberless religions." In modern political times, "Jeffersonians are no longer at the helm," distinguishing "injuries," as he did, from heresies or sins. Under the umbrella of the state's "police power" and the "general-welfare" clause of the Constitution, government now "bulged out of its revolutionary garments." The result was to confuse the distinction between "the protection of inalienable rights and the closing of Sunday movies."[123]

It was not until the 1940s that a Catholic theorist took on the crucial task of reformulating Catholic thought on separation in the light of the American situation.[124] Father John Courtney Murray, editor of *Theological Studies*, worked out a theory of religious liberty as being "explicitly the product of a twentieth-century insight into the exigencies of the personal and political consciousness." In his view, the point was not to read Pope John XXIII back into Pope Leo XIII, but to see that now "religious pluralism is theologically the human condition." The First Amendment in a lay state has the function to protect and promote religious freedom not because of the "rationalist-individualist conception of man, as if the human person were somehow first an individual and only in the second instance a social being," but because the American Constitution and Bill of Rights have historically altered the traditional state function of public care for religion.[125] In 1963 and 1964, Murray was recognized at the Vatican Council as the American expert on religious freedom, drafting the statement on religious liberty for the second and third sessions of the Second Vatican Council. In the American context, his lucid presence sharply highlighted the extent to which many separationist Protestants simply read their anti-Catholic religious prejudices and Protestant individualism into the First Amendment, thus theologizing it, rather than treating it as a secular legal rule for a lay state that acknowledges the primacy of the citizen, not the believer.

"Theologians of the First Amendment, whether Protestant or secularist," he pointed out, "are accustomed to appeal to history. They stress the importance of ideological factors in the genesis of the American concepts of freedom of religion and separation of church and state. However, these essays in theological history are never convincing." He acknowledged, however, that "the fear of Roger Williams, that the state would corrupt the church, or the fear of Thomas Jefferson, that the church would corrupt the state," converged in their common metaphor of "a wall of separation"; but he wished to read the First Amendment instead in the spirit of the pragmatic lawyer whose prose has "not the ring of a trumpet," but something "more like the dry rustle of a lawyer's sheaf of parchment."[126] From this perspective, it is "an article of peace," and it does not forbid governmental aid to religion "when it represents a legitimate accommodation of the public service to the religious and spiritual needs of the people," as is traditionally recognized in military chaplaincies and tax exemption for religious properties.[127]

Catholic controversialists, however, had their own dogmatists about the First Amendment. James M. O'Neill, challenging the separationism of Blanshard, Dawson, Moehlman, Pfeffer, and Justice Rutledge, confidently declared that no important question in American history could be "more completely and definitely determined than the question as to what *is* the *purpose* of the religious clause of the First Amendment." It is, he asserted, simply to prevent any "monopolistic government favor given by law to *one religious group.*" O'Neill's confident emphasis on cooperation, not separation, ignored the House's rejection of the Senate's narrow form of the "establishment" clause in the debate over the First Amendment, as well as many state restrictions against even indirect aid to religious schools; and he tended to blur Jefferson's position with his own reading of the First Amendment, finding separation of church and state devoid of "specific constitutional meaning," because it does not occur as a phrase in American constitutions. Even so, he thought that parochial schools rightfully deserve not "full public aid," but "some token grant."[128] In 1965, mainline Protestants, including Baptists, joined with Catholics to support a child-benefit rationale for the Elementary and Secondary Education Act, designed to benefit educationally deprived children without reference to separationist strictures, even though the usual alliance would soon yield priority to new debates about civil disobedience, civil religion, and the public role of the churches.[129]

Dispute over Jefferson's "wall" and particular policies about religion and education reflect the tensions of American religious pluralism. Even separating the Virginia Statute from the First Amendment can illustrate that pluralism of perspective. Joseph H. Brady, for a conservative example, added to his historical argument against the Rutledge doctrine a protest against the incorporation of the First Amendment into the Fourteenth because it provides "any atheist or secularist with the tools with which to design and execute sweeping changes in the Christian,

American way of life."[130] A Protestant interpreter of our history, Franklin H. Littel, instead affirms the coming of a "post-Protestant" America, growing out of its traditional "carry-over of many sorts of establishment from the past, some unquestioned even yet and others still being fought out." For him, the separation of the religious and political covenants *is* "the genius of the American experiment – not 'separation of church and state' (a misnomer, for we have *never* had it)."[131] From a secular and humanist perspective, suspicious of parochial education, philosopher Sidney Hook can agree that there never has been a "wall" in America, just some efforts with "a modest success" to build one, because there is "no evidence that the enlightened philosophy of Jefferson and Madison with respect to relations of the state to religion was shared by a majority of their legislative contemporaries," nor can it be assumed that their views " 'came to be incorporated not only in the Federal Constitution but likewise in most of our States,' " as Justice Clark maintained in the *Schempp* case. The Founders "were not legislating for the states when they forbade the establishment of a religion for the nation." Far from erecting "a high and impregnable" wall of separation, "they probably would have swallowed prayer and Bible reading, to which they were prone on many public occasions, without the slightest constitutional embarrassment." Religious neutrality, it follows, should be based not on dubious history, but on the "wisdom of a democratic policy."[132]

Even ardent separationists like the Adventists have recently been tempted by the welfare state's economic benefits to move closer to accepting a "wall," more like the serpentine one on Jefferson's campus, as the Court itself has confusingly come to see it as "a blurred, indistinct and variable barrier depending on all the circumstances of a particular relationship."[133] Still, whatever the limitations or merits of Jefferson's metaphor, the canonization of the Virginia Statute will continue to make good sense for most Jews, Unitarians, agnostics, and atheists insofar as it made civic room for them in a bold and novel conception of full religious freedom. Too simple by half in their usual historical fusing of the First Amendment with the Virginia Statute, their appreciation of Jefferson, nevertheless, rightly perceives that his universal view of religious liberty is jugular for a "post-Protestant" era. In this respect at least, as John Adams memorably remarked on his deathbed, "Thomas Jefferson still survives."

Whether "something there is that doesn't love a wall," or whether, as Frost's poem also says, "good fences make good neighbors," the Supreme Court's decision to read the First Amendment into the Fourteenth with respect to the "religion" clauses fulfills Madison's hopes, which were disappointed in 1789. The word "liberty" in the "due-process" clause of the Fourteenth Amendment has to be given legal content, and inevitably it will have a developing meaning in a changing society. No Court is likely to reverse this tradition of over forty years, in spite of some current conservative urgings to do so. But it is quite another matter for the Court, historians, political scientists, and politicians to base a modern interpretation of the "religion" clause on a specious history that conflates the statute with the First Amendment. Distinguishing them historically does not make the settlement of 1789 static and absolute, any more than conflating them provides a sound basis for a Jeffersonian view of separation between church and state. Historical analysis cannot settle current issues of high policy, but it can clear the air of partisan gerrymandering of the past.

What the statute and the Constitution have in common is the recognition that the political order has secular justifications and entitlements that are not religious matters. In the clarity of their recognition, Jefferson and Madison were more Virginian than American. The delegates to the Constitutional Convention could easily agree (except for those from North Carolina) to forbid any religious tests for federal offices because it was taken for granted that different assumptions prevailed in a diverse union of states, whose religious diversity would be protected by what Madison called the "compound republic," which in some respects was to be taken as a national system and in other respects as a league of independent states. If Jefferson's statute has become rationalized, the reasons lie not in the intentions of the Framers at Philadelphia, but in the increasing religious diversity that immigration has brought to the United States, and the pressure that the ideal of equal rights has exerted on the Supreme Court in a post-Protestant society of believers and unbelievers.

NOTES

1 Merrimon Cuninggim, *Freedom's Holy Light* (New York, 1925), p. 55.
2 A. Arnold Wettstein, "Religionless Religion in the Letters and Papers from Monticello," *Religion in Life* 45 (Summer 1976): 152–9.
3 Quoted in Donovan Fitzpatrick and Saul Saphire, *Navy Maverick: Uriah Phillips Levy* (New York, 1963), p. 128.
4 Thomas Jefferson, *Autobiography*, in *The Life and Selected Writings of Thomas Jefferson*, ed. Adrienne Koch and William Peden (New York, 1944), p. 47.
5 *Selection of Eulogies . . . in Honor of John Adams and Thomas Jefferson* (Hartford, Conn., 1826), p. 134. Only three of nineteen speeches – those by John Tyler, William Wirt, and Henry Potter – make much of the Virginia Statute.
6 Merrill D. Peterson, *The Jefferson Image in the American Mind* (New York, 1962), p. 387.

7   Rembert Gilman Smith, *Politics in a Protestant Church* (Atlanta, 1930), p. 199.

8   *Thomas Jefferson Then and Now, 1743–1943: A National Symposium,* ed. James Waterman Wise (New York, 1943), p. 51.

9   Franklin Hamlin Littel, *From State Church to Pluralism: A Protestant Interpretation of Religion in American History* (Garden City, N.Y., 1962), p. 155.

10 Quoted in Patricia Barrett, *Religious Liberty and the American Presidency: A Study in Church–State Relations* (New York, 1963), p. 21.

11 Ibid., p. 161.

12 Herbert Butterfield, *The Whig Interpretation of History* (New York, 1951).

13 Morton G. White, *The Philosophy of the American Revolution* (New York, 1978), p. 201.

14 Thomas Cooper, *Lectures on the Elements of Political Economy,* 2d ed. (Columbia, S.C., 1830), Appendix 5.

15 An Act for Establishing Religious Freedom, in *Life and Selected Writings of Jefferson,* p. 313.

16 *Reynolds* v. *United States,* 98 U.S. 145 (1878).

17 David Little, "Thomas Jefferson's Religious Views and Their Influence on the Supreme Court's Interpretation of the First Amendment," *Catholic University of America Law Review* 26 (Fall 1974): 72.

18 Sadie Bell, *The Church, the State, and Education in Virginia* (Philadelphia, 1930), p. 156.

19 A. E. Dick Howard, *Commentaries on the Constitution of Virginia* (Charlottesville, Va., 1974), 1:300.

20 *Perry's* Case, 3 Va. 632–4 (1846).

21 *Bacon* Case, 7 Va. 604, 609, 611, 612 (1850).

22 Quoted in Bell, *Church, State, and Education,* p. 519.

23 George W. McDaniel, "The Bible in Its Place," *Plain Talk,* December 19, 1927, pp. 98, 96.

24 Bell, *Church, State, and Education,* pp. 519, 521–2.

25 Quoted in Leland W. Meyer, *The Life and Times of Colonel Richard M. Johnson of Kentucky* (New York, 1932), p. 261.

26 Ibid., pp. 382–3.

27 Anson Phelps Stokes and Leo Pfeffer, *Church and State in the United States,* rev. ed. (New York, 1964), p. 186.

28 E. Milton Altfeld, *The Jew's Struggle for Religious and Civil Liberty in Maryland,* (1924; New York, reprint, 1970), p. 17.

29 Ibid., pp. 67, 70, 75.

30 Stokes and Pfeffer, *Church and State,* pp. 247–8.

31 Jonathan Elliot, ed., *Debates in the Several State Conventions on the Adoption of the Federal Constitution* (Washington, D.C., 1836), 4:199.

32 Jacob Henry, speech in the North Carolina House of Delegates, in *Cornerstones of Religious Freedom in America,* ed. Joseph L. Blau, rev. ed. (New York, 1964), pp. 95–6.

33 *Proceedings and Debates of the Convention of North Carolina* (Raleigh, N.C.,

1836), pp. 240. Weldon N. Edwards also cited Jefferson and criticized making the political issue of slavery a religious one (Ibid., pp. 216–17).

34 Stokes and Pfeffer, *Church and State,* p. 72.

35 Quoted from an address before Congress in Peter Guilday, *The Life and Times of John England, First Bishop of Charleston, 1786–1842* (New York, 1927), 2:59.

36 William G. McLoughlin, *New England Dissent: The Baptists and the Separation of Church and State* (Cambridge, Mass., 1971), 2:619, n. 10, 785, 1008.

37 Ibid., 2:931–3.

38 Ibid., 2:1067, 1229.

39 Ibid., 2:1004.

40 Abraham Bishop, oration delivered in Wallingford (New Haven, Conn., 1801), pp. 17, 13, 41, 68.

41 William McLoughlin, *Isaac Backus and the American Pietistic Tradition* (Boston, 1967), p. 149.

42 Bishop, oration, pp. 27–8.

43 Quoted in Stokes and Pfeffer, *Church and State,* p. 244.

44 Alexis de Tocqueville, *Democracy in America,* ed. J. P. Mayer and Max Lerner, trans. George Lawrence (New York, 1966), 1:270.

45 Stephen Colwell, *The Position of Christianity in the United States in Its Relations with Our Political Institutions . . .* (Philadelphia, 1854), pp. 36, 103.

46 *Donahoe* v. *Richards,* 38 Me. 376, 390 (1854).

47 Ibid., 412.

48 Quoted from Article XI of Jefferson's bill for public education (1811) in Robert M. Healey, *Jefferson on Religion in Public Education* (New Haven, Conn., 1962), p. 208.

49 Robert Michaelsen, *Piety in the Public School* (New York, 1970), pp. 84, 87–8.

50 *Minor* v. *Board of Education,* in Robert G. McCloskey, *The Bible in the Public Schools* (New York, 1967), pp. 9, 94, 147.

51 Ibid., pp. 410–11, 415, 437.

52 Thomas Jefferson to Peter Carr, August 10, 1787, *The Portable Thomas Jefferson,* ed. Merrill D. Peterson (New York, 1975), p. 427; Jefferson to Ezra Stiles, June 25, 1819, *Alexander Hamilton and Thomas Jefferson,* ed. Frederick C. Prescott (New York, 1934), p. 393.

53 Grotius, "A Vindication of Thomas Jefferson against the Charges contained in a Pamphlet entitled 'Serious Consideration,' etc.," *The Monthly Magazine and American Review* 3 (December 1800): 447–52.

54 Robert Baird, *Religion in America,* abridged ed. (New York, 1970), pp. 103, 275.

55 *Hale* v. *Everett,* 53 N.H. 9, 89 (1868).

56 Ibid., 114, 97.

57 Francis E. Abbot, "Nine Demands of Liberalism," cited in Sidney Warren, *American Freethought, 1860–1914* (New York, 1943), p. 163. Presbyterians were the most active endorsers of the Christian movement.

58 Quoted in William Addison Blakely, *American State Papers on Freedom in Religion* (Washington, D.C. 1949), p. 532.

59 Francis May Holland, *Liberty in the Nineteenth Century* (New York, 1899), pp. 233–43.

60 Warren, *American Freethought*, p. 115; C. H. Cramer, *Royal Bob: The Life of Robert G. Ingersoll* (New York, 1952).

61 Carl Zollmann, "The Relation of Church and State," in *Studies in Religious Education*, ed. Philip Henry Lotz (Nashville, Tenn., 1931), pp. 422–3.

62 Jeremiah J. Crowley, *Romanism a Menace to the Nation* (Aurora, Mo., 1912), pp. 623, 625.

63 William Jennings Bryan, "The Statute for Establishing Religious Freedom," in *The Writings of Thomas Jefferson*, ed A. A. Lipscomb (Washington, D.C., 1905), 8: v.

64 Quoted in Ferenc Morton Szasz, *The Divided Mind of Protestant America, 1880–1930* (University, Ala., 1982), p. 121.

65 Bryan, "The Statute," pp. viii–ix.

66 Albert C. Dieffenbach, *Religious Liberty, the Great American Illusion* (New York, 1927), pp. 10, 105, 121.

67 Peterson, *The Jefferson Image*, p. 303.

68 Joseph Fort Newton, "Thomas Jefferson and the Religion of America," *Forum* 78 (December 1927): 891–3, 894.

69 John Dewey, ed., *The Living Thoughts of Thomas Jefferson* (Philadelphia, 1940), p. 24.

70 John Dewey, "Religion and Our Schools," in *Characters and Events*, ed. Joseph Ratner (New York, 1928), 2:508, 514, 516.

71 Horace M. Kallen, *Secularism Is the Will of God: An Essay in the Social Philosophy of Democracy and Religion* (New York, 1954), pp. 26, 217.

72 Ibid., pp. 215, 30.

73 Ibid., pp. 172, 141–2, n. 1.

74 Vashti McCollum, *One Woman's Fight* (Boston, 1961), pp. 164–5.

75 Blau, *Cornerstones of Religious Freedom*, pp. 311, 312–16, 318.

76 McCollum, *One Woman's Fight*, p. 26. See also Lloyd Morain and Mary Morain, *Humanism as the Next Step: An Introduction for Liberal Protestants, Catholics, and Jews* (Boston, 1954), p. 73, in which the child's discovery of his or her religious identity in school is seen as "tragic."

77 McCollum, *One Woman's Fight*, pp. 201, 217.

78 Madalyn Murray O'Hair, *Freedom Under Siege: The Impact of Organized Religion on Your Liberty and Your Pocketbook* (Los Angeles, 1974), p. 108, cites the statute as "true freedom" versus the argument for parochial schools as a parent's free choice.

79 Frank Swancara, *The Separation of Religion and Government* (New York, 1950), pp. 17, 89.

80 Frank Swancara, *Thomas Jefferson versus Religious Oppression* (New York, 1969), p. 123.

81 Jefferson to John Adams, November 13, 1818, and August 15, 1820, *Life and Selected Writings of Jefferson*, pp. 690, 701.

82 Felix Frankfurter, "The Permanence of Jefferson," address of Mr. Justice Felix Frankfurter on the Bicentennial, April 13, 1943 (Washington, D.C., 1943), p. 5.

83 William J. Brennan, Jr., *An Affair with Freedom: A Collection of His Opinions and Speeches*, ed. Stephen J. Friedman (New York, 1967), p. 125.

84 *Everson v. Board of Education*, 330 U.S. 1 (1947), in *Cases on Church and State in the United States*, comp. Mark DeWolfe Howe (Cambridge, Mass., 1952), pp. 90, 92.

85 *West Virginia State Board of Education v. Barnette*, 319 U.S. 624 (1943), and *Jones v. Opelika*, 316 U.S. 584 (1942), cited in Blakely, *American State Papers*, pp. 586, 611.

86 *Everson v. Board of Education*, cited in ibid., p. 800.

87 Quoted in H. N. Hirsch, *The Enigma of Felix Frankfurter* (New York, 1981), pp. 193, 169.

88 Quoted in Gerald T. Dunne, *Hugo Black and the Judicial Revolution* (New York, 1977), p. 267.

89 Quoted from a radio address in Charlotte Williams, *Hugo L. Black: A Study in Judicial Process* (Baltimore, 1950), p. 27.

90 Dunne, *Hugo Black*, p. 269.

91 Hugo L. Black, *A Constitutional Faith* (New York, 1969), p. 53.

92 Quoted in Fowler V. Harper, *Justice Rutledge and the Bright Constellation* (Inidanapolis, 1965), pp. 76, 79.

93 F. William O'Brien, *Justice Reed and the First Amendment: The Religious Clauses* (Washington, D.C., 1958), p. 159.

94 John C. Bennett, *Christians and the State* (New York, 1958), pp. 234, 248–9.

95 V. T. Thayer, *The Attack upon the American Secular School* (Boston, 1951), pp. 90, 78.

96 Frank J. Sorauf, *The Wall of Separation: The Constitutional Politics of Church and State* (Princeton, N.J., 1976), pp. 370, 245, 106.

97 Quoted in Powhatan W. James, *George W. Truett* (Nashville, Tenn., 1939), p. 3.

98 Joseph Martin Dawson, *A Thousand Months to Remember* (Waco, Tex. 1964), p. 194.

99 Ibid., p. 203.

100 Ibid., p. 258.

101 Quoted in Lynn Dumeuil, *Freemasonry and American Culture, 1880–1930* (Princeton, N.J., 1984), pp. 142, 125.

102 Joseph Martin Dawson, *Baptists and the American Republic* (Nashville, Tenn., 1956), p. 42.

103 Dawson, *A Thousand Months*, p. 258.

104 Theodore Powell, *The School Bus Law: A Case Study in Education, Religion, and Politics* (Middletown, Conn., 1960), p. 177.

105 Conrad Henry Moehlman, *The Wall of Separation Between Church and State* (Boston, 1951), p. 75.

106 William C. Adams, "American Public Opinion in the 1960's on Two Church –State Issues," *Journal of Church and State* 17 (Autumn 1975): 485.

107 Letter to James Monroe, April 12, 1785, quoted in Charles F. James, *Documentary History of the Struggle for Religious Liberty in Virginia* (Lynchburg, Va., 1900), p. 130.

108 Thomas Cary Johnson, *Virginia Presbyterianism and Religious Liberty in Colonial and Revolutionary Times* (Richmond, 1907), pp. 118, 120.

109 United Presbyterian Church, *Relations Between Church and State in the United States of America* (Philadelphia, 1963), pp. 19, 25–7.

110 Sam J. Ervin, Jr., *Preserving the Constitution* (Charlottesville, Va., 1984), p. 27. Actually, the phrasing of the clauses reflects Samuel Livermore and Fisher Ames, no friends of Madison's aims (Cushing Strout, *The New Heavens and New Earth: Political Religion in America* [New York, 1974], pp. 95–7).

111 Ervin, *Preserving the Constitution*, p. 230.

112 Ibid., pp. 235, 247, 356.

113 Quoted in M. Searle Bates, *Religious Liberty: An Inquiry* (New York, 1945), pp. 365–6.

114 Quoted in Powell, *School Bus Law*, p. 18.

115 Donald E. Boles, *The Bible, Religion, and the Public Schools*, rev. ed. (New York, 1963), pp. 127–8.

116 Frank H. Yost and Alvin W. Johnson, *Separation of Church and State in the United States* (Minneapolis, 1948), pp. 11–12; Eric Syme, *A History of SDA Church–State Relations in the United States* (Mountain View, Calif., 1973), p. 121.

117 Max J. Kohler, "Phases in the History of Religious Liberty in America, with Special Reference to the Jews," *Publications of the American Jewish Historical Society* 11 (1903): 66.

118 Charles S. Liebman, *The Ambivalent American Jew: Politics, Religion, and Family in American Jewish Life* (Philadelphia, 1973), pp. 152, 158.

119 Blau, *Cornerstones of Religious Freedom*, pp. xiii, 7, 12, 30.

120 Sorauf, *Wall of Separation*, p. 160.

121 See letters to the editor by Blau and Pfeffer, New York Times, June 19, 1985. For a Catholic charge of "establishing" secularism, see Francis Canavan, *Politics, Pluralism and Schools* (New York, 1965), p. 11.

122 Leo Pfeffer, *God, Caesar, and the Constitution* (Boston, 1975), pp. 159, 29, 31.

123 Clarence Manion, "Are Church and State Separate?" *Commonweal*, June 13, 1928, pp. 153–4.

124 For the traditional view, see John A. Ryan, "Comments on the 'Christian Constitution of States,' " in *The State and the Church*, ed. John A. Ryan and Moorhouse F. X. Millar (New York, 1930), pp. 33–39.

125 John Courtney Murray, "The Problem of Religious Freedom," *Theological Studies* 25 (December 1944): 568–9, 574, 535.

126 John Courtney Murray, "Civil Unity and Religious Integrity," in *We Hold These Truths: Catholic Reflections on the American Proposition* (Garden City, N.Y., 1964), pp. 64, 72, 84.
127 John Courtney Murray, "Is It Justice?" in ibid., p. 151.
128 James M. O'Neill, *Catholics in Controversy* (New York, 1954), pp. 23, 18, 202, 209.
129 Dean M. Kelley, "Confronting the Danger of the Moment," in *Church, State, and Public Policy: The New Shape of the Church–State Debate* ed. Joy Mechling (Washington, D.C., 1978), p. 14; "John Coleman's Summary," in ibid., p. 92.
130 Joseph H. Brady, *Confusion Twice Confounded; The First Amendment and the Supreme Court: An Historical Study* (South Orange, N.J., 1954), pp. 122, 132, 173, 143.
131 Littel, *From State Church to Pluralism*, p. 100.
132 Sidney Hook, *Religion in a Free Society* (Lincoln, Neb., 1967), pp. 43–44, 64, 65, 67, 50.
133 *Lemon v. Kurtzman*, 91 U.S. 2105, 2112 (1971); see also Syme, *History of SDA*, p. 146.

9

Religion and Civil Virtue in America: Jefferson's Statute Reconsidered

DAVID LITTLE

In identifying the "larger historical, societal, and constitutional context" of the controversy in the 1770s and 1780s surrounding Jefferson's Statute for Religious Freedom, James Smylie mentions the "debate over the importance of religion as a source of virtue and the need of society for religion and virtue."[1] That was not the only important subject, but it was crucial. As we undertake to reconsider Jefferson's statute two hundred years later, the subject is still crucial.

Along with the other Founding Fathers, Jefferson would surely have agreed with George Mason's dire assessment of the predicament of the young republic:

> Whether our Independence shall prove a Blessing or a Curse must depend upon our own Wisdom and Folly, Virtue or Wickedness; judging of the future from the Past, the Prospect is not promising. Justice and Virtue are the vital Principles of republican Government; but among us, a Depravity of Manners and Morals prevails, to the Destruction of all Confidence between Man & Man.[2]

The central problem raised by this troubled observation concerned the exact role of religious belief and practice in overcoming the "Depravity of Manners and Morals" and inspiring "Justice and Virtue," "the vital Principles of republican Government."

The same concern with the relation of religion and civil virtue is widely expressed today by national leaders and commentators, and the Founding Fathers, including Jefferson, feature prominently in their statements. At a prayer breakfast in Dallas in August 1984, President Ronald Reagan invoked "our forefathers" in supporting his claim that what binds us as a people, what gives us our common purpose, what motivates and mobilizes our sense of civic responsibility is a set of shared religious beliefs and values. "Religion," states the president, "[has] played not only a strong role in our national life, it [has from the beginning] played a positive role. . . . But in the 1960s, this began to change. We began to make great steps toward secularizing our nation and removing religion from its honored place." Or, again, in perhaps his most well-known comment, "The truth is, politics and morality are inseparable, and as morality's foundation is religion, religion and politics are related."

The connection of religion and American civil life has also been affirmed by Secretary of Education William J. Bennett. In an address to the Knights of Columbus delivered in August 1985, Bennett decried "the assault of secularism on religion," as exhibited, he believed, in a number of recent Supreme Court decisions. For Bennett, the need of the American republic for a common religion was consistently underscored in the utterances of the Founding Fathers.

> Was Jefferson wrong when he asserted [in the *Notes on Virginia*[3]] that the liberties of a nation cannot be thought secure "when we have removed their only firm basis – a conviction in the minds of the people that these liberties are of the gift of God"? Has subsequent history made the wisdom of our Founders obsolete? I do not believe so.

Finally, Richard John Neuhaus, in a much-publicized recent book, *The Naked Public Square*, came to the same conclusions. Neuhaus states that "the American experiment . . . is not only derived from religiously grounded belief, it continues to depend upon such belief."[4] Because overzealous secularists are insensitive to this reality, they allow and frequently encourage the stripping bare of our civil order of its natural religious garb, and thus make way for the disintegration of our communal life. They have forgotten, writes Neuhaus, that "the values and virtues that the [American] polity assumed were [from the beginning] chiefly the business of religion."[5]

What shall we make of this Reagan-Bennett-Neuhaus thesis concerning the view of Jefferson? With all his avowed concern for establishing civic virtue in the young republic, did Jefferson believe that shared religious belief was indispensable for achieving that end? The short answer is that he, like other Founders, was deeply ambivalent on the subject and argued at different times in different ways.

On the one side, Reagan, Bennett, and Neuhaus are not entirely wrong. It is easy to collect passages from Jefferson's writings and from the writings of the other Founders similar to the quotation about the liberties of a nation being the gift of God. The impulse to develop an American civil religion came, no doubt, from two sources: the Judaic and Constanti-nian-Christian traditions, in which the idea of a national religion was central; and the classical republican tradition, for which public religion provided the cement for civil unity, and at least part of the basis for civil virtue.

Accordingly, the claims of Professor Thomas E. Buckley, S.J., that Jefferson was committed to a version of "political theology" are certainly partly right.[6] Buckley points out that although as president, Jefferson refrained from mandating public prayer and religious proclamations, he "did not display religious indifference in the executive office."[7] In both inaugural addresses, he emphasized the importance to the nation of "that Infinite Power which rules the destinies of the universe,"[8] of "that Being in whose hands we are, . . . who has covered our infancy with His Providence and our riper years with His wisdom and power."[9] More concretely,

> Jefferson himself – albeit with a caution from Secretary of State Madison, who feared someone might sniff out "a principle, not according with the exemption of Religion from Civil power" – approved a treaty with the Kaskaskia tribe that granted one hundred dollars annually for seven years for "the support of a priest" who would minister to the Indians and teach school. The treaty also committed the government to allocate three hundred dollars to help build the church.[10]

Buckley concludes that while Jefferson is properly remembered as the father of the doctrine of church–state separation,

> he should also be counted as one who helped establish and promote a theological vision of America's place within salvation history. As president, he consolidated elements of a national faith that he had articulated a quarter of a century before. . . . Far from being a twentieth-century–style secularist or advocating a national polity indifferent to religion, Jefferson publicly expressed what became the American faith – a complex of ideas, values, and symbols related to and dependent on a transcendent reality we call God.[11]

Nor were Jefferson's expressions of a "national faith" or his readiness to lend governmental support to certain religious activities, such as "civilizing" the Indians, incidental or exhibited merely for the sake of public relations. In much that he wrote, Jefferson inclined to reduce all that seemed to him important in religion to a basic set of moral and social duties, intuited directly by an inborn "moral sense."[12] These duties, in turn, inspired the "social dispositions" necessary for a harmonious civil order. In other words, what is essential to religion – the basic prohibitions against murder, stealing, plundering, or bearing false witness – is also essential to a healthy society. So understood, "religion" and "civil virtue" are interdependent terms.[13]

Jefferson occasionally supported these views by critical comparative analysis of various religious traditions. He tried to demonstrate that once the common moral denominator of all religions has been isolated, it is then possible to detach and dispense with the respective "dogmas" of the different traditions. Religious dogmas are, declared Jefferson, "totally unconnected with morality."[14] Since dogmas, rather than basic moral outlook, divide and alienate religions from one another, hostility can be overcome only by distilling away the "inferior" portions and finding common agreement around the moral heart of religious belief.

Jefferson devoted considerable attention to trying to show how this is so with respect to Christianity. His expurgated version of the New Testament, *The Life and Morals of Jesus of Nazareth,* was an attempt, as he put it, to "pick out the diamonds from the dunghills" in Christian Scriptures.[15] Stripped of all extranaeous doctrinal accretions, what was left was a "system of morals, . . . which, if filled up in the style and spirit of the rich fragments [Jesus] left us, would be the most perfect and sublime that has ever been taught by man."[16] Thus properly understood, Jesus's moral message epitomizes the heart of all true religion, and thereby provides a firm foundation for civic life.

There is, then, much in Jefferson's writings in favor of a "common sense religion" that is closely connected with the basic moral sense commonly available, as he thought, to human beings in general. Influenced as he was by the Scottish Common Sense School, Jefferson believed that the essentials of morality and religion are directly perceivable by a kind of sixth sense, closer in character to the normal sense than to the operations of reason. Just as the "sense of right and wrong . . . is as much a part of [human] nature as the sense of hearing, seeing, feeling, . . . as much a part of man as his leg or arm . . . ,"[17] so, for Jefferson, the true God is "nature's God," as referred to in the Declaration of Independence, a deity to be discovered by direct sense experience, and not by tortuous theological speculation.

This general attitude reflected a broader philosophical conviction, according to which Jefferson strongly devalued, at times, rational or theoretical reflection, of which theological speculation was, of course, one example. Strongly committed as he was to a sense-intuitionist theory, he frequently disparaged what he called the "uncertain combinations of the head."[18] "The practice of morality being necessary for the well-being of society, our Creator has taken care to impress its precepts indelibly on our hearts that they shall not be effaced by the subtleties of our brain."[19]

Jefferson now and again differentiated sharply between "facts" of a moral or natural-scientific sort, which he believed are securely knowable by direct sensation, and "opinions," which, as the deposits of rational abstraction, he regarded as a less reliable and more readily dispensable source of knowledge. In short, Jefferson's recurring suspicion of theory and of abstract systems of belief is an example of naïve empiricism, a perspective that, of course, accounts for the antitheoretical side of his thought.[20]

Accordingly, Jefferson found it natural to conclude that his "self-evident," nonmetaphysical God, manifested in the "pure and simple unity of the Creator of the universe," would similarly manifest himself to Jefferson's compatriots. Thanks to their membership in the "new order of the ages," Americans needed no longer to be encumbered by Old World superstitions, by the theological "charlatanry of the mind" that was perpetrated by the dominant groups in Europe to keep the ignorant in bondage.

By 1822, indeed, it appeared to Jefferson that the religious views that seemed to him so obvious were in the process of sweeping the land and soon would become "the general religion of the United States."[21] Such a religion would undoubtedly help to strengthen the moral foundations of the American civil order. Jefferson, of course, believed that these religious views would gain broad adherence because of their persuasive power, because of their simple self-evidence. Enforcement of the general religion of the United States was both inappropriate and unnecessary.

There are, then, rather elaborate grounds for arguing that up to a point, Jefferson did believe in some voluntary version of an American civil religion, that he did envision a certain kind of religious foundation for civil unity and virtue in the new American republic. However, it is a serious mistake to infer from these convictions that that was *all* Jefferson believed. On inspection, his commitments were much more complicated. Considered altogether, they were, in fact, not entirely consistent with one another, which leads to the conclusion that he, like many Americans who came after him, had not worked out a thoroughly consistent approach to the tangled question of religion and civil virtue.

Alongside Jefferson's expressions of support for a political or civil religion that is taken to undergird civic duties, there is a very different and competing theme, one more closely associated with the Statute for Religious Freedom, as well as with some things Jefferson had to say in his *Notes on Virginia* and in some of his letters, and with Madison's "Memorial and Remonstrance Against Religious Assessments," which deserves to be considered alongside Jefferson's statute.[22] The central theme in these documents suggests that civil unity and virtue do *not* rest in common religious beliefs and values, but in a shared belief in the natural right of every citizen to the sovereignty of conscience. The foundation of civil unity and virtue is, consequently, not religious, but lies in a relatively independent "civil-moral" sphere that is regarded as distinctly secular.

Whether this second theme ought to be given more weight in the interpretation of Jefferson (and Madison) is no doubt an unanswerable question. It is, however, worth remembering that the Virginia Statute and the "Memorial and Remonstrance" are of special significance, since they have, explicitly and intentionally, a *legislative,* or civil institutional, objective. They are not offhand or purely rhetorical statements, as are some of the frequently quoted utterances by Jefferson and Madison in favor of an American civil religion.

Interestingly enough, both Jefferson's statute and Madison's "Memorial and Remonstrance" were conceived in reaction to a widespread belief at the time that is reminiscent of the claims of Reagan, Bennett, and Neuhaus. As one opponent of the statute put it, "Without religion 'tis hard to say what formulation there should be for any such mutual trust and confidence among men as is necessary for the support of government, the very being of society."[23] Or, in words that have an uncanny contemporary ring to them, Samuel Stanhope Smith, a leading Presbyterian theologian and president of both Hampden-Sydney College and the College of New Jersey (Princeton), put the case for the religious foundations of the republic quite graphically in a sermon entitled "Religion Necessary to National Prosperity."

> Where have we seen a people, under the full influence of religious and moral principle, in the full vigor of frugal and virtuous habits, which has fallen prey to internal disorders, or to foreign domination?
>
> The belief of the principles of religion, and the practice of its duties, under some form which is calculated profoundly to impress the public mind with the sentiment of God, and the righteous government of his Providence over human affairs, is essential to the prosperity of nations.
>
> The necessity of religion to the interests of civil society arises out of the necessity of morals. . . .
>
> But, when the ties of religion are once broken from the mind . . . public sentiment is absorbed in private interest – public virtue is lost. Sensuality insulates every citizen; he has no country but self; all the energies of patriotism are enfeebled.

When a nation has abandoned religion, the firmest basis of civil government is dissolved. Voluptuousness and effeminacy, avarice and prodigality, a restless ambition, dark treacheries, and a universal disregard of justice, which are the natural consequences of a general impiety, accumulate every species of misery on a wretched people, forsaken of God, and lost to virtue.[24]

In fact, it was sentiments like these that lay behind the groundswell in the late 1770s and early 1780s in Virginia for what was called a Bill Concerning Religion, which was placed before the General Assembly in 1779. That bill favored multiple establishment of Protestant denominations, in contrast to the system of single Anglican Establishment. Proponents of the bill did not believe that any injustice would be done to people like "Jews, Mohammadans, Atheists or Deists," whose organizations would not be supported under the distinctly Protestant stipulations enshrined in the measure. It was, after all, the common good of all citizens that was being promoted by establishing Protestant Christianity and, thereby, undergirding public virtue. Therefore, even the members of excluded groups would benefit from such a bill and should, accordingly, pay their fair share.

Although as we have seen, Jefferson did at times link religion and civil virtue in his own way, when it came to composing the Statute for Religious Freedom, he and his ally, Madison, were thoroughly unpersuaded by the sort of arguments that the Reverend Samuel Stanhope Smith and other proponents of the Bill Concerning Religion had put forward. In fact, in opposing those arguments, Jefferson and Madison took the quite radical line that no necessary link exists between religion and civil virtue. However much it may diverge from what they said elsewhere, this proposition is, at bottom, what the statute and the "Memorial and Remonstrance" are all about.[25]

There are two points of importance here, one explicit and one implicit – although no less salient. The first and obvious concern of both documents is that any civil enforcement of religious belief and practice[26] not only does not contribute to the kind of civil virtue necessary for preserving a free government and the blessings of liberty, *but actually works to undermine such virtue.* Jefferson underscored this point several times in the statute. In the preamble, he wrote:

all attempts to influence [the mind] by temporal punishments or burthens, or by civil incapacitations, tend only to beget habits of hypocrisy and meanness. . . .
[Well aware] . . . that therefore the proscribing any citizen as unworthy [of] the public confidence by laying upon him an incapacity of being called to offices of trust and emolument, unless

he profess or renounce this or that religious opinion, is depriving him injuriously of those privileges and advantages to which in common with his fellow-citizens he has a natural right; that it tends only to corrupt the principles of that religion it is meant to encourage, by bribing with a monopoly of worldly honours and emoluments, those who will externally profess and conform to it.

Similarly, Madison wrote in the "Memorial and Remonstrance":

Because experience witnesseth that ecclesiastical establishments, instead of maintaining purity and efficacy of Religion, have had a contrary operation. During almost fifteen centuries has the legal establishment of Christianity been on trial. What have been its fruits? More or less in all places, pride and indolence in the Clergy, ignorance and servility in the laity, in both, superstition, bigotry and persecution.[27]

The objective of comments like these is to turn the tables on the proponents of established religion and on their contention that without a civilly prescribed religion, the nation would go to pieces. For Jefferson and Madison, on the contrary, established religion of any sort contributes to the moral and civil corruption of the social order. It predictably produces "hypocrisy, injustice, intemperence, immoderation, tyranny, and intolerance" – hardly the sort of civic behavior necessary for preserving and edifying a free society.

The second point is that the basis for "the vital Principles of republican Government," the principles of "Justice and Virtue," derive not from a common religion, but from the common respect of all citizens and the common design of all public institutions for protecting the free exercise of diverse religious and even nonreligious and irreligious expression. Such an idea is avowedly the implication of Jefferson and Madison's doctrine of the sovereignty of conscience.

In employing this doctrine, Jefferson and Madison presupposed a crucial distinction of longstanding significance in the Western Christian tradition between what was called the "internal forum," or conscience, and the "external forum," or civil government. Accordingly, human beings were believed to be subject to "two laws" and "two governments" – one an inner law of the spirit, enforced by reason and reflection of the mind and heart; and the other, an outer law, enforced, finally, by the magistrate's sword.

According to this view, the internal forum – the conscience – is primary and thus "sovereign," while the external forum – the civil government – is secondary. Therefore, the essential job of the government is to protect and encourage by all appropriate means the operation of the internal forum – the free exercise of conscience. Jefferson clearly had this distinction in mind when he wrote in the statute: "[I]t is time enough for the rightful purposes of civil government, for its officers to interfere when principles break out into overt acts against peace and good order"; or when he stated in his *Notes on Virginia:* "It does me no injury for my neighbor to say there are twenty gods or no God. It neither picks my pocket or breaks my leg."[28]

As we have said, these thoughts were not original with Jefferson. Moreover, they did not originate with the Enlightenment, as has often mistakenly been claimed, or with John Locke, who employed them, to be sure, or even with Locke's major sources, the independent and left-wing Puritans of the seventeenth century.

The Christian tradition had long differentiated between the two tables of the Decalogue: the first through fourth commandments refer to duties owed directly to God; they are typically the "religious" commandments. The fifth through tenth commandments refer to the duties owed to fellow human beings; they are typically the "moral" commandments.

The second table, or moral commandments, protect against outward bodily injury or arbitrary abuse, such as theft, unlawful killing, and libel, and, as a consequence, may be enforced by outward physical restraint and punishment – that is, the use of legitimate civil coercion. Moreover, the idea that human beings have a relatively well-developed "natural" capacity to know right from wrong when it comes, in general, to these outward moral matters is assumed. Human beings do not, as a rule, need any special enlightenment or inspiration to know that the direct and deliberate infliction of severe bodily pain or injury on another human being simply for the fun of it or for sheer personal gain is wrong and ought to be restrained – forcibly, if necessary. Because human beings are supposed to know such things, they may be held morally responsible or accountable and may be justly punished for violations, merely because they are human beings.

Set apart from the outward moral sphere, according to the tradition on which Jefferson drew, is the inner sphere, the strictly religious sphere. If morality, at bottom, concerns the regulation of physical, or outward, injury by physical, or outward, means, religion concerns the regulation of the inner, or spiritual, life by inner, or spiritual, means. This implies that the life of the spirit may not be regulated by outward, or physical, coercion. It must, that is, be left completely free to follow its own inner laws and dictates. Therefore, a much greater range of personal discretion and determination must be permitted in the "things of the spirit" than in the "things of the body."

Finally, according to this tradition, the very idea of having a con-

science that is understood to be a part of natural human equipment requires that human beings recognize and respect the difference between
the inner and the outer side of human experience. This point is particularly important. The central distinction would lose its force if it were not
possible to assume that human beings are able to differentiate, in some
general way, between the "law of the sword" and the "law of the spirit."

And this assumption obviously underlies the statute and the "Memorial and Remonstrance." Madison, in part borrowing some phrases from
George Mason, enunciated it with special force.

> Because we hold it for a fundamental and undeniable truth, "that
> Religion or the duty which we owe to our Creator and the man-
> ner of discharging it, can be directed only by reason and convic-
> tion, not by force or violence." The Religion then of every man
> must be left to the conviction and conscience of every man; and
> it is the right of every man to exercise it as these may dictate.
> This right is in its nature an unalienable right.[29]

The same assumption is also presupposed in Jefferson's frequent references in the statute to freedom of religion as a "natural right." "[W]e are
free to declare, and do declare, that the rights hereby asserted are of the
natural rights of mankind, and that if any act shall be hereafter passed to
repeal the present, or to narrow its operation, such act will be an infringement of natural right."

We need to emphasize that although Jefferson was not always consistent about the distinction between "religion" and "morality," a distinction that clearly underlies the statute, he did on occasion stand by that
distinction and take its full consequences. In 1814, he wrote to Thomas
Law: "Some have made the love of God the foundation of morality. . . .
[But] if we did a good act merely from the love of God and a belief that
it is pleasing to him, whence arises the morality of the Atheist[s]? . . .
Their virtue must have some other foundation."[30] And it is this idea of a
ground of morality taken as independent of religion that can be understood to lie behind Jefferson's famous statement in the statute: "[Well
aware] that our civil rights have no dependence on our religious opinions . . ."

Incidentally, Jefferson would have to intend this point to stand whether
people agreed with his own particular religious formulations or not. On
the logic of the statute, as we are outlining it, one might or might not
accept Jefferson's theological remarks about "Almighty God" and "the
Holy author of our religion" in the preamble, without altering what one
is still "by nature" morally responsible to know and respect in the civil

sphere. Otherwise, in contradiction to the whole point of the statute, "our civil rights" would, in fact, be dependent on (Jefferson's) particular religious opinions!

It is, then, the free exercise of conscience to espouse and act on now one religious belief, now another, and now none at all, that constitutes the foundation of civil virtue in the Statute for Religious Freedom (and in the "Memorial and Remonstrance"). "Our rulers," wrote Jefferson in *Notes on Virginia,* "can have no authority over such natural rights, only as we have submitted to them. The rights of conscience we never submitted; we could not submit."[31]

It is true that some have wondered whether the statute actually is intended to protect religiously conscientious actions, as well as beliefs. However, the statement "it is time enough for the rightful purposes of civil government, for its officers to interfere when principles break out into overt acts against peace and good order" clearly suggests that as long as actions (as well as beliefs) do not break out against peace and good order, they are fully protected.

If the central burden of Jefferson's statute and Madison's "Memorial and Remonstrance" is that human beings are morally bound by nature to recognize and respect the limits of physical power in favor of the rights of the inner life of "reason and conviction," it follows that that natural moral knowledge itself becomes the foundation of an enduring and just civil order and of the duties and obligations of civic responsibility.

What is, on this line of reasoning, *not* the case is that a just and desirable political order must presuppose a set of commonly held religious beliefs. On the contrary, that is just what it must not do. It must, to be sure, respect the opportunity for serious religious inquiry, reflection, encounter, and exchange. At the same time, such inquiry must include the full and equal opportunity "to say that there are twenty gods or no God," so that beliefs of that kind "shall in no wise diminish, enlarge, or affect . . . civil capacities." Of course, according to this view, a just and desirable political order must make sure that free religious expression and practice do not infringe on the rightful moral restrictions against arbitrary bodily injury and coercive abuse. But beyond those requirements, individual conscience is sovereign.

We ought to stress, in passing, that to understand that the idea of conscience lies behind Jefferson's formulations in the statute and elsewhere is to see that the alleged contradiction in the statute, mentioned by Professor Pocock, between the deleted reference to the involuntariness of opinion and belief, and the statement that God created the mind free, actually makes perfectly good sense.[32] On a traditional understanding of the working of conscience in the Christian tradition, there is no contradiction in saying that conscience compels (or "binds") in its own right and, therefore, that one ought to be free from being compelled or restrained by one's fellows. Analogously, many a good Calvinist Baptist during Jefferson's time saw no problem in arguing for the restraint of civil coercion in religious affairs precisely in order to allow God to exercise his sovereign dominion over conscience. For Jefferson, every bit as much as for the Baptists who supported the statute, the important point was that what counts as compelling evidence for holding a religious belief must be left up to each person's conscientious determination.

We also need to stress that just as the "complexity" of Jefferson's views shows up in his notions concerning religion and civil virtue, so diversity shows up in his thoughts on the religious deliberations of conscience. As we saw earlier, Jefferson from time to time disparaged theoretical reflection; in matters of religion, morals, and science, he frequently looked askance at thinking too much, at putting too much confidence in the "uncertain combinations of the head." Sometimes Jefferson wrote as though religious truths, like moral and scientific truths, were so self-evident, so clear to common sense, as to permit of no reasonable doubt, no deliberative struggle.

In 1787, however, he recommended to his nephew Peter Carr a most rigorous process of conscientious deliberation in religious matters, a process of strenuous rational analysis and criticism, and plainly open, in Jefferson's mind, to the possibility of religious unbelief.

> In the first place, divest yourself of all bias in favor of novelty and singularity of opinion. Indulge them in any other subject rather than that of religion. *It is too important, and the consequences of error may be too serious.* On the other hand, shake off all the fears and servile prejudices, under which weak minds are servilely crouched. Fix reason firmly in her seat, and call to her tribunal every fact, every opinion. Question with boldness even the existence of a God; because, if there be one, he must more approve of the homage of reason, than that of blindfolded fear. . . .
>
> Do not be frightened from this inquiry by any fear of its consequences. If it ends in a belief that there is no God, you will find incitements to virtue in the comfort and pleasantness you feel in its exercise, and the love of others which it will procure you. If you find reason to believe there is a God, a consciousness that you are acting under his eye, and that he approves you, will be a vast additional incitement; if that there be a future state, the hope of a happy existence in that increases the appetite to deserve it; if that Jesus was also a God, you will be comforted by a belief

of his aid and love. In fine, I repeat, you must lay aside all prejudice on both sides. . . . Your own reason is the only oracle
given you by heaven, *and you are answerable, not for the rightness,
but uprightness of the decision.*[33]

The closing comment is, of course, an assertion of the centrality of conscientiousness in religious matters. It is the main point of remarks like
these that the virtues of conscientiousness – of scrupulous honesty, rigorous self-examination of belief, relentless consideration and evaluation
of alternative points of view, and persistent application of principle to
practice – constitute the fundamental ideals of a free society, whatever
may be the particular conclusions in favor of belief or unbelief of a given
individual at a given time.

While Jefferson (and Madison) held religious beliefs influenced by the
Enlightenment, and thus in many ways quite unorthodox with respect
to traditional Christianity, the identification of conscience, together with
the radical social and political implications of its right to freedom, was
strongly connected, as we have hinted, to an important part of the Christian tradition. To be exact, the strongest connection was to the "free-
church" strand of the tradition, represented most characteristically by
Roger Williams, the Puritan founder of the Rhode Island colony in the
1630s.

Well over one hundred years before Jefferson and Madison delivered
their one-two punch on behalf of religious freedom in the 1780s, Williams had worked out the central arguments that appear in the statute
and the "Memorial and Remonstrance." That is, no doubt, one important reason why the Baptists, who in the eighteenth century rediscovered
Williams, found themselves drawn so naturally to support the statute.

Williams's whole position circulated around the basic distinction between the "inner" and the "outer" life, between "religion" and "morality," as those terms were developed and applied by Jefferson and Madison. Williams supported his case from two different, but to his mind
compatible, points of view – a natural-rational perspective and a specifically Christian perspective.

From a rational point of view, Williams thought it self-evident that
there exists an inalterable distinction between the "sword of the spirit"
and the "sword of steel." To try to convince a person of the truth of
something by threatening injury to or by imprisoning that person is simply to be mistaken about how the mind and spirit actually work.[34]

This point, of course, provides the basis for the related distinction that
Williams, like Jefferson and Madison, drew between religion and morality. Against the beliefs of the established church in the Massachusetts Bay

Colony, Williams asserted that to confound "the nature of civil and moral goodness with religious [goodness], is as far from goodness as darkness is from light."[35] Moral and civil virtue among a people do not depend on a set of prescribed and shared religiously based beliefs and values.

> There is a moral virtue, a moral fidelity, ability and honesty, which other men (beside Church-members) are, by good nature and education, by good laws and good examples, nourished and trained up in, so that the civil places need not be monopolized into the hands of Church-members (who sometimes are not fitted for them), and *all others deprived of their natural and civil rights and liberties.*[36]

For Williams, the same conclusions follow from what he regarded as authentic Christian belief. Early Christianity, which was for him and for the free-church tradition valid Christianity, had gone out of its way to set believers apart from the civil order and thereby to establish a "free zone" for intense, personal devotion and responsibility, independent of "external" worldly control and guidance. The implication is that true religious belief is an inward, voluntary matter between an individual and God and that, consequently, all individuals ought to be left free to negotiate their own personal affiliation with God in keeping with the dictates of their own best inner judgment. In short, if one is to be left free by the civil realm to choose a particular religious belief, then it follows that one must also be left free to dissent from that belief and to choose another belief or to choose no religious belief at all.

It is this sort of reasoning that, from a theological point of view, underlies Williams's recurrent emphasis on the difference between the "religious" and the "moral" tables of the Decalogue and therefore adds weight to his argument for a relatively independent and generally available "natural moral law." And it is this sort of reasoning that supports the undeniable conclusion that Williams was, after all, a firm believer in the possibility and desirability of a "secular" civil order.

It would, incidentally, be a mistake to infer from this that religion has nothing to do with morality and the civil order. That was not Williams's view, nor is that the implication of his thought, as his own vigorous involvement in political affairs throughout his life makes clear. He simply believed (as did Jefferson and Madison) that the connections had to be worked out by each individual, alone or in groups, on the basis of independent conscientious consideration. For Williams, that could happen only in a society in which the civil order knew, and knew profoundly, its secular limitations – knew, that is, that religious belief and values are, from a civil point of view, never settled, never closed, but are forever open to what Williams described as continual "chewing and rational weighing." Too much emphasis on an easy compatibility between religion and the civil order would dampen the vitality inherent in Williams's vision. It would corrupt religion and debase the civil order, as Williams believed had happened over and again in the bloody experience of post-Constantinian Christianity. The same vision as well as the same fears found their way into Jefferson's statute and Madison's "Memorial and Remonstrance."

In sum, whatever the differences in philosophical and theological detail, the general themes of Williams's work are remarkably consonant with the general themes of the statute and the "Memorial and Remonstrance." For our purposes, that consonance is particularly strong at the point of arguing to disqualify shared religious belief as one of the constituents of civil virtue in a desirable political order.

I stress the continuity among Williams, Jefferson, and Madison in order to support the claim that the sort of values advanced by Jefferson and Madison, especially in the documents we have been reviewing, are rooted in an important part of the Christian tradition and are not simply the result of "Enlightenment indifferentism," or some such.

But this admission does not, be it noted, strengthen the case of Reagan, Bennett, and Neuhaus. On the contrary, what it proves is that the Christian tradition itself, especially certain parts of it, transmitted doctrines of freedom of conscience, natural rights, and a secular civil order that were later elaborated and institutionalized by the writings and efforts of Jefferson and Madison in the 1780s.

In the light of our discussion, we can now understand that statements like President Reagan's – "as morality's foundation is religion, religion and politics are related" – or Neuhaus's – "the American experiment . . . is not only derived from religiously grounded belief, it continues to depend upon such belief" – cannot confidently be taken to represent all parts of the American tradition.

Clearly, such views are not without some historical foundation. The idea that there is a necessary connection between shared religion and civil virtue is a popular and recurring one in American history. It even has echoes, as we saw, in some of the thinking of Thomas Jefferson and other Founders. Still, there are strong counterthemes as well. Anyone who wishes to go on advocating the Reagan-Bennett-Neuhaus thesis will have to face up to and deal in detail with the considerations put forward by Williams, Jefferson, and Madison designed to challenge the link between a set of shared religious beliefs and civil virtue.

My own view is that the considerations regarding freedom of conscience, natural rights, and a secular civil order, advanced by Williams and by Jefferson and Madison in what must be regarded as some very significant national documents, present formidable obstacles to the views of Reagan, Bennett, and Neuhaus. The distinction between an inner and an outer sphere of experience, between the religious and the moral dimension of life, so essential to a belief in free conscience and religious liberty, strikes me as indispensable to the whole idea of a liberal democratic order.

> Certain it is [writes Leo Pfeffer] that religious liberty is the progenitor of most other civil liberties. Out of the victory in the struggle for freedom of worship as one's conscience dictates came victory in the struggle for freedom to print religious tracts [and, therefore, eventually freedom of the press]. . . . [F]reedom to assemble politically can be traced to the struggle of freedom to assemble religiously.[37]

If Williams, Jefferson, and Madison were correct, this connection is more than a historical accident. It is the result of a profound similarity between the very notion of a natural right – of a fundamental moral right – and the distinction between the inner and the outer life that Williams, Jefferson, and Madison assumed to be so important.

For what is the idea of a fundamental moral right other than that every human being should be entitled to have protection against unwarranted outside interference or manipulation, especially of a coercive or an injurious sort? Such rights are supposed, in large measure, to guarantee and enforce an independent sphere of "personal operations" – an internal forum of conscientious deliberation – that is conducted according to the "laws of mind and spirit," rather than according to the "laws of fist and club."

The constitutional consequence for us as a people has been, of course, the development of a system of legally protected civil rights and liberties that only expands, as Leo Pfeffer suggests, the original right to free religious inquiry, exchange, assembly, and dissemination of ideas into our broader notions of free speech, free assembly, free press, and other freedoms. For Williams, Jefferson, and Madison, all these civil rights and liberties flow, finally, from the elemental right of free conscience, which, as Jefferson eloquently put it, "we have never submitted, we could not submit."

Unless we assume with Williams, Jefferson, and Madison that the distinction between two sets of laws – inner and outer, according to which human beings understand and conduct their lives – is intelligible and tells us something about ourselves, it would be hard to know how we could continue to affirm or embrace the prescriptions of the Statute for Religious Freedom. The very idea of the sovereignty of conscience, as it has developed and as it has become institutionalized in American life, unquestionably presupposes a doctrine of the human person that could not be surrendered without surrendering the entire frame of reference from which our basic civil institutions gain their meaning.

The same is true of the distinction between religion and morality. Unless we believe with Williams, Jefferson, and Madison that whatever the word "morality" may come to mean in different contexts, it refers, at bottom, to a basic and fixed core of virtues and vices, including a fundamental "harm principle," that is readily identifiable regardless of religious belief, it would be impossible to make any sense of our common inclination to identify "secular" limits of permissibility with respect to the "free exercise of religion."

I conclude that there are good reasons for proceeding with the utmost caution, care, and discipline in the face of claims like those of President Reagan, Secretary Bennett, and Richard Neuhaus, that a liberal society can survive only by means of its members affirming and sharing a particular set of religious beliefs and values. That proposition is open to serious question and doubt, according to some salient strands of thought that are deeply embedded in both our civil and our religious past.

NOTES

1 James H. Smylie, "Jefferson's Statute for Religious Freedom: Historical, Societal, and Constitutional Contexts" (Typescript), p. 2.

2 Quoted in ibid., p. 12.

3 Thomas Jefferson, *Notes on the State of Virginia,* in *Life and Selected Writings of Thomas Jefferson,* ed. Adrienne Koch and William Peden (New York: Random House, 1944), pp. 278–9.

4 Richard John Neuhaus, *The Naked Public Square* (Grand Rapids, Mich.: Eerdmans, 1984), p. 95.

5 Ibid., p. 141.

6 Thomas E. Buckley, S.J., "The Political Theology of Thomas Jefferson," included in this volume, pp. 75–107, cited with permission.

7 Ibid., p. 95.

8 Thomas Jefferson, Inaugural Address, March 4, 1801, cited in ibid., p. 94; see also *Life and Selected Writings of Thomas Jefferson,* p. 325.

9 Thomas Jefferson, Second Inaugural Address March 4, 1805, quoted in Buckley, "Political Theology," p. 95; see also *Life and Selected Writings of Thomas Jefferson,* p. 345.

10 Buckley, "Political Theology," p. 96; [Madison to Jefferson], in Message to Congress, October 17, 1803, *A Compilation of All the Treaties Between the United States and the Indian Tribes Now in Force as Laws* (Washington, D.C., 1873), p. 425.

11 Buckley, "Political Theology," p. 96.
12 See David Little, "The Origins of Perplexity: Civil Religion and Moral Belief in the Thought of Thomas Jefferson," in *American Civil Religion*, ed. R. E. Jones and D. G. Jones (New York: Harper & Row, 1974), pp. 199–200.
13 Ibid.
14 Quoted in Daniel Boorstin, *The Lost World of Thomas Jefferson* (Boston: Beacon Press, 1960), p. 162.
15 Thomas Jefferson, *The Life and Morals of Jesus of Nazareth, Extracted Textually from the Gospels of Matthew, Mark, Luke and John* (Boston: Beacon Press, 1951).
16 Thomas Jefferson, "Syllabus of an Estimate of the Merit of the Doctrines of Jesus," in *Life and Selected Writings of Thomas Jefferson*, pp. 568–70.
17 Ibid., pp. 430–1.
18 Ibid., p. 404.
19 Quoted in Charles B. Sanford, *The Religious Life of Thomas Jefferson* (Charlottesville: University of Virginia Press, 1984), p. 51.
20 See, especially, Boorstin, *Lost World of Thomas Jefferson*, pp. 128ff, for an able discussion of this side of Jefferson's thought.
21 Jefferson to James Smith, December 8, 1822, *Life and Selected Writings of Thomas Jefferson*, pp. 703–4.
22 See Thomas E. Buckley, S.J., *Church and State in Revolutionary Virginia, 1776–1787* (Charlottesville: University of Virginia Press, 1977), pp. 130–6.
23 Quoted in ibid, p. 141.
24 Quoted in Fred J. Hood, "Presbyterianism and the New American Nation, 1783–1826: A Case Study in Religion and National Life," (Ph.D. diss., Princeton University, 1968).
25 My interpretation of Jefferson's statute and related thoughts modifies my earlier account of Jefferson's ideas on religion and civil life, as represented, for example, in "The Origins of Perplexity" and in "Thomas Jefferson's Religious Views and Their Influence on the Supreme Court's Interpretation of the First Amendment," *Catholic University Law Review* 26 (Fall 1976): 57–72. While I believe that those earlier essays do represent one side of Jefferson's thought, I now think that there is more complexity than I realized.
26 I believe that the statute covers actions as well as beliefs, as I point out on p. 247.
27 James Madison, "Memorial and Remonstrance," *Papers of James Madison*, ed. Robert A. Rutland and William M. E. Rachal (Chicago: University of Chicago Press, 1973), 8:301.
28 Jefferson, *Notes on Virginia*, in *Life and Selected Writings of Thomas Jefferson*, p. 275.
29 Madison, "Memorial and Remonstrance," in *Papers of James Madison*, 8:299.
30 Jefferson to Thomas Law, June 13, 1814, *Life and Selected Writings of Thomas Jefferson*, p. 637. Emphasis added.
31 Jefferson, *Notes on Virginia*, in ibid., pp. 274–5.
32 See J. G. A. Pocock, "Religious Freedom and the Desacralization of Politics:

From the English Civil Wars to the Virginia Statute," included in this volume, pp. 43–73. While Professor Pocock is clearly correct to emphasize, as he does, how irregular, compared with standard Christian conceptions, was Jefferson's view of religion as "a system of opinions" (p. 60), he overlooks both the complexity of Jefferson's attitude toward religion (including the role of rational deliberation in forming religious beliefs) and the consonance between parts of the Christian tradition and Jefferson's concern with freedom of conscience.

I believe, too, that Professor Pocock oversimplifies the contrast between Jefferson and "that distinguished resident of Lynchburg whom I seriously suggest ought to be with us today . . ." (p. 61). Many a free-church Baptist, who would no doubt report an experience of the immediate "pentecostal action of the Spirit" that Pocock opposes to Jefferson's religious ideas, would also be deeply at odds with the Reverend Falwell's "new Constantianism." With respect to preserving the freedom of the spirit as far as civil restraint is concerned, many free-church Christians, filled as they are with the Spirit, stand closer to Jefferson than to Falwell.

33 Jefferson to Peter Carr, August 10, 1787, *Life and Selected Writings of Thomas Jefferson*, pp. 431–2. Emphasis added.

34 I have developed Williams's views on these matters and have argued for the "complexity" of his influence on Anglo-Saxon theories of religious liberty in "Roger Williams and the Separation of Church and State," in *Religion and the State*, ed. James E. Wood, Jr. (Waco, Tex.: Baylor University Press, 1985), pp. 3–23.

35 Roger Williams, *The Bloody Tenant Yet More Bloody*, in *Complete Writings of Roger Williams* (New York: Russell & Russell, 1964), 4:406.

36 Ibid., 4:365. Emphasis added.

37 Leo Pfeffer, *Liberties of an American: The Supreme Court Speaks* (Boston: Beacon Press, 1956), p. 31.

10

The Priority of Democracy to Philosophy

RICHARD RORTY

Thomas Jefferson set the tone for American liberal politics when he said "it does me no injury for my neighbor to say that there are twenty Gods or no God."[1] His example helped make respectable the idea that politics can be separated from beliefs about matters of ultimate importance – that shared beliefs among citizens on such matters are not essential to a democratic society. Like many other figures of the Enlightenment, Jefferson assumed that a moral faculty common to the typical theist and the typical atheist suffices for civic virtue.

Many Enlightenment intellectuals were willing to go further and say that since religious beliefs turn out to be inessential for political cohesion, they should simply be discarded as mumbo jumbo – perhaps to be replaced (as in twentieth-century totalitarian Marxist states) with some sort of explicitly secular political faith that will form the moral consciousness of the citizen. Jefferson again set the tone when he refused to go that far. He thought it enough to privatize religion, to view it as irrelevant to social order but relevant to, and possibly essential for, individual perfection. Citizens of a Jeffersonian democracy can be as religious or irreligious as they please as long as they are not "fanatical." That is, they must abandon or modify opinions on matters of ultimate importance, the opinions that may hitherto have given sense and point to their lives, if these opinions entail public actions that cannot be justified to most of their fellow citizens.

This Jeffersonian compromise concerning the relation of spiritual perfection to public policy has two sides. Its absolutist side says that every human being, without the benefit of special revelation, has all the beliefs necessary for civic virtue. These beliefs spring from a universal human faculty, conscience – possession of which constitutes the specifically human essence of each human being. This is the faculty that gives the individual human dignity and rights. But there is also a pragmatic side. This side says that when the individual finds in her conscience beliefs that are relevant to public policy but incapable of defense on the basis of beliefs common to her fellow citizens, she must sacrifice her conscience on the altar of public expediency.

The tension between these two sides can be eliminated by a philosophical theory that identifies justifiability to humanity at large with truth. The Enlightenment idea of "reason" embodies such a theory: the theory that there is a relation between the ahistorical essence of the human soul and moral truth that ensures that free and open discussion will produce "one right answer" to moral as well as to scientific questions.[2] Such a theory guarantees that a moral belief that cannot be justified to the mass of mankind is "irrational," and thus is not really a product of our moral faculty at all. Rather, it is a "prejudice," a belief that comes from some other part of the soul than "reason." It does not share in the sanctity of conscience, for it is the product of a sort of pseudoconscience – something whose loss is no sacrifice, but a purgation.

In our century, this rationalist justification of the Enlightenment compromise has been discredited. Contemporary intellectuals have given up the Enlightenment assumption that religion, myth, and tradition can be opposed to something ahistorical, something common to all human beings qua human. Anthropologists and historians of science have blurred the distinction between innate rationality and the products of acculturation. Philosophers such as Heidegger and Gadamer have given us ways of seeing human beings as historical all the way through. Other philosophers, such as Quine and Davidson, have blurred the distinction between permanent truths of reason and temporary truths of fact. Psychoanalysis has blurred the distinction between conscience and the emotions of love, hate, and fear, and thus the distinction between morality and prudence. The result is to erase the picture of the self common to Greek metaphysics, Christian theology, and Enlightenment rationalism: the picture of an ahistorical nature center, the locus of human dignity, surrounded by an adventitious and inessential periphery.

The effect of erasing this picture is to break the link between truth and justifiability. This, in turn, breaks down the bridge bewteen the two sides of the Enlightenment compromise. The effect is to polarize liberal social theory. If we stay on the absolutist side, we shall talk about inalienable "human rights" and about "one right answer" to moral and political dilemmas without trying to back up such talk with a theory of human nature. We shall abandon metaphysical accounts of what a right is while nevertheless insisting that everywhere, in all times and cultures, members of our species have had the same rights. But if we swing to the pragmatist side, and consider talk of "rights" an attempt to enjoy the benefits of metaphysics without assuming the appropriate responsibilities, we shall still need something to distinguish the sort of individual conscience we respect from the sort we condemn as "fanatical." This can only be something relatively local and ethnocentric – the tradition of a particular community, the consensus of a particular culture. According to this view, what counts as rational or as fanatical is relative to the group to which we think it necessary to justify ourselves – to the body of shared belief that determines the reference of the word "we." The Kantian identification with a central transcultural and ahistorical self is thus replaced by a quasi-Hegelian identification with our own community, thought of as a historical product. For pragmatist social theory, the question of whether justifiability to the community with which we identify entails truth is simply irrelevant.

Ronald Dworkin and others who take the notion of ahistorical human "rights" seriously serve as examples of the first, absolutist, pole. John Dewey and, as I shall shortly be arguing, John Rawls serve as examples of the second pole. But there is a third type of social theory – often dubbed "communitarianism" – which is less easy to place. Roughly speaking, the writers tagged with this label are those who reject both the individualistic rationalism of the Enlightenment and the idea of "rights," but, unlike the pragmatists, see this rejection as throwing doubt on the institutions and culture of the surviving democratic states. Such theorists include Robert Bellah, Alasdair MacIntyre, Michael Sandel, Charles Taylor, the early Roberto Unger, and many others. These writers share some measure of agreement with a view found in an extreme form, both in Heidegger and in Horkheimer and Adorno's *Dialectic of Enlightenment*. This is the view that liberal institutions and culture either should not or cannot survive the collapse of the philosophical justification that the Enlightenment provided for them.

There are three strands in communitarianism that need to be disentangled. First, there is the empirical prediction that no society that sets aside the idea of ahistorical moral truth in the insouciant way that Dewey recommended can survive. Horkheimer and Adorno, for example, suspect that you cannot have a moral community in a disenchanted world because toleration leads to pragmatism, and it is not clear how we can prevent "blindly pragmatized thought" from losing "its transcending quality and its relation to truth."[3] They think that pragmatism was the inevitable outcome of Enlightenment rationalism and that pragmatism is not a strong enough philosophy to make moral community possible.[4] Second, there is the moral judgment that the sort of human being who is produced by liberal institutions and culture is undesirable. MacIntyre, for example, thinks that our culture – a culture he says is dominated by "the Rich Aesthete, the Manager, and the Therapist" – is a *reductio ad absurdum* both of the philosophical views that helped create it and of those now invoked in its defense. Third, there is the claim that political institutions "presuppose" a doctrine about the nature of human beings and that such a doctrine must, unlike Enlightenment rationalism, make clear the essentially historical character of the self. So we find writers like Taylor and Sandel saying that we need a theory of the self that incorporates Hegel's and Heidegger's sense of the self's historicity.

The first claim is a straightforward empirical, sociological-historical one about the sort of glue that is required to hold a community together. The second is a straightforward moral judgment that the advantages of contemporary liberal democracy are outweighed by the disadvantages, by the ignoble and sordid character of the culture and the individual human beings that it produces. The third claim, however, is the most puzzling and complex. I shall concentrate on this third, most puzzling, claim, although toward the end I shall return briefly to the first two.

To evaluate this third claim, we need to ask two questions. The first is whether there is any sense in which liberal democracy "needs" philosophical justification at all. Those who share Dewey's pragmatism will say that although it may need philosophical articulation, it does not need philosophical backup. On this view, the philosopher of liberal democracy may wish to develop a theory of the human self that comports with the institutions he or she admires. But such a philosopher is not thereby justifying these institutions by reference to more fundamental premises, but the reverse: He or she is putting politics first and tailoring a philosophy to suit. Communitarians, by contrast, often speak as though political institutions were no better than their philosophical foundations.

The second question is one that we can ask even if we put the opposition between justification and articulation to one side. It is the question of whether a conception of the self that, as Taylor says, makes "the community constitutive of the individual"[5] does in fact comport better with liberal democracy than does the Enlightenment conception of the self. Taylor summarizes the latter as "an ideal of disengagement" that defines a "typically modern notion" of human dignity: "the ability to act on one's own, without outside interference or subordination to outside authority." On Taylor's view, as on Heidegger's, these Enlightenment notions are closely linked with characteristically modern ideas of "efficacy, power, unperturbability."[6] They are also closely linked with the contemporary form of the doctrine of the sacredness of the individual conscience – Dworkin's claim that appeals to rights "trump" all other appeals. Taylor, like Heidegger, would like to substitute a less individualistic conception of what it is to be properly human – one that makes less of autonomy and more of interdependence.

I can preview what is to come by saying that I shall answer "no" to the first question about the communitarians' third claim and "yes" to the second. I shall be arguing that Rawls, following up on Dewey, shows us how liberal democracy can get along without philosophical presuppositions. He has thus shown us how we can disregard the third communitarian claim. But I shall also argue that communitarians like Taylor are right in saying that a conception of the self that makes the community constitutive of the self does comport well with liberal democracy. That is, if we *want* to flesh out our self-image as citizens of such a democracy with a philosophical view of the self, Taylor gives us pretty much the right view. But this sort of philosophical fleshing-out does not have the importance that writers like Horkheimer and Adorno, or Heidegger, have attributed to it.

Without further preface, I turn now to Rawls. I shall begin by pointing out that both in *A Theory of Justice* and subsequently, he has linked his own position to the Jeffersonian ideal of religious toleration. In an article called "Justice as Fairness: Political not Metaphysical," he says that he is "going to apply the principle of toleration to philosophy itself," and goes on to say:

> The essential point is this: as a practical political matter no general moral conception can provide the basis for a public conception of justice in a modern democratic society. The social and historical conditions of such a society have their origins in the Wars of Religion following the Reformation and the development of the principle of toleration, and in the growth of constitutional government and the institutions of large market economies. These conditions profoundly affect the requirements of a workable conception of political justice: such a conception must allow for a diversity of doctrines and the plurality of conflicting, and indeed incommensurable conceptions of the good affirmed by the members of existing democratic societies.[7]

We can think of Rawls as saying that just as the principle of religious toleration and the social thought of the Enlightenment proposed to bracket many standard theological topics when deliberating about public policy and constructing political institutions, so we need to bracket many standard topics of philosophical inquiry. For purposes of social theory, we can put aside such topics as an ahistorical human nature, the nature of selfhood, the motive of moral behavior, and the meaning of human life.

We treat these as irrelevant to politics as Jefferson thought questions about the Trinity and about transubstantiation.

Insofar as he adopts this stance, Rawls disarms many of the criticisms that, in the wake of Horkheimer and Adorno, have been directed at American liberalism. Rawls can agree that Jefferson and his circle shared a lot of dubious philosophical views, views that we might now wish to reject. He can even agree with Horkheimer and Adorno, as Dewey would have, that these views contained the seeds of their own destruction. But he thinks that the remedy may be not to formulate better philosophical views on the same topics, but (for purposes of political theory) benignly to neglect these topics. As he says:

> since justice as fairness is intended as a political conception of justice for a democratic society, it tries to draw solely upon basic intuitive ideas that are embedded in the political institutions of a democratic society and the public traditions of their interpretation. Justice as fairness is a political conception in part because it starts from within a certain political tradition. We hope that this political conception of justice may be at least supported by what we may call "overlapping consensus," that is, by a consensus that includes all the opposing philosophical and religious doctrines likely to persist and gain adherents in a more or less just constitutional democratic society.[8]

Rawls thinks that "philosophy as the search for truth about an independent metaphysical and moral order cannot . . . provide a workable and shared basis for a political conception of justice in a democratic society."[9] So he suggests that we confine ourselves to collecting, "such settled convictions as the belief in religious toleration and the rejection of slavery" and then "try to organize the basic intuitive ideas and principles implicit in these convictions into a coherent conception of justice."[10]

This attitude is thoroughly historicist and antiuniversalist.[11] Rawls can wholeheartedly agree with Hegel and Dewey against Kant and can say that the Enlightenment attempt to free oneself from tradition and history, to appeal to "Nature" or "Reason," was self-deceptive.[12] He can see such an appeal as a misguided attempt to make philosophy do what theology failed to do. Rawls's effort to, in his words, "stay on the surface, philosophically speaking" can be seen as taking Jefferson's avoidance of theology one step further.

On the Deweyan view I am attributing to Rawls, no such discipline as "philosophical anthropology" is required as a preface to politics, but only history and sociology. Further, it is misleading to think of his view as Dworkin does: as "rights-based" as opposed to "goal-based." For the notion of "basis" is not in point. It is not that we know, on antecedent philosophical grounds, that it is of the essence of human beings to have rights, and then proceed to ask how a society might preserve and protect these rights. On the question of priority, as on the question of the relativity of justice to historical situations, Rawls is closer to Walzer than to Dworkin.[13] Since Rawls does not believe that for purposes of political theory, we need think of ourselves as having an essence that precedes and antedates history, he would not agree with Sandel that for these purposes, we need have an account of "the nature of the moral subject," which is "in some sense necessary, non-contingent and prior to any particular experience."[14] Some of our ancestors may have required such an account, just as others of our ancestors required such an account, of their relation to their putative Creator. But *we* – we heirs of the Enlightenment for whom justice has become the first virtue – need neither. As citizens and as social theorists, we can be as indifferent to philosophical disagreements about the nature of the self as Jefferson was to theological differences about the nature of God.

This last point suggests a way of sharpening up my claim that Rawls's advocacy of philosophical toleration is a plausible extension of Jefferson's advocacy of religious toleration. Both "religion" and "philosophy" are vague umbrella terms, and both are subject to persuasive redefinition. When these terms are broadly enough defined, everybody, even atheists, will be said to have a religious faith (in the Tillichian sense of a "symbol of ultimate concern"). Everybody, even those who shun metaphysics and epistemology, will be said to have "philosophical presuppositions."[15] But for purposes of interpreting Jefferson and Rawls, we must use narrower definitions. Let "religion" mean, for Jefferson's purposes, disputes about the nature and the true name of God – and even about his existence.[16] Let "philosophy" mean, for Rawls's purposes, disputes about the nature of human beings and even about whether there is such a thing as "human nature."[17] Using these definitions, we can say that Rawls wants views about man's nature and purpose to be detached from politics. As he says, he wants his conception of justice to "avoid . . . claims about the essential nature and identity of persons."[18] So presumably, he wants questions about the point of human existence, or the meaning of human life, to be reserved for private life. A liberal democracy will not only exempt opinions on such matters from legal coercion, but also aim at disengaging discussions of such questions from discussions of social policy. Yet it will use force against the individual conscience, just insofar as conscience leads individuals to act so as to threaten democratic institutions. Unlike Jefferson's, Rawls's argument against fanaticism is not that it threatens truth about the characteristics of an antecedent meta-physical and moral order by threatening free discussion, but *simply* that it threatens freedom, and thus threatens justice. Truth about the exis-tence or nature of that order drops out.

The definition of "philosophy" I have just suggested is not as artificial and ad hoc as it may appear. Intellectual historians commonly treat "the nature of the human subject" as the topic that gradually replaced "God" as European culture secularized itself. This has been the central topic of metaphysics and epistemology from the seventeenth century to the pres-ent, and, for better or worse, metaphysics and epistemology have been taken to be the "core" of philosophy.[19] Insofar as one thinks that political conclusions require extrapolitical grounding – that is, insofar as one thinks Rawls's method of reflective equilibrium[20] is not good enough – one will want an account of the "authority" of those general principles.

If one feels a need for such legitimation, one will want either a reli-gious or a philosophical preface to politics.[21] One will be likely to share Horkheimer and Adorno's fear that pragmatism is not strong enough to hold a free society together. But Rawls echoes Dewey in suggesting that insofar as justice becomes the first virtue of a society, the need for such legitimation may gradually cease to be felt. Such a society will become accustomed to the thought that social policy needs no more authority than successful accommodation among individuals, individuals who find themselves heir to the same historical traditions and faced with the same problems. It will be a society that encourages the "end of ideology," that takes reflective equilibrium as the only method needed in discussing so-cial policy. When such a society deliberates, when it collects the princi-ples and intuitions to be brought into equilibrium, it will tend to discard those drawn from philosophical accounts of the self or of rationality. For such a society will view such accounts not as the foundations of political institutions, but as, at worst, philosophical mumbo jumbo, or, at best, relevant to private searches for perfection, but not to social policy.[22]

In order to spell out the contrast between Rawls's attempt to "stay on the surface, philosophically speaking" and the traditional at-tempt to dig down to "philosophical foundations of democracy," I shall turn briefly to Sandel's *Liberalism and the Limits of Justice*. This clear and forceful book provides very elegant and cogent arguments against the attempt to use a certain conception of the self, a certain metaphysical view of what human beings are like, to legitimize liberal politics. Sandel attributes this attempt to Rawls. Many people, including myself, initially took Rawls's *Theory of Justice* to be such an attempt. We read it as a continuation of the Enlightenment attempt to ground our moral intuitions on a conception of human nature (and, more specifically, as a neo-Kantian attempt to ground them on the notion of "rationality"). However, Rawls's writings subsequent to *A Theory of Justice* have helped us realize that we were misinterpreting his book, that we had overemphasized the Kantian and underemphasized the Hegelian and Deweyan elements. These writings make more explicit than did his book Rawls's metaphilosophical doctrine that "what justifies a conception of justice is not its being true to an order antecedent to and given to us, but its congruence with our deeper understanding of ourselves and our aspirations, and our realization that, *given our history and the traditions embedded in our public life,* it is the most reasonable doctrine *for us.*"[23]

When reread in the light of such passages, *A Theory of Justice* no longer seems committed to a philosophical account of the human self, but only to a historico-sociological description of the way we live now.

Sandel sees Rawls as offering us "deontology with a Humean face" – that is, a Kantian universalistic approach to social thought without the handicap of Kant's idealistic metaphysics. He thinks that this will not work, that a social theory of the sort that Rawls wants requires us to postulate the sort of self that Descartes and Kant invented to replace God – one that can be distinguished from the Kantian "empirical self" as having various "contingent desires, wants and ends," rather than being a mere concatenation of beliefs and desires. Since such a concatenation – what Sandel calls a "radically situated subject"[24] – is all that Hume offers us, Sandel thinks that Rawls's project is doomed.[25] On Sandel's account, Rawls's doctrine that "justice is the first virtue of social institutions" requires backup from the metaphysical claim that "teleology to the contrary, what is most essential to our personhood is not the ends we choose but our capacity to choose them. And this capacity is located in a self which must be prior to the ends it chooses."[26]

But reading *A Theory of Justice* as political rather than metaphysical, one can see that when Rawls says that "the self is prior to the ends which are affirmed by it,"[27] he need not mean that there is an entity called "the self" that is something distinct from the web of beliefs and desires that that self "has." When he says that "we should not attempt to give form to our life by first looking to the good independently defined,"[28] he is not basing this "should" on a claim about the nature of the self. "Should" is not to be glossed by "because of the intrinsic nature of morality"[29] or "because a capacity for choice is the essence of personhood," but by something like "because *we* – we modern inheritors of the traditions of religious tolerance and constitutional government – put liberty ahead of perfection."

This willingness to invoke what *we* do raises, as I have said, the specters of ethnocentrism and of relativism. Because Sandel is convinced that Rawls shares Kant's fear of these specters, he is convinced that Rawls is looking for an " 'Archimedean point' from which to assess the basic structure of society" – a "standpoint neither compromised by its implication in the world nor dissociated and so disqualified by detachment."[30] It is just this idea that a standpoint can be "compromised by its implication in the world" that Rawls rejects in his recent writings. Philosophically inclined communitarians like Sandel are unable to envisage a middle ground between relativism and a "theory of the moral subject" – a theory that is not about, for example, religious tolerance and large market economies, but about human beings as such, viewed ahistorically. Rawls is trying to stake out just such a middle ground.[31] When he speaks of an "Archimedean point," he does not mean a point outside history, but simply the kind of settled social habits that allow much latitude for further choices. He says, for example,

> The upshot of these considerations is that justice as fairness is not at the mercy, so to speak, of existing wants and interests. It sets up an Archimedean point for assessing the social system without invoking a priori considerations. The long range aim of society is settled in its main lines irrespective of the particular desires and needs of its present members. . . . There is no place for the question whether men's desires to play the role of superior of inferior might not be so great that autocratic institutions should be accepted, or whether men's perception of the religious practices of others might not be so upsetting that liberty of conscience should not be allowed.[32]

To say that there is no place for the questions that Nietzsche or Loyola would raise is not to say that the views of either are unintelligible (in the sense of "logically incoherent" or "conceptually confused"). Nor is it to say that they are based on an incorrect theory of the self. Nor is it *just* to say that our preferences conflict with theirs.[33] It is to say that the conflict between these men and us is so great that "preferences" is the wrong word. It is appropriate to speak of gustatory or sexual preferences, for these do not matter to anybody but yourself and your immediate circle. But it is misleading to speak of a "preference" for liberal democracy.

Rather, we heirs of the Enlightenment think of enemies of liberal democracy like Nietzsche or Loyola as, to use Rawls's word, "mad." We do so because there is no way to see them as fellow citizens of our constitutional democracy, people whose life plans might, given ingenuity and good will, be fitted in with those of other citizens. They are not crazy because they have mistaken the ahistorical nature of human beings.

They are crazy because the limits of sanity are set by what *we* can take seriously. This, in turn, is determined by our upbringing, our historical situation.[34]

If this short way of dealing with Nietzsche and Loyola seems shockingly ethnocentric, it is because the philosophical tradition has accustomed us to the idea that anybody who is willing to listen to reason – to hear out all the arguments – can be brought around to the truth. This view, which Kierkegaard called "Socratism" and contrasted with the claim that our point of departure may be simply a historical event, is intertwined with the idea that the human self has a center (a divine spark, or a truth-tracking faculty called "reason") and that argumentation will, given time and patience, penetrate to this center. For Rawls's purposes, we do not need this picture. We are free to see the self as centerless, as a historical contingency all the way through. Rawls neither needs nor wants to defend the priority of the right to the good as Kant defended it, by invoking a theory of the self that makes it more than an "empirical self," more than a "radically situated subject." He presumably thinks of Kant as, although largely right about the nature of justice, largely wrong about the nature and function of philosophy.

More specifically, he can reject Sandel's Kantian claim that there is a "distance between subject and situation which is necessary to any measure of detachment, is essential to the ineliminably *possessive* aspect of any coherent conception of the self."[35] Sandel defines this aspect by saying, "I can never fully be constituted by my attributes . . . there must always be some attributes I *have* rather than am." On the interpretation of Rawls I am offering, we do not need a categorical distinction between the self and its situation. We can dismiss the distinction between an attribute of the self and a constituent of the self, between the self's accidents and its essence, as "merely" metaphysical.[36] If we are inclined to philosophize, we shall want the vocabulary offered by Dewey, Heidegger, Davidson, and Derrida, with its built-in cautions against metaphysics, rather than that offered by Descartes, Hume, and Kant.[37] For if we use the former vocabulary, we shall be able to see moral progress as a history of making rather than finding, of poetic achievement by "radically situated" individuals and communities, rather than as the gradual unveiling, through the use of "reason," of "principles" or "rights" or "values."

Sandel's claim that "the concept of a subject given prior to and independent of its objects offers a foundation for the moral law that . . . powerfully completes the deontological vision" is true enough. But to suggest such a powerful completion to Rawls is to offer him a poisoned gift. It is like offering Jefferson an argument for religious tolerance based on exegesis of the Christian Scriptures.[38] Rejecting the assumption that the moral law needs a "foundation" is just what distinguishes Rawls from Jefferson. It is just this that permits him to be a Deweyan naturalist who needs neither the distinction between will and intellect nor the distinction between the self's constituents and its attributes. He does not *want* a "complete deontological vision," one that would explain *why* we should give justice priority over our conception of the good. He is filling out the consequences of the claim that it is prior, not its presuppositions.[39] Rawls is not interested in conditions for the identity of the self, but only in conditions for citizenship in a liberal society.

Suppose one grants that Rawls is not attempting a transcendental deduction of American liberalism or supplying philosophical foundations for democratic institutions, but simply trying to systematize the principles and intuitions typical of American liberals. Still, it may seem that the important questions raised by the critics of liberalism have been begged. Consider the claim that we liberals can simply dismiss Neitzsche and Loyola as crazy. One imagines these two rejoining that they are quite aware that their views unfit them for citizenship in a constitutional democracy and that the typical inhabitant of such a democracy would regard them as crazy. But they take these facts as further counts against constitutional democracy. They think that the kind of person created by such a democracy is not what a human being should be.

In finding a dialectical stance to adopt toward Nietzsche or Loyola, we liberal democrats are faced with a dilemma. To refuse to argue about what human beings should be like seems to show a contempt for the spirit of accommodation and tolerance, which is essential to democracy. But it is not clear how to argue for the claim that human beings ought to be liberals rather than fanatics without being driven back on a theory of human nature, on philosophy. I think that we must grasp the first horn. We have to insist that not every argument need to be met in the terms in which it is presented. Accommodation and tolerance must stop short of a willingness to work within any vocabulary that one's interlocutor wishes to use, to take seriously any topic that he puts forward for discussion. To take this view is of a piece with dropping the idea that a single moral vocabulary and a single set of moral beliefs are appropriate for every human community everywhere, and to grant that historical developments may lead us to simply *drop* questions and the vocabulary in which those questions are posed.

Just as Jefferson refused to let the Christian Scriptures set the terms in which to discuss alternative political institutions, so we either must refuse to answer the question "What sort of human being are you hoping to produce?" or, at least, must not let our answer to this question dictate our answer to the question "Is justice primary?"[40] It is no more evident that democratic institutions are to be measured by the sort of person they create than that they are to be measured against divine commands. It is not evident that they are to be measured by anything more specific than the moral intuitions of the particular historical community that has created those institutions. The idea that moral and political controversies should always be "brought back to first principles" is reasonable if it means merely that we should seek common ground in the hope of attaining agreement. But it is misleading if it is taken as the claim that there is a natural order of premises from which moral and political conclusions are to be inferred – not to mention the claim that some particular interlocutor (for example, Neitzsche or Loyola) has already discerned that order. The liberal response to the communitarians' second claim must be, therefore, that even if the typical character types of liberal democracies *are* bland, calculating, petty, and unheroic, the prevalence of such people may be a reasonable price to pay for political freedom.

The spirit of accommodation and tolerance certainly suggests that we should seek common ground with Neitzsche and Loyola, but there is no predicting where, or whether, such common ground will be found. The philosophical tradition has assumed that there are certain topics (for example, "What is God's will?" "What is man?" "What rights are intrinsic to the species?") on which everyone has, or should have, views and that these topics are prior in the order of justification to those at issue in political deliberation. This assumption goes along with the assumption that human beings have a natural center that philosophical inquiry can locate and illuminate. By contrast, the view that human beings are centerless networks of beliefs and desires and that their vocabularies and opinions are determined by historical circumstance allows for the possibility that there may not be enough overlap between two such networks to make possible agreement about political topics, or even profitable discussion of such topics.[41] We do not conclude that Nietzsche and Loyola are crazy because they hold unusual views on certain "fundamental" topics; rather, we conclude this only after extensive attempts at an exchange of political views have made us realize that we are not going to get anywhere.[42]

One can sum up this way of grasping the first horn of the dilemma I sketched earlier by saying that Rawls puts democratic politics first, and philosophy second. He retains the Socratic commitment to free exchange of views without the Platonic commitment to the possibility of universal agreement – a possibility underwritten by epistemological doctrines like Plato's Theory of Recollection[43] or Kant's theory of the relation between pure and empirical concepts. He disengages the question of whether we ought to be tolerant and Socratic from the question of whether this strategy will lead to truth. He is content that it should lead to whatever intersubjective reflective equilibrium may be obtainable, given the contingent make-up of the subjects in question. Truth, viewed in the Platonic way, as the grasp of what Rawls calls "an order antecedent to and given to us," is simply not relevant to democratic politics. So philosophy, as the explanation of the relation between such an order and human nature, is not relevant either. When the two come into conflict, democracy takes precedence over philosophy.

This conclusion may seem liable to an obvious objection. It may seem that I have been rejecting a concern with philosophical theories about the nature of men and women on the basis of just such a theory. But notice that although I have frequently said that Rawls *can be content* with a notion of the human self as a centerless web of historically conditioned beliefs and desires, I have not suggested that he *needs* such a theory. Such a theory does not offer liberal social theory a *basis*. If one *wants* a model of the human self, then this picture of a centerless web will fill the need. But for purposes of liberal social theory, one can do without such a model. One can get along with common sense and social science, areas of discourse in which the term "the self" rarely occurs.

If, however, one has a taste for philosophy – if one's vocation, one's private pursuit of perfection, entails constructing models of such entities as "the self," "knowledge," "language," "nature," "God," or "history," and then tinkering with them until they mesh with one another – one *will* want a picture of the self. Since my own vocation is of this sort, and the moral identity around which I wish to build such models is that of a citizen of a liberal democratic state, I commend the picture of the self as a centerless and contingent web to those with similar tastes and similar identities. But I would not commend it to those with a similar vocation but dissimilar moral identities – identities built, for example, around the love of God, Nietzschean self-overcoming, the accurate representation of reality as it is in itself, the quest for "one right answer" to moral questions, or the natural superiority of a given character type. Such persons need a more complex and interesting, less simple-minded model of the self – one that meshes in complex ways with complex models of such things as "nature" or "history." Nevertheless, such persons may, for pragmatic rather than moral reasons, be loyal citizens of a liberal democratic society. They may despise most of their fellow citizens, but be prepared to grant that the prevalence of such despicable character types is a lesser evil than the loss of political freedom. They may be ruefully grateful that their private senses of moral identity and the models of the human self that they develop to articulate this sense – the ways in which they deal with their aloneness – are not the concern of such a state. Rawls and Dewey have shown how the liberal state can ignore the difference between the moral identities of Glaucon and of Thrasymachus, just as it ignores the difference between the religious identities of a Catholic archbishop and a Mormon prophet.

There is, however, a flavor of paradox in this attitude toward theories of the self. One might be inclined to say that I have evaded one sort of self-referential paradox only by falling into another sort. For I am presupposing that one is at liberty to rig up a model of the self to suit oneself, to tailor it to one's politics, one's religion, or one's private sense of the meaning of one's life. This, in turn, presupposes that there is no "objective truth" about what the human self is *really* like. That, in turn, seems a claim that could be justified only on the basis of a metaphysico-epistemological view of the traditional sort. For surely if anything is the province of such a view, it is the question of what there is and is not a "fact of the matter" about. So my argument must ultimately come back to philosophical first principles.

Here I can only say that if there were a discoverable fact of the matter about what there is a fact of the matter about, then it would doubtless be metaphysics and epistemology that would discover that meta-fact. But I think that the very idea of a "fact of the matter" is one we would be better off without. Philosophers like Davidson and Derrida have, I think, given us good reason to think that the *physis–nomos, in se–ad nos,* and objective–subjective distinctions were steps on a ladder that we can now safely throw away. The question of whether the reasons such philosophers have given for this claim are themselves metaphysico-epistemological reasons, and if not, what sort of reasons they are, strikes me as pointless and sterile. Once again, I fall back on the holist's strategy of insisting that reflective equilibrium is all we need try for – that there is no natural order of justification of beliefs, no predestined outline for argument to trace. Getting rid of the idea of such an outline seems to me one of the many benefits of a conception of the self as a centerless web. Another benefit is that questions about whom we need justify ourselves to – questions about who counts as a fanatic and who deserves an answer – can be treated as just further matters to be sorted out in the course of attaining reflective equilibrium.

I can, however, make one point to offset the air of light-minded aestheticism I am adopting toward traditional philosophical questions. This is that there is a moral purpose behind this light-mindedness. The encouragement of light-mindedness about traditional philosophical topics serves the same purposes as does the encouragement of light-mindedness about traditional theological topics. Like the rise of large market economies, the increase in literacy, the proliferation of artistic genres, and the insouciant pluralism of contemporary culture, such philosophical superficiality and light-mindedness helps along the disenchantment of the world. It helps make the world's inhabitants more pragmatic, more tolerant, more liberal, more receptive to the appeal of instrumental rationality.

If one's moral identity consists in being a citizen of a liberal polity, then to encourage light-mindedness will serve one's moral purposes. Moral commitment, after all, does not require taking seriously all the matters that are, for moral reasons, taken seriously by one's fellow citizens. It may require just the opposite. It may require trying to josh them out of the habit of taking those topics so seriously. There may be serious reasons for so joshing them. More generally, we should not assume that the aesthetic is always the enemy of the moral. I should argue that in the recent history of liberal societies, the willingness to view matters aesthetically – to be content to indulge in what Schiller called "play" and to discard what Nietzsche called "the spirit of seriousness" – has been an important vehicle of moral progress.

I have now said everything I have to say about the third of the communitarian claims that I distinguished at the outset: the claim that the social theory of the liberal state rests on false philosophical presuppositions. I hope I have given reasons for thinking that insofar as the communitarian is a critic of liberalism, he should drop this claim and should instead develop either of the first two claims: the empirical claim that democratic institutions cannot be combined with the sense of common purpose that predemocratic societies enjoyed, or the moral judgment that the products of the liberal state are too high a price to pay for the elimination of the evils that preceded it. If communitarian critics of liberalism stuck to these two claims, they would avoid the sort of terminal wistfulness with which their books typically end. Heidegger, for example, tells us that "we are too late for the gods, and too early for Being." Unger ends *Knowledge and Politics* with an appeal to a *Deus absconditus*. MacIntyre ends *After Virtue* by saying that we "are awaiting not for a Godot, but for another – doubtless very different – St. Benedict."[44] Sandel ends his book by saying that liberalism "forgets the possibility that when politics goes well, we can know a good in common that we cannot know alone," but he does not suggest a candidate for this common good.

Instead of thus suggesting that philosophical reflection, or a return to religion, might enable us to re-enchant the world, I think that communitarians should stick to the question of whether disenchantment has, on balance, done us more harm than good, or created more dangers than it has evaded. For Dewey, communal and public disenchantment is the price we pay for individual and private spiritual liberation, the kind of liberation that Emerson thought characteristically American. Dewey was as well aware as Weber that there is a price to be paid, but he thought it well worth paying. He assumed that no good achieved by earlier societies would be worth recapturing if the price were a diminution in our ability to leave people alone, to let them try out their private visions of perfection in peace. He admired the American habit of giving democracy priority over philosophy by asking, about any vision of the meaning of life, "Would not acting out this vision interfere with the ability of others to work out their own salvation?" Giving priority to that question is no more "natural" than giving priority to, say, MacIntyre's question "What sorts of human beings emerge in the culture of liberalism?" or Sandel's question "Can a community of those who put justice first ever be more than a community of strangers?" The question of which of these questions is prior to which others is, necessarily, begged by *everybody*. Nobody is being any more arbitrary than anybody else. But that is to say that nobody is being arbitrary at all. Everybody is just insisting that the beliefs and desires they hold most dear should come first in the order of discussion. That is not arbitrariness, but sincerity.

The danger of re-enchanting the world, from a Deweyan point of view, is that it might interfere with the development of what Rawls calls "a social union of social unions,"[45] some of which may be (and in Emerson's view, should be) very small indeed. For it is hard to be both enchanted with one version of the world and tolerant of all the others. I have not tried to argue the question of whether Dewey was right in this judgment of relative danger and promise. I have merely argued that such a judgment neither presupposes nor supports a theory of the self. Nor have I tried to deal with Horkheimer and Adorno's prediction that the "dissolvent rationality" of the Enghlightenment will eventually cause the liberal democracies to come unstuck.

The only thing I have to say about this prediction is that the collapse of the liberal democracies would not, in itself, provide much evidence for the claim that human societies cannot survive without widely shared opinions on matters of ultimate importance – shared conceptions of our place in the universe and our mission on earth. Perhaps they cannot survive under such conditions, but the eventual collapse of the democracies would not, in itself, show that this was the case – any more than it would show that human societies require kings or an established religion, or that political community cannot exist outside of small city-states.

Both Jefferson and Dewey described America as an "experiment." If the experiment fails, our descendants may learn something important. But they will not learn a philosophical truth, any more than they will learn a religious one. They will simply get some hints about what to watch out for when setting up their next experiment. Even if nothing else survives from the age of the democratic revolutions, perhaps our descendants will remember that social institutions *can* be viewed as experiments in cooperation rather than as attempts to embody a universal and ahistorical order. It is hard to believe that this memory would not be worth having.

NOTES

I am grateful to David Levin, Michael Sandel, J. B. Schneewind, and A. J. Simmons for comment on earlier drafts of this paper.

1   Thomas Jefferson, *Notes on the State of Virginia,* Query XVII, in *The Writings of Thomas Jefferson,* ed. A. A. Lipscomb and A. E. Bergh (Washington, D.C., 1905), 2: 217.

2   Jefferson included a statement of this familiar Scriptural claim (roughly in the form in which it had been restated by Milton in *Areopagitica*) in the preamble to the Virginia Statute for Religious Freedom: "truth is great and will prevail if left to herself, . . . she is the proper and sufficient antagonist to error, and has nothing to fear from the conflict, unless by human interposition disarmed of her natural weapons, free argument and debate, errors ceasing to be dangerous when it is permitted freely to contradict them" (ibid., 2: 302).

3   Max Horkheimer and Theodor W. Adorno, *Dialectic of Enlightenment* (New York: Seabury Press, 1972), p. xiii.

4   "For the Enlightenment, whatever does not conform to the rule of computation and utility is suspect. So long as it can develop undisturbed by any outward repression, there is no holding it. In the process, it treats its own ideas of human rights exactly as it does the older universals . . . Enlightenment is totalitarian" (ibid., p. 6). This line of thought recurs repeatedly in communitarian accounts of the present state of the liberal democracies; see, for example, Robert Bellah, Richard Madsen, William Sullivan, Ann Swidler, and Steven Tipton, *Habits of the Heart: Individualism and Commitment in American Life* (Berkeley: University of California Press, 1985): "There is a widespread feeling that the promise of the modern era is slipping away from us. A movement of enlightenment and liberation that was to have freed us from superstition and tyranny has led in the twentieth century to a world in which ideological fanaticism and political oppression have reached extremes unknown in previous history" (p. 277).

5   Charles Taylor, *Philosophy and the Human Sciences,* vol. 2 of *Philosophical Papers* (Cambridge: Cambridge University Press, 1985), p. 8.

6   Ibid., p. 5.

7 John Rawls, "Justice as Fairness: Political not Metaphysical," *Philosophy and Public Affairs* 14 (1985): 225. Religious toleration is a constantly recurring theme in Rawls's writing. Early in *A Theory of Justice* (Cambridge, Mass.: Harvard University Press, 1971), when giving examples of the sort of common opinions that a theory of justice must take into account and systematize, he cites our conviction that religious intolerance is unjust (p. 19). His example of the fact that "a well-ordered society tends to eliminate or at least to control men's inclinations to injustice" is that "warring and intolerant sects are much less likely to exist" (p. 247). Another relevant passage (which I shall discuss below) is his diagnosis of Ignatius Loyola's attempt to make the love of God the "dominant good": "Although to subordinate all our aims to one end does not strictly speaking violate the principles of rational choice . . . it still strikes us as irrational, or more likely as mad" (pp. 553–4).

8 Rawls, "Justice as Fairness," pp. 225–6. The suggestion that there are many philosophical views that will *not* survive in such conditions is analogous to the Enlightenment suggestion that the adoption of democratic institutions will cause "superstitious" forms of religious belief gradually to die off.

9 Ibid., p. 230.

10 Ibid.

11 For Rawls's historicism see, for example, *Theory of Justice,* p. 547. There, Rawls says that the people in the original position are assumed to know "the general facts about society," including the fact that "institutions are not fixed but change over time, altered by natural circumstances and the activities and conflicts of social groups." He uses this point to rule out, as original choosers of principles of justice, those "in a fuedal or a caste system," those who are unaware of events such as the French Revolution. This is one of many passages that make clear (at least read in the light of Rawls's later work) that a great deal of knowledge that came late to the mind of Europe is present to the minds of those behind the veil of ignorance. Or, to put it another way, such passages make clear that those original choosers behind the veil exemplify a certain modern type of human being, not an ahistorical human nature. See also p. 548, where Rawls says, "Of course in working out what the requisite principles [of justice] are, we must rely upon current knowledge as recognized by common sense and the existing scientific consensus. We have to concede that as established beliefs change, it is possible that the principles of justice which it seems rational to choose may likewise change."

12 See Bellah et al., *Habits of the Heart,* p. 141, for a recent restatement of this "counter-Enlightenment" line of thought. For the authors' view of the problems created by persistence in Enlightenment rhetoric and by the prevalence of the conception of human dignity that Taylor identifies as "distinctively modern," see p. 21: "For most of us, it is easier to think about to get what we want than to know exactly what we should want. Thus Brian, Joe, Margaret and Wayne [some of the Americans interviewed by the authors] are each in his or her own way confused about how to define for themselves such things as the nature of success, the meaning of freedom, and the re-

quirements of justice. Those difficulties are in an important way created by the limitations in the common tradition of moral discourse they – and we – share." Compare p. 290: "the language of individualism, the primary American language of self-understanding, limits the way in which people think."

To my mind, the authors of *Habits of the Heart* undermine their own conclusions in the passages where they point to actual moral progress being made in recent American history, notably in their discussion of the civil-rights movement. There, they say that Martin Luther King, Jr., made the struggle for freedom "a practice of commitment within a vision of America as a community of memory" and that the response King elicited "came from the reawakened recognition by many Americans that their own sense of self was rooted in companionship with others who, though not necessarily like themselves, nevertheless shared with them a common history and whose appeals to justice and solidarity made powerful claims on our loyalty" (p. 252). These descriptions of King's achievement seem exactly right, but they can be read as evidence that the rhetoric of the Enlightenment offers at least as many opportunities as it does obstacles for the renewal of a sense of community. The civil-rights movement combined, without much strain, the language of Christian fellowship and the "language of individualism," about which Bellah and his colleagues are dubious.

13 See Michael Walzer, *Spheres of Justice* (New York: Basic, 1983), pp. 312 ff.

14 Michael Sandel, *Liberalism and the Limits of Justice* (Cambridge: Cambridge University Press, 1982), p. 49.

15 In a recent, as yet unpublished, paper, Sandel has urged that Rawls's claim that "philosophy in the classical sense as the search for truth about a prior and independent moral order cannot provide the shared basis for a political conception of justice" presupposes the controversial metaphysical claim that there is no such order. This seems to me like saying that Jefferson was presupposing the controversial theological claim that God is not interested in the name by which he is called by human beings. Both charges are accurate, but not really to the point. Both Jefferson and Rawls would have to reply, "I have no arguments for my dubious theological-metaphysical claim, because I do not know how to discuss such issues, and do not want to. My interest is in helping to preserve and create political institutions that will foster public indifference to such issues, while putting no restrictions on private discussion of them." This reply, of course, begs the "deeper" question that Sandel wants to raise, for the question of whether we *should* determine what issues to discuss on political or on "theoretical" (for example, theological or philosophical) grounds remains unanswered. (At the end of this paper, I briefly discuss the need for philosophers to escape from the requirement to answer questions phrased in vocabularies they wish to replace, and in more detail in "Beyond Realism and Anti-Realism," in *Wo steht die sprachanalytische Philosophie heute?*, ed. Herta Nagl-Docekal et al. [forthcoming].)

16 Jefferson agreed with Luther that philosophers had muddied the clear waters

of the gospels. See Jefferson's polemic against Plato's "foggy mind" and his claim that "the doctrines which flowed from the lips of Jesus himself are within the comprehension of a child; but thousands of volumes have not yet explained the Platonisms engrafted on them; and for this obvious reason, that nonsense can never be explained" (*Writings of Thomas Jefferson,* 14: 149).

17 I am here using the term "human nature" in the traditional philosophical sense in which Sartre denied that there was such a thing, rather than in the rather unusual one that Rawls gives it. Rawls distinguishes between a "conception of the person" and a "theory of human nature," where the former is a "moral ideal" and the latter is provided by, roughly, common sense plus the social sciences. To have a theory of human nature is to have "general facts that we take to be true, or true enough, given the state of public knowledge in our society," facts that "limit the feasibility of the ideals of person and society embedded in that framework" ("Kantian Constructivism in Moral Theory," *Journal of Philosophy* 77 [1980]: 534).

18 Rawls, "Justice as Fairness," p. 223.

19 In fact, it has been for the worse. A view that made politics more central to philosophy and subjectivity less would both permit more effective defenses of democracy than those that purport to supply it with "foundations" and permit liberals to meet Marxists on their own, political, ground. Dewey's explicit attempt to make the central philosophical question "What serves democracy?" rather than "What permits us to argue for democracy?" has been, unfortunately, neglected. I try to make this point in "Philosophy as Science, as Metaphor, and as Politics," in *The Institution of Philosophy*, ed. Avner Cohen and Marcello Dascal (Totowa, N.J.: Rowman and Allenfield, forthcoming).

20 That is, give-and-take between intuitions about the desirability of particular consequences of particular actions and intuitions about general principles, with neither having the determining voice.

21 One will also, as I did on first reading Rawls, take him to be attempting to supply such legitimation by an appeal to the rationality of the choosers in the original position (the position of those who, behind a veil of ignorance that hides them from their life chances and their conceptions of the good, select from among alternative principles of justice) served simply "to make vivid . . . the restrictions that it seems reasonable to impose on arguments for principles of justice and therefore on those principles themselves" (*Theory of Justice*, p. 18).

But this warning went unheeded by myself and others, in part because of an ambiguity between "reasonable" as defined by ahistorical criteria and as meaning something like "in accord with the moral sentiments characteristic of the heirs of the Enlightenment." Rawls's later work has, as I have said, helped us come down on the historicist side of this ambiguity; see, for example, "Kantian Constructivism": "the original position is not an axiomatic (or deductive) basis from which principles most fitting to the conception of the person most likely to be held, at least implicitly, in a democratic society"

(p. 572). It is tempting to suggest that one could eliminate all reference to the original position from *A Theory of Justice* without loss, but this is as daring a suggestion as that one might rewrite (as many have wished to do) Kant's *Critique of Pure Reason* without reference to the thing-in-itself. T. M. Scanlon has suggested that we can, at least, safely eliminate reference, in the description of the choosers in the original position, to an appeal to self-interest in describing the motives of those choosers. ("Contractualism and Utilitarianism," in *Utilitarianism and Beyond*, ed. Bernard Williams and Amartya Sen [Cambridge: Cambridge University Press, 1982]). Since justifiability is, more evidently than self-interest, relative to historical circumstance, Scanlon's proposal seems to be more faithful to Rawls's overall philosophical program than Rawls's own formulation.

22   In particular, there will be no principles or intuitions concerning the universal features of human psychology relevant to motivation. Sandel thinks that since assumptions about motivation are part of the description of the original position, "what issues at one end in a theory of justice must issue at the other in a theory of the person, or more precisely, a theory of the moral subject" (*Liberalism and the Limits of Justice*, p. 47). I would argue that if we follow Scanlon's lead (note 17) in dropping reference to self-interest in our description of the original choosers and replacing this with reference to their desire to justify their choices to their fellows, then the only "theory of the person" we get is a sociological description of the inhabitants of contemporary liberal democracies.

23   Rawls, "Kantian Constructivism," p. 519. Italics added.

24   Sandel, *Liberalism and the Limits of Justice*, p. 21. I have argued for the advantages of thinking of the self as just such a concatenation; see "Postmodernist Bourgeois Liberalism," *Journal of Philosophy* 80 (1983): 583–9 and "Freud and Moral Reflection," in *The Pragmatists' Freud*, ed. Joseph E. Smith and William Kerrigan (Baltimore: Johns Hopkins University Press, 1986). When Sandel cites Robert Nozick and Daniel Bell as suggesting that Rawls "ends by dissolving the self in order to preserve it" (*Liberalism and the Limits of Justice*, p. 95), I should rejoin that it may be helpful to dissolve the metaphysical self in order to preserve the political one. Less obliquely stated: It may be helpful, for purposes of systematizing our intuitions about the priority of liberty, to treat the self as having no center, no essence, but *merely* as a concatenation of beliefs and desires.

25   "Deontology with a Humean face either fails as deontology or recreates in the original position the disembodied subject it resolves to avoid" (ibid., p. 14).

26   Ibid., p. 19.

27   Rawls, *Theory of Justice*, p. 560.

28   Ibid.

29   It is important to note that Rawls explicitly distances himself from the idea that he is analyzing the very idea of morality and from conceptual analysis as the method of social theory (ibid., p. 130). Some of his critics have sug-

gested that Rawls is practicing "reductive logical analysis" of the sort characteristic of "analytic philosophy"; see, for example, William M. Sullivan, *Reconstructing Public Philosophy* (Berkeley: University of California Press, 1982), pp. 94ff. Sullivan says that "this ideal of reductive logical analysis lends legitimacy to the notion that moral philosophy is summed up in the task of discovering, through the analysis of moral rules, both primitive elements and governing principles that must apply to any rational moral system, *rational* here meaning 'logically coherent' " (p. 96). He goes on to grant that "Nozik and Rawls are more sensitive to the importance of history and social experience in human life than were the classic liberal thinkers" (p. 97). But this concession is too slight and is misleading. Rawls's willingness to adopt "reflective equilibrium" rather than "conceptual analysis" as a methodological watchword sets him apart from the epistemologically oriented moral philosophy that was dominant prior to the appearance of *A Theory of Justice.* Rawls represents a reaction against the Kantian idea of "morality" as having an ahistorical essence, the same sort of reaction found in Hegel and in Dewey.

30 Sandel, *Liberalism and the Limits of Justice,* p. 17.

31 ". . . liberty of conscience and freedom of thought should not be founded on philosophical or ethical skepticism, nor on indifference to religious and moral interests. The principles of justice define an appropriate path between dogmatism and intolerance on the one side, and a reductionism which regards religion and morality as mere preferences on the other" (Rawls, *Theory of Justice,* p. 243). I take it that Rawls is identifying "philosophical or ethical skepticism" with the idea that everything is just a matter of "preference," even religion, philosophy, and morals. So we should distinguish his suggestion that we "extend the principle of toleration to philosophy itself" from the suggestion that we dismiss philosophy as epiphenomenal. That is the sort of suggestion that is backed up by reductionist accounts of philosophical doctrines as "preferences" or "wish fulfillments" or "expressions of emotion" (see Rawls's criticism of Freudian reductionism in ibid., pp. 539ff.). Neither psychology nor logic nor any other theoretical discipline can supply non-question-begging reasons why philosophy should be set aside, any more than philosophy can supply such reasons why theology should be set aside. But this is compatible with saying that the general course of historical experience may lead us to neglect theological topics and bring us to the point at which, like Jefferson, we find a theological vocabulary "meaningless" (or, more precisely, useless). I am suggesting that the course of historical experience since Jefferson's time has led us to a point at which we find much of the vocabulary of modern philosophy no longer useful.

32 Ibid., pp. 261–2.

33 The contrast between "mere preference" and something less "arbitrary," something more closely related to the very nature of man or of reason, is invoked by many writers who think of "human rights" as requiring a philosophical foundation of the traditional sort. Thus my colleague David Little, commenting on my "Solidarity or Objectivity?" (*Post-Analytic Philosophy,*

ed. John Rajchman and Cornel West [New York: Columbia University Press, 1985]), says "Rorty appears to permit criticism and pressure against those societies [the ones we do not like] *if we happen to want to* criticize and pressure them in pursuit of some interest or belief we may (at the time) have, and for whatever ethnocentric reasons we may happen to hold those interests or beliefs" ("Natural Rights and Human Rights: The International Imperative," in *Natural Rights and Natural Law: The Legacy of George Mason,* ed. Robert P. Davidow [Fairfax, Va.: George Mason University Press, 1986], pp. 67–122; italics in original). I would rejoin that Little's use of "happen to want to" presupposes a dubious distinction between necessary, built-in, universal convictions (convictions that it would be "irrational" to reject) and accidental, culturally determined convictions. It also presupposes the existence of such faculties as reason, will, and emotion, all of which the pragmatist tradition in American philosophy and the so-called existentialist tradition in European philosophy try to undercut. Dewey's *Human Nature and Conduct* and Heidegger's *Being and Time* both offer a moral psychology that avoids oppositions between "preference" and "reason."

34   "Aristotle remarks that it is a peculiarity of men that they possess a sense of the just and the unjust and that their sharing a common understanding of justice makes a polis. Analogously one might say, in view of our discussion, that a common understanding of justice as fairness makes a constitutional democracy" (Rawls, *Theory of Justice,* p. 243). In the interpretation of Rawls I am offering, it is unrealistic to expect Aristotle to have developed a conception of justice as fairness, since he simply lacked the kind of historical experience that we have accumulated since his day. More generally, it is pointless to assume (with, for example, Leo Strauss) that the Greeks had already canvassed the alternatives available for social life and institutions. When we discuss justice, we cannot agree to bracket our knowledge of recent history.

35   Sandel, *Liberalism and the Limits of Justice,* p. 20.

36   We can dismiss other distinctions that Sandel draws in the same way. Examples are the distinction between a voluntarist and a cognitive account of the original position (ibid., p. 121), that between "the identity of the subject" as the "product" rather than the "premise" of its agency (ibid., p. 152), and that between the question "Who am I?" and its rival as "the paradigmatic moral question," "What shall I choose?" (ibid., p. 153). These distinctions are all to be analyzed away as products of the "Kantian dualisms" that Rawls praises Hegel and Dewey for having overcome.

37   For some similarities between Dewey and Heidegger with respect to anti-Cartesianism, see my "Overcoming the Tradition," in Richard Rorty, *Consequences of Pragmatism* (Minneapolis: University of Minnesota Press, 1982). For similarities between Davidson and Derrida, see Samuel Wheeler, "Indeterminancy of French Translation," in *Essays on 'Inquiries into truth and interpretation,'* ed. Ernest LePore (Oxford: Basil Blackwell, 1986).

38   David Levin has pointed out to me that Jefferson was not above borrowing

such arguments. I take this to show that Jefferson, like Kant, found himself in an untenable halfway position between theology and Deweyan social experimentalism.

39 Sandel takes "the primacy of the subject" to be not only a way of filling out the deontological picture, but also a necessary condition of its correctness: "If the claim for the primacy of justice is to succeed, if the right is to be prior to the good in the interlocking moral and foundational senses we have distinguished, then some version of the claim for the primacy of the subject must succeed as well" (*Liberalism and the Limits of Justice*, p. 7). Sandel quotes Rawls as saying that "the essential unity of the self is already provided by the conception of the right" and takes this passage as evidence that Rawls holds a doctrine of the "priority of the self" (ibid., p. 21). But consider the context of this sentence. Rawls says: "The principles of justice and their realization in social forms define the bounds within which our deliberations take place. The essential unity of the self is already provided by the conception of right. Moreover, in a well-ordered society this unity is the same for all; everyone's conception of the good as given by his rational plan is a subplan of the larger comprehensive plan that regulates the community as a social union of social unions" (*Theory of Justice*, p. 563). The "essential unity of the self," which is in question here, is simply the system of moral sentiments, habits, and internalized traditions that is typical of the politically aware citizen of a constitutional democracy. This self is, once again, a historical product. It has nothing to do with the nonempirical self, which Kant had to postulate in the interests of Enlightenment universalism.

40 This is the kernel of truth in Dworkin's claim that Rawls rejects "goal-based" social theory, but this point should not lead us to think that he is thereby driven back on a "rights-based" theory.

41 But one should not press this point so far as to raise the specter of "untranslatable languages." As Donald Davidson has remarked, we would not recognize other organisms as actual or potential language users – or, therefore, as persons – unless there were enough overlap in belief and desire to make translation possible. The point is merely that efficient and frequent communication is only a necessary, not a sufficient, condition of agreement.

42 Further, such a conclusion is *restricted* to politics. It does not cast doubt on the ability of these men to follow the rules of logic or their ability to do many other things skillfully and well. It is thus not equivalent to the traditional philosophical charge of "irrationality." That charge presupposes that inability to "see" certain truths is evidence of the lack of an organ that is essential for human functioning generally.

43 In Kierkegaard's *Philosophical Fragments*, to which I have referred earlier, we find the Platonic Theory of Recollection treated as the archetypal justification of "Socratism" and thus as the symbol of all forms (especially Hegel's) of what Bernard Williams has recently called "the rationalist theory of rationality" – the idea that one is rational only if one can appeal to universally accepted criteria, criteria whose truth and applicability all human beings can

find "in their heart." This is the philosophical core of the Scriptural idea that "truth is great, and will prevail," when that idea is dissociated from the Pauline idea of "a New Being" (in the way that Kierkegaard refused to dissociate it).

44 See Jeffrey Stout's discussion of the manifold ambiguities of this conclusion in "Virtue Among the Ruins: An Essay on MacIntrye," *Neue Zeitschrift für Systematische Theologie und Religionsphilosophie* 26 (1984): 256–73, especially, 269.

45 This is Rawls's description of "a well-ordered society (corresponding to justice as fairness)" (*Theory of Justice*, p. 527). Sandel finds these passages metaphorical and complains that "intersubjective and individualistic images appear in uneasy, sometimes unfelicitious combination, as if to betray the incompatible commitments contending within" (*Liberalism and the Limits of Justice*, pp. 150ff.). He concludes that "the moral vocabulary of community in the strong sense cannot in all cases be captured by a conception that [as Rawls has said his is] 'in its theoretical basis is individualistic.' " I am claiming that these commitments will look incompatible only if one attempts to define their philosophical presuppositions (which Rawls himself may occasionally have done too much of), and that this is a good reason for not making such attempts. Compare the Enlightenment view that attempts to sharpen up the theological presuppositions of social commitments had done more harm than good and that if theology cannot simply be discarded, it should at least be left as fuzzy (or, one might say, "liberal") as possible. Oakeshott has a point when he insists on the value of theoretical muddle for the health of the state.

Elsewhere Rawls has claimed that "there is no reason why a well-ordered society should encourage primarily individualistic values if this means ways of life that lead individuals to pursue their own way and to have no concern for the interest of others" ("Fairness to Goodness," *Philosophical Review* 84 [1975]: 550). Sandel's discussion of this passage says that it "suggests a deeper sense in which Rawls' conception is individualistic," but his argument that this suggestion is correct is, once again, the claim that "the Rawlsian self is not only a subject of possession, but an antecedently individuated subject" (*Liberalism and the Limits of Justice*, p. 61 ff.). This is just the claim I have been arguing against by arguing that there is no such thing as "the Rawlsian self" and that Rawls "takes for granted that every individual consists of one and only one system of desires" (ibid., p. 62), but it is hard to find evidence for this claim in the texts. At worst, Rawls simplifies his presentation by imagining each of his citizens as having only one such set, but this simplifying assumption does not seem central to his view.

11

Madison's "Detached Memoranda": Then and Now

LEO PFEFFER

Introduction

For all practical purposes, Madison's "Memorial and Remonstrance" was discovered by the Supreme Court in *Everson* v. *Board of Education* (1947).[1] In that case, both Justice Hugo L. Black's majority opinion[2] and Justice Wiley B. Rutledge's dissenting opinion[3] placed great emphasis on it in support of their contrary opinions on the constitutionality of using tax-raised funds to finance transportation to religious schools – Rutledge so much so that he deemed it worthwhile to set it forth in its entirety as an appendix to his dissenting opinion, which argued unconstitutionality.

It is not unprecedented for both prevailing and dissenting opinions in a case to invoke the same authority – usually a court decision but often, as in *Everson*, a nonjudicial document. In that case, however, it seemed fairly clear that the "Memorial and Remonstrance" was more supportive of the dissenting than of the majority opinion, impelling Justice Robert H. Jackson, in his dissenting opinion, to note that

> the Court's opinion marshals every argument in favor of state aid and puts the case in its most favorable light, but much of its reasoning confirms my conclusions that there are no good grounds upon which to support the present legislation. In fact, the undertones of the opinion, advocating complete and uncompromising separation of Church from State, seem utterly discordant with its conclusion yielding support to their commingling in educational matters. The case which irresistibly comes to mind as the most fitting precedent is that of Julia who, according to Byron's reports, "whispering 'I will ne'er consent,' – consented."[4]

First Prayer in Congress as depicted in 1889, printed as the frontispiece to the Reverend Edward J. Giddin's *American Christian Rulers* (New York, 1890). Courtesy of the Virginia State Library.

It is hardly disputable that the "Memorial and Remonstrance" was a significant factor in defeating a Virginia measure to finance religious instruction and in the enactment a year later of Thomas Jefferson's Statute for Religious Freedom.[5] Nor can there be any doubt that together, the "Memorial and Remonstrance" and the Virginia Statute furnished a historic basis for the adoption, five years later, of an amendment to the Constitution that opens with the words "Congress shall make no law respecting an establishment of religion, or prohibiting the free exercise thereof."

Virginia, however, was not the only state that disestablished a church before the First Amendment became part of the Constitution, and states other than Virginia enacted statutes guaranteeing religious liberty before the First Amendment was adopted. New York, for example, adopted a constitution that abrogated all laws "which may be construed to establish or maintain any particular denomination of Christians or their ministers" and guaranteed forever the "free exercise of religious profession and worship without discrimination or preference."[6] Moreover, neither the Virginia experience nor the adoption of the First Amendment effected immediate disestablishment in all the states; that did not come to Connecticut until 1818[7] and to Massachusetts until 1833.[8]

Since the *Everson* decision, Madison's "Memorial and Remonstrance" has been cited, relied on, rejected, distinguished, interpreted, and reinterpreted in court decisions, books, articles, professorial lectures, public debates, and scholarly conferences – literally innumerable times. In substance, the "Memorial and Remonstrance" presents a fifteen-point sociopolitical foundation for the basically integral unity of religious freedom and church–state separation, at least insofar as it relates to the use of tax-raised funds to finance churches and religion.[9]

In 1946, a year before the *Everson* decision was handed down, another document expressing Madison's philosophy in this arena of constitutional law became known to judges, lawyers, and scholars. The October issue of the *William and Mary Quarterly* (subtitled a *Magazine of Early American History, Institutions and Culture*),[10] carried in its "Notes and Documents" section the text of a manuscript written by Madison and entitled by him "Detached Memoranda." The manuscript, folded and tied securely with a shoestring, was among the papers of William Cabell Rives, who in 1856 had been appointed by Congress to prepare Madison's papers for publication. It was discovered by Elizabeth Fleet in the course of her research in preparing a biography of Rives and was annotated by her before publication.

The publication of the "Detached Memoranda" aroused no great interest, not even among constitutional-law scholars or political historians.

Actually, part of the document had appeared in the March 1914 issue of *Harper's Magazine,* under the title "Aspects of Monopoly One Hundred Years Ago," with an introduction by Gaillard Hunt.[11] Black made a passing reference to the Fleet article in footnote 12 of the *Everson* opinion: "In a recently discovered collection of Madison's papers, Madison recollected that his Remonstrance 'met with the approbation of the Baptists, the Presbyterians, the Quakers, and the few Roman Catholics, universally; of the Methodists in part, and even of not a few of the Sect [Episcopalians] formerly established by law. . . .' Fleet, Madison's 'Detached Memorandum [*sic*].' "[12] Rutledge's reference to it in his dissenting opinion is even more summary. After describing the "Memorial and Remonstrance" as "Madison's complete, though not his only, interpretation of religious liberty," he advised the reader, in a footnote, to "[s]ee also" the Fleet article.[13]

A passing reference is found in Justice Felix Frankfurter's concurring opinion in *McGovern* v. *Maryland* (1961).[14] Thereafter "Detached Memoranda" was not mentioned by the Supreme Court until it handed down its opinion in 1970 in *Walz* v. *Tax Commission.*[15] It was referred to again in the 1983 case of *Marsh* v. *Chambers.*[16]

What is significant with respect to the date of its writing is that Madison's "Detached Memoranda" interprets the Constitution and the Bill of Rights and, unlike the Declaration of Independence, does not rest exclusively on the laws of nature or nature's God, on Madison's own "Memorial and Remonstrance," or on Jefferson's Virginia Statute for Religious Freedom, although all are reported, confirmed, and defended. It would seem, therefore that the "Detached Memoranda" would be the best source for determining the intended meaning of the "religion" clauses of the First Amendment (and the provision in Article VI of the Constitution forbidding religious tests for public office), at least by the primary draftsman of both the Constitution and the First Amendment. It is the purpose of this paper to examine how judicial interpretation and application coincide with or differ from Madison's as expressed by him in the "Detached Memoranda."

As set forth in the Fleet article, the "Detached Memoranda" covers some thirty-two pages. Of these, only nine, under the heading "Monopolies, Perpetuities, Corporations, Ecclesiastical Endowments," are devoted to the subject of religion as it relates to government.

It is uncertain when the "Detached Memoranda" was written. William Cabell Rives, who edited *Letters and Other Writings of James Madison* in 1868, stated that Madison had written it "subsequent to his retirement from the presidency in 1817,"[17] and Hunt dated it "before 1832."[18] Fleet suggested that "all the memoranda were hastily jotted down within a few years after Madison's retirement from the presidency."[19] We know that the "Detached Memoranda" was written at a time when the First Amendment's "religion" clauses were not applicable to the states, but the Court in *Cantwell v. Connecticut* (1940)[20] and in *Everson v. Board of Education* (1947)[21] ruled that under the "due-process" clause of the Fourteenth Amendment, both the "free-exercise" and the "establishment" clauses apply to the states to the same extent as to the federal government.

Church, State, and the "Detached Memoranda"

The "Detached Memoranda" considers eight issues relating to religion that have reached the Supreme Court in one way or another since the Constitution was adopted: (1) ecclesiastical monopolies; (2) incorporation of churches; (3) grants of public lands to churches; (4) tax exemption of religious entities; (5) the Deity in governmental documents; (6) congressional chaplaincies; (7) military chaplaincies; and (8) religious proclamations by the government.

Ecclesiastical Monopolies

Monopolies, said Madison, although sometimes useful, should be granted with caution and guarded with strictness against abuse. The Constitution limits their permissibility to two cases: copyrights and inventions.[22]

It is Madison's concern about ecclesiastical monopolies that we discuss here.[23] The danger of silent accumulations of wealth in the United States, Madison said, had not received the attention that it should have. He noted that the excessive wealth of ecclesiastical corporations and its misuse in many European countries had long been a topic of complaint. In some, the church had amassed perhaps half the nation's property.

> Are the U.S. duly awake to the tendency of the precedents they are establishing, in the multiplied incorporations of Religious Congregations with the faculty of acquiring and holding property real as well as personal? Do not many of these acts give this faculty, without limit either as to time or as to amount? And must not bodies, perpetual in their existence, and which may be always gaining without ever losing, speedily gain more than is useful, and in time more than is safe? Are there not already examples in the U.S. of ecclesiastical wealth equally beyond its object and the foresight of those who laid the foundation of it?[24]

Madison found no objection to grants in perpetuity of public lands, as long as they were made according to rules of impartiality and for a valuable consideration (that is, fair price).[25] (It might be suggested that to do otherwise would, under later Supreme Court opinions, violate the "establishment" clause, which imposes an obligation of governmental neutrality, not hostility, toward religion. As the Supreme Court was later to rule in a host of cases, the clause is violated by laws that inhibit religion no less than by those that advance it.)

Incorporation of Churches

Madison's opposition to "multiplied incorporation of Religious Congregations" could not be translated into constitutional law with respect to state-chartered churches, since more than a century would pass before the "religion" clauses of the First Amendment would be held applicable to the states. This, however, was not the case where national (congressional) charters were involved: "Strongly guarded as is the separation between Religion & Govt in the Constitution of the United States the danger of encroachment by Ecclesiastical Bodies, may be illustrated by precedents already furnished in their short history."[26]

This paragraph refers to four legislative acts, the first three by Congress and the fourth by the Kentucky legislature. The first was a measure seeking to incorporate the Episcopal Church in Alexandria (then part of the District of Columbia and hence within the jurisdiction of Congress). Madison's message stated two reasons for vetoing the bill to incorporate the church.[27] The first, in the opening paragraph of the veto message, reads: "Because the bill exceeds the rightful authority to which governments are limited by the essential distinction between civil and religious functions, and violates in particular the article of the Constitution of the United States which declares that 'Congress shall make no law respecting a religious establishment [sic].' "[28]

Congress has apparently had little difficulty is disregarding Madison's views and granting corporate charters to churches in the District of Columbia and other territories subject to congressional lawmaking jurisdiction. Thus in 1844, Congress incorporated Georgetown University, a Jesuit institution, and in 1887, the Catholic University. In 1893, it incorporated American University, a Methodist institution, and in 1896, it incorporated the same Episcopal Church of the Diocese of Washington, D.C., that Madison had refused to allow to be incorporated.[29] Moreover, despite Madison's views, today, four decades after the Court in the *Everson* case ruled the "establishment" clause applicable to the states, religious-incorporation laws are common throughout the nation. But it

should be noted that the first reason Madison gave for the veto anticipated by some 130 years the rationale of the Supreme Court's decision
in *Walz* v. *Tax Commission* (1970),[30] which declared unconstitutional laws
having the effect of excessive governmental entanglement with religion.

One further comment on the corporation aspect of the "Detached
Memoranda" is in order. The power to create implies the power to destroy, and the power of government to incorporate a church may well
imply the power to destroy it. Recent governmental efforts to destroy
religious bodies that are called "cults" may well testify to this. So, too,
was the action of Congress with respect to the Church of Jesus Christ of
Latter-Day Saints (Mormons), which had been established as a religious
corporation in Utah while Utah was still a territory of the United States.
The Mormons' adherence to polygamy as religious obligation resulted
in a variety of efforts to invoke legal (as well as illegal) methods of achieving
its destruction. All others having proved ineffective, Congress enacted a
law repealing the charter it had granted the church and declaring its properties forfeit. This finally achieved the government's purpose (which was
not the destruction of the church, but its discontinuance of the practice
of plural marriage), notwithstanding the church's claimed constitutional
right to the free exercise of religion.[31] Adherence to Madison's construction of the "establishment" clause with reference to the Episcopal Church
in Alexandria would have eliminated the charter-repeal sanction, for
Congress would not have had the power to grant the charter in the first
place.

The other reason for Madison's action is set forth in the second paragraph in his veto message:

> Because the bill vests in the said incorporated church an author-
> ity to provide for the support of the poor and the education of
> poor children of the same, an authority which, being altogether
> superfluous if the provision is to be the result of pious charity,
> would be a precedent for giving to religious societies as such a
> legal agency in carrying into effect a public and civil duty.[32]

This paragraph of the veto message anticipated the statement made by
Jeremiah Black, a noted constitutional lawyer:

> The manifest object of the men who framed the institutions of
> this country, was to have a State without religion and church
> without politics – that is to say, they meant that one should
> never be used as an engine for the purposes of the other. . . . For
> that reason they built a wall of complete and perfect partition
> between the two.[33]

It is difficult to avoid the conclusion that by sanctioning incorporation, the government is allowing itself to be used "as an engine for the purposes of" religion. Churches do not have to be incorporated in order to fulfill their religious mission.

This second stated reason for Madison's veto is considerably more relevant to contemporary controversy than is the incorporation of religious institutions. It touches on two strongly debated constitutional questions: (1) the utilization of churches as instruments of government to provide for the noneducational needs of the poor; and (2) the provision of funds for the education of poor children. In neither case, Madison said, is the "establishment" clause in any way implicated if these missions are financed by voluntary contributions to churches made by the public at large. But if tax-raised funds are utilized for these purposes, the clause is violated.

The issue with respect to the noneducational-funding aspect reached the Supreme Court in the 1899 case of *Bradfield* v. *Roberts*.[34] The Court held it constitutional to consummate a contract under which the federal government would erect a hospital in Washington, D.C., and pay a specified sum for each poor patient sent to it by the Commissioners of the District of Columbia. The contract was made not with the Catholic Church, but with the Catholic Sisters of Charity, a duly formed purely secular corporation. That the hospital was to be conducted under the auspices (that is, influence or patronage) of the Catholic Church did not render the contract unconstitutional, according to the Court.

Bradfield v. *Roberts* became the foundation of the Hospital Surety and Construction Act of 1946, generally known as the Hill-Burton Act, and of state statutes providing for the use of tax-raised funds for the support of hospitals. The case for validity seems to be simple: There is, after all, nothing religious about removing a cancerous tumor or repairing a defective heart.

But what of Catholic hospitals in which crucifixes hang on the walls of all the rooms, including those utilized by all patients? And what of Jewish hospitals that allow only kosher food to be eaten and do not include bread on its menus during the Passover holidays? And what of hospitals – Catholic, Protestant, or Jewish – that for religious reasons do not allow abortions, even when called for by the health of the patient?

As long as a hospital is entirely private, in the sense that it receives no tax-raised funds, there is no question that it has the right to impose any of these restrictions. If, however, a hospital elects to receive Hill-Burton funds or their state equivalent, it would seem to be of doubtful fairness or constitutionality to allow it the privilege of imposing religious restrictions on its services. The basic premise is that services financed by taxes imposed on persons of all religions or none should be available to persons of all religions or none. This is implicit in the *Bradfield* v. *Roberts* opinion, and its consequence is that not only must hospital walls be devoid of religious symbols other than those hung adjacent to the beds of those patients who request them, but also generally accepted medical treatments – such as blood transfusions or abortions – should not be excluded because of religious inhibitions.

This is substantially what the Supreme Court, beginning with *Lemon* v. *Kurtzman* (1971),[35] has held in the relevant cases involving elementary and secondary schools, and the rationale of these cases would seem to be equally applicable to hospitals.

Not so, said the Supreme Court in *Harris* v. *McRae* (1980),[36] a suit challenging the constitutionality of a statute forbidding the use of Medicaid funds to finance abortions "except where the life of the mother would be endangered if the fetus were carried to term; or except for such medical procedures necessary for the victims of rape or incest, when such rape or incest has been reported promptly to a law enforcement agency or public health service."

Although the Court divided 5 to 4 in deciding the case, there was no disagreement with respect to the claim that this contested provision violated the "establishment" clause. The statute was not unconstitutional, the Court said, simply because it "happens to coincide or harmonize with the tenets of some or all religions. That the Judaeo-Christian religions oppose stealing does not mean that a State or the Federal Government may not, consistent with the Establishment Clause, enact laws prohibiting larceny."[37]

Insofar as "the education of poor children" is concerned, what was futile with respect to the first ground for Madison's veto has proved to be in substantive part less futile with respect to the second. Incorporated or not, churches cannot constitutionally act as an agency of government for that purpose. The Supreme Court's most recent decisions on this subject – *Aguilar* v. *Felton* (1985),[38] *School District of the City of Grand Rapids* v. *Ball* (1985),[39] and *Wallace* v. *Jaffree* (1985)[40] – stand for the proposition that tax-raised funds may not be used to finance secular instruction in religious schools or prayers, even silent ones, in the public schools.

Grants of Public Lands to Churches

Madison's second veto referred to in the "Detached Memoranda" was to a bill granting certain land to a Baptist church in Mississippi Territory.[41] The veto message reads in part:

Because the bill in reserving a certain parcel of land of the United States for the use of said Baptist Church comprises a principle and a precedent for the appropriation of funds of the United States for the use and support of religious societies, contrary to this article of the Constitution which declares that "Congress shall make no law respecting a religious establishment [*sic*]."[42]

It is noteworthy that the proposed grant was perhaps not so much a giveaway as it would seem to be. The Baptist church had been built on public land as the result of an error in surveying, and the grant was designed to correct that unfortunate mistake.[43] Nevertheless, to Madison, the grant would have violated the "establishment" clause, since the error could easily be rectified by the entirely constitutional sale to the church of the government-owned land. Moreover, conveyance of the land free of charge would require taxpayers to pay for an error committed by the church's surveyors, a consequence that could hardly be deemed equitable.

The constitutional question that faced Madison with respect to the Baptist church in Mississippi reached the Supreme Court in the 1982 case of *Valley Forge Christian College* v. *Americans United for Separation of Church and State*.[44] In 1949, Congress had enacted a law designating as "surplus" any federal government property that had outlived its usefulness. It authorized the government to sell or lease such property to nonprofit, tax-exempt educational institutions for consideration that took into account "any benefit which has accrued or may accrue to the United States" from the transferee's use of the property.

Acting under the statute, the Secretary of Education, for no monetary consideration, conveyed to the Northeast Bible College (which later changed its name to Valley Forge Christian College) land on which had been located the government-owned Valley Forge General Hospital, but was no longer used for that or any other purpose. The transaction was challenged by Americans United for Separation of Church and State and some of its officers, the latter suing in their capacity as taxpayers. Unfortunately for Americans United and its officers, the Supreme Court did not rely on Madison's precedent or reach the merits of their claim.

In *Flast* v. *Cohen* (1968),[45] the Supreme Court had ruled that taxpayers can sue (technically, have standing to sue) governmental officials for an injunction forbidding them to expend tax-raised funds to aid parochial schools. But, said Justice Rehnquist in his opinion for the majority of five in the *Valley Forge* case, *Flast* v. *Cohen* challenged action taken by Congress under its authority conferred by the "taxing and spending" clause of Article I, Section 8, of the Constitution. In the *Valley Forge* case, however, the government was acting pursuant to that part of Article IV, Section 3, that reads: "The Congress shall have power to dispose of and make all needful rules and regulations respecting the territory or other property belonging to the United States." Therefore, Rehnquist concluded, taxpayers have no standing to sue, and their case must be thrown out of court. The consequence was that the Valley Forge Christian College could, as the rightful and complete owner of the property, do anything it wanted with it, including using it as a church or a parochial school or selling it and using the proceeds to erect or maintain church or parochial-school buildings elsewhere.

In short, the college won on a technicality, but in the world of realities, there is no difference between victories so won and any other victories.

Tax Exemption of Religious Entities

The "Detached Memoranda" speaks of a case in which Madison "withheld his signature" from a bill that he believed to be an encroachment by ecclesiastical bodies on the separation between church and state.[46] This was only the second time that a president had exercised what was later to become known as a "pocket veto," a power conferred on presidents by Article I, Section 7(2), of the Constitution.[47]

In the "Detached Memoranda," Madison did not identify the measure that he had vetoed, other than by declaring the measure to be a violation of the "establishment" clause. Research discloses that he was referring to A Bill for the Relief of Bible Societies in the United States (excepting from duty all plates, etc. imported for such societies), which had been passed in 1816.[48]

In *Walz* v. *Tax Commission* (1970),[49] the majority of the Court voted to uphold the constitutionality of a measure granting tax exemption to religious organizations for properties used solely for religious worship. In the Court's opinion, Justice Burger referred to a statute, enacted in 1813, that authorized a refund for duties paid by religious societies on the importation of religious articles (in that case, plates for printing Bibles).[50] Madison did not veto this bill, nor three years later did he veto A Bill for the Relief of the Baltimore and Massachusetts Bible Societies (remitting duty on plates imported by the Baltimore Society and paying a drawback to the Massachusetts Bible Society for bibles imported to the United States and there re-exported).

How, then, can Madison's acceptance of these two measures be reconciled with his pocket-veto rejection of the one referred to in the "Detached Memoranda"? One possible explanation may be that the accepted measures were private bills, applicable to only specifically named societies (those in Baltimore and Massachusetts), whereas the vetoed bill, although using the same language as the accepted ones, was a general bill, applicable to all Bible societies in the nation.

This, however, is hardly an adequate explanation. An unconstitutional bill does not become constitutional just because it is limited to two states rather than applying to all. Moreover, the two measures that Madison did veto within ten days after they were presented to him – those concerning the incorporation of the Episcopal Church in Alexandria and the grant of land to a Baptist church in Mississippi Territory – were in substantial effect private bills, even more so than were the importation bills, which he signed.

In his majority opinion in the *Walz* case, Burger made no reference to the "Detached Memoranda," but Justice Brennan, in his concurring opinion, did.[51] The arguments set forth in the "Detached Memoranda," he suggested, "represented at most an extreme view of church–state relations, which Madison himself may have reached only late in life." The basic principles in the "Detached Memoranda," however, are the same as those in Madison's "Memorial and Remonstrance," written when he was only thirty-five years old.

Justice Douglas, too, in his dissenting opinion, referred to the "Detached Memoranda," specifically mentioning the sentence: "Strongly guarded as is the separation between Religion & Govt in the Constitution of the United States the danger of encroachment by Ecclesiastical Bodies, may be illustrated by precedents already furnished in their short history."[52] He cited Madison's reference to "the attempt in Kentucky, for example, where it was proposed to exempt Houses of Worship from taxes."[53] He did not, however, refer to Madison's pocket veto, even though it dealt specifically with the issue before the Court in the *Walz* case and supported the position that Douglas took. Douglas admitted that "what Madison would have thought of the present state of subsidy to churches – a tax exemption as distinguished from an outright grant – no one can say with certainty."[54]

It may be that the explanation for Madison's apparent inconsistency lies in the arena of realpolitik. Madison would not say no to the petitioners in the first two Bible-tariff cases, but, by resorting to the pocket veto, he could prevent making the exemption in Baltimore and Massachusetts the law of the whole nation.

The fourth piece of legislation referred to in the "Detached Memoranda" in relationship to ecclesiastical encroachments on the constitutional mandate of church–state separation dealt with an attempt in Kentucky "to exempt Houses of Worship from taxes."[55] Unfortunately, Madison did not indicate when this apparently unsuccessful effort had taken place. What we do know is that the entry dated January 21, 1816, in the *Journal of the House of Representatives* (1815–16) of the commonwealth of Kentucky notes that the governor approved and signed "an act for exempting from taxation houses devoted to public worship, and seminaries of learning, and the ground on which they are erected."[56]

This is the exact opposite of what Madison wrote. Hence, two alternatives seem possible: Either Madison was mistaken about what had happened in Kentucky, or he wrote the "Detached Memoranda" (or at least this section) after the Kentucky act had been passed but before the news of it reached him. Neither alternative is acceptable based on other historical evidence, and the confusion remains.

The Deity in Governmental Documents

In the "Detached Memoranda," Madison referred briefly to the history of the proposed Virginia measure to provide for teachers of the Christian religion, his "Memorial and Remonstrance" opposing it, and the ensuing adoption of Jefferson's Virginia Statute for Religious Freedom. Referring to Jefferson's statute, Madison wrote:

> In the course of the opposition to the bill in the House of Delegates, which was warm and strenuous from some of the minority, an experiment was made on the reverence entertained for the name and sanctity of the Saviour, by proposing to insert the words "Jesus Christ" after the words "our lord" in the preamble, the object of which, would have been, to imply a restriction of the liberty defined in the bill, to those professing his religion only. The amendment was discussed, and rejected by a vote of against (See letter of J.M. to Mr. Jefferson dated   ) [omissions in original].
>
> The opponents of the amendment having turned the feeling as well as judgment of the House against it, by successfully contending that the better proof of reverence for that holy name would be not to profane it by making it a topic of legislative discussion, and particularly by making his religion the means of abridging the natural and equal rights of all men, in defiance of his own declaration that his Kingdom was not of this world.[57]

This deletion of the name Jesus Christ was not the last word on this subject in the history of our Constitution.[58] In *Vidal* v. *Girard's Executors* (1843),[59] the Supreme Court ruled that "the Christian religion is part of the common law" of all the states in the Union: "It is unnecessary for us to consider what would be the legal effect of a device . . . for the establishment of a school or college for the propagation of Judaism, or Deism, or any other form of infidelity. Such a case is not to be presumed in to exist in a Christian country."[60]

Some fifty years later, in the case of *Church of Holy Trinity* v. *United States*, (1892)[61] the Court ruled that "this is a Christian nation" and tendered as evidence the following oath required in the Delaware Constitution of all state employees: "I profess faith in God the Father, and in Jesus Christ His only Son, and in the Holy Ghosts, One God blessed he for evermore, and I do acknowledge the Holy Scripture of the Old and New Testament to be given by divine inspiration." As late as 1931, the Supreme Court could assert that "we are a Christian people . . . acknowledging with reverence the duty of obedience to the will of God."[62]

World War II and Hitler's determination to destroy every Jew in Europe and, perhaps, in the world, successful only to the extent of destroying 6 million Jews, had the effect of making Americans, including Supreme Court justices, somewhat more conscious of the fact that the concept of a Christian nation was no longer acceptable to the American conscience. So in lieu thereof came the "Judeo-Christian" formula. While Madison's "Memorial and Remonstrance" served to effect defeat of the proposal to insert the name Jesus Christ in Jefferson's proposed Statute for Religious Freedom, the statute still was allowed to open with the words, "Whereas Almighty God hath created the mind free," and to refer to "the holy Author of our religion . . . [the] Lord both of body and mind." Yet only a year later, Madison was able to draft and obtain enactment of a Constitution for the United States that omits any reference not only to "Jesus Christ," but even to "God" or "the Lord."[63]

Congressional Chaplaincies

"Is the appointment of Chaplains in the two Houses of Congress consistent with the Constitution, and with the pure principle of *religious freedom?*" Madison asked in the "Detached Memoranda."[64] He answered:

> [A] law appointing Chaplains establishes a religious worship for the national representatives, to be performed by ministers of religion, elected by a majority of them; and these are to be paid out of the national taxes. Does not this involve the principle of a *national establishment* applicable to a provision for a religious worship for the Constituent as well as of the representative Body, approved by the majority and conducted by ministers of religion paid by the entire nation?[65]

Thus Madison invoked both the "free-exercise" and the "establishment" clauses of the First Amendment as barriers to congressional chaplaincies. In the next paragraph, he asserted that the employment of chaplains also constitutes a "palpable violation of equal rights as well as Constitutional Principles," implying impermissibility even if there were no First Amendment.

This is quite understandable, inasmuch as the mandate of equal protection of the laws was not made part of the Constitution until the adoption of the Fourteenth Amendment in 1868; and even then, it was inapplicable to the federal government until it was read into the "due-process" clause of the Fifth Amendment in the 1954 case of *Barrows* v. *Jackson*.[66] Instead, Madison invoked the natural-law principles of the "divine rights of conscience," or, as Jefferson worded it in the Declaration of Independence, "the laws of nature":

> The tenets of the Chaplain elected [Madison continued] shut the door of worship against the members whose creeds and consciences forbid a participation in that of the majority. To say nothing of other sects, this is the case with that of Roman Catholics and Quakers who have always had numbers in one or both of the Legislative branches. Could a Catholic clergyman ever hope to be appointed a Chaplain?[67] To say that his religious principles are obnoxious or that his sect is small, is to lift the veil at once and exhibit in its naked deformity the doctrine that religious truth is to be tested by numbers, or that the major sects have a right to govern the minor.
>
> If Religion consists in voluntary acts of individuals, singly or voluntarily associated, and if it be proper that public functionaries, as well as their constituents should discharge their religious duties, let them, like their constituents, do so at their own expense. How small a contribution from each member of Congress would suffice for the purpose! How just would it be in its principle! How noble in its exemplary sacrifice to the genius of the Constitution; and the *divine rights of conscience!* Why should the expense of a religious worship for the Legislature, be paid by the public, more than that for the Executive or Judiciary branches of the Government?[68]

The post of legislative chaplain is as close to being a political sinecure as our government system allows.[69] Except in the well-attended and well-televised sessions of Congress, the chaplain need not be present when a session opens each day.

What Madison wrote in the "Detached Memoranda" cannot easily be reconciled with what he did when he was a member of the House of Representatives. In that capacity, he served on a joint committee of six (three from each House) chosen in 1789 to nominate candidates to be government-paid chaplains in both Houses.[70] It is hardly an adequate answer that this occurred before the First Amendment ban on laws respecting an establishment of religion became part of the Constitution. If he felt that the practice was wrong, First Amendment or no First Amendment, he should have said that it violated the "divine rights of conscience," and certainly not have been a participant in effecting it. More important, the last operative words of the Constitution (of which Madison was chief draftsman) expressly state that "no religious test shall ever be required as a qualification to any office or public trust under the United States."[71] One cannot easily assume that he did not consider a person's status as clergyman of some recognized faith a prerequisite for appointment as chaplain. Under Article VI of the Constitution, an atheist is eligible for appointment as congressional chaplain.

It should be noted that after Madison succeeded Jefferson as rector of the University of Virginia in 1826, he approved the appointment of a chaplain for religious instruction as long as his salary was paid by the voluntary contributions of the students' parents.[72] This, however, was at a time long before the First Amendment was held applicable to the states, and Article VI seemed to be limited to Federal officials. (Jefferson, his predecessor and the founder of the university, would not allow the setting aside of a room for religious worship and denied a specific request to hold religious services in university buildings on Sundays.)[73]

In a real sense, all this is irrelevant. If, as Madison argued, the practice of appointing congressional chaplains violates the Constitution, the fact that Madison himself was a transgressor is hardly conclusive. In the *Walz* case, Burger was not content with noting that tax exemption for churches was a common practice when the Constitution and the First Amendment were adopted; he tested the practice by the purpose, effect, and entanglement standard and found that it passed that test.[74] In *Marsh* v. *Chambers* (1983),[75] Burger did not subject legislative chaplaincies to the same test.[76]

In that case, a rather courageous member of the Nebraska legislature brought suit challenging the constitutionality of a longstanding practice of starting each day the legislature met with a prayer recited by a salaried chaplain. At the time the suit was brought, the chaplain had occupied the office for sixteen years, and during most of this period, his prayers were Christological. This had come to an end in 1980, as indicated by footnote 14 of the majority opinion: "[Chaplain] Palmer characterizes his prayers as 'non-sectarian,' 'Judeo Christian,' and with 'elements of the American civil religion.' App. 75 and 87. (Deposition of Robert E. Palmer). Although some of his earlier prayers were often explicitly Christian, Palmer removed all references to Christ after a 1980 complaint from a Jewish legislator."[77]

In the *Marsh* case, the district court held, and it was this holding that was appealed, that the state's appropriation of funds used to pay the chaplain's salary was unconstitutional, but that the practice itself was not.[78] (In this respect, it was echoing Madison's position.) The court of appeals (echoing Jefferson's) went further and ruled that the practice was unconstitutional in its entirety and that it did not matter whether or not the chaplain received salary for his services.[79] The Supreme Court decided that both lower courts were wrong and held that the practice itself was valid and so, too, was the chaplain's receipt of monetary compensation for his services.[80] The Court, in an opinion by Burger, held immaterial the fact that the chaplain had served for sixteen years; he noted that for the twenty years between 1949 and 1969, one chaplain had served in the United States Senate.[81]

In reaching their decisions, both lower courts had relied on the purpose, effect, and entanglement test, but, beyond mentioning this fact, the Supreme Court paid no further attention to it. Burger relied exclusively on history. Perhaps he did so because, as Brennan suggested in his dissenting opinion, the Nebraska law could not escape invalidation under any of the facets in the three-pronged test of constitutionality, especially the one relating to Burger's own contribution in *Walz* v. *Tax Commission*.[82]

In his recitation of history, Burger could hardly pretend that the "Detached Memoranda" never existed. He disposed of it in a short footnote.[83] To Brennan, the "Detached Memoranda" was more significant and relevant to the issue before the Court in the *Marsh* case than Burger considered it to be. In his dissenting opinion, he quoted, not as a footnote but in its body, the two paragraphs quoted above, answering in the negative the question whether the appointment of congressional chaplains is consistent with the Constitution.[84] Brennan also suggested that "Madison's later views [in the "Detached Memoranda"] may not have represented so much a change of *mind* as a change of *role,* from a member of Congress engaged in the hurley-burley of legislative activity to the detached observer engaged in unrepressed reflection."[85] The difficulty with this rationalization is that, what Madison voted for in the First Congress cannot be easily reconciled with what he had written five years earlier in the "Memorial and Remonstrance."

Military Chaplaincies

Madison was no more reconciled to military chaplaincies than he was to congressional chaplaincies, and (with one possible exception, to which we will return shortly) he was no more successful with respect to the former than he was with respect to the latter. He wrote:

> Better also to disarm in the same way the precedent of Chaplainships for the army and navy, than erect them into a political authority in matters of religion. The object of this establishment is seducing; the motive to it is laudable. But is it not safer to adhere to a right principle, and trust to its consequences, than confide in the reasoning however specious in favor of a wrong one. Look thro' the armies and navies of the world, and say whether in the appointment of their ministers of religion, the spiritual interest of the flocks or the temporal interest of the Shepherds, be most in view: whether here, as elsewhere the political care of religion is not a nominal more than a real aid. If the spirit of armies be devout, the spirit out of the armies will never be less so; and a failure of religious instruction and exhortation from a voluntary source within or without, will rarely happen: and if such be not the spirit of armies, the official services of their teachers are not likely to produce it. It is more likely to flow from the labours of a spontaneous zeal. The armies of the Puritans had their appointed Chaplains; but without these there would have been no lack of public devotion in that devout age.[86]

Noteworthy here is Madison's reference to "a political authority in matters of religion," a concept that in recent constitutional-law terminology has been called "the (impermissible) entanglement of government with religion."[87]

Madison recognized that in one area, there might be some apparent justification for government-supplied military chaplains:

> The case of navies with insulated crews may be less within the scope of these reflections. But it is not entirely so. The chance of a devout officer, might be of as much worth to religion, as the service of an ordinary chaplain. (Were it admitted that religion has a real interest in the latter.) But we are always to keep in mind that it is safer to trust the consequences of a right principle, than reasonings in support of a bad one.[88]

Opponents of military chaplaincies today recognize, as did Madison, the need of many soldiers for spiritual help, particularly in periods of stress and crisis. They agree with him that the churches could provide this even more effectively and certainly more honestly if the chaplains were not part of the military establishment, if they were paid by the churches rather than by the government, and – it might be added – if they did not wear military uniforms and did not hold military rank. Godly men, he could have added, are human too, and in the military, they want good efficiency reports, promotions in rank, and decorations. To achieve these, they are strongly tempted to use their spiritual influence with the soldiers in a way that would further the political goal of winning a war. The following incident, which was reported in the March 1, 1967, issue of the Jewish Telegraph Agency *Daily News Bulletins,* illustrates:

> A U.S. Army private who embarked on a "death fast" because he claimed his religious conviction as an Orthodox Jew prevented him from serving an army practicing violence in Viet Nam, has been taken into custody and confined in a mental ward. . . .
>
> Defense Department officials disclosed that the Army is trying to get rabbis to convince [Private Robert] Levy that the war is righteous and his fast unjustified.

The exception referred to above is found in the case of *Laird* v. *Anderson* (1972).[89] The Supreme Court refused to review a Court of Appeals decision ruling violative of the "establishment" clause the regulations in the military academies that require cadets and midshipmen to attend religious services in order to make them better and more effective combat officers.[90] These regulations, the Court held, violate the clause because they utilize religion to further the secular cause of winning wars.

It must be recognized that Madison's suggestion that the "chance of a devout officer, might be of as much worth to religion, as the service of an ordinary chaplain" seems to sanction violation of the First Amendment mandate of church–state separation, which forbids governmental use of religion as an instrument to achieve a secular end, even, at least according to Madison, one as important as winning a war. Moreover, in selecting military officers, the authorities would naturally consider their devoutness, which would hardly be reconcilable with the ban on religious tests for public office imposed by Article VI of the Constitution.

It should be noted that the two wars in which the United States had been engaged before Madison wrote the "Detached Memoranda," the Revolutionary War and the War of 1812, had taken place on American soil, where churches and pastors were available. The same could not be said of our combat in Japan, Korea, and Vietnam, and one cannot assume that there would be available enough volunteer ministers who would, or financially could, leave their pulpits and their families for unpaid service at a battlefront thousands of miles away from home should their churches be unable or unwilling to pay them as they pay their missionaries.

In his concurring opinion in *Abington School District* v. *Schempp* (1963),[91] Brennan recognized that military chaplaincies may not be easily reconciled with the "establishment" clause, and yet be defensible under the "free-exercise" clause:

> There are certain practices conceivably violative of the Establishment Clause, the striking down of which might seriously interfere with certain religious liberties also protected by the First Amendment. Provisions for churches and chaplains at military establishments for those in the armed services may afford one such example. . . . It is argued that such provisions may be assumed to contravene the Establishment Clause, yet be sustained on constitutional grounds as necessary to secure to the members of the Armed Forces and prisoners those rights of worship guaranteed under the Free Exercise Clause. Since government has deprived such persons of the opportunity to practice their faith at places of their choice, the argument runs, government may, in order to avoid infringing the free exercise guarantees, provide substitutes where it requires such persons to be.[92]

Finally, in more recent years, the Supreme Court has held that neither the "establishment" nor the "free-exercise" mandate is absolute; what would ordinarily be deemed violations are constitutionally permissible if necessary to accomplish a compelling state purpose and are tailored to do so in the least restrictive manner under the circumstances. Viewed in this light, the army's effort "to get rabbis to convince Levy that the war [was] righteous" was not quite as horrendous as it would seem at first glance.

Religious Proclamations by the Government

To Madison, presidential religious proclamations "recommending thanksgiving and fasts" were "shoots from the same root with the other legislative acts reviewed" in the "Detached Memoranda." Although the proclamations may be only recommendations, they imply religious actions not delegated "to the political rulers."[93] Actions of Congress, such as in laws making Thanksgiving, Christmas, or New Year's Day official holidays, and expression of a combined resolution by Congress and Proclamation by the President, such as the designation of 1983 as the "Year of the Bible," may also imply religious actions.

Madison listed five objections to religious proclamations:[94]

1. Governments ought not to interpose themselves in relation to

matters not within their authority to do so with effect: "An *advisory* government is a contradiction in terms [Madison's emphasis]."

2. Members of a government cannot in any sense be regarded as possessing a trust from their constituents to advise them on matters of faith or conscience. In their individual capacites, as distinct from their official status, they can unite to make recommendations of any sort whatever, but they must make it clear that they are speaking as individuals.

3. Presidential recommendations "seem to imply and certainly nourish the erroneous ideal of a *national* religion [Madison's emphasis]." This idea, of "theocracy," just as it related to the Jewish nation,[95] had been improperly adopted by many nations that embraced Christianity and was "too apt to lurk in the bosoms even of Americans," who, in general, were "aware of the distinction between religious and political Societies."

4. The tendency of the practice was to narrow the recommendation to the standard of the predominant sect. The first proclamation, dated July 1, 1795, recommended a day of thanksgiving that "embraced all who believed in a supreme ruler of the Universe."[96] "That of Mr. Adams called for a *Christian* worship."[97] The proclamations issued by Madison were critized by many for using the general terms used by Washington rather than Adams's specific term "Christian."[98]

5. The last, but not the least, objection was "the liability of the practice to [become] a subserviency to political views; to the scandal of religion, as well as the increase of party animosity." Washington's proclamation, issued just after the insurrection in Pennsylvania "and at a time when the public mind was divided on several topics, was so construed by many." Hamilton, Secretary of Treasury, in a marginal note on the draft proclamation wrote: "In short the proclamation ought to savour as much as possible of religion, and not too much of having a political object[ive]."[99]

Madison concluded the part of the "Detached Memoranda" to which this paper is addressed by noting that

during the administration of Mr. Jefferson no religious proclamation was issued. It being understood that his successor [Madison] was disinclined to such interpositions of the Executive and by some supposed moreover that they might originate with more propriety with the Legislative Body, a resolution was passed requesting him to issue a proclamation.

It was thought not proper to refuse a compliance altogether; but a form and language were employed, which were meant to deaden as much as possible any claim of political right to enjoin religious observances by resting these expressly on the voluntary compliance of individuals, and even by limiting the recommendation to such as wished simultaneous as well as voluntary performance of a religious act on the occasion.[100]

Jefferson had no problem in refusing to issue proclamations for prayers or fasts. Writing to Reverend Samuel Miller, he explained: "Fasting and prayer are religious exercises; the enjoining them an act of discipline. Every religious society has a right to determine for itself the times for these exercises, and the objects proper for them, according to their own particular tenets; and the right can never be safer than in their hands, where the Constitution has deposited it."[101]

Like Jefferson, President Andrew Jackson did feel it "proper to refuse a compliance altogether." He refused to issue a proclamation for prayer because he believed that he would be "transcending the limits presented by the Constitution for the President, and might disturb the security which religion now enjoys in the country, in its complete separation from the political concerns of the General Government."[102]

With the exceptions of Jefferson and Jackson, and partly that of Madison, however, American presidents have found no constitutional or other problem in issuing proclamations for prayer or thanksgiving. The basic questions relating to the constitutionality of governmental involvement in religious celebrations did not reach the Supreme Court until the 1984 case of *Lynch* v. *Donnelly*.[103]

The case involved a taxpayer's challenge to the funding of the placing and maintaining of a crèche, or nativity scene, in the heart of the shopping district of Pawtucket, Rhode Island. By a vote of 5 to 4, the Court, in an opinion by Burger, upheld the constitutionality of the city's action. He was persuaded that the city had had a valid secular purpose for including a crèche in a Christmas display, that it had not impermissibly advanced religion, and that it had not created an excessive entanglement between church and state.

To support his decision, Burger stated in footnote 2:

> The day after the First Amendment was proposed, Congress urged President Washington to proclaim "a day of public thanksgiving and prayer, to be observed by acknowledging with grateful hearts, the many and signal favours of Almighty God." President

Washington proclaimed November 26, 1789, a day of thanksgiving to "offe[r] our prayers and supplications to the Great Lord and Ruler of Nations, and beseech Him to pardon our national and other transgressions. . . ."

Presidents Adams and Madison also issued thanksgiving proclamations, as have almost all our presidents.[104]

This joinder of Washington, Adams, and Madison is not complete, and to some extent it is misleading. As the "Detached Memoranda" discloses, Washington, Adams, and Madison did issue religious proclamations, but they were not identical. Washington's embraced "all who believed in a supreme ruler of the Universe." Adams's called for a Christian worship. Madison certainly did not endorse Adams's proclamation; he felt it not proper to refuse altogether compliance with a congressional resolution requesting him to issue a proclamation, so he worded it "to deaden as much as possible any claim of political right to enjoin religious observances."[105]

In his majority opinion, Burger, quite naturally, made no mention of the "Detached Memoranda," but neither did Brennan in his dissenting opinion, perhaps because it was not until 1836, the year in which Madison died, that any state granted a legal recognition to Christmas as a public holiday.[106] Brennan did, however, echo the spirit, if not the words, of the "Detached Memoranda":

> The nativity scene is clearly distinct in its purpose and effect from the rest of the Hodgson Park display for the simple reason that it is the only one rooted in a biblical account of Christ's birth. It is the chief symbol of the characteristically Christian belief that a divine Savior was brought into the world and that the purpose of this miraculous birth was to illuminate a path toward salvation and redemption. For Christians, that path is exclusive, precious and holy. But for those who do not share these beliefs, the symbolic re-enactment of the birth of a divine being who has been miraculously incarnated as a man stands as a dramatic reminder of their differences with Christian faith. To be so excluded on religious grounds by one's elected government is an insult and an injury that, until today, could not be countenanced by the Establishment Clause.[107]

As a footnote, quoting Martin Buber, he added: "For Christians, of course, the essential message of the nativity is that God became incarnate in the person of Christ. But just as fundamental to Jewish thought is the belief in the non-incarnation of God."[108] To these quoted words of Brennan and Buber should be added those that begin an essay by Norman Redlich (like Buber, a Jew), dean of New York University School of Law: "The United States Supreme Court's decision in the Pawtucket, R. I. creche case insults American Jews and all others who do not share what the Court's majority perceives as the country's dominant belief, Christianity."[109]

As a final note, it should be added that President Reagan's Solicitor General, Rex E. Lee, undoubtedly at the president's direction, intervened in the *Lynch* case and in his argument to the Supreme Court urged it to uphold the constitutionality of the crèche. It is a reasonable assumption that Madison would never have intervened.

Conclusion

A good case can be made for the premise that no single American contributed as much as, and certainly none more than, Madison to this nation's making church–state separation a fundamental, constitutionally protected principle. The history of the "Detached Memoranda" testifies quite clearly that at times, his reach exceeded his grasp. Tax exemption and legislative chaplaincies, among others, are examples.

But even with respect to tax exemption, it should be noted that the Supreme Court in the *Walz* case held only that it is a constitutionally permissible privilege; it refused to hold, as urged in the amicus curiae briefs of the National Council of Churches and the Synagogue Council of America, that it is a constitutionally protected right, and therefore immune from legislative repeal or even limitations.[110] Moreover, although the Court did not find it necessary to pass on the issue in *Diffenderfer* v. *Central Baptist Church of Miami* (1972)[111] (because the challenged statute was repealed while the case was pending), for all practical purposes, it is the law of the land that income earned by churches from nonreligious business enterprises is constitutionally taxable.

Above all, it was Madison, more than anyone else, who established the constitutional law forbidding the use of tax-raised funds to finance the operations of religious schools and mandating the exclusion of religious instruction and teacher-organized prayer in the public schools; his "Memorial and Remonstrance" led to the Virginia Statute for Religious Freedom, which, in turn, led to *Everson* v. *Board of Education, McCollum* v. *Board of Education,* and the many Supreme Court decisions that are the offspring of both these cases.

Madison's credo, from which he rarely departed throughout his life, is perhaps best epitomized in a paragraph of a letter he wrote to Edward Everett of Massachusetts in 1824:

The settled opinion here is that religion is essentially distinct from civil Government, and exempt from its cognizance; that a connection between them is injurious to both; that there are causes in the human breast which ensure the perpetuity of religion without the aid of the law; that rival sects, with equal rights, exercise mutual censorships in favor of good morale; that if new sects arise with absurd opinions or over-heated imagination,[112] the proper remedies lie in time, forbearance, and example; that a legal establishment of religion without a toleration could not be thought of, and with a toleration, is no security for public quiet and harmony, but rather a source itself of discord and animosity; and, finally, that these opinions are supported by experience, which has shown that every relaxation of the alliance between law and religion, from the partial example of Holland to its consummation in Pennsylvania, Delaware, New Jersey, etc., has been found as safe in practice as it is sound in theory. Prior to the Revolution the Episcopal Church was established by law in this State. On the Declaration of Independence it was left, with all other sects, to a self-support. And no doubt exists that there is much more religion among us now than there ever was before the change, and particularly in the sect which enjoyed the legal patronage. This proves rather more than that the law is not necessary to the support of religion.[113]

It is perhaps most appropriate to close this paper with Madison's almost sermonic plea to the American people:

Ye States of America, which retain in your Constitutions or Codes, any aberration from the sacred principle of religious liberty, by giving to Caesar what belongs to God, or joining together what God has put asunder, hasten to revise and purify your systems, and make the example of your Country as pure and compleat, in what relates to the freedom of the mind and its allegiance to its maker, as in what belongs to the legitimate objects of political and civil institutions.[114]

NOTES

1   330 U.S. 1.
2   Ibid., at 12–14.
3   Ibid., at 37 ff.
4   Ibid., at 19.
5   Part of the text of the Virginia Statute is set forth in ibid., at 28.

6   Francis N. Thorpe, *Federal and State Constitutions, Colonial Charters and Other Organic Laws* (Washington, D.C.: Government Printing Office, 1909), pp. 1889–90.
7   Anson Phelps Stokes and Leo Pfeffer, *Church and State in the United States* (New York: Harper & Row, 1964), p. 75.
8   Ibid., 77–8.
9   As early as 1776, Thomas Paine, in his pamphlet *Common Sense,* anticipated the First Amendment in stating that "as to religion, I hold it to be the indisputable duty of government to protect all conscientious professors thereof, and I know of no other business which government hath to do therewith."
10 *William and Mary Quarterly,* 3d ser., 3 (1946): 534.
11 In this essay, the *William and Mary* article will be referred to as "Fleet," and the *Harper's* article, as "Hunt."
12 330 U.S., at 12.
13 Ibid., at 37 and footnote 21.
14 366 U.S. 420. The case involved a challenge to the constitutionality of Sunday closing laws. "Only in Virginia and Rhode Island," Frankfurter wrote, "had the ideal of complete church–state separation been realized." As authority for Virginia, he cited the "Detached Memoranda" (ibid., at 486, footnote 43).
15 397 U.S. 664.
16 103 S. Ct. 3330.
17 Fleet, p. 534.
18 Ibid.
19 Ibid., p. 535.
20 310 U.S. 296.
21 330 U.S. 1.
22 Article I, Section 8, of the Constitution reads in part: "The Congress shall have power . . . to promote the progress of science and useful arts, by securing for limited times to authors and inventors the exclusive right to their respective writings and discoveries."
23 In discussing ecclesiastical monopolies, Madison dealt with government-granted monopolies, not with those that are economically developed.
24 Fleet, p. 557.
25 Ibid., p. 552.
26 Ibid., p. 555.
27 The bill was vetoed on February 21, 1811 (ibid., n. 47).
28 *Messages and Papers of the Presidents,* ed. James D. Richardson (Washington, D.C., 1896–99), 1: 489.
29 Anson Phelps Stokes, *Church and State in the United States* (New York: Harper & Brothers, 1950), 3: 414.
30 397 U.S. 664.
31 *Church of Latter-Day Saints* v. *United States,* 136 U.S. 1 (1896).
32 *Messages and Papers of the Presidents,* 1: 490.
33 Jeremiah Black, *Essays and Speeches* (New York: Appleton, 1885), p. 53.

34 175 U.S. 291.

35 403 U.S. 602.

36 448 U.S. 297.

37 Ibid., at 319.

38 105 S. Ct. 3232.

39 105 S. Ct. 3216.

40 105 S. Ct. 2479.

41 Fleet, p. 555. Hunt gives only the year (p. 490).

42 *Messages and Papers of the Presidents,* 1: 490.

43 Irving Brant, "Madison: On the Separation of Church and State," *William and Mary Quarterly,* 3d ser., 8 (1951): 18.

44 454 U.S. 464.

45 392 U.S. 83.

46 Fleet, p. 555.

47 The first veto, also by Madison, was of a naturalization bill passed in 1812.

48 The source for this is U.S. Congress, House, House Document No. 493, 70th Cong., 2d sess., p. 2.

49 397 U.S. 664.

50 Ibid., at 677. The reference is to 6 Stat. 116 (1813).

51 Ibid., at 684, footnote 5.

52 Ibid., at 712–13.

53 Ibid., at 713.

54 Ibid.

55 Fleet, p. 555. The author of this essay wishes to express his appreciation to Laurel Welch, librarian of the Kentucky Historical Association, for her assistance in his presentation of this aspect of the tax-exemption question.

56 Commonwealth of Kentucky, *Journal of the House of Representatives,* p. 245.

57 Fleet, p. 556.

58 For a fuller discussion of the use of the name of God in government documents, see Leo Pfeffer, "The Deity in American Constitutional History," *Journal of Church and State* 23 (Spring 1981): 215–39.

59 2 How (43 U.S.) 127.

60 Ibid., at 198.

61 143 U.S. 457, at 469.

62 *United States* v. *Macintosh,* 283 U.S. 605, at 625.

63 In a literal sense, this is not quite accurate. Article VII of the Constitution, as adopted, reads in part: "Done in convention by the unanimous consent of the States present the Seventeenth day of September in the year of our Lord one thousand seven hundred and eighty seven, and of the independence of the United States of America the Twelfth. In witness whereof we have hereunto subscribed our names." Official government documents generally no longer use the phrase "year of our Lord," but the abbreviation A.D. is quite often used, and B.C. is always used.

64 Fleet, p. 558. Emphasis added.

65 Ibid. Emphasis added.

66   346 U.S. 249.
67   In 1832, a few years after this was written, Charles Constantine Pise, a Catholic priest, was elected chaplain of the Senate. Four years later, Andrew Jackson appointed, and the Senate confirmed the appointment of, Roger Taney, a Roman Catholic, to the Chief Justiceship of the Supreme Court.
68   Fleet, pp. 558–9. Emphasis added.
69   It is also a religious sinecure. Indeed, the word "sinecure" has a religious etymology, from the Latin *beneficium sine cura,* "benefice without care." Webster's *Third New International Dictionary* defines "sinecure" as (1) "an ecclesiastical benefice without cure of souls," and (2) "an office or position that requires little or no work and that usually provides a sermon."
70   *Annals of Congress,* 1: 18, cited in Stokes, *Church and State in the United States,* 1: 456.
71   Article VI, paragraph 3.
72   Robert F. Butts, *The American Tradition in Religion and Education* (Boston: Beacon Press, 1950), p. 130.
73   Ibid., p. 128.
74   Under this test, a court must decide if (1) there is a secular legislative purpose, (2) a primary effect of the challenged practice either advances or inhibits religion, and (3) it avoids excessive government entanglement with religion.
75   463 U.S. 783.
76   The constitutionality of legislative chaplaincies was considered in the Massachusetts case of *Colo* v. *Treasurer* (392 N.E. 2d 1195 [1979]). The state's highest court, in upholding the constitutionality of the practice, did cite and quote from Madison's "Detached Memoranda," but decided the case under the purpose-effect-entanglement test and found that it passed that test. In *Elliot* v. *White* (23 F. 2d 997 [1928]), a federal court suit challenging payment of salaries to congressional and army chaplains was dismissed on the grounds that taxpayers do not have standing to bring such a suit.
77   463 U.S., at 793, footnote 14.
78   504 F. Supp. 585 (1980).
79   675 F. 2d 288 (1981).
80   *Marsh* v. *Chambers,* 463 U.S. 783 (1983).
81   Ibid., at 794, footnote 17.
82   Ibid., at 796.
83   Ibid., at 791, footnote 12.
84   Ibid., at 807–808.
85   Ibid., at 815.
86   Fleet, pp. 559–60.
87   See, for example, *Walz* v. *Tax Commission,* 397 U.S. 664, at 674 (1970); *Lemon* v. *Kurtzman,* 403 U.S. 602, at 629–30 (1971).
88   Fleet, p. 559.
89   409 U.S. 1076.
90   466 F. 2d 283 (1972).

91   374 U.S. 203. It should be noted that the free-exercise justification is valid
     only with respect to conscripted members of the armed forces.
92   Ibid., at 296.
93   Fleet, p. 560.
94   Ibid., pp. 560–2.
95   The term "theocracy" was coined by Josephus, a Jewish historian of the
     first century A.D., to describe the polity of the Jews in the era of the Second
     Temple (*Encyclopaedia Judaica*, s. v. "Theocracy").
96   Fleet, p. 561. Washington had issued an earlier proclamation on October
     3, 1789, but it was at the request of Congress, not on his own initiative.
97   Fleet, p. 561. Madison's emphasis.
98   Ibid.
99   Ibid.
100 Ibid., p. 562; Hunt, p. 495.
101 Thomas Jefferson to Samuel Miller, January 23, 1808, *Writings of Thomas
     Jefferson*, Monticello ed., ed. Andrew A. Lipscomb and Albert Ellery Bergh
     (Washington, D.C., 1905), 10: 428–30.
102 Quoted in Stokes, *Church and State in the United States*, 3: 181.
103 465 U.S. 668. For a more complete discussion of this case, see Leo Pfeffer,
     Religion, State and the Burger Court (Buffalo, N.Y.: Prometheus Books, 1984),
     pp. 113–26.
104 *Lynch* v. *Donnelly*, 465 U.S., at 675, footnote 2.
105 In 1982, Reagan signed a congressional resolution proclaiming 1983 to be
     the "Year of the Bible . . . in recognition of both the formative influence
     the Bible has been for our Nation, and our national need to study and apply
     the teachings of the Holy Scripture." A decision by the United States Dis-
     trict Court in California rejected a suit challenging the validity of the pro-
     clamation under the "establishment" clause. The court ruled that since the
     proclamation had no force of law, imposed no penalties or sanctions of any
     kind, and did not authorize the president to exact any particular behavior
     from any individual, it could not be adjudged unconstitutional (*Zwerling*
     v. *Reagan*, 576 F. Supp. 1373 [1983]).
106 *Lynch* v. *Donnelly*, 465 U.S., at 723.
107 Ibid., at 708.
108 Ibid., at 708, footnote 14.
109 Norman Redlich, "Nativity Ruling Insults Jews," *New York Times*, March
     26, 1984, p. A-19.
110 Pfeffer, *Religion, State and the Burger Court*, pp. 4–5; Dean Kelley, *Why
     Churches Should Not Pay Taxes* (New York: Harper & Row, 1977), pp. 44–
     5.
111 404 U.S. 412.
112 Today, they are called "cults," but are as much entitled to First Amend-
     ment protection as are accepted and respected religious faiths (*Larson* v.
     Valente, 456 U.S. 228 [1982]). "The constitutional [that is, "establishment"
     clause] prohibition of denominational preferences," the Court said in that

case, which involved Reverend Moon's Unification Church, "is inexorably connected with the continuing vitality of the Free Exercise Clause" (ibid., at 245). The Court quoted in support of this assertion Madison's statement in *The Federalist,* No. 52: "Security for civil rights must be the same as that for religious rights: it consists in one case in a multiplicity of interests and in the other of sects."

113 Quoted in Stokes, *Church and State in the United States,* 1: 396–7.
114 Fleet, p. 555.

12

The Supreme Court and the Serpentine Wall

A. E. DICK HOWARD

Almost from the beginning of the republic, the United States Supreme Court has been an arena for issues with momentous political overtones. Few critics of the modern Court can have been more upset by the Court's decisions than Thomas Jefferson and Spencer Roane were by John Marshall's opinions in cases such as *Marbury* v. *Madison* (1803) and *Cohens* v. *Virginia* (1821).[1]

In recent years, especially since the advent of the Warren Court, the Supreme Court's docket has tended to mirror the country's social and political struggles. Imitating the example set by the NAACP's Legal Aid and Defense Fund, public-interest groups have often gone to court to further their cause.

What liberal groups, such as the ACLU or NAACP, can do, conservative groups can do, too. Both in and out of court, groups such as the Washington Legal Foundation, the Free Congress Foundation, and the Center for Judicial Studies, all strongly conservative, are urging an agenda that typically includes an effort to curb what is perceived as judicial activism on the bench.

Such conservative organizations have a natural ally in the Reagan administration. One account calls them a "budding and influential cadre of conservative activists providing the intellectual underpinning for the Reagan Administration's stances on busing, abortion, school prayer, crime, and civil rights."[2]

The Reagan administration, riding the crest of the president's electoral triumphs in 1980 and 1984, has directed considerable effort at moving the country in new directions. Much of that effort is, of course, directed at Congress and at public opinion. Another avenue is the courts, both their personnel and their opinions. It was estimated that as early as the end of 1985, President Reagan would have appointed even more federal judges than the record number (245) chosen by President Carter.[3]

Ultimately, any administration must reckon with the Supreme Court. For years, ever since President Nixon appointed four justices (Burger, Blackmun, Powell, and Rehnquist) to the Court in the late 1960s and early 1970s, there has been unending speculation as to whether and when a "conservative" majority might come into being on the Court. One of the paradoxes of the Burger Court was the extent to which, despite appointments by Republican presidents (no vacancies occurred during the Carter presidency), the Court was often an activist tribunal.[4] Examples might include the Court's 1972 decision striking down capital-punishment laws as then administered in the states, decisions expanding opportunities for litigants to sue under the general federal civil-rights statute (42 U.S.C. § 1983), and, of course, the decision in *Roe* v. *Wade* (1973), which grounds a woman's abortion right in the Constitution.[5]

In the Term ending in the summer of 1984, however, it appeared as though, after so many years of directionless searching, the Court might be moving into a new direction, with a working conservative majority at last in control. In the 1983 Term, the Court handed down several major opinions portending a more conservative mood. Among them were decisions upholding the Reagan administration's restrictions on travel to Cuba, limiting the use of racial quotas in employment cases, narrowing the reach of the federal law banning sex discrimination in colleges that receive federal assistance, creating the first significant exception to *Miranda,* and making inroads on the Fourth Amendment's exclusionary rule.[6] One observer said that the Court had entered an era of "aggressive majoritarianism," that it was a Court "that sees the Constitution through the eyes of mainline America."[7] The ACLU's Burt Neuborne called it a "genuinely appalling Term," in which the Court had functioned "not as a vigorous guardian of the individual, but as a cheerleader for the government."[8] Conservatives were pleased, but thought the Court had not yet moved far enough to the right. The Free Congress Research and Education Foundation's Patrick B. McGuigan said that the Court in 1983 and 1984 had moved "slightly toward a more constructionist, conservative reading of the Constitution" but that "significant progress is still needed in the years ahead."[9]

One of the opinions of the 1983 Term was *Lynch* v. *Donnelly.*[10] In that case, a majority of the justices rejected a challenge to the display by the city of Pawtucket, Rhode Island, of a city-owned crèche in a public park at the Christmas season. The previous Term, the Court had decided two important religion cases – one permitting the Nebraska legislature to use public funds to pay a legislative chaplain, and the other upholding a Minnesota tuition-credit statute whose principal beneficiaries were parents of children in parochial schools.[11] Taken together, the three cases could be read to portend a significant shift in the Supreme Court's approach to cases arising under the establishment clause of the First Amendment. As the 1984 Term opened, attention was riveted on several important religion cases, and the stage was set for further major judicial pronouncements about church–state relations.[12]

In the pages that follow, I propose to explore (1) in brief, the evolution of the Supreme Court's thinking about establishment clause cases, (2) the arguments made in briefs filed in parties and by amici (including the government) before the Court in four of the religion cases heard during the 1984 Term, and (3) the decisions in those cases and the implications that may be drawn from them.

The Establishment Clause in the Supreme Court

One hears so much about Thomas Jefferson and the "wall of separation" between church and state that one might suppose that Jefferson was the author of the First Amendment and that "wall of separation" is its key phrase. In fact, Jefferson was not even a member of the First Congress, which drafted the First Amendment, and his "wall of separation" came into the lexicon of American politics years later, with a letter he wrote to the Danbury Baptists in 1802.[13]

Jefferson and his fellow Virginian James Madison were the guiding light for Justice Hugo L. Black, when that jurist wrote the seminal establishment clause case in the modern Supreme Court, *Everson v. Board of Education* (1947).[14] Tracing the events in Virginia that led to Madison's drafting of the "Memorial and Remonstrance" and to the enactment of Jefferson's Bill for Establishing Religious Liberty, Black concluded that the First Amendment was meant to provide "the same protection against governmental intrusion on religious liberty as the Virginia statute."[15]

Everson was the subject of much criticism. Erwin Griswold labeled Black an "absolutist," and Paul Kauper said, "Nothing in the historical research to date lends authority to Justice Black's broad interpretation" of the First Amendment.[16] Such objections notwithstanding, *Everson* has been for forty years the benchmark against which positions on the meaning of the establishment clause have been measured. Ironically, *Everson* itself suggested the difficulties of drawing lines under the First Amendment: Despite Black's separationist language, he concluded that the practice challenged in the case (New Jersey's reimbursing parents of parochial-school children for the cost of bus transportation) was constitutional.

In the years since *Everson,* the justices have struggled with the meaning and application of the establishment clause. Oftentimes, the judgment calls have been as close as those at Wimbledon. In 1948, the Court struck down an Illinois released-time program (under which religious instructors were permitted to come into public-school classrooms), but four years later, the justices upheld a New York program that released students to receive religious instruction off the public-school grounds.[17] In the early 1960s, the Court ruled against the saying of prayers and against the reading of the Bible in public schools, but the justices voted to sustain Sunday closing laws, on the theory that, notwithstanding their religious origins, they now served a secular purpose.[18]

Individual justices seemed uncertain about the proper course for the Court. Justice William O. Douglas, writing the opinion upholding released-time programs off public-school premises, declared, "We are a religious people whose institutions presuppose a Supreme Being."[19] Ten years later, however, Douglas confessed that he had changed his mind about *Everson,* whose result (upholding the New Jersey law) he thought "in retrospect to be out of line with the First Amendment."[20]

Between 1969 and 1971, President Nixon appointed four justices to the Court. The advent of these new faces came at the same time that the Court began to see yet more church-and-state cases on its docket. In his first term on the Court, Chief Justice Warren Burger read the First Amendment as permitting "benevolent neutrality" by government toward religion. Thus in *Walz* v. *Tax Commission* (1970), he wrote for a near-unanimous Court (only Douglas dissenting) upholding property-tax exemptions for religious property.[21]

Cases like *Walz* and the previous decision in *Board of Education* v. *Allen* (1968) (permitting New York to lend textbooks to students in parochial schools) encouraged legislators who saw in the notion of "benevolent neutrality" a green light for more extensive state aid to parochial schools.[22] In a string of decisions in the 1970s, however, the Court struck down a variety of parochiaid programs. The key case was *Lemon* v. *Kurtzman* (1971), invalidating a Rhode Island statute giving salary supplements to teachers in nonpublic schools and a Pennsylvania act authorizing the "purchase" by the state of "secular" educational services from private schools.[23] In a 1973 decision, *Committee for Public Education & Religious Liberty* v. *Nyquist,* a divided court struck down three New York programs – direct grants to private schools for "maintenance and repair" of facilities and equipment, a tuition-reimbursement plan for low-income parents of children in private schools, and tax deductions for parents who did not qualify for tuition reimbursement.[24] In *Meek* v. *Pittenger* (1975), the Court invalidated several Pennsylvania programs, including the loan of instructional equipment and materials to parochial schools and the provision of "auxiliary" services, such as counseling, testing, and speech and hearing therapy.[25] In *Wolman* v. *Walter* (1977), the Court relaxed the barriers only slightly, permitting Ohio to provide specialized diagnostic, guidance, and other services to students in religious schools if the services were not performed on school premises.[26]

Even from this brief survey, one can see how fine the lines tended to be drawn. Because of *Allen*, it was all right to lend textbooks to parochial-school students, but *Meek* and *Wolman* forbade the lending of instructional materials and equipment for use in religious schools. The state could reimburse parents for the cost of getting their children to and from parochial schools (*Everson*), but could not pick up the tab for field trips from those schools, such as to museums and art galleries (*Wolman*). Specialized counseling and therapy that could not be provided on a parochial school's premises (*Meek*) could be provided off grounds (*Wolman*).

Mathematicians have their calipers, but judges must settle for "tests." Establishment clause litigation in the Supreme Court has produced a three-part test summed up as follows in Chief Justice Burger's opinion in *Lemon* v. *Kurtzman:* "First, the statute must have a secular legislative purpose; second, its principal or primary effect must be one that neither advances nor inhibits religion . . . ; finally, the statute must not foster 'an excessive entanglement with religion.' "[27] An additional inquiry (although not formally a separate "test" in the Court's cases) asks whether a program carries a "potentially divisive political effect," that is, tends to stir political controversy along sectarian lines.[28]

Both the Court's analytical techniques and the results it has reached in establishment clause cases have provoked various criticisms. Some justices, such as White and Rehnquist, have thought the Court's approach too demanding and unrealistic. They, and some of the commentators, especially dislike the "entanglement" test, seeing it operate as a kind of Catch-22 (the more a state does to avoid the "effect" of aiding religion, the more likely it is to run into "entanglement" problems).[29] Justice Stevens, however, thinks that through its three-part analysis, the Court has simply encouraged the states "to search for new ways of achieving forbidden ends"; he has suggested abandoning the three-part analysis altogether and returning to Black's *Everson* opinion.[30]

While the Court's decisions of the 1970s often reached separationist results, there were also some justices who, in dissent, thought that a challenged program (such as aid to parochial schools) should be upheld as being "general-welfare" legislation (that is, viewing students rather than religious schools as the program's beneficiaries).[31] They have complained of the majority's striking down a statute because of "speculation" about potential dangers (such as subsidizing religious indoctrination), rather than requiring evidence that the evils implicated under the establishment clause have actually come about on the facts of the case.[32] Such dissenters hoped that in time a majority of the justices would abandon the notion of a "wall of separation," that separation would give way to accommodation.

Accommodation in the 1980s

The 1980s opened with only a hint of the doctrinal shifts that that decade would soon see. Ten years earlier, in 1970, the New York legislature had appropriated public funds to reimburse nonpublic schools for performing various services, including the testing of students. Tests for which a school could be reimbursed under the 1970s law included not only tests prepared by the state itself, but also the more common and familiar tests prepared by the school's own teachers. In 1973, the Supreme Court struck down this statute as violating the establishment clause.[33]

On the heels of the 1973 decision, the New York legislature immediately sought to patch up its statute. A revised law, enacted in 1974, directed state repayment of nonpublic schools' costs incurred in complying with certain examinations and reports required by state law; omitted was any reimbursement for tests prepared and administered by the schools' teachers. When this version of the New York law reached the Supreme Court, in *Committee for Public Education & Religious Liberty* v. *Regan* (1980), it was upheld.[34]

Justice White, speaking for a five-man majority, reasoned that the grading of tests furnished by the state itself was a function having a secular purpose and primarily a secular effect. It did not make the arrangements unconstitutional that the state made cash payments to the schools, including church-related schools, to administer the tests.[35]

Some might view *Regan* as but a minor adjustment in the body of doctrine developed in the 1970s. After all, in *Wolman* v. *Walter,* the Court had upheld an Ohio statute supplying nonpublic-school students with standardized tests and scoring services used in the public schools.[36] In either case – that from Ohio and that from New York – the private school was being relieved of the cost of grading examinations required and furnished by the state. But Justice Blackmun, dissenting in *Regan,* thought the Court was taking "a long step backwards" by rewarding New York for its persistence in looking for ways to aid parochial schools. New York's laws channeled as much as $10 million a year to private schools, most of which were sectarian, and thus relieved those schools of direct costs they would have been obliged to incur had there been no reimbursement. Justice Blackmun read *Wolman* as reaffirming *Meek* v. *Pittinger's* finding that direct aid to a religious school's educational function advances the sectarian enterprise as a whole.[37]

Blackmun's dissent in *Regan* reads like the pessimistic report of a field commander who, reviewing the disposition of his troops, finds that some of his soldiers have gone over to the enemy camp. Blackmun saw three groupings on the Court: (1) those justices who, being of a permissive mind, "would rule in favor of almost any aid a state legislature saw fit to provide"; (2) those justices who, at the other extreme, "would rule against aid of almost any kind"; and (3) those justices in the center. Until now, he thought, the separationists and the centrists had joined "to make order and a consensus" – in such decisions as *Lemon, Meek,* and *Wolman*. Some of those who had joined to invalidate, Blackmun lamented, now "depart and validate."[38]

The pace of readjustment quickened in 1983. In *Mueller* v. *Allen* (1983) the Court, over the dissent of four justices, upheld a Minnesota statute allowing state taxpayers, in computing their income tax, to deduct expenses (up to a stated amount) incurred in providing tuition, textbooks, and transportation for their children.[39] Justice Rehnquist, writing for the majority, invoked the principle of "neutrality" in upholding the statute. He thought it significant that *all* parents, whether their children were in public or in private schools, could claim the deduction.[40]

In formal terms, Justice Rehnquist's opinion in *Mueller* conforms to the three-part analysis of purpose, effect, and entanglement laid down in *Lemon*. In fact, in Rehnquist's skilled hands, *Mueller* became an opinion markedly different in spirit and result from the parochiaid cases of the 1970s. The opinion is striking in several respects:

1. Throughout, the opinion in *Mueller* reflects a notable deference to legislative judgments. In concluding that the Minnesota statute has a secular purpose, Rehnquist was willing to hypothesize purposes that *might* have been in the legislators' minds. Rehnquist conceded that the statute's legislative history throws little light on its actual purposes, but added that the "absence of such evidence does not affect our treatment of the statute."[41]

Likewise, in asking whether the Minnesota statute has the forbidden effect of advancing religion, Rehnquist called for "substantial deference" to the legislature's judgment in light of the broad latitude traditionally accorded by the Court to classifications created by state tax statutes.[42] Rehnquist thus sought to treat the Minnesota statute, not so much as raising sensitive questions of church and state, but as calling for the more relaxed judicial response appropriate to tax classifications in general.

2. The key to *Mueller* lies in Rehnquist's taking the Minnesota statute at face value. Public schools in Minnesota may charge tuition only for students living outside the district.[43] In the 1978/79 school year, only 79 public-school students paid tuition (of about 815,000 students in public schools). About 90,000 students were enrolled in private schools that charged tuition; over 95 percent of those students attended sectarian schools.[44]

In earlier parochiaid cases, such as *Nyquist* and *Sloan v. Lemon* (both decided in 1973), the Court explicitly had taken note of the way in which the programs at issue in those cases worked mainly to the benefit of parents whose children attended sectarian schools. In *Sloan,* for example, the Court thought it significant that more than 90 percent of the children attending nonpublic schools in Pennsylvania were in religious schools.[45]

A like approach to the Minnesota statute would surely have put it in jeopardy. Rehnquist rejected, however, a "statistical" approach, preferring instead to rely on the statute's facial neutrality.[46]

3. Justice Rehnquist's opinion makes no secret of its policy grounding. Private schools and their patrons, he pointed out, "make special contributions" to the public good. In particular, he submitted, the tax benefits extended by the statute "can fairly be regarded as a rough return" for the benefits the state and taxpayers generally reap from parents' sending their children to private schools.[47]

Mueller does not directly impeach the vitality of *Nyquist.* But Justice Rehnquist's opinion – marked by deference, impressed by neutrality, and concerned for equity – is not ultimately compatible with the earlier opinion.

A week after *Mueller,* the Court showed that relaxing the three-part establishment test is but one avenue for upholding state accommodations of religion. In *Marsh v. Chambers* (1983), the majority by-passed the *Lemon* test altogether. In *Marsh,* Chief Justice Burger rejected an establishment clause challenge to Nebraska's longstanding practice of paying a chaplain to open legislative sessions.[48]

The Court of Appeals for the Eighth Circuit had applied in *Marsh* the traditional three-part test and had concluded that Nebraska's practice violated all three prongs of the test.[49] In looking to history, however, Burger sidestepped the three-part test altogether. Burger found Nebraska's practice to be "deeply imbedded in the history and tradition of this country." That history includes the action of the First Congress – the same sessions that voted to submit the First Amendment to the states for ratification – in appointing a chaplain to open sessions with a prayer.[50]

How broad an exception to the Court's usual approach to establishment clause cases is carved out in *Marsh?* Justice Brennan, in dissent, thought – perhaps "hoped" would be the better word – the exception was a narrow one, posing little threat "to the overall fate" of the establishment clause.[51]

The use of history to reject an establishment clause challenge is but one aspect of Burger's *Marsh* opinion. There is a second, albeit less explicit, theme. In speeches and other public statements, the former Chief Justice has often voiced his concern about the overburdening of the courts in a litigious age.[52] In his role as legal reformer, Burger unquestionably would like to see the American people making less use of the courts to air their grievances. As author of the *Marsh* opinion, Burger treated the practice there challenged, legislative prayers, as being essentially marginal when compared with other establishment clause issues – a "mere shadow" rather than a "real threat."[53]

The ink was hardly dry on *Mueller* and *Marsh* before the Court, early in the next term, heard arguments in a case that received far broader public attention and commentary than had either the Minnesota or the Nebraska case. In *Lynch* v. *Donnelly*, the justices reviewed a challenge to the Pawtucket, Rhode Island, display of a city-owned crèche in a public park at the Christmas season.[54]

Once again, as in *Mueller* and *Marsh*, the majority of the justices were persuaded that the challenged practice did not offend the establishment clause. Chief Justice Burger, writing the Court's opinion, observed that the crèche was displayed alongside more secular seasonal figures, such as Santa Claus and his reindeer. Burger concluded that the crèche, rather than carrying an explicitly sectarian message, served to engender "a friendly community spirit of good will in keeping with the season."[55]

The Chief Justice's opinion in *Lynch* is not quite like either *Mueller* or *Marsh*, although it carries something of the flavor of both. It resembles *Mueller* insofar as, while applying the three-part establishment clause test, it has little trouble in finding all three aspects of the test satisfied. It resembles *Marsh* insofar as a fair proportion of *Lynch* is devoted to history. But taken in its entirety, Burger's *Lynch* opinion paints with a broader brush than either of its predecessors. The air of accommodation is even stronger, the implications for other cases more far-reaching, in *Lynch* than in either *Mueller* or *Marsh*.

In *Lynch*, Burger made accommodation the central focus. Conceding that the notion of a "wall of separation" might be a "useful figure of speech," Burger downplayed this "metaphor" as "not a wholly accurate description" of the "practical" relationship existing in fact between church and state. As Burger read the Constitution, far from requiring complete separation of church and state, it "affirmatively mandates accommodation" by government of religion.[56]

Lynch shows how such accommodation can be upheld. In deciding that Pawtucket's display of the crèche is permissible, Burger found at least three ways to put the use of the crèche in some larger context. In so doing, he sought to defuse the argument that the crèche is to be seen in its specifically religious setting.

1. As to the immediate physical setting of the crèche, Justice Brennan, writing for the four dissenters, argued that the city's interest in celebrating the season and in promoting good will (and retail sales in the local stores) can readily be accomplished by the rest of the display (Santa Claus, reindeer, wishing wells, and other non-Christian symbols), minus the crèche. Brennan thus singled out the crèche as a "distinctively religious element" in the display.[57] Burger, by contrast, treated the crèche as simply one element in the seasonal display.[58]

2. Burger further merged the display of the crèche into the larger tradition of observing the Christmas holiday. This celebration, he noted, was of twenty centuries' standing in the Western world and had been marked in this country for two hundred years "by the people, by the Executive Branch, by the Congress, and the courts." It would, Burger thought, be ironic to forbid the use of the crèche ("this one passive symbol") "at the very time people are taking note of the season with Christmas hymns and carols in public schools and other public places."[59]

3. Burger measured the issue of the crèche against other practices previously upheld by the Court. To conclude that the primary effect of displaying the crèche would be to advance religion, Burger argued, would require the Court to view it as "more beneficial to and more an endorsement of" religion than those practices already sustained – the loan of textbooks to students in parochial schools, reimbursement of parents for the cost of transporting their children to parochial schools, tax exemptions for churches, legislative prayers, and the like.[60]

Lynch is not simply a replay of *Marsh,* although history is invoked in both cases. In *Marsh,* the Court was able to point to historical practices extending back to the First Congress itself – hence to the time and place of the First Amendment's drafting. In *Lynch,* the majority could invoke no such unbroken historical chain. Indeed, at the time of the First Amendment's adoption, there was as yet no general pattern of the celebration of Christmas either by religious sects or by the public. It was the mid-nineteenth century in America before Christmas had come to be a widely observed holiday recognized by state and federal laws.[61]

Thus *Lynch* turns not so much on history as on some more general notion of tradition and custom. To the extent that the opinion may be characterized as turning on history, it is not so much the history of the display of crèches or even the celebration of Christmas as it is the place that the opinion's author sees religion as having in American public life. "There is," Burger submitted, "an unbroken history of official acknowledgement by all three branches of government of the role of religion in American life from at least 1789." And Burger gave examples – executive orders and other proclamations recognizing days of thanksgiving, "In God We Trust" on coins, the Pledge of Allegiance's inclusion of the phrase "under God," public galleries' display of religious art, and such.[62]

One reads the majority opinion in *Lynch* with the distinct impression that its author is seeking to settle (as far as one opinion can) the acceptability of a broad range of public acknowledgments of religion. "We are unable to perceive," Burger wrote, "the Archbishop of Canterbury, the Vicar of Rome, or other powerful religious leaders behind every public acknowledgement of the religious heritage long officially recognized by the three constitutional branches of government. Any notion that these symbols pose a real danger of establishment of a state church is far-fetched indeed."[63]

In sum, by 1984, a majority of the justices appeared to have carried the Court far from any strictly separationist view of the "wall of separation" and a long way toward a congenial accommodation of religion by public authorities. For those who wanted to deflect an establishment clause attack on state benefits to or accommodation of religion, the decisions in *Mueller, Marsh,* and *Lynch* offered a variety of techniques. Among them were a more relaxed application of the three-part *Lemon* test, an unwillingness to delve deeply into underlying motives, a deference to legislative judgment, an ability to see a broad "neutral" classification whose benefits were not confined to religious groups, the grounding of a practice in history or tradition, and an acceptance of arguments implicating concerns for equity or free exercise.

The 1984 Term: Briefs and Arguments

The Court's 1984 Term opened with an air of expectancy. Attention centered above all on several religion cases pending on the Court's docket. The cases seemed to raise the whole spectrum of religious liberty and church-and-state concerns. From Michigan came a challenge to a plan under which Grand Rapids's public-school district sent public teachers into church schools to teach selected subjects. From Alabama came the constitutionality of a state law allowing up to one minute of silence in public-school classrooms for "meditation or voluntary prayer." From Connecticut came a state court's decision striking down a statute forbidding an employer to require an employee to work on a day designated by the employee as his Sabbath. As the new Term got under way, the

Court accepted another major case – the decision of a federal court in New York enjoining a federal program that paid the salaries of public-school teachers who taught remedial courses in parochial schools. And there were yet other religion cases on the Term's docket.[64]

Interest in the religion cases tended to overshadow interest in other cases being argued in the 1984 Term. A *New York Times* correspondent thought the Term was "shaping up as a potential watershed in the constitutional relationship between government and religion." Any of the Court's major religion cases could, she mused, "be the vehicle that Chief Justice Warren E. Burger and his allies on the Court have been seeking for a fundamental revision of the Court's doctrines on the separation of church and state."[65] A pair of *Washington Post* reporters, noting the predictions that the Court's conservative decisions of the previous Term might portend the long-awaited Burger Court reversal of the tides of the Warren years, said, "If a 'counterrevolution' happens this term, most expect it to come in the field of religion."[66]

The religion cases of the 1984 Term attracted, in addition to the parties' arguments, amicus briefs from a broad spectrum of groups and organizations. Just in the four principal cases already mentioned (from Michigan, Alabama, Connecticut, and New York), amicus briefs were filed by groups as widely divergent as the American Civil Liberties Union, the American Jewish Congress, Americans United for Separation of Church and State, the AFL-CIO, the Christian Legal Society, the Moral Majority, and the Catholic League for Religious and Civil Rights.[67]

Coincident with the surge in religion cases on the Court's docket was rising attention to religion as a political issue. In addition to the perennial attempts to amend the Constitution to permit some form of prayer in public schools, Congress, in July 1984, enacted the Equal Access Act, intended to require a local school system to allow religious groups to use public-school property (for example, for Bible-study groups) if the local school board allows other noncurricular clubs to meet in the school.[68] The fall of 1984 saw, of course, President Reagan's reelection campaign, in which explicit appeals were made both to fundamentalist Protestants and to Catholics.[69]

Given the emergence of religion in politics, it is hardly surprising that the Reagan administration's Justice Department made itself heard in briefs filed in the cases being argued in the Supreme Court's 1984 Term. In one case, that involving the use of federal funds to send public-school teachers into New York's parochial schools, the United States was a party. In the other cases, however, the government had only the standing of an amicus curiae. In the Alabama moment-of-silence case, for example, the United States explained its interest in the case by pointing to the possible implications of a decision in the case for federal measures undertaking "governmental accommodation of religion," such as giving religious holidays to federal employees.[70] In all four of the principal cases, the United States, either as party or as amicus curiae, took a position favoring what the government saw to be measures accommodating religious practices.[71]

Some indication of the expectations raised by the Court's recent decisions – especially those in *Mueller, Marsh,* and *Lynch* – may be gleaned from a reading of briefs filed by parties and amici in the 1984 Term religion cases. For present purposes, the four cases (from Alabama, Michigan, Connecticut, and New York) will serve. (Several other cases on that Term's docket are omitted from consideration here.)[72]

The four cases raised a range of establishment clause issues. Two – the Michigan and New York cases – were parochiaid cases and thus raised issues involving state aid to religious institutions. The Alabama moment-of-silence case brought the question of government activities allegedly promoting religion in the classroom. The Connecticut case raised the question how far government can go to oblige employers or others in the private sector to accommodate their fellow citizens' religious beliefs and practices.

The facts of the four cases were as follows. In *School District of the City of Grand Rapids* v. *Ball,* the school district provided classes, at public expense, to students in parochial schools in classrooms located in and leased from those schools. There were two programs. One, the Shared Time program, sent public employees to the religious schools to teach various courses – some remedial, and some enrichment. The other, Community Education, hired, on a part-time basis, teachers, most of whom were regular employees of the private schools to which they were then assigned by the public-school district to teach after-school courses.

In *Aguilar* v. *Felton,* New York City used federal funds – provided under Title I of the Elementary and Secondary Education Act of 1965 – to pay the salaries of public-school employees who taught courses in parochial schools on those schools' premises. A principal difference between the Title I program and that in Grand Rapids was that Title I required that funds be directed to educationally deprived children living in areas with a high concentration of low-income families.

In *Wallace* v. *Jaffree,* a 1978 Alabama statute (not at issue before the Supreme Court) had authorized a one-minute period of silence in public schools for "meditation." At issue in *Wallace* was the constitutionality of a 1981 statute authorizing a period of silence "for meditation or voluntary prayer."

In *Estate of Thornton* v. *Caldor, Inc.,* a Connecticut statute provided:

"No person who states that a particular day of the week is observed as his Sabbath may be required by his employer to work on such day. An employee's refusal to work on his Sabbath shall not constitute grounds for his dismissal."

A review of the briefs filed in the 1984 Term's religion cases makes clear the extent to which parties or amici hoping for further accommodationist opinions from the Court drew sustenance from *Mueller, Marsh,* and *Lynch.* Charles H. Wilson, of Williams and Connolly (and an old hand at church-and-state litigation), filed the appellants' brief in *Aguilar* v. *Felton.*[73] He began his argument with a section entitled "Governing Constitutional Principles" and opened with the statement, "This Court has repeatedly cautioned against a rigid, absolutist view of the Establishment Clause," citing *Lynch.* And he pointed to the Court's "most recent Establishment Clause decisions'" (citing *Mueller, Marsh,* and *Lynch*) as embodying "nondoctrinaire realism." In those three cases, he submitted, "the Court has realistically assessed the dangers posed by the challenged statute or practice and has discounted hypothetical and speculative concerns."[74] Briefs filed in other 1984 Term cases place similar reliance on *Mueller, Marsh,* and *Lynch* to bolster various accommodationist arguments advanced in those briefs.[75]

"Accommodation" is the thread that runs through the briefs defending the programs at issue in the Michigan, New York, Alabama, and Connecticut cases. In *Wallace* v. *Jaffree,* Governor Wallace invoked *Lynch* as giving "new life to the theory of accommodation."[76] The Solicitor General, also defending Alabama's moment-of-silence law, declared the object of the First Amendment's religion clauses to be "toleration and accommodation, not the removal of all traces of religion from our public life."[77] Indeed, in the briefs filed in the 1984 Term, arguments for "accommodation" bid fair to replace "neutrality" as the favored talisman of those opposed to strict separation.[78]

These arguments for accommodation frequently go beyond simply saying that it is permissible; commonly, the briefs argue that accommodation is mandatory. John W. Whitehead, a Manassas, Virginia, attorney with considerable experience in religion clause cases, signed an amicus brief in *Wallace* v. *Jaffree* for the Freedom Council, a group with close ties to Pat Robertson's Christian Broadcasting Network. In a spirited defense of Alabama's moment-of-silence statute, he declared that "First Amendment neutrality *mandates* that the public school present no affront to the spiritual needs and concerns of its students."[79] The Legal Foundation of America (quartered at Houston's South Texas College of Law) argued, "Accommodation of religion (and not merely 'toleration') is required by the Constitution. . . ."[80] In making the argument for man-

datory accommodation, parties and amici were able to cite Chief Justice
Burger's statement in *Lynch* that the Constitution "affirmatively mandates accommodation, not merely tolerance, of all religions. . . ."[81]

Politics, they say, makes strange bedfellows. So does Supreme Court
litigation. In the moment-of-silence case, groups of a more conservative
bent tended to advance broad arguments for accommodation. Liberal
groups, such as the ACLU and the American Jewish Congress, sought
to narrow that concept. While accepting that accommodation is appropriate to further free-exercise values, the ACLU called accommodation
"a narrowly crafted analytical framework" and resisted appellants' efforts to "transform" accommodation by allowing it to be invoked, even
in the absence of any impediment to the free exercise of religion.[82] The
American Jewish Congress thought the ultimate question in *Wallace* was
"the proper scope of the accommodation doctrine" – whether government could "under the guise of accommodation, use the compulsory
education system for 'the promotion of religion.' "[83]

In light of the respective postures of amici attacking and defending the
Alabama law, it is intriguing to consider the arguments advanced regarding Connecticut's Sabbatarian law. *Thornton* found the ACLU, the
Anti-Defamation League of B'nai B'rith, and Americans United for Separation of Church and State – all groups strongly identified with a separationist philosophy – lined up in support of Connecticut's statute.
Americans United and the ACLU took cautious positions in favor of
accommodation; indeed, the ACLU (joined by the American Jewish
Committee) thought that requirements imposed on private employers
must be "reasonable." Hence these amici suggested remand of the case
to determine whether requiring deference to Thornton's religious practices would, on the facts of the case, have imposed such an undue burden
on his employer or his co-workers as to violate the establishment clause.[84]

The Anti-Defamation League took a more unqualified stance. Its defense of Connecticut's law invoked *Lynch*'s statement that the Constitution "affirmatively mandates accommodation" of religion.[85] As one
compares the briefs in *Wallace* with those in *Thornton,* one is struck by
the way in which interest groups of such disparate temperament – the
conservative groups favoring the moment-of-silence law and the liberal
groups supporting the Sabbatarian statute – find uses for the doctrine of
accommodation. Jewish groups, in particular, would have reason to be
concerned about practices tending to religious observances in public schools
(where the dominant influences are likely to be Christian), yet they could
see strong appeal in Sabbatarian statutes (especially for employees who
might be Orthodox Jews). The arguments for accommodation in the
1984 Term briefs show how malleable is the concept and how one's at-

titude to it turns heavily on just whose religious beliefs and practices are being accommodated and in what context.

Closely allied with arguments for accommodation are invocations of free exercise. Thus the proponents of parochiaid, moments of silence, and a day off for Sabbatarians sought to do more than simply deflect establishment clause challenges; they grounded those practices in the Constitution itself – in the free-exercise clause. In *Aguilar*, the Solicitor General argued that to deny Title I services to students in religious schools "is to burden their exercise of a constitutional right."[86]

Amici in *Wallace* were especially vocal about believers' free-exercise interests in being able to pray in public schools. For the Moral Majority, William Bentley Ball, a seasoned practitioner of religious-liberty cases, observed that "numerous intervenors" in *Wallace* had told the Court that Alabama's law "gives positive recognition to prayer, a 'quintessential religious practice'. . . . and allows their children to participate in that practice as a practice publicly deemed worthy of recognition." Millions of children, he argued, are compelled to attend public school, yet "none may presently exercise liberty of religious observance within those schools."[87]

Among the values urged on the Court in accommodationist briefs in the 1984 Term were those of diversity and pluralism. In his separate opinion in *Wolman* v. *Walter*, Justice Powell had spoken of the "educational alternative" offered by parochial schools, of the "wholesome competition" they offer to public schools.[88] More generally, in *Lynch* v. *Donnelly*, Chief Justice Burger had read the establishment clause in light of a constitutional tradition that encourages "diversity and pluralism."[89] The 1984 briefs urged the pending cases as implicating just such values. Thus the Solicitor General defended both Title I and the Grand Rapids program as promoting diversity and pluralism (citing *Lynch*).[90] The Council for American Private Education, in support of Title I, developed at length the argument (strongly relying on Powell in *Wolman*) that aid to children in parochial schools bolsters pluralism in education.[91] In *Wallace*, the Solicitor General took the broad position that a government practice accommodating religious needs "makes an important point about toleration and pluralism." Alabama's moment-of-silence law, he argued, was "uniquely suited" as a "lesson in toleration."[92]

The popular debate over religion and politics often rages with charges that the public schools are teaching "secular humanism." These allegations found their way into the 1984 Term briefs. In its *Wallace* brief, the Moral Majority argued that excluding religious observances from public schools results not in neutrality, but in a "religious preference" – that is, "tax-supported secularism." Citing examples of educators' belief that they have a duty to teach values (of citizenship, relations with others, sexual standards, and such), the Moral Majority complained that "secular humanism" is being established as the religion of the public school:

> This widespread kind of programming is mentioned, not to deny that schools may teach values, but to point out that, in our public schools today, *all* of these programs must be presented *without* traditional Judeo-Christian value judgments and are presented *with* nontheistic value judgments. They thus constitute what is known as Secular Humanism. Secular Humanism is a religion. It is now awarded a legally preferred status and is supported by taxes extracted from all taxpayers.[93]

In another *Wallace* brief, the Freedom Council placed the moment-of-silence case at the center of an ideological struggle between religion and secularism. Quoting Harvard's Harvey Cox (*The Secular City*), the council declared secularism to be "a menace to freedom because it seeks to impose its ideology through the organs of the State."[94]

Authors of some briefs saw evidence of hostility to religion in the very opinions of the state and federal courts being reviewed by the Supreme Court. The Catholic League for Religious and Civil Rights criticized the Second Circuit in *Aguilar* not only for having misapplied the *Lemon* test, but also for having embraced a more pernicious error: a view of religion "in and of itself, as an evil." In the League's view, the court had treated religion as a "contaminant."[95] The Solicitor General avoided such strong language, but in *Thornton,* he reached a similar conclusion: that the Connecticut Supreme Court had made the establishment clause "an instrument of hostility to religion."[96]

If the erring judges were viewed as hostile to religion, the accommodationist briefs looked to legislative bodies, both state and federal, to be more sympathetic to the religionists' agenda. Alabama's moment-of-silence and Connecticut's Sabbatarian law were simply accommodations of religion, hence not an establishment, briefs argued for deference to legislative judgments. The Solicitor General pressed this argument in both cases. Noting in *Wallace* that about half the states have thought it "appropriate" to have a moment of silence, the Solicitor General declared: "How serious is the need for a particular religious accommodation (where not required by the Free Exercise Clause) is primarily a question of public policy, for legislatures to assess."[97] Likewise, in *Thornton,* the Solicitor General urged that when it comes to accommodating religion, "there is a wide scope for legislative discretion – 'room for play in the joints' " (quoting Chief Justice Burger's opinion in *Walz*).[98]

The Solicitor General's arguments for deference to legislative judgments in the religion cases parallel the position that he had taken, again as amicus, when the Court had heard arguments (in the 1982 Term) in a case involving the constitutionality of an ordinance enacted in Akron, Ohio, limiting access to abortions. In the Akron case, as in the religion cases, the Solicitor General argued for the Court to take a position more deferential to state and local perceptions of the right balancing of interests than previous cases (*Roe* v. *Wade* and its sequels in the abortion context, *Lemon* and its progeny in the religion area) might call for.[99] In either area, of course, religion or abortion, deference to local political instincts would encourage more laws restricting abortion and more measures accommodating religion.

Just how substantial such deference might be may be inferred from petitioner's brief in *Thornton*. In a brief signed by Washington attorney Nathan Lewin, well known at the Supreme Court bar, petitioner argued that the Connecticut statute ought to be treated as an antidiscrimination statute. Hence the proper standard of review would be a rationality standard.[100] Were such an argument to be accepted, it is hard to imagine a more relaxed standard of review.[101] If a statute need have only a rational relation to some legitimate state objective, then accommodation would be easily accomplished.

The themes that run through many of the briefs filed in the 1984 Term cases may thus be clearly identified. Among them are arguments that the First Amendment permits or even requires accommodation of religion, that the laws being reviewed in those cases further free exercise of religion (thus vindicate a constitutional right), that the statutes promote diversity and pluralism, that the judicial opinions being appealed from are hostile to religion, and that where the state seeks to accommodate religion, the courts should be deferential to legislative judgments about the scope and range of such accommodation.

Such arguments must inevitably be translated into legal standards. If accommodation is to be attained, by what legal litmus paper is the Supreme Court to measure a statute whose defenders say it accommodates and whose challengers say it violates the establishment clause? The accommodationist briefs filed in the 1984 Term take several tacks in charting the legal course.

The broadest attack on the use of the establishment clause by the courts was mounted in *Wallace* v. *Jaffree*. The Center for Judicial Studies, as amicus, argued that the Fourteenth Amendment was not intended to apply any of the provisions of the Bill of Rights against the states. Alternatively, the Center maintained that even were some of the provisions of the Bill of Rights intended to apply to the states, the establishment clause was not among them.[102] Ever since Justice Black, in his famous dissent in *Adamson* v. *California* (1947), advanced his "incorporation" theory, scholars have debated the historical evidence on the reach of the Fourteenth Amendment.[103] Charles Fairman and Raoul Berger, among others, have concluded that those who framed and ratified the Fourteenth Amendment did not intend to make the Bill of Rights applicable to the states.[104] The founder of the Center for Judicial Studies, James McClellan – he is both a historian and a lawyer – emphatically agrees with the Fairman–Berger thesis.[105] Charles Rice, a law professor at Notre Dame who is often conspicuous in conservative legal circles, wrote the Center's brief in *Wallace* and obviously is of the same mind as McClellan.[106]

The argument for (as it were) disestablishing the establishment clause actually succeeded in the federal district court in which *Wallace* was tried. Judge W. B. Hand decided that "the United States Supreme Court has erred in its reading of history," and he accordingly ruled that the establishment clause places no limit on the states.[107] The Eleventh Circuit Court of Appeals had little difficulty reversing Judge Hand. As the appellate court saw it, the Supreme Court "is the ultimate authority on the interpretation of our Constitution and laws; its interpretations may not be disregarded."[108]

Persuading the justices of the Supreme Court to change their collective minds on basic doctrine is never an easy task. The difficulties of asking the Court to hold that the establishment clause (not to mention the Bill of Rights generally) does not apply to the states are daunting. Whatever the debate among scholars, even those justices who think the Court has gone too far in its establishment clause decisions have shown no inclination to turn the clock back on the basic question of the establishment clause's application to the states. The prevailing view on the Court was summed up in a 1963 opinion's statement that arguments that the establishment clause does not limit the states are "untenable and of value only as academic exercises."[109] In *Wallace* itself, while Governor Wallace's counsel no doubt would have agreed with McClellan's thesis, Wallace's brief reluctantly granted in a footnote appellants' understanding that, in agreeing to hear the case, the Supreme Court had excluded from review the issue of the Fourteenth Amendment's incorporation of the establishment clause.[110] In light of the scope of review in *Wallace* and of the remote prospects that the Court would, in any event, reconsider the establishment clause's application to the states, one must conclude that the center's brief in *Wallace* was written with a view to the long run. If the justices will not listen now, maybe their successors will. Or if the Court turns a deaf ear, perhaps the center's appeal is to the judgment of a larger audience – perhaps, if nothing else, to let it be known that, whatever the odds, someone is willing to "fight the good fight."[111]

Those who wrote accommodationist briefs in the 1984 Term, taking heart from the trend of Supreme Court cases, were quite willing to take the establishment clause as having some kind of application to the states. If the justices were suitably receptive, then legislators would, by this approach, have ample breathing room to accommodate religion.

A pervasive theme of the accommodationist briefs is their portrayal of the decisions being appealed from as relying on speculation and will-o'-the-wisp abstractions to strike down programs presenting no concrete dangers of a kind against which the establishment clause was meant to protect. Again and again, the briefs hammer home the theme: Do not rely on "per se" rules; look instead to the actual record in the case at bar.

> The Solicitor General saw *Grand Rapids* as providing "an opportunity for this Court to assess the actual operations and effects of a program which is characteristic of many programs adopted across the country. In this case, unlike many others that have reached this Court, there is an extensive factual record documenting these operations and effects over a period of six years."[112]

Thus the Solicitor General sought to distance *Grand Rapids* from the Court's more separationist decisions – "unlike many others that have reached this Court" – such as *Wolman* v. *Walter* and *Meek* v. *Pittenger*.[113] In his *Aguilar* brief, the Solicitor General took special pains to weaken *Meek's* precedential impact by comparing the record in the two cases. *Aguilar*, he said, had come to the Court "after a full trial on the merits by two district courts, with an extensive factual record covering a period of 16 years of Title I operations." *Meek*, by contrast, saw the Court reviewing a decision by a "three-judge district court, upholding the program on a sparse evidentiary record" involving a program that had been in existence "barely a year."[114]

Petitioners in *Grand Rapids* made essentially the same point by insisting over and over in their brief that the Court of Appeals had used a "per se" approach to decide the case, rather than sifting the factual evidence. There is hardly a page in petitioners' brief in which they do not talk about the Court of Appeals' having used a "per se" rule.[115] In their reply brief, petitioners make the "per se" argument even more central, organizing the brief around attacks on "per se" methodology ("I.   Introduction – Respondents' Per Se Approach") and its unhappy consequences ("III.   Consequences of the Per Se Rule – Exaggeration through Mischaracterization" and "IV.   Consequences of the 'Per Se Rule' – Ignoring the Record").[116] Throughout their briefs in *Aguilar* and *Grand Rapids,* both petitioners, the government, and other amici sought to paint the

Court of Appeals' majority as absolutists, blinded by stereotypes and abstractions, insensitive to the actual record in the case.[117]

Another avenue explored in the 1984 Term briefs was that of history. The inspiration for invoking the lessons of history was found, of course, in Chief Justice Burger's opinions in *Marsh* and *Lynch*. The attorneys general of six states filed an amicus brief in *Wallace* using *Marsh* and *Lynch* as the point of departure for a history lesson: how the First Amendment's framers had intended government to have the power to designate times appropriate for general prayer.[118] Governor Wallace's brief celebrated history's being "recovered" in *Marsh* and *Lynch* and becoming "part of the case law."[119]

Just as Burger devoted a considerable space to history in the Nebraska chaplain and Pawtucket crèche cases, so do several of the *Wallace* briefs. The Freedom Council saw no conflict between the Alabama statute and the intentions of the framers of the First Amendment, as revealed "in their words, deeds, and history." That evidence, set out at some length, included actions of Jefferson and Madison as well as other history showing governmental actions "in support of our religious heritage."[120]

The *Wallace* brief filed by the Center for Judicial Studies was devoted entirely to history. Part of the brief (as described above) argued that the Fourteenth Amendment was not intended to apply the establishment clause to the states. The brief's final section argued that even assuming the establishment clause's applicability, the clause was not intended "to prevent any government from encouraging religion and morality through prayer."[121] In support of that position, the Center invited the Court's attention to "significant new research, and newly discovered historical material" that had come to light since the Court's 1963 decision in *Schempp* – the opinion that had dismissed objections to the Court's reading of the establishment clause as "untenable" and mere "academic exercises."[122] Among the scholars relied on were Mark DeWolfe Howe, James McClellan, and Robert L. Cord, all of whom have accused the Supreme Court of having abused history in its establishment clause cases.[123]

McClellan's influence is obvious far beyond the brief filed by his Center for Judicial Studies. He testified at the trial in the district court, and his testimony was quoted in the district judge's opinion.[124] Indeed, in that opinion, Judge Hand said, "If this opinion will accomplish its intent, which is to take us back to our original historical roots, then much of the credit for the vision lies with Professor James McClellan and Professor Robert L. Cord."[125] Moreover, in the Supreme Court, in addition to the center's brief, McClellan's ideas are strongly reflected in Governor Wallace's brief as appellant. A striking proportion of the brief is given over to history (twelve pages to the Northwest Ordinance).[126] Particular emphasis is placed on the views of Justice Story, quoting from McClellan's biography of Story.[127] "It seems more than a coincidence," appellant noted, "that the revival of the concept of accommodation in *Lynch* is linked to the reliance for the first time in modern religion cases to Justice Joseph Story's writings."[128]

Inevitably, parties and amici in the 1984 religion cases had to address the three-part *Lemon* test – purpose, effect, and entanglement. By the fall of 1984, that test had become increasingly embattled. In March, in his opinion in *Lynch*, Chief Justice Burger had emphasized the Court's "unwillingness to be confined to any single test or criterion in this sensitive area" and reminded his readers of two cases (*Marsh* and *Larson* v. *Valente*) in which the *Lemon* test had not been applied at all.[129] Small wonder that Justice Brennan, dissenting in *Lynch*, had worried that "the Court's less than vigorous application of the *Lemon* test suggests that its commitment to those standards may only be superficial."[130]

In the 1984 Term's parochiaid cases, those who defended Title I and the Grand Rapids program made no effort to avoid the *Lemon* test; they simply argued that it should be considered to have been satisfied. As the Solicitor General put it, the *Lemon* test, "sensitively applied, would seem to furnish an appropriate 'framework of analysis' . . . for governmental programs of assistance to the education of children attending nonpublic schools."[131] Petitioners in *Grand Rapids*, labeling the Court of Appeals' methodology as imposing a "per se" requirement, maintained that if that court had "relied upon the 'three-pronged test' as a guide to its inquiry," the outcome would have been "markedly different."[132] In the parochiaid cases, therefore, the dispute was not over the appropriate analytical framework, but over its application.

The quarrel over *Lemon* broke out into the open in the moment-of-silence and, even more so, in the Connecticut Sabbath-law case. In *Wallace*, the Legal Foundation of America complained that the *Lemon* test "fails to protect accommodation of religion or even to recognize it as a countervailing consideration" and feared that "it would obliterate the free exercise clause if consistently applied."[133] Other accommodationist briefs in *Wallace*, however, appeared content to apply the three-part test and find it to have been met.[134]

Thornton produced the sharpest attacks on *Lemon*'s test. The Solicitor General argued that the purpose and effect tests "seem less apt" when "the very purpose of the challenged program is to accommodate private religious beliefs. . . ." To ask about purpose and effect, he thought, "may seem artificial – even circular – in the context of religious accommodations, where the government's action, by definition, explicitly turns on considerations of religion." The court below had fallen into a "semantic trap, which litigants can manipulate at will to make all forms of religious accommodation – or none – appear to violate the Establishment Clause."[135] Nathan Lewin, for the petitioner in *Thornton,* was more direct: The three-part test, he argued, "is *not* the correct constitutional yardstick by which to determine the validity of a law protecting religious observance." Petitioner's standard was that of the "rational basis" test: "When a State acts to guarantee to religious observers the cherished freedom freely to exercise their religion, its action should be upheld if the law rationally furthers the legitimate, articulated State purpose of protecting religious freedom and if the law has no invidious discrimination that denies equal protection of the laws."[136]

Closely associated with the three-part test – but never quite accepted as an independent, or fourth, query – is the question whether a challenged governmental program has a "divisive political potential."[137] In *Mueller,* Justice Rehnquist viewed the political-divisiveness argument as being "confined to cases where direct financial subsidies are paid to parochial schools or to teachers in parochial schools."[138] In *Lynch,* Chief Justice Burger thought no enquiry into political divisiveness was called for, since the case did not involve a "direct subsidy" to a religious institution.[139]

Accommodationist briefs in the 1984 Term took two approaches to rebuffing claims that the challenged programs would stir religious controversy. One approach was to argue that the case at bar involved no "direct subsidy"; hence the political-divisiveness issue did not arise. In the parochiaid case, the program's defenders thought the short answer to the political-divisiveness argument was that funds spent on the programs did not flow to the parochial schools (paychecks going instead to teachers hired as public employees).[140]

The other tack was to criticize the political-divisiveness doctrine or ask the Court to repudiate it outright. In *Grand Rapids* (where the Court of Appeals had made much of the program's potential for such controversy), the Solicitor General agreed with Justice O'Connor that guessing what divisive potential a program might have is simply "too speculative an enterprise."[141] Moreover, such inquiry seemed in conflict with the political system's commitment to "uninhibited, robust, and wide-open" debate on public issues.[142] The author of the Council for Private Education's amicus brief in *Aguilar,* Professor Edward M. Gaffney, Jr., has himself been a critic of the political-divisiveness doctrine.[143] In his brief, Professor Gaffney thought it time for the Court "to repudiate the political divisiveness test as a formal component of Establishment Clause jurisprudence."[144]

The 1984 Term: The Results

Those who expected the Supreme Court, in deciding the 1984 Term's religion cases, to continue its apparent trend toward accommodation found their hopes dashed. In early June 1985, the Court ruled against Alabama's moment-of-silence law.[145] Later the same month, the justices found against Connecticut's Sabbatarian statute.[146] The final blow fell on July 1, when the Court held that both the Grand Rapids program and the New York City Title I program violated the First Amendment.[147] In all four cases, the establishment clause challenges were upheld, and the accommodationist arguments rejected.

In both *Wallace* v. *Jaffree* and *Estate of Thornton* v. *Caldor, Inc.*, the opinions turned on narrow grounds. In *Wallace*, Justice Stevens needed only the "purpose" criterion to decide the case. Not only was there the evidence of the sponsor's intention that the bill be enacted in order "to return voluntary prayer" to the public schools, but also the statute had no secular purpose. To the argument that the statute was best understood as a permissible accommodation of religion, Stevens responded that at the time of the bill's enactment, no government practice impeded students from silent prayer at the beginning of a school day; hence there was no need to accommodate individuals' religious needs.[148]

Both the Solicitor General and appellants in *Wallace* had sought, as a matter of tactics, to paint the case as having direct implications for moment-of-silence statutes throughout the country. The Solicitor General used a broad brush: "The legislatures of twenty-four states have concluded that the practice at issue here, a moment of silence for the purpose of silent meditation," was appropriate to accommodate students' desire to pray.[149] Governor Wallace's brief objected to looking at a sponsor's motives to distinguish among "identically worded statutes."[150]

In fact, so peculiar was the record in *Wallace* that the Court's final decision does not appear to call into question the validity of a moment-of-silence statute free of the taint of the impermissible motives that Justice Stevens found attached to the Alabama law. It is not likely that litigation in another state would produce a record showing the enactment of a statute redundant of existing moment-of-silence legislation, save for adding reference to prayer. The concurring opinions in *Wallace* drive home the case's uniqueness. Justice O'Connor wrote her concurring opinion for the express purpose of explaining "why moment of silence laws in other States do not necessarily manifest the same infirmity" as did Alabama's law.[151] Justice Powell said, "I agree fully with Justice O'Connor's assertion that some moment of silence statutes may be constitutional. . . ."[152] Justice Stevens's opinion implies a like view, as he noted that the legislative intent to return prayer to public schools is "quite different from merely protecting every student's right to engage in voluntary prayer during an appropriate moment of silence during the school day."[153] Even discounting the clear implication of Stevens's statement, Powell and O'Connor, together with the three dissenters (Burger, White, and Rehnquist) make a clear majority on the Court for validation of some form of moment-of-silence statute.

The Court's decision in *Thornton,* striking down the Connecticut law requiring employers to accommodate the wishes of Sabbath observers among their employees, may at first blush seem a surprising opinion – especially so when one discovers that the majority opinion was written by one of the Court's most ardent accommodationists, the Chief Justice. The opinion turns, however, on narrow grounds. It was the categorical nature of the preference given to Sabbatarian employees, as compared with other employees, that brought the statute down. Chief Justice Burger, in a very brief opinion, described the law as arming Sabbatarian observers "with an absolute and unqualified right" not to work on their Sabbath. "The State thus commands that Sabbath religious concerns automatically control . . . ; the statute takes no account of the convenience or interests of the employer or those of other employees who do not observe a Sabbath."[154]

Thornton does not necessarily call into question other laws requiring employers to accommodate employees' religious preferences. Requiring only "reasonable" accommodations would answer Burger's principal objection to the Connecticut statute. And extending the required accommodation to all religious practices, not just observance of a Sabbath, would remove the obvious preference accorded Sabbatarians over others. A statute framed along these lines would be more likely to stand as an antidiscrimination law than as favoritism to a particular religious practice.[155]

Neither *Wallace* nor *Thornton* would seem to be a significant setback to those favoring government accommodation of religion. Neither the principle of allowing a moment of silence nor that of requiring employers to give at least some degree of accommodation to employees' religious practices seems significantly endangered by the respective opinions.

The Court's decisions in *Grand Rapids* and *Aguilar,* however, have broader implications. Those cases deal, of course, with core establishment concerns – the channeling of public funds in ways that might advance religion. And Justice Brennan, who wrote the majority opinions in both cases, reasserted the separationist principles of the pre-1980 parochiaid cases. In *Grand Rapids,* invoking the "effect" branch of the *Lemon* test, Brennan found three ways in which the challenged programs could advance religion: the risk of state-subsidized indoctrination, the close identification of government and religion, and a subsidy to the parochial school's religious mission.[156] In *Aguilar*, Brennan rested on two findings of "entanglement": the pervasive monitoring required to ensure that teachers paid with public funds would not engage in religious indoctrination, and the administrative cooperation between the public- and parochial-school systems entailed in carrying out the program.[157]

Several comments may be made about the implications and significance of the Alabama, Connecticut, Michigan, and New York cases.

1. A majority of the justices, as *Grand Rapids* and *Aguilar* make clear, are prepared to hold the line in parochiaid cases – a line established in the 1970s, a line unquestionably separationist in character. Notwithstanding his kinds words about the importance of private schools in earlier cases (notably in *Wolman* v. *Walter*), Justice Powell stands with that majority. The majority is, however, a slim one; both *Grand Rapids* and *Aguilar* were decided by 5 to 4 votes. One may no more expect these two decisions to quiet demands for aid to parochial schools than did *Lemon* or any of its sequels. It is doubtful that legislative ingenuity has run out of ideas.

2. Justice Brennan's two opinions invoke just the sort of talk about "risks" and "dangers" that the proponents of parochiaid, in their briefs, fought so valiantly to squelch. Thus Brennan, in *Aguilar*, spoke of the "substantial risk" that teachers would convey a religious message, the danger that teachers in the environment of religious schools "may" well conform their instruction to that environment. Brennan was well aware that "no evidence of specific incidents of religious indoctrination" had been adduced in the case; the absence of such evidence was "of little significance" in light of Brennan's observation that neither students and their parents nor school officials would have had any incentive to complain, even had there been indoctrination.[158] In *Aguilar*, Brennan assumed, again as a prophylactic measure, the scope of pervasive monitoring that spells entanglement.[159]

3. *Lemon*'s three-part test continues to be as near to common ground for the Court's analysis of establishment clause cases as there is. Justice Rehnquist continues to be a vocal critic of the *Lemon* test, arguing that it lacks grounding in the history of the First Amendment and that it has not provided workable standards for deciding establishment clause cases.[160] Justice O'Connor, while not ready to jettison *Lemon*, thinks its standards should be "reexamined and refined"; her approach would ask whether government action endorses religion.[161] But Justice Powell, uneasy at tampering with doctrine used in so many establishment clause cases, wrote

a concurring opinion in *Wallace* expressly "to respond to criticism" of *Lemon*. That case, Powell submitted,

> identifies standards that have proven useful in analyzing case after case both in our decisions and in those of other courts. It is the only coherent test a majority of the Court has ever adopted. Only once since our decision in *Lemon, supra,* have we addressed an Establishment Clause issue without resort to its three-pronged test. . . . *Lemon, supra,* has not been overruled or its test modified. Yet, continued criticism of it could encourage other courts to feel free to decide Establishment Clause cases on an *ad hoc* basis.[162]

In all four of the religion cases handed down in June and July 1985, the three-part test was the basis for analysis. Indeed, it is interesting that in Chief Justice Burger's opinion in *Thornton,* the test is applied without comment and as a matter of course.[163]

4. The political-divisiveness doctrine survives, but remains the subject of intense debate. Justice O'Connor thought there was little support in the record in *Aguilar* that "New York's admirable Title I program has ignited any controversy other than this litigation."[164] (Indeed, O'Connor voiced doubts about even the institutional dimensions of the entanglement test. Pointing to the "anomalous results" occasioned by the Court's use of the entanglement standard, she concluded, "If a statute lacks a purpose or effect of advancing or endorsing religion, I would not invalidate it merely because it requires some ongoing cooperation between church and state or some state supervision to ensure that state funds do not advance religion.")[165]

The 1984 Term's cases brought a spirited defense of the political-divisiveness doctrine from Justice Powell. In his concurring opinion in *Wolman* v. *Walter,* Powell had commented that in the twentieth century, "we are quite far removed from the dangers that prompted the Framers to include the Establishment Clause" in the Constitution. As to religious controversy, Powell had gone on to say, "The risk of significant religious or denominational control over our democratic processes – or even of deep political division along religious lines – is remote, and when viewed against the positive contributions of sectarian schools, any such risk seems entirely tolerable in light of the continuing oversight of this Court."[166]

The nature and scope of the aid programs at issue in *Grand Rapids* and *Aguilar* obviously tested the limits of Powell's tolerance. Concurring in these two cases, Powell recalled his own opinion in *Wolman,* but said, nonetheless, that "there is a likelihood whenever direct governmental aid is extended to some groups that there will be competition and strife among them and others to gain, maintain, or increase the financial support of government. . . ." Powell found the potential for such divisiveness (as well as government entanglement in the administration of parochial schools) a "strong additional reason" for striking down the Title I and Grand Rapids programs.[167]

5. The 1985 cases reveal the limits to the distance that arguments about history (whether of the First Amendment or of religion in American life) will carry the present Court. Encouraged by the uses of history in *Marsh* and *Lynch,* petitioners and amici laid large doses of history before the Court in briefs filed in the 1984 Term.[168] Justice Rehnquist used his *Wallace* dissent to develop at length a view of history showing why it is a mistake for the Court to freight the establishment clause with Jefferson's "misleading metaphor" about a "wall of separation." Reviewing the debates in the First Congress, the Northwest Ordinance, and the views of Joseph Story and Thomas Cooley, among other evidence, Rehnquist concluded that the "wall of separation" should be "frankly and explicitly abandoned."[169]

Whatever the arguments over rhetoric and metaphors, history did not avail in the 1984 Term to save any of the four programs or practices being reviewed. Commentators will surely continue to hammer away at the theme of bad history making bad law. For now, however, efforts to move toward greater accommodation by invoking the lessons of history seem likely to have greater effect at the margins (such as in the crèche and legislative chaplain cases) than in bringing about major revisions of doctrine.

6. All in all, the decisions of the 1984 Term were surely disappointments for accommodations. In spirit and result, the decisions of June and July 1985 were hardly like the more deferential decisions of the early 1980s. As surprised as many pundits and other Court-watchers were by the later decisions, however, the contrast between the decisions of 1983 and 1984 and those of 1985 is perhaps less marked than appears at first glance. *Mueller* upheld accommodation by validating the Minnesota tuition-credit statute. That program involved no contact between the state and the parochial schools; the programs in Grand Rapids and New York City, by contrast, sent teachers onto the premises of religious schools to engage in classroom instruction. Putting limits to *Mueller* is far easier than it would have been to cabin the reach of *Aguilar* and *Grand Rapids* had the programs at issue in those cases been approved. In understanding the two July 1985 decisions, one should not overlook the massive amount of

money involved in many parochiaid programs and the intense pressures to create and expand such plans. Such awareness seems to have informed the Court's thinking throughout its experience with parochiaid cases.

As to nonfinancial government accommodation of religion, the narrowness of the *Wallace* and *Thornton* decisions leaves much room to speculate about further efforts to build on *Marsh* and *Lynch*. The Court will not be receptive to efforts to reconsider its decisions of the 1960s banning religious exercise (such as teacher-led prayer) in public schools, but *Wallace* leaves the door open to provisions for moments of silence – so long as they are not tainted with a religious purpose, as was found in the Alabama statute. *Thornton* puts no considerable obstacle in the path of legislation to require employers to undertake reasonable accommodations of employees' religious practices. When he is in dissent, Chief Justice Burger is quick to accuse the Court of results displaying "hostility" to religion, but the Connecticut statute was so categorical in its preference for Sabbatarians that Burger felt no discomfort in putting himself at the head of an 8 to 1 majority.[170]

However one compares the cases upholding accommodation with those limiting it, the ideological and analytical battle lines are well drawn. Both Attorney General Edwin Meese, III, and Secretary of Education William J. Bennett have been sharply critical of the Court's church–state decisions of the 1984 Term.[171] Moreover, there is evidence that the Reagan administration will take more aggressive stands in Supreme Court cases than it did in the past. The former Solicitor General, Rex Lee, said that he saw his job as winning cases, not as reaching some larger audience.[172] But briefs being filed as the 1985 Term opens (for example, asking the Court to overrule *Roe* v. *Wade*) suggest, as one account put it, that the Reagan administration "appears to have concluded that there are more important goals than winning cases."[173]

In future religion cases, whatever the accommodationists' tactics, they will surely draw on the encouragement of *Mueller, Marsh,* and *Lynch,* and will continue to make forays seeking to breach the wall of separation. Separationists, well aware of the closeness of some of their victories (as in *Aguilar* and *Grand Rapids*) and the erosion at other points in the wall (as in the 1983 and 1984 cases), will continue to try to extend the line of precedents keeping government and religion apart. Chief Justice Rehnquist will continue to ask for a new vision based on old insights; Justice Brennan will keep before us the dangers of mixing church and state. Only when Americans cease to care deeply about religion and politics alike will the Court find that it no longer has to concern itself with the contours of the establishment clause.

NOTES

1   1 Cranch 137 (1803); 6 Wheat. 264 (1821).
2   *Washington Post,* August 9, 1985, p. A1.
3   *Washington Post,* August 8, 1985 p. A23.
4   See A. E. Dick Howard, "The Burger Court: A Judicial Nonet Plays the Enigma Variations," 43 *Law and Contemporary Problems* 7 (1980).
5   *Furman* v. *Georgia,* 408 U.S. 238 (1972) (capital punishment); *Maine* v. *Thiboutot,* 448 U.S. 1 (1980) (§ 1983); *Owen* v. *City of Independence,* 445 U.S. 622 (1980) (§ 1983); *Roe* v. *Wade,* 410 U.S. 113 (1973) (abortion).
6   *Regan* v. *Wald,* 104 S. Ct. 3026 (1984) (travel to Cuba); *Firefighters* v. *Stotts,* 104 S. Ct. 2576 (1984) (employment); *Grove City College* v. *Bell,* 104 S. Ct. 1211 (1984) (sex discrimination); *New York* v. *Quarles,* 104 S. Ct. 2626 (1984) (*Miranda* warnings); *United States* v. *Leon,* 104 S. Ct. 3405 (1984) (exclusionary rule); *Nix* v. *Williams,* 104 S. Ct. 2501 (1984) (exclusionary rule).
7   Geoffrey R. Stone, "O.T. 1983 and the Era of Aggressive Majoritarianism: A Court in Transition," 19 *Georgia Law Review* 15 (1984).
8   ACLU News Release, July 6, 1984.
9   *Judicial Notice* 1 (July–August 1984) (newsletter of Judicial Reform Project, Free Congress Research and Education Foundation).
10   104 S. Ct. 1355 (1984). In the autumn of 1984, the *California Law Review* sponsored a symposium on the religion clauses that offers a comprehensive analysis of the cases up to and including *Lynch:* Kent Greenawalt, "Religion as a Concept in Constitutional Law," 72 *California Law Review* 753 (1984); Philip E. Johnson, "Concepts and Compromise in First Amendment Religious Doctrine," 72 *California Law Review* 817 (1984); John H. Mansfield, "The Religion Clauses of the First Amendment and the Philosophy of the Constitution," 72 *California Law Review* 847 (1984).
11   *Marsh* v. *Chambers,* 463 U.S. 783 (1983); *Mueller* v. *Allen,* 463 U.S. 388 (1983).
12   See the section in this paper entitled "The 1984 Term: Briefs and Arguments."
13   Thomas Jefferson to Committee of the Danbury Baptist Association, January 2, 1802, *The Life and Selected Writings of Thomas Jefferson,* ed. Adrienne Koch and William Peden (New York, 1944), pp. 332–3.
14   330 U.S. 1 (1947).
15   330 U.S., at 13.
16   Erwin N. Griswold, "Absolute is in the Dark – A Discussion of the Approach of the Supreme Court to Constitutional Questions," 8 *Utah Law Review* 167 (1963); Paul G. Kauper, "Everson v. Board of Education: A Product of the Judicial Will," 15 *Arizona Law Review* 307, 317 (1973).
17   *McCollum* v. *Board of Education,* 333 U.S. 203 (1948); *Zorach* v. *Clauson,* 343 U.S. 306 (1952).
18   *Engel* v. *Vitale,* 370 U.S. 421 (1962) (New York Board of Regents prayer);

School District of Abington Township v. *Schempp,* 374 U.S. 203 (1963) (Bible reading, Lord's Prayer); *McGowan* v. *Maryland,* 366 U.S. 420 (1961) (Sunday closing laws).

19 *Zorach* v. *Clauson,* 343 U.S. 306, 313 (1952).
20 *Engel* v. *Vitale,* 370 U.S., at 443 (Douglas, J., concurring).
21 397 U.S. 664, 676 (1970).
22 392 U.S. 236 (1968).
23 403 U.S. 602 (1971).
24 413 U.S. 756 (1973).
25 421 U.S. 349 (1975).
26 433 U.S. 229 (1977).
27 403 U.S., at 612–13.
28 See *Lemon* v. *Kurtzman,* 403 U.S. 602, 622–4 (1971); *Committee for Public Education & Religious Liberty* v. *Nyquist,* 413 U.S. 756, 795–6 (1973).
29 See *Meek* v. *Pittenger,* 421 U.S. 349, 394 (Rehnquist, J., dissenting in part); *Roemer* v. *Board of Public Works,* 426 U.S. 736, 768–9 (1976) (White, J., concurring). For commentators' criticisms of the entanglement test, see, for example, Jesse Choper, "The Religious Clauses of the First Amendment: Reconciling the Conflict," 41 *University of Pittsburgh Law Review* 673, 680 (1980); Philip B. Kurland, "The Irrelevance of the Constitution: The Religion Clauses of the First Amendment and the Supreme Court," 24 *Villanova Law Review* 3, 19 (1978–9).
30 *Wolman* v. *Walter,* 433 U.S. 229, 265–6 (1977) (Stevens, J., concurring in part and dissenting in part).
31 See, for example, *Committee for Public Education & Religious Liberty* v. *Nyquist,* 413 U.S. 756, 803–5 (1973) (Burger, C. J., concurring in part and dissenting in part).
32 See, for example, *Lemon* v. *Kurtzman,* 403 U.S. 602, 667–9 (1971) (White, J., concurring in part and dissenting in part).
33 *Levitt* v. *Committee for Public Education,* 413 U.S. 472 (1973).
34 444 U.S. 646 (1980).
35 444 U.S., at 657–9.
36 433 U.S. 229 (1977).
37 444 U.S., at 666 (Blackmun, J., dissenting).
38 444 U.S., at 664 (Blackmun, J., dissenting).
39 463 U.S. 388 (1983).
40 463 U.S., at 398.
41 463 U.S., at 395–6 n.4.
42 463 U.S., at 396.
43 Minn. Stat. § 123.39 (5) (1985).
44 463 U.S., at 391.
45 413 U.S., at 830 (1973).
46 463 U.S., at 401.
47 463 U.S., at 401–2.
48 463 U.S., 783 (1983).

49   675 F.2d 228 (8th Circuit 1982), reversed, 463 U.S. 783.

50   463 U.S., at 786.

51   463 U.S., at 795 (Brennan, J., dissenting).

52   Warren E. Burger, "The State of Justice," 70 *American Bar Association Journal* 62 (1984); Symposium, "Rx for an Overburdened Supreme Court: Is Relief in Sight?" 66 *Judicature* 394 (1983).

53   463 U.S., at 795, quoting *School District of Abington Township* v. *Schempp, 374 U.S.*, at 308 (Goldberg, J., concurring).

54   104 S. Ct. 1355.

55   104 S. Ct., at 1365.

56   104 S. Ct., at 1359.

57   104 S. Ct., at 1378–80 (Brennan, J., dissenting).

58   104 S. Ct., at 1369.

59   104 S. Ct., at 1365.

60   104 S. Ct., at 1363–4.

61   See generally James H. Barnett, *The American Christmas: A Study in National Culture* (New York, 1954); Robert J. Meyers, *Celebrations: The Complete Book of American Holidays* (Garden City, N.Y., 1972).

62   104 S. Ct., at 1360.

63   104 S. Ct., at 1360–1.

64   *Judicial Notice,* 1.

65   *New York Times,* August 6, 1984, p. A16.

66   *Washington Post,* September 30, 1984, p. A4.

67   Assessments of the actual impact of amicus briefs on Supreme Court opinions must in good part be speculation. One study has documented the percentages of Supreme Court opinions from 1969 to 1981 that cited amicus briefs. Karen O'Connor and Lee Epstein, "Court Rules and Workload: A Case Study of Rules Governing Amicus Curiae Participation," 8 *Justice Systems Journal* 35, 42 (1983). But such statistics tell little about the actual influence of amicus briefs. There is no doubt that in recent years, the number of amicus briefs filed in the Court have greatly increased. See Bruce J. Ennis, "Effective Amicus Briefs," 33 *Catholic University Law Review* 603 (1984). Aside from their impact on the Court, it is fair to suppose that many briefs are filed with other audiences in mind, especially those who give financial or other support to the group filing the brief. See Leo Pfeffer, "Amici in Church–State Litigation," 44 *Law and Contemporary Problems*. 83, 108 (1981); Stephen L. Wasby, "How Planned Is 'Planned Litigation'?" 1984 *American Bar Foundation Research Journal* 83, 116. On the amicus brief in general, see Samuel Krislov, "The Amicus Curiae Brief: From Friendship to Advocacy," 72 *Yale Law Journal* 694 (1963).

68   Equal Access Act, 98 Stat. 1302 (1984).

69   See *New York Times,* August 12, 1984, p. E1.

70   *Wallace* v. *Jaffree,* Brief Amicus of the United States, pp. 1–2.

71   *Aguilar* v. *Felton,* Brief of the Secretary of Education; *School District of the City of Grand Rapids* v. *Ball,* Brief Amicus of the United States; *Wallace* v.

Jaffree, Brief Amicus of the United States; *Estate of Thornton* v. *Caldor, Inc.*, Brief Amicus of the United States.

72 Among the more interesting were *Jensen* v. *Quaring*, No. 83-1944, and *Board of Trustees of the Village of Scarsdale* v. *McCreary*, No. 84-277. The question in *Jensen* was whether Nebraska's requiring a photograph on a driver's license infringed the free exercise of religion of a driver who read the second commandment's prohibition against graven images literally. The *Scarsdale* case brought before the Court the Second Circuit's decision that Scarsdale, New York, could not rely on the establishment clause in denying private citizens' request to display a crèche in a public park owned by the village. I have not included either case for discussion in the body of this paper, as the Court divided 4 to 4 in both cases (Justice Powell not participating), and thus there were no opinions. See 105 S. Ct. 2355 (1985); 53 USLW 4431 (March 27, 1985).

73 See, generally, Charles H. Wilson, "ESEA Title I Litigation – A National View," 27 *Catholic Lawyer* 231 (1982).

74 *Aguilar* v. *Felton*, Brief for Appellants, pp. 17, 20–1.

75 See, for example, *Aguilar* v. *Felton*, Brief of Appellant Chancellor, pp. 16, 19, Brief Amicus of the Council for American Private Education et al., pp. 11, 22; *Wallace* v. *Jaffree*, Brief of Appellant George C. Wallace, pp. 33, 36, Brief Amicus of the Legal Foundation of America, pp. 7–8, Brief Amicus of the States' Attorneys General, pp. 18–22; *Estate of Thornton* v. *Caldor, Inc.*, Brief of Petitioner, p. 21.

76 *Wallace* v. *Jaffree*, Brief of Appellant George C. Wallace, p. 33.

77 *Wallace* v. *Jaffree*, Brief Amicus of the United States, p. 12.

78 See, for example, *Aguilar* v. *Felton*, Brief of Appellant, pp. 24–6, Brief of Appellant Chancellor, p. 16; *Wallace* v. *Jaffree*, Brief Amicus of the Christian Legal Society, pp. 3–7; *Estate of Thornton* v. *Caldor, Inc.*, Brief of Petitioner, p. 20, Brief Amicus of the United States, pp. 15, 24.

79 *Wallace* v. *Jaffree*, Brief Amicus of the Freedom Council, p. 21.

80 *Wallace* v. *Jaffree*, Brief Amicus of the Legal Foundation of America, p. 3.

81 104 S. Ct., at 1359.

82 *Wallace* v. *Jaffree*, Brief Amicus of the ACLU et al., pp. 21–2.

83 *Wallace* v. *Jaffree*, Brief Amicus of the American Jewish Congress, p. 1.

84 *Estate of Thornton* v. *Caldor, Inc.*, Brief Amicus of the ACLU and the American Jewish Committee, pp. iii–iv.

85 *Estate of Thornton* v. *Caldor, Inc.*, Brief Amicus of the Anti-Defamation League of B'nai B'rith, p. 6.

86 *Aguilar* v. *Felton*, Brief of the Secretary of Education, p. 47.

87 *Wallace* v. *Jaffree*, Brief Amicus of the Moral Majority, Inc., pp. 6–7. See also Brief Amicus of the Legal Foundation of America, pp. 6, 8–10; Brief Amicus of the Freedom Council, pp. 16–20.

88 433 U.S., at 262 (Powell, J., concurring in part and dissenting in part).

89 104 S. Ct., at 1363.

90 *Aguilar* v. *Felton*, Brief of the Secretary of Education, p. 47; *School District of the City of Grand Rapids* v. *Ball*, Brief Amicus of the United States, p. 9.

91 *Aguilar* v. *Felton*, Brief Amicus of the Council for American Private Education, pp. 3–7.

92 *Wallace* v. *Jaffree*, Brief Amicus of the United States, pp. 19–20.

93 *Wallace* v. *Jaffree*, Brief Amicus of the Moral Majority, Inc., pp. 14–16.

94 *Wallace* v. *Jaffree*, Brief Amicus of the Freedom Council, p. 29, quoting Harvey Cox, *The Secular City: Secularization and Urbanization in Theological Perspective* (New York, 1965), p. 18.

95 *Aguilar* v. *Felton*, Brief Amicus of the Catholic League for Religious and Civil Rights, p. 6.

96 *Estate of Thornton* v. *Caldor, Inc.*, Brief Amicus of the United States, p. 29.

97 *Estate of Thornton* v. *Caldor, Inc.*, Brief Amicus of the United States, pp. 23–4.

98 *Estate of Thornton* v. *Caldor, Inc.*, Brief Amicus of the United States, p. 24.

99 See Brief Amicus of the United States in *City of Akron* v. *Akron Center for Reproductive Rights*, Nos. 81-746, 81-1623, pp. 17–19. In its subsequent decision, the Court rejected the government's suggestion to adopt a more deferential posture in abortion cases. See 462 U.S., at 416 (1983); compare 462 U.S., at 452 (O'Connor, J., dissenting).

100 *Estate of Thornton* v. *Caldor, Inc.*, Brief of Petitioner, pp. 22–7.

101 See, for example, *Williamson* v. *Lee Optical*, 348 U.S. 483, 487–91 (1955); *Heart of Atlanta Motel, Inc.* v. *United States*, 379 U.S. 241, 262 (1964).

102 *Wallace* v. *Jaffree*, Brief Amicus of the Center for Judicial Studies, pp. 3–19.

103 332 U.S. 46, 71–2 (1947) (Black, J., dissenting). As to the states being subject to the establishment clause, see Justice Black's opinion in *Everson* v. *Board of Education*, 330 U.S. 1.

104 See Charles Fairman, "Does the Fourteenth Amendment Incorporate the Bill of Rights?" 2 *Stanford Law Review* 5 (1949); Raoul Berger, *Government by Judiciary: The Transformation of the Fourteenth Amendment* (Cambridge, Mass., 1977), p. 156, n. 95.

105 "Black's sweeping hypothesis, feebly argued, has apparently secured a foothold in the Court." James McClellan, *Joseph Story and the American Constitution* (Norman, Okla., 1971), pp. 151–9.

106 See, for example, Charles E. Rice, "The Problem of Unjust Laws," 26 *Catholic Lawyer* 278 (1981).

107 *Jaffree* v. *Board of School Commissioners*, 554 F. Supp. 1104, 1128 (S.D. Ala. 1983).

108 *Jaffree* v. *Wallace*, 705 F.2d 1526, 1532 (11th Circuit 1983).

109 *School District of Abington Township* v. *Schempp*, 374 U.S. 203, 217 (1963).

110 *Wallace* v. *Jaffree*, Brief of Appellant George C. Wallace, p. 37, n. 51.

111 "*Benchmark* (a publication of the Center for Judicial Studies) subscribes to the maxim that Rule of Law demands adherence to the original intent of the Constitution, and that a deliberate departure from the true import and

sense of its enumerated powers or general principles is the establishment of a new constitution." James McClellan, "Editor's Brief," *Benchmark: A Bimonthly Report on the Constitution and the Courts* 1 (1983): 1–2.

112 *School District of the City of Grand Rapids* v. *Ball,* Brief Amicus of the United States, p. 10.

113 433 U.S. 229 (1977); 421 U.S. 349 (1975).

114 *School District of the City of Grand Rapids* v. *Ball,* Brief of the Secretary of Education, p. 43.

115 See, for example, *School District of the City of Grand Rapids* v. *Ball,* Joint Brief of Petitioners, pp. 20, 32, 36, 39, 40, 42, 43, 44, 45.

116 *School District of the City of Grands Rapids* v. *Ball,* Joint Reply Brief of Petitioners, pp. 1–3, 5, 9–11.

117 In addition to passages cited in notes 40–44, see, for example, *Aguilar* v. *Felton,* Brief of Appellants, pp. 17–23, Brief Amicus of the Catholic League for Religious and Civil Rights, p. 5, Brief Amicus of the Council for American Private Education, pp. 8–9, Brief Amicus for the National Jewish Commission on Law and Public Affairs, pp. 3, 7.

118 *Wallace* v. *Jaffree,* Brief Amicus of the States' Attorneys General, p. 20.

119 *Wallace* v. *Jaffree,* Brief of Appellant George C. Wallace, p. 36.

120 *Wallace* v. *Jaffree,* Brief Amicus of the Freedom Council, pp. 4–16.

121 *Wallace* v. *Jaffree,* Brief Amicus of the Center for Judicial Studies, p. 20.

122 374 U.S., at 217.

123 See Mark D. Howe, *The Garden and the Wilderness: Religion and Government in American Constitutional History* (Chicago, 1965), p. 31; McClellan, *Joseph Story and the American Constitution,* p. 142; James McClellan, "The Making and Unmaking of the Establishment Clause," in *A Blueprint for Judicial Report,* ed. Patrick B. McGuigan and Randall R. Rader (Washington, D.C., 1981), pp. 295, 319; Robert L. Cord, *Separation of Church and State: Historical Fact and Current Fiction* (New York, 1982), pp. 15, 144–5.

124 554 F. Supp., at 1114–15.

125 554 F. Supp, at 1113, n. 5.

126 *Wallace* v. *Jaffree,* Brief of Appellant George C. Wallace, pp. 17–29.

127 McClellan, *Joseph Story and the American Constitution.*

128 *Wallace* v. *Jaffree,* Brief of Appellant George C. Wallace, p. 33.

129 104 S. Ct., at 1362. See *Marsh* v. *Chambers,* 463 U.S. 783 (1983); *Larson* v. *Valente,* 456 U.S. 228 (1982). In *Larson,* the Court applied a more rigorous standard (strict scrutiny) than that of *Lemon,* but went on to hold the state law invalid under the *Lemon* analysis as well. See 456 U.S., at 251–5.

130 104 S. Ct., at 1370–1 (Brennan, J., dissenting).

131 *School District of the City of Grand Rapids* v. *Ball,* Brief Amicus of the United States, p. 11, quoting *Committee for Public Education & Religious Liberty* v. *Nyquist,* 413 U.S. 756, 761, n. 5.

132 *School District of the City of Grand Rapids* v. *Ball,* Joint Brief of Petitioners, p. 23.

133 *Wallace* v. *Jaffree,* Amicus Brief of the Legal Foundation of America, p. 15.

134   See *Wallace* v. *Jaffree,* Brief Amicus of the United States, pp. 18–22, Brief Amicus of the Freedom Council, pp. 23–8, Brief Amicus of the States' Attorneys General, pp. 14–19.

135   *Estate of Thornton* v. *Caldor, Inc.,* Brief Amicus of the United States, pp. 26–7.

136   *Estate of Thornton* v. *Caldor, Inc.,* Brief of Petitioner, p. 9.

137   See *Lemon* v. *Kurtzman,* 403 U.S. 602, 622 (1971).

138   463 U.S., at 403–4, n. 11.

139   104 S. Ct., at 1364–5.

140   *Aguilar* v. *Felton,* Brief of Appellants, p. 48; *School District of the City of Grand Rapids* v. *Ball,* Joint Reply Brief of Petitioners, p. 15.

141   *School District of the City of Grand Rapids* v. *Ball,* Brief Amicus of the United States, p. 24, quoting *Lynch* v. *Donnelly,* 104 S. Ct. at (O'Connor, J., concurring).

142   *School District of the City of Grand Rapids* v. *Ball,* Brief Amicus of the United States, p. 24, quoting *New York Times Co.* v. *Sullivan,* 376 U.S. 254, 270 (1964).

143   See Edward N. Gaffney, "Political Divisiveness along Religious Lines," 24 *St. Louis University Law Journal* 205 (1980).

144   *Aguilar* v. *Felton,* Brief Amicus of the Council for American Private Education et al., p. 19. By contrast, the ACLU's brief in *Wallace* argued that cases like that one "demonstrate that 'political divisiveness' is an acute element of Establishment Clause concern" and suggested that the Court "should reconsider the independent significance of political divisiveness in Establishment Clause jurisprudence." Brief Amicus of the ACLU, p. 43, n. 31.

145   *Wallace* v. *Jaffree,* 105 S. Ct. 2479 (1985).

146   *Estate of Thornton* v. *Caldor, Inc.,* 105 S. Ct. 2914 (1985).

147   *School District of the City of Grand Rapids* v. *Ball,* 105 S. Ct. 3216 (1985); *Aguilar* v. *Felton,* 105 S. Ct. 3232 (1985).

148   105 S. Ct., at 2489–93 and n. 45.

149   *Wallace* v. *Jaffree,* Brief Amicus of the United States, p. 10.

150   *Wallace* v. *Jaffree,* Brief of Appellant George C. Wallace, p. 14.

151   105 S. Ct., at 2496 (O'Connor, J., concurring).

152   105 S. Ct., at 2493 (Powell, J., concurring).

153   105 S. Ct., at 2491.

154   105 S. Ct., at 2918.

155   Cf. Title VII of the Civil Rights Act of 1964, 42 U.S.C. § 2000, which requires employers to give reasonable accommodation to employees' religious practices unless to do so would cause "undue hardship."

156   105 S. Ct., at 3223–30.

157   105 S. Ct., at 3237–9.

158   105 S. Ct., at 3238–9.

159   105 S. Ct., at 3237–9. Justice Rehnquist was exasperated that the Court should strike down the Grand Rapids and New York City programs when

"not one instance of attempted religious inculcation" existed in the record in either case (105 S. Ct., at 3232 [Rehnquist, J., dissenting]).

160 105 S. Ct., at 2517–20 (Rehnquist, J., dissenting).

161 *Wallace* v. *Jaffree,* 105 S. Ct., at 2497 (O'Connor, J., concurring). See Justice O'Connor's concurring opinion in *Lynch* v. *Donnelly,* 104 S. Ct., at 1366–70.

162 105 S. Ct., at 2493–94 (Powell, J., concurring).

163 "In setting the appropriate boundaries in Establishment Clause cases, the Court has frequently relied on our holding in *Lemon, supra,* for guidance, and we do so here." 105 S. Ct., at 2917.

164 105 S. Ct., at 3247 (O'Connor, J. dissenting).

165 105 S. Ct., at 3248 (O'Connor, J., dissenting).

166 433 U.S., at 263 (Powell, J., concurring in part and dissenting in part).

167 105 S. Ct., at 3240 (Powell, J., concurring). Powell concurred in the Court's opinions, as well as its judgments, in both cases (105 S. Ct. at 3239).

168 See the section in this paper entitled "The 1984 Term: Briefs and Argumentation."

169 105 S. Ct., at 2508–20 (Rehnquist, J., dissenting).

170 For charges of "hostility," see *Aguilar* v. *Felton,* 105 S. Ct., at 3242–3 (Burger, C. J., dissenting); *Wallace* v. *Jaffree,* 105 S. Ct., at 2507–8 (Burger, C. J., dissenting).

171 Speaking at the American Bar Association's annual convention in Washington, Meese said that the Constitution's framers would find the Court's views "somewhat bizarre." *Washington Post,* July 10, 1985, p. A1.

172 "But my audience in the final analysis is not millions, not thousands or even hundreds, but nine." *New York Times,* July 18, 1985, p. 18. For such views, Lee was excoriated by James McClellan, who laid at Lee's feet the "primary responsibility" for the administration's failure to make "inroads against the Imperial Judiciary." Lee, said McClellan, "misunderstands both his own role and that of the Court." McClellan concluded, "To say that he [Lee] is not suited for the task to which he has been assigned is to understate the case for his prompt removal." "Editor's Brief: A Lawyer Looks at Rex Lee," *Benchmark* 1 (March–April 1984): 1, 2, 16.

173 *New York Times,* July 18, 1985, p. 18.

Index

Abbott, Francis E., 213–14
Abercrombie, James, 75
Abington School District v. *Schempp*, 7, 224, 228, 302, 333
abortion, 291, 314, 330
accommodation, 268, 269, 321–2, 325, 326–8, 329, 330–2, 334–5, 336; permitted/mandated by Constitution, 326–7, 330; rejection of, 336–7, 340–1; in Supreme Court religion cases, 318–23; in Virginia struggle for religious liberty, 161–3
Act Against Blasphemy, An (Mass. statute), 171–5
Act for Incorporating the Protestant Episcopal Church (Va.), 157
Act of Toleration (England), 141, 142; *see also* Toleration Act of 1689
Act respecting Publick Worship and Religious Freedom, An (Mass.), 184
Adams, John, 39, 40, 78, 80, 179, 191, 192, 193, 213, 218, 228; death of, 96; religious proclamations, 303, 305; religious thought of, 65
Adams, Samuel, 179, 192
Adams v. *Howe*, 184
Adamson v. *California*, 330–1
"Address to the Anabaptist Preachers Imprisoned in Caroline County," 143
adiaphora, 49
adiaphorism, 59
Adorno, Theodor, 261, 262, 264, 273; *Dialectic of Enlightenment*, 259

aestheticism, 271–2
AFL-CIO, 324
After Virtue (MacIntyre), 272
Age of Constantine, 2
agnostics, 202, 213, 228
agreement, universal, 269–70
Aguilar v. *Felton*, 291, 325, 326, 328, 329, 332–3, 335, 337, 338, 339–40, 341
Akron, Ohio, 330
Alabama, 5; moment-of-silence case, 323, 324, 325, 326, 327, 328, 329, 333, 336–7, 338–41
Alexandria: Episcopal Church, 288, 289, 294
America: as "experiment," 273–4
American Civil Liberties Union (ACLU), 215, 217, 225, 313, 314, 324, 327
American colonies: established church in, 2–3; religion and liberty of conscience in, 23–42; religious belief in, 64–5
"American creed," 4, 7
American Freedom and Catholic Power (Blanshard), 219
American Humanist Association, 217
American Jewish Committee, 327
American Jewish Congress, 223, 225, 324, 327
American Museum of Natural History, 214
American people: shared past for, 80; social and religious composition of, 202
American pluralism: Jeffersonian religious liberty and, 201–35

"American proposition, the," 3, 7
American Revolution, 69, 127, 128, 145, 301; and Anglican Establishment, 27–8, 38; religion in, 68; and religious diversity, 29–30
American Unitarian Association, 217
American University, 288
Americans for Public Schools, 223
amicus briefs: Supreme court religion cases, 324–5, 326, 327, 328, 330, 331, 332–3, 334, 335, 340
Amish, 11
Andover, 188
Andros, Sir Edmund, 28
Anglican Church (Established church) (Va.), vii, 7, 67, 152–6, 243; disestablishment of, viii; Jeffersonian case against, 85–92; see also Church of England; Episcopal Church
Anglican Way: in American colonies, 24–8, 29, 30, 36, 37, 38, 40
Anglicans, 35, 39–40
Annapolis Convention, 125
Anne, queen of England, 56, 57
anti-Catholic sentiment, 210, 215, 218, 219, 226
Antichrist, 50
Anti-Defamation League of B'nai B'rith, 327
antinomianism, 47–8, 51, 59
"anti-papist oath" (Mass.), 176
Appeal to the Public (Chandler), 27
"Archimedean point," 266
Areopagitica (Milton), 31, 274n2
argumentation, 267, 268, 271
Aristotle, 46, 280n34
Articles of Confederation, 114
assessment (Va.), 109, 113, 115–17, 119–21, 122–3, 127–8, 129, 146–7, 150–1
assessment bill (Va.), 159, 222; petitions against, 146–56, 158
Assize Act (1784), 125
Athanasians, 65
atheism, 54, 57, 58, 68, 224
atheists, 25, 202, 213, 228; excluded from toleration, 131n9, 176
Athens, 43
Augustine, bishop of Hippo, 44–5, 46; De Civitate Dei, 43
authority: and disestablishment (Va.), 82–

3; fallibility of, 88; locus of, 46–54, 55, 56, 59, 60, 62–3, 69, 128; limitations of civil, 84–5; and struggle over Virginia Statute, 139
autonomy, 260, 261
Avery, Joseph, 182
Avery v. The Inhabitants of Tyringham, 182

Backus, Isaac, 39, 179, 192, 209
Bacon, Francis, 54
Bacon, Jarvis C., 205
Bailyn, Bernard, 81
Baird, Robert: Religion in America, 213
Baker, Eliphalet, 186
Baker v. Fales, 186–7
Ball, William Bentley, 328
Bancroft, George: History, 222
Baptist Association of Virginia, 223
Baptist Church, 3
Baptist Joint Committee on Public Affairs, 221
Baptists, 29, 61, 202, 217; and aid to parochial schools, 227; in American colonies, 26, 35, 37, 39–40, 41n9, 70; and assessment bill (Va.), 123; and Bible reading in schools, 205–6; and disestablishment, 208–9; and establishment (Va.), 116; in New England, 192; and religious freedom, 221–22; and religious liberty for Catholics, 203, 204, 206; and separation of church and state, 221; southern, 11; and struggle for religious liberty in Massachusetts, 179, 180, 189, 191, 192; and support for Virginia statute, viii, 248, 249; and tax support for religion in Massachusetts, 183–4, 186, 198n11; in Virginia struggle for religious freedom, 140–1, 142, 143, 144, 146, 147, 148, 151–6, 157, 158–61, 162; see also Separate Baptists
Baptists of Virginia, The (Ryland), 160–1
Barnes, Thomas, 183
Barnes v. First Parish in Falmouth, 182–3, 192
Barrows v. Jackson, 297
Beckley, John, 76, 96
Being and Time (Heidegger), 280n33
belief(s), 10–11, 12–13, 16, 52, 60; duty of, 204; privacy of, 90; privileging, 17;

as religion, 19; religion as system of, existing in mind, 61–6, 163, 204, 205, 213, 247–8; in thought of Jefferson, 77, 86–7

belief/action distinction, 14, 88, 204–5, 247

Bell, Daniel, 278n24

Bellah, Robert, 80, 96, 259, 276n12

Benchmark (journal), 346n111

Bennett, John C.: *Christians and the State,* 220

Bennett, William J., 5, 8, 18, 238, 242, 251–2, 253, 341

Berger, Raoul, 331

Berkeley, George, 28, 78

Berns, Walter, 15–16

Bible: King James Version, 190, 199n119, 211–12; public reading of, 228

Bible reading in schools, 205–6, 210–12, 214, 215, 217–18, 316; opposition to, 223, 224

biblical tradition, 17–19

bigamy, 204

Bill Concerning Religion (Va.), 243

Bill for Establishing a Provision for the Teachers of the Christian Religion, A (Va.), 115, 146–7

Bill of Rights, ix, x, 129–30, 190, 206, 208, 226; applicability of, to states, x, 6, 211, 330, 331; interpreted in Madison's "Detached Memoranda," 286; political/religious indifference in, 57; separation of church and state in, 66

Bill for the Relief of Bible Societies in the United States, A, 293–4

Bill for the Relief of the Baltimore and Massachusetts Bible Societies, A, 293–4

Bill on Crimes and Punishments (Va.), 123

bills of rights, 128

Bishop, Abraham, 209, 210

Black, Hugo L., 218–20, 222, 225, 283, 286, 315, 317, 330–1

Black, Jeremiah, 289

Blackmun, Harry A., 314, 318–19

Blaine, James G., 215

Blaine Amendment, 224

Blair, James, 25

Blanshard, Paul, 218, 227; *American Freedom and Catholic Power,* 219; "Bus Wedge, The," 222

blasphemy, 171–5, 179

Blau, Joseph L., 225

"Blue Laws," 162

Board of Education, v. *Allen,* 316, 317

Board of Trustees of the Village of Scarsdale v. *McCreary,* 345n72

Bonhoeffer, Dietrich, 202

Borah, William E., 203

"bourgeois liberty," 163

Bowdoin, James, 179, 192

Bradfield v. *Roberts,* 290, 291

Brady, Joseph H., 227–8

Bray, Thomas, 25–6, 30, 36

Brennan, William J., Jr., 218, 222, 299, 302, 305–6, 320–1, 322, 334, 337–8, 341

Brethren, 35

Brown, O. B., 207

Bryan, William Jennings, 215

Buber, Martin, 305, 306

Buckley, Thomas E., S. J., 239

Bunyan, John, 33

Burger, Warren E., 293, 294, 298, 299, 304–5, 314, 316, 317, 320, 321–3, 324, 327, 328, 329, 333, 334, 335, 337, 339, 341

Burger Court, 314

Burke, Edmund, 65, 71; *Speech on Conciliation with America,* 64

Burlamaqui, Jean Jacques, 102n54

"Bus Wedge, The" (Blanshard), 222

Calvert, George, 1st Baron Baltimore, 25, 35–6

Calvinism, 211

Cambridge Platonists, 58

Cannon, Joseph W., 184

Cannon, Josiah, 192

Cantwell v. *Connecticut,* 4–5, 11, 14, 287

capital punishment laws, 314

Carr, Peter, 213, 248–9

Carter, James, 12, 314

Catholic League for Religious and Civil Rights, 324, 329

Catholic Sisters of Charity, 290

Catholic University, 288

Catholicism, 23, 217; in Maryland, 34–6

Catholics, 35, 91, 131n9, 134n28, 191–2, 202; and aid to parochial schools, 211,

Catholics (*cont.*)
227; in American colonies, 24, 41n9;
danger to religious freedom from, 221;
distrust of (Mass.), 176–8, 182; in England, 56, 57; impact of Virginia Statute on, 225–7; in Maryland, 25, 26;
prejudice against, 210, 215, 218, 219,
226; and religion in public schools, 206,
211–12, 224; religious liberty for, 203–
4, 207–8, 209, 222
Center for Judicial Studies, 313, 330, 331,
333
Chandler, Thomas Bradbury, 38; *Appeal to
the Public,* 27
Charles I, king of England, 56
Charles II, king of England, 55, 56, 57
Chesterton, G. K., 4
Cheverus, Jean, 177–8, 191, 192
Christian Broadcasting Network, 326
Christian Legal Society, 324
Christianity, 66, 210, 251; assessments for
support of (Va.), 113; church-state
problem in, 43–8; and civil government, viii, 92; common core of, in
U.S., 211; in common law of U.S.,
295–6; distinction between civic order
and, 250, 251; establishment of, 119–
20, 244; establishment of, in Massachusetts, 173–4, 175, 178, 179–87, 183;
freedom of conscience in, 249; of Jefferson, 76, 94, 96; morality in, 240; not
part of common law, 84; presupposed
in religious liberty (Va.), 82; separation
of religion and government in, 245–6,
251; and state, 120–1, 151–2, 206; as
state religion, 63, 117, 214, 221
Christianity and Crisis, 220
Christians and the State (Bennett), 220
Christmas, 305, 322
Church: authority of, 62–3; in thought of
Jefferson, 89–91, 103n64; views of, in
Virginia struggle for religious liberty,
152–6
Church Establishment: in England, 55–61
Church of England: in American colonies,
23–8; dissent in, 33; established by law
in England, 47; king as head of, 57; and
Restoration, 56; in Virginia, 2–3, 82–4,
110, 115–16; *see also* Anglican Church;
Episcopal Church

Church of Holy Trinity v. *United States,* 296
Church of Jesus Christ of Latter-Day
Saints (Mormons), 204, 289
church-state relations, xi, 109, 221, 228; in
American colonies, 29–30, 37–8; assumptions in, 1–2; conflict over, 217–
18; cooperation in, 220, 227; in exploration and discovery, 23–4; in history
of Christianity, 43–8; Jews and, 224–5;
Madison's "Detached Memoranda" in
decisions re, 287–306; in Supreme
Court religion cases, 315, 321, 323,
324, 341; in thought of Jefferson, ix,
77, 78, 84–5; in Virginia, 115, 127–8,
130; *see also* separation of church and
state
churches: grants of public land to, 287,
291–3; as instruments of government,
289, 290–1; public role of, 227; *see also*
religious taxation
Cincinnati School Board, 212, 213
citizenship, 43–4, 268, 270, 272; and religion, 54
civil authority: limitations of (Jefferson),
84–5
civil capacities: freedom of religion and,
11–13
civil-contractual basis: in petitions re religious liberty in Virginia, 149–50, 152
civil disobedience, 227
civil government, *see* government
civil liberty, x; and religious liberty,
110–12
civil order, 250–1; foundation of, 247
civil religion, 7, 54, 63, 66, 96, 227; Jefferson and, 77–8, 95–6, 238–40, 241
civil rights, ix, 64, 252; distinct from religious opinions, 204, 246–7; government and, 128; of Jews, 224; moral personality as basis for, 68; protection of,
130; and religion, 86, 90, 92, 201;
republican government, 126–30
civil rights movement, 276n12
civil-rights statute, 314
civil society: and coercion, 163; primacy
of, 69; and religion, 118–21; *see also* society
civil virtue: basis of, 244; religion and,
237–55, 257
civitas Dei, 44–5, 62

civitas terrena, 45, 62.
Claiborne, William, 36
Clarendon Code (England), 33
Clark, Mark, 221
Clark, Tom C., 19, 222, 228
Clarke, John, 32
clergy, 54, 55; licensing of (Va.), 113, 143;
  magistracy and, 51; role of, in thought
  of Jefferson, 59, 89–91, 92; as symbolic
  figures, 153–4, 156; tax support for,
  92, 146, 181; *see also* priests
Cleveland, Grover, 214
coercion, 7, 163, 263; of belief, 213; as
  component of Establishment, 12, 13,
  17; of conscience, 263–4; in religion, 7,
  191, 201, 209, 248
Coercive Acts (England), 110
Cohens v. *Virginia*, 313
College of New Jersey (Princeton), 242; *see
  also* Princeton [college]
College of William and Mary, 90, 91, 144
Colo v. *Treasurer*, 310n76
Colwell, Stephen, 210
*Committee for Public Education and Religious
  Liberty* v. *Nyquist*, 316, 320
*Committee for Public Education and Religious
  Liberty* v. *Regan*, 318
Common Faith (Dewey), 16
common law: Christianity in, 84, 295–6
Common Law, The (Holmes), 175
common religion, 238; and civic virtue,
  250; *see also* civil religion; shared religious belief
"common sense religion," 240
communication, 46, 281n41
Communism, 217
communitarianism, 259–61, 266, 269,
  272–3
community, 260; of church, 162; constitutive of self, 260, 261; moral, 259; moral
  vocabulary of, 282n45
compelling state purpose, 302; *see also* purpose criterion
comprehension, 56–7
Conant, James B., 221
Confederation, 124, 126
congressional chaplaincies, 287, 296–9
Congregational Way (New England), 24
Congregationalism, 2–3, 174; in American
  colonies, 28, 29–30, 37, 38–9, 40, 41n9

Congregationalists, 91; in American colonies, 26, 191, 192; and Harvard College, 188–9; and tax-supported religion
  in Massachusetts, 181, 186, 187
Congress, 206–7; powers of, 114, 124–5
Connecticut, 32, 35; Anglicanism in, 28,
  39–40; Congregationalism in, 29–30;
  disestablishment in, 285; impact of Virginia Statute in, 209–10; religious liberty in, 37; Sabbatarian law, 323, 324,
  325, 326, 327, 329, 334, 336, 337, 338–
  41
conscience, 117, 257–8, 259; force used
  against, when democratic institutions
  threatened, 263; and public policy, 258;
  sacredness of, 260; *see also* freedom of
  conscience; rights of conscience; sovereignty of conscience
conscientious objectors, 103n65
conscientiousness (religious), 248–9
consensus: and establishment in Virginia,
  147–56; overlapping, 262; religious, in
  American colonies, 24
conservative groups, 313; and accommodation, 327; and Supreme Court, 313–
  15
Constantine, 43, 45, 48, 64
Constantinian-Christian tradition, 239
Constitution (Va.), 81–2, 83, 111, 112,
  120, 123, 150; religious liberty in,
  145–46
Constitution (U.S.), 4, 178, 191, 192, 208;
  "general-welfare" clause, 226; interpreted in Madison's "Detached Memoranda," 286; monopolies in, 287; Protestantism as basis of, 210; religious tests
  forbidden in, 298; separation of church
  and state in, 66, 203–4; strict construction of, 119; Virginia Statute and, ix–x,
  229
Constitutional Convention, 126, 127,
  136n64, 229
constitutional government, 265
constitutional law, 285, 306
Continental Congress, 39, 78, 79, 83, 111,
  130
convictions, 280n33
Cooley, Thomas, 340
Cooper, Thomas, 91, 204
cooperation: in church-state relations, 220,

cooperation (*cont.*)
227; social institutions as experiments in, 274
Cord, Robert L., 6, 7, 8, 10, 15, 17, 333
Corwin, E. S., 220
Cotton, John, 31–2
Council for American Private Education, 328, 335
Council of Nicaea, 64
counter-Enlightenment, 275n12
Cox, Harvey: *The Secular City*, 329
crèches, 223; constitutionality of public, 304–6, 314–15, 321–3, 333
criminal prosecutions: Massachusetts, 171–5, 179
Critique of Pure Reason (Kant), 278n21
Cromwell, Oliver, 52
"Crystal Cathedral" case, 8
cults, 11, 289; First Amendment protection of, 211n112
culture: and judgment of sanity/fanaticism, 259, 263–4, 265, 266–7; liberal democratic, 259–60
Curtis, Benjamin, 175

Dante Alighieri, 45
Davidson, Donald, 258, 267, 271, 281n41
Davies, Samuel, 159
Dawson, Joseph Martin, 221–2, 227
De Civitate Dei (Augustine), 43
Dearborn, Henry, 178
Decalogue, 245, 250
Declaration of Independence, vii, 3, 4, 76, 80, 81, 84, 86, 118, 297; God in, 240; principle of consent in, 216; significance of, 78
Declaration of Rights (Mass.), 172, 173, 174, 179, 182, 189, 190
Declaration of the Causes and Necessity for Taking Up Arms, 79–80
deism, 62, 63, 68, 211; of Madison, 110; in Virginia Statute, 161, 162
deist-humanist school, 15–17
deists, 66; religious liberty for, 209
Delaware: Anglicanism in, 26–7; Constitution, 296
democracy, 127, 277n19; and civil rights, 129; factions in, 129, 191; persons created by, 268, 269, 273; priority of, to

philosophy, 71, 257–82; religion of, 216
Democracy in America (Tocqueville), x
democratic institutions, 272
Democratic Party, 215
deontology, 265, 268, 278n25
Derrida, Jacques, 267, 271
Descartes, René, 265, 267
Destutt de Tracy, Antoine, 61
"Detached Memoranda" (Madison), 285–312
determinism, 61
Dewey, John, 17, 259, 261, 262, 264, 267, 271, 273, 277n19, 279n29, 280n36; *Common Faith*, 16; *Human Nature and Conduct*, 280n33; *The Living Thoughts of Thomas Jefferson*, 216
Dialectic of Enlightenment (Adorno), 259
Diffenderfer v. Central Baptist of Miami, 306
Dirksen, Everett, 223
disabilities (component of Establishment), 12
discrimination, 192–3
disenchantment, 272–3
disengagement, 260
disestablishment, 3, 30, 64, 203, 285; Jefferson and, 81, 82, 83, 84, 85–92, 131n12; in Madison, 113; in Massachusetts, 184, 185, 186–7; in New England, 209–10; in South Carolina, 208; in Virginia, 112, 149–50, 156–7, 208, 285
dissent, viii; in American colonies, 27, 29, 30–1; freedom of, 250; modes of, in Virginia struggle for religious liberty, 82, 83–4, 155; suppression of, in England, 33
dissenters, vii, 219; in American colonies, 24; English Protestant, 134n33; and tax support for religion in Massachusetts, 183–4, 185
dissenters in Virginia, 91, 103n65, 110–11, 112–13, 116, 117, 149–50, 156–61, 162; petitions to Assembly, 146–7, 148–9; and Virginia statute, 139–69
Dissenting interest: in English Restoration, 55–7, 59, 64
District of Columbia: incorporation of churches, 288

diversity, 27, 229; in England, 33; invoked in Supreme Court religion cases, 328, 330
"divine rights of conscience," 297, 298; *see also* rights of conscience; sovereignty of conscience
divisive political potential test, 317, 335, 339–40
Documentary History of the Struggle of Religious Liberty in Virginia (James), 160
dogma(s), 240
dogmatism, 279n31
Douglas, William O., 220, 222, 223, 294, 316
Dutch in American colonies, 26
Dutch Reformed Church, 24, 26, 41n9
Dworkin, Ronald, 259, 260, 263, 281n40

ecclesiastical monopolies, 287–8
Edwards, Morgan, 158
"effect" test (establishment clause litigation), 317, 319–20, 322, 334, 337–8
Eisenhower, Dwight D., 71
Elementary and Secondary Education Act, 227, 325
Eliot School, Boston, 199n119
Elizabeth I, queen of England, 50
Elliot v. *White,* 310n76
Emerson, Ralph Waldo, 174, 213, 273
Encyclopédie, ix, 93, 156, 163
Enfield, William, 73n28
Engel v. *Vitale,* 7
England, John, 208
England: Civil War(s), 33, 36, 48, 50–2, 56; moderate religion in, 64; religious freedom in, 50–1; religious toleration in, 36–7; Restoration politics in, 33, 55–61, 64
English Reformation, 48–9, 50–1, 54–5
Enlightenment, 17, 19, 55, 70, 245, 248, 263, 264, 275n12, 282n45; American expression of, 202; Jefferson and, viii, 13; Protestant, 66; religion in, 13, 14, 15, 16; social thought of, 261
Enlightenment rationalism, 257, 258, 259, 260, 262, 273
"entanglement" test (establishment clause litigation), 300, 317, 319, 334, 338

"enthusiasm," 58, 62, 63, 64, 66, 67; Plato as founder of, 73n28
enthusiasts, 25, 26, 37
episcopacy, 25, 27, 29, 38, 84; in English Restoration, 55
Episcopal Church, 222; establishment of, 84, 156–7, 307; *see also* Anglican Church; Church of England
Episcopal Church of the Diocese of Washington, 288
Episcopalians, 90, 91, 104n79, 130, 189; disagreements among (Va.), 122–3; tax rights of (Mass.), 181
epistemology, 264, 271
Equal Access Act, 324
equal protection of the laws (principle), 297
equal rights, 229; in religious liberty, 121–2; in thought of Madison, 120
equal separation, 12
equality, vii
equality before the law, 128
error: rights of, 23, 33, 52, 226
Ervin, Sam J., Jr., 223
Essay Concerning Human Understanding (Locke), 59
establishment, viii, 206–7, 228; in American colonies, 24, 26, 27–8, 29–30, 33, 37, 38, 39–40, 41n9; components of, 12; and corruption, 117; dangers in, 119–20; forbidden in Constitution, 228; and Harvard College, 188–90; Jefferson opposed to, 244; Madison on, 110, 112, 113, 120–1, 307; in Massachusetts, 171–99; multiple, viii, 243; Protestant, 207–8; resistance to, 31–40; in South Carolina, 208; in Virginia, 110, 112, 113, 147, 158
establishmentarianism, 24
Establishmentarians (Va.), 146; and assessment bill, 152–6, 162
Estate of Thornton v. *Caldor, Inc.,* 325–6, 327, 329, 330, 334–5, 336, 337, 339, 341
Ethical Culture Society, 217
ethics, 211
ethnocentrism, 266, 267
evangelicalism, 71, 202, 206; in Virginia, 140–6, 162–3

evangelicals: concept of law of, 161–2
Everett, Edward, 306–7
Everson v. *Board of Education*, 6, 219–20, 221, 225, 283, 285, 286, 287, 288, 306, 315–16, 317
evolution: teaching of, 206, 215
existentialism, 280n33
experience: redemption through, 45–6

Fairman, Charles, 331
faith: salvation through, 45, 47
Falwell, Jerry, 71
fanaticism, 37, 259, 263–4
Federal Council of Churches, 223
federal reform: Madison's efforts toward, 125–7
Federalist, The, No. 10, 191
Federalists, 75, 76, 94, 209, 210
Fifth Amendment: "due-process" clause, 297
Fifth Monarchists, 33
Fincastle Resolutions, 149
First Amendment, 6, 19, 109, 174, 192, 203, 209, 216, 217, 285, 298; Baptists and, 222; broad meaning of, 223; cults protected under, 311n112; and government role in religion, 15; incorporation into Fourteenth, 11, 227–9; legal development of reasoning in, 14; and separation of church and state, 220–1, 224, 301; theology of, 226–7; Virginia Statute and, ix–x, 3, 4–5, 225, 228
First Amendment "establishment" clause, 7, 8, 219, 227, 288; applicability to states of, 287, 288, 331–2, 333; and church-state relations, 289, 290, 291, 292, 301, 302, 311n105; in Supreme Court religion cases, 225, 315–23, 326, 327, 328, 329, 330–2, 335, 336, 337–9, 341
First Amendment "free-exercise" clause, 10–11, 12, 14, 287; and church-state relations, 297, 302; in Supreme Court religion cases, 328
First Amendment religion clauses, 222, 223; applicability to states of, 5, 6, 206, 215, 217, 287, 288, 298; meaning of, 229, 286; purpose of, 227; in Supreme Court religion cases, 218–20

Flast v. *Cohen,* 223, 292
Fleet, Elizabeth, 285, 286–7
Foote, William Henry, 158, 160
Foster, Edmund, 178
Founding Fathers: 207, intent of, 3, 6, 212, 217, 229, 333, 346n111; and relation of religion to civic virtue, 237–8; religious views of, 15
Fourteenth Amendment, 5, 6, 225, 297; "due-process" clause, 5, 6, 229, 287; First incorporated into, 11, 227–9; reach of, 330–1, 333
Frankfurter, Felix, 218–20, 286
Franklin, Benjamin, 17, 18, 78, 214
free assembly, 252
free-church tradition, 249, 250
Free Congress Research and Education Foundation, 313, 314
free inquiry: religion of, 68, 69–70
free press, 31, 252
Free Religious Association, 214
free speech, 252
free will, 61
freedom, vii; as signal value in Jefferson, 76–7; threatened by fanaticism, 264
Freedom Council, 326, 329, 333
freedom from religion, 34, 67, 76, 250
freedom of conscience, 82, 192, 279n31; basis of, 112; in Christian tradition, 251; in colonial America, 23–42; and public support of religion (Mass.), 180, 183; in thought of Jefferson, 9, 146; *see also* rights of conscience; sovereignty of conscience
freedom of religion, *see* religious freedom (liberty)
freedom of thought, 93, 250, 279n31
Freedom Under Siege (O'Hair), 218
freethinkers, 202, 213–14, 215
fundamentalism, 71, 215–16

Gadamer, Hans-Georg, 258
Gaffney, Edward M., Jr., 335
Gage, Thomas, 80
Garrison, Winfred E., 1–2
Gaston, William, 208
Geertz, Clifford, 14, 15
General Conference of American Rabbis, 217

gentry authoritarians (Va.): and dissenters, 139, 142, 147, 156
George III, king of England, 56, 79, 81
George Washington University, 207
Georgetown University, 288
Georgia: Anglicanism in, 26, 27
German Reformed [church], 24, 41n9
Gerry, Elbridge, 127, 184
Gibbon, Edward, 44
Glorious Revolution, 36
God, 68; concern with, replaced by emphasis on the human, 264; debates about, 15–19; duty toward, in thought of Madison, 118–19; in governmental documents, 287, 295–6; in Massachusetts law, 173–4, 175, 184; nature of, 54; rational knowledge of, 59–60; in thought of Jefferson, 77, 79, 80, 84, 86–7, 89, 93–4, 95, 97, 204, 240, 241, 263
God, Caesar, and the Constitution (Pfeffer), 225
Gospel: invoked in Virginia struggle for religious liberty, 150–1; see also Word of God
government, 150, 212; "benevolent neutrality" toward religion by, 288, 316, 319; Christianity and, 92; constitutional, 265; constitutionality of involvement of, in religious celebrations, 304–6; debates about God in, 15–19; enforcement of religion by, undermines civic virtue, 243–4; factions in, 191; Jefferson's proposed form of, 80–1; natural-law philosophy of origins of, 78–9; power of, to destroy churches, 289; and prevention of rights, 126–30; and religion, 77, 78, 93, 117, 178, 201, 210, 223, 244–5; religious proclamations by, 287, 302–6; right of, to interfere with religious opinion to preserve peace and order, 174, 204–5, 247; and rights of citizens, 86, 87–9, 93; secularization of, 214; and sovereignty of conscience, 244–6
Government Intervention in Religious Affairs (Kelley), 11
governmental documents: Deity in, 287, 295–6

Grant, U.S., 215
Great Awakening, 37, 38, 62
Great Case of Liberty of Conscience, The (Penn), 33–4
Great Revival of 1785, 161
Great Seal of the United States, 80
Greek city: Christian Church and, 43–5
Green, William, 203
Gregory VII, pope, 50
Griswold, Erwin, 315
Gwatkin, Thomas ("Hoadleianus"), 144

Hamilton, Alexander, 303
Hampden-Sydney College, 149, 157, 242
Hand, W. B., 331, 333
Hanover Awakening, 149
Hare Krishna, 11
Harlan, John Marshall, 222
"harm principle," 253
Harper's Magazine, 286
Harrington, James, 54
Harris v. McRae, 291
Harrison, Benjamin, 123
Harvard College, 173–4, 188–90
Harvard Divinity School, 188
Healey, Robert W., 9, 16
Hegel, Georg W. F., 260, 262, 279n29, 280n36, 281n43
Heidegger, Martin, 258, 259, 260, 261, 267, 272; Being and Time, 280n33
Henley, Samuel, 144
Henry, Jacob, 208
Henry, Patrick, 3, 83, 112, 114, 115, 116, 117, 124
Henry IV, emperor, 50
Henry VIII, king of England, 45, 48–9
Higher Education Facilities Act of, 1963, 223
historical experience: and philosophical understanding, 279n31, 280n34
historicity: of self, 248, 258, 259, 260, 262, 263, 265, 266–7, 270, 281n39
history, 262; invoked in Supreme Court religion cases, 320–1, 322–3, 333–44; and moral development, 265, 266, 268–9; in thought of Jefferson, 79–80, 84, 85
Hitler, Adolf, 296
Hoadly, bishop of Bangor, 62

Hoadly, George, 212
Hobbes, Thomas: *Leviathan,* 51, 53
Hobbism, 57, 58
Holland, Francis May: *Liberty in the Nineteenth Century,* 214
Holmes, Obadiah, 32
Holmes, Oliver Wendell, Jr.: *The Common Law,* 175
Holy Cross College, 198n111
Home, Henry, 102n54
Honeyman, James, 28
Hook, Sidney, 228
Horkheimer, Max, 259, 261, 262, 264, 273
Hospital Surety and Construction Act of 1946 (Hill-Burton Act), 290–1
hospitals: federal funding for sectarian, 290–1
hostility to religion (claim), 329, 330, 341
Howe, Mark De Wolfe, 186, 333
Hubbard, Samuel, 178, 192
Hughes, John, 211
human beings: ahistorical essence of, 258, 266; created by liberal democracy, 268, 269, 273; legitimation of views of, 264; nature of, 260, 261, 263, 264, 265, 268–9, 270; nature of, presupposed in political institutions, 260–1, 263, 265
human dignity, 275n12
human nature, 263, 264, 265; theory of, 277n17
Human Nature and Conduct (Dewey), 280n33
human rights, 263; ahistorical, 258–9, 261–2
Hume, David, 63–4, 68, 265, 267
Hunt, Gaillard, 286

idéologie, 67
ideology, 61; in American concept of freedom of religion, 226–7; among heirs to Jefferson, 202
immigrants, immigration, 202, 210–11, 221, 229
imperium, 46, 48, 49, 69
Imprisoned Preachers and Religious Liberty in Virginia (Little), 160
incarnation, 45, 46
Incarnation, 44, 45–6, 54
incorporation, 5–6, 11, 287, 288–91

incorporation bill (Va.), 115–16, 117, 123
"incorporation" theory (Justice Black), 330–1
Independent Reflector (Livingston), 84
Indians (in America), 95, 96, 207, 239
indifference, 75, 95, 96; in religion/politics relationship, 57, 64
indifferentism, 251
individualism, 221, 225, 226, 282n45; language of, 276n12; religious, 213
Indulgence (policy), 56–7, 58
Ingersoll, Robert, 214, 215
Inglis, Charles, 27
inner/outer experience distinction: and religious basis of civil order, 247, 249–50, 252–53
instrumental rationality, 272
intellect, 44; *see also* mind; reason
intellectual liberty, ix
intellectuals: and freedom of religion, 54
interdependence, 261
intolerance, 30, 210–11, 279n31
Ireland, James, 160
irrationality, 281n42
irreligion: charges of, against Jefferson, 76, 77, 93–5, 213; *see also* freedom from religion
IRS, 11
Isaac, Rhys, 70

Jackson, Andrew, 207, 304
Jackson, Robert H., x, 283
James, Charles F.: *Documentary History of the Struggle of Religious Liberty in Virginia,* 160
James, William, 60
James· Edward the Old Pretender, 56
James I, king of England, 50, 55
James II, king of England, 36, 56, 57
James VI, king of Scotland, 55
Jefferson, Thomas, 120, 122, 123–4, 262, 268, 273, 280n38, 333; and American liberal politics, 257–8; anti-theology stance of, 262, 263, 276n16; arguments over views of, 9–10, 75–6; *Autobiography* of, 203; death of, 96–7; draft constitution for Virginia of, 131n12; and early struggles for religious liberty in Virginia, 141, 144–5, 146, 163; Enlightenment assumptions of, 13; indif-

ference of, to religion/irreligion, 13, 75, 88, 257; *The Life and Morals of Jesus of Nazareth*, 240; and Madison, 113, 114, 129–30, 132n12; *Notes on the State of Virginia*, 13, 75, 76, 84, 85, 86–7, 88, 89, 90, 94, 100n34, 241, 245, 247; policies and practices of, re establishment of religion, 19; political theology of, 47, 75–107, 239; presidency of, ix–x, 94–6; and question of proselytizing among slaves, 163; as rector, University of Virginia, 298; and relation of religion to civic virtue, 237, 238–42, 243–9, 250, 251–3; and religious liberty, 12, 30, 40, 55, 201–35; and religious proclamations, 303–4; religious thought of, 15, 16–17, 18–19, 58, 63–4, 65, 66, 67–8, 95–6, 213, 218, 248–9, 257–8, 263; and religious toleration, 263, 267–8; *A Summary View of the Rights of British America*, 79, 80; and Supreme Court decisions, 313; *see also* Declaration of Independence; Virginia Statute for Religious Freedom; "wall of separation" metaphor
Jeffersonian Republicans, 39–40
Jehovah's Witnesses, 11, 219
Jensen v. *Quaring*, 345n72
Jesuits, 90
Jesus Christ, 44, 45, 46, 59–60, 64, 66, 67, 68, 216; magistracy and, 69; name in government documents, 295, 296; real presence of, 67
Jewish law: Christian Church and, 43, 44
Jewish Telegraph Agency: *Daily News Bulletin*, 301
Jews, 35, 91, 202, 296, 306; and accommodation principle, 327; impact of Virginia Statute on, 224–5, 228; prejudice against, 210; and religion in public schools, 206, 212, 224; religious liberty for, 203, 207–8, 209
John XXIII, pope, 226
Johnson, Alvin W., and Frank H. Yost: *Separation of Church and State in the United States*, 224
Johnson, Richard M., 207
Jones, Joseph, 114
Josephus, 311n95
Judaic tradition: national religion in, 239

Judeo-Christian tradition, 3–4, 296; formal privilege for, 13, 17–19
judicial activism, 313, 314
judicial interpretation/application: religion clauses of First Amendment, 286, 287–306
jure divino, 47, 55, 56
justice, 45, 128; basis for concept of, 261, 262, 263, 265; as fairness, 262, 266, 280n34; as first virtue of democratic society, 262, 263, 264, 265, 268, 273; philosophy as basis for political conception of, 276n15; principles of, 277n21, 279n31, 281n39; shared understanding of, 280n34; theory of, 278n22; threatened by fanaticism, 264
"Justice as Fairness" (Rawls), 261
justifiability, 278n21; and truth, 258–9

Kallen, Horace M., 216–17
Kames, Lord, 102n54
Kant, Immanuel, 262, 265, 266, 267, 269–70, 281n38, 281n39; *Critique of Pure Reason*, 278n21
Kantian dualisms, 280n36
Kaskaskia Indians, 10, 239
Kauper, Paul, 315
Kelley, Dean M.: *Government Intervention in Religious Affairs*, 11
Kennedy, John F., 203–4, 222
Kennedy, Thomas, 207–8, 224
Kentucky, 207, 294, 295
Kierkegaard, Sören, 267; *Philosophical Fragments*, 281n43
king, 45; as head of church, 48–9, 50–1, 55–6, 57
King, Martin Luther, Jr., 276n12
kingdom of God, 46, 48
Kirkland, John, 188
Knapp, Samuel L., 177, 192
Kneeland, Abner, 172–5, 192
Knowledge and Politics (Unger), 272
Know-Nothing Party, 210
Ku Klux Klan, 203, 219

Laird v. *Anderson*, 301
languages, untranslatable, 281n41
Larson v. *Valente*, 334
Latitudinarians, 58–9, 62, 66
Laud, William, 50

Law, Thomas, 246
law: lack of, in struggle for religious liberty in Virginia, 142–43; Madison's respect for, 119, 120; and religion, 307; separation of church and state in, 213, 214
law of nature, *see* natural law
Lee, Ann, 63
Lee, Rex E., 306, 341
Lee, Richard Henry, 78, 115, 124
Legal Foundation of America, 326–7, 334
legal tradition (U.S.): persuasive-coercive distinction in, 3–4
legislative chaplaincies, 7, 209, 306, 314–15, 320–1
legislative judgments: Supreme Court deference to, 319, 239–30
Leland, John, 39, 184, 192, 209, 221
Lemon v. *Kurtzman*, 291, 316, 317, 319, 323, 329, 330, 334–5, 337–9
Leo XIII, pope, 226
Lerner, Max, 220
Leviathan (Hobbes), 51, 53
Levin, David, 280n38
Levy, Uriah Phillips, 202–3
Lewin, Nathan, 330, 335
liberal democracy: enemies of, 266–7; and "need" for philosophical justification, 259, 260, 261–4, 272–4
liberal institutions and culture, 259, 273–4
Liberal Party, 224
liberal politics, 257
liberal social theory, 272; polarization of, 258–9
liberal society, 70
liberalism: criticisms of, 71, 262, 268–9, 272; Enlightenment, 163; Jews and, 224; in religion, 58, 59
Liberalism and the Limits of Justice (Sandel), 264–8
liberals, viii, 313; and Supreme Court religion cases, 327
liberation (individual), 273
libertarians: in struggle for religious liberty in Virginia, 145, 162–3
Liberty Hall, 157
Liberty in the Nineteenth Century (Holland), 214
Life and Morals of Jesus of Nazareth, The (Jefferson), 240

Liguori, Alfonso de', 177
Lincoln, Abraham, 4
litigation: in religious taxation issue (Mass.), 181–4; *see also* Supreme Court religion cases
Littel, Franklin H., 228
Little, David, 204–5, 279n33
Little, Lewis Peyton: *Imprisoned Preachers and Religious Liberty in Virginia*, 160
Lives of Virginia Baptist Ministers, 160
Living Thoughts of Thomas Jefferson, The (Dewey), 216
Livingston, William: *Independent Reflector*, 84
Locke, John, 38, 58, 59–60, 63, 102n54, 120, 245; *Essay Concerning Human Understanding*, 59; on freedom of religious opinion, 132n12; influence on Jefferson of, 84, 89, 103n64; influence on Madison of, 118; *Letters on Toleration*, 59, 84, 91, 112; theory of toleration of, 176–7; *Treatise on Government*, 59
Logos, 44
Lombard, Ichabod, 181
Lombard, Lemuel, 181
Lonergan, Bernard, 77
"loyalty oath" (Mass.), 176
Loyola, Saint Ignatius, 266, 267, 268, 269
Luther, Martin, 46, 276n16
Lutherans, 24, 35, 41n9
Lynch v. *Donnelly*, 304–5, 306, 314–15, 321–3, 326, 327, 328, 333, 334, 335, 340, 341

McClellan, James, 331, 333, 334
McCollum, Vashti: *One Woman's Flight*, 217–18
McCollum v. *Board of Education*, 306
McDaniel, George W., 206
McGovern v. *Maryland*, 286
McGuigan, Patrick B., 314
MacIntyre, Alasdair, 259–60, 273; *After Virtue*, 272
Madison, James, ix, 10, 13, 140, 184, 210, 215, 221, 239, 233; and civic religion, 78; "Detached Memoranda," 285–312; development of political thought of, 124–30; and drafting of Constitution, 298; and establishment of religion, 19; and First Amendment, 223; and free

exercise of religion by public officials, 12–13; "Memorial and Remonstrance Against Religious Assessments," viii, 43, 109, 118–24, 125, 130, 148, 150, 154, 155, 156, 241–2, 243, 244, 246, 247, 249, 251, 283–5, 286, 294, 295, 296, 315; and relation of religion to civic virtue, 243, 244, 246, 247, 249, 250, 251, 252, 253; and religious liberty, 30, 40, 55, 190–3, 203, 206–7, 212, 219; religious views of, 15, 109–10; as Secretary of State, 96; and separation of church and state, 225, 228–9; and struggle for religious liberty in Virginia, 81, 82, 83, 145, 146–7, 163; and veto of grant of public lands to churches, 291–2, 294; and veto of incorporation of Episcopal Church in Alexandria, 288–90, 291, 294; and Virginia Statute, viii, 1, 3, 7, 92–3, 109–38, 156, 222

Madison, James (bishop), 90, 144

magistracy, 64; locus of authority in, 46, 47–8, 49, 50–3, 55, 56, 59, 62, 66, 69, 70

Maine: impact of Virginia Statute on, 210–11

Maine Literary and Theological Institution (Waterville College; later Colby College), 198n111

majority(ies), 5; tyranny of, 210

majority rule, 126, 216; and minority rights, 125, 126–8; in tax-supported religion, 185–6

Malone, David Dudley, 215

man: political nature of, 43, 44; *see also* human beings

Mann, Horace, 211

Marbury v. *Madison,* 313

Marsh v. *Chambers,* 286, 298–9, 320–1, 322, 323, 326, 333, 334, 340, 341

Marshall, John, 313

Maryland: Act of Toleration, 36; Anglicanism in, 24, 25–6, 29, 36, 37; impact of Virginia Statute on, 207–8; religious freedom in, 35–7

Mason, George, 78, 111, 112, 120, 122, 145, 237, 246

Masonic lodges, 63

Masons, 221

Massachusetts, ix; Anglicanism in, 28, 40; Congregationalism in, 29–30; Constitution, 172, 173, 174, 175, 176, 177–9, 180, 182–3, 184, 185, 187, 188–9, 190, 191; criminal prosecutions in religious matters in, 171–5; and disestablishment, 285; and establishment, 171–99; impact of Virginia Statute in, 209–10; religious conformity in, 31–2; religious test for office in, 175–9

Massachusetts Bay Colony, 249–50

materialism, 54

Matignon, Francis, 177, 181–2

Mayhew, Jonathan, 28–9

Mead, Sidney, 16–17, 96

Meade, William, 157, 158, 160

Medicaid, 291

Meek v. *Pittenger,* 316–17, 319, 332

Meese, Edwin, III, 5, 8, 341

"Memorial and Remonstrance Against Religious Assessments" (Madison), viii, 43, 109, 118–24, 125, 130, 148, 150, 154, 155, 156, 241–2, 243, 244, 246, 247, 249, 251, 283–5, 286, 294, 295, 296, 315

Memorials of Methodism in Virginia, 160

Mencken, H. L., 215

Mennonites, 35, 103n65, 134n28, 148

mental reservation, 177

metaphysics, 65, 264, 267, 271

Methodists, 35, 62, 143, 189, 206; in Virginia struggle for religious liberty, 147, 162

Michigan, 323, 324, 325, 326, 338–41

Middle Colonies, 30; Anglicanism in, 24, 26–8, 37, 38

military academies, 7

military chaplaincies, 227, 287, 299–302

millennialism, 48, 53

Miller, Samuel, 304

Miller, William Lee, 11

Milton, John, 50–1; *Areopagitica,* 31, 274n2

mind: belief and, 86; freedom of, 82; primacy of, 161; religion existing in, 163; religious beliefs, involuntary result of impact of evidence on, 204, 205, 213; and religious experience, 60, 61–6

ministerial authority, 47–8, 51, 53

Minnesota, 319–20

minorities, 36; rights of, 94

Miranda v. *Arizona,* 314
missionaries, Anglican, 28, 29, 35, 36, 38
Mississippi, 5
Missouri Synod Lutherans, 11
moderation: in politics of religion, 59
Moehlman, Conrad, 227
Molière, 96
moment-of-silence cases, 323, 324–5, 326, 327, 328, 329, 334, 336–7, 341
monarchy, 27, 49
Moon, Rev. Sun Myung, 312n112
moral identity, 271, 272
moral law, 268
Moral Majority, 324, 328–9
moral personality, 68
moral philosophy, 279n29
moral progress, 267, 276n12
moral right, fundamental, 252
moral sense, 102n54, 239–40, 245–6; common, 257
moral subject: theory of, 266, 278n22
morality: ahistorical essence of, 279n29; as basis of civic order, 247; politics and, 238; and prudence, 258; and religion, 116, 183, 211, 239–41, 245, 246, 249–50, 251–2, 253; in thought of Jefferson, 86, 90, 213
Moravians, 35, 62
Morgan, Richard E., 14
Morton, Marcus, 174, 175
Mount Vernon Conference, 114
Mueller v. *Allen,* 319–20, 321, 323, 326, 335, 340, 341
Murphy, Frank, 219
Murray, John Courtney, 3, 181, 198n118, 226
myth, 258
"myth of origin," 80

NAACP: Legal Aid and Defense Fund, 313
Naked Public Square, The (Neuhaus), 238
national church, 59; prohibited by First Amendment, 220
National Council of Churches, 306
national faith (U.S.), 78, 80, 93, 95, 96–7; expressed in public schools, 224; *see also* shared religious belief
National Liberal League, 214, 218
National Reform Association, 214

national religion, 7; sources of, 239; *see also* civil religion
National Religious Liberty Association, 224
natural law, 80, 250, 297; origins of government in, 78–9; respect of government for, 128
natural religion, 63; language of, in Virginia petitions, 149–50, 152
natural right(s), 16, 204, 210, 252; in Christian tradition, 251; of conscience, 86, 242 (*see also* rights of conscience); freedom of religion as, 83, 85–6, 92, 93, 97, 246; government and, 78–9, 80; respect of government for, 128; in Virginia struggle for religious liberty, 154–5
Nebraska, 7, 320–1, 333
neoconservatism, 15, 17–18
Neuborne, Burt, 314
Neuhaus, Richard John, 242, 251–2, 253; *The Naked Public Square,* 238
neutrality: and obligation of government, 288; religious, 228
"neutrality" principle: in Supreme Court religion cases, 319–20, 323, 326
New England: Anglicanism in, 28–9, 38; Congregational Way in, 24; Congregationalism in, 37; establishment in, 117; impact of Virginia Statute on, 208–11; religious liberty in, 39
New England Way, 39
New Hampshire, 30; constitution, 213–14
New Jersey, 30; Anglicanism in, 27
New Lights, 26, 161, 162, 163; *see also* Separate Baptists
New World, 31, 33
New York, 30, 89; Anglicanism in, 27; freedom of religion in, 285
New York City, 8; aid to parochial schools in, 318–19, 324, 325, 326, 336, 338–41
Newton, Isaac, 58
Newton, Joseph Fort, 216
Nicholas, George, 118, 122, 146–7
Nicholas, Robert Carter, 84, 89
Nicholas, Wilson Cary, 118
Niebuhr, Reinhold, 220
Nietzsche, Friedrich, 266, 267, 268, 269, 272
Nixon, Richard, 314, 316

Noah, Mordecai M., 210
North Carolina, 229; Anglicanism in, 26, 27; impact of Virginia Statute on, 208; and Supreme Court, 208
Northeast Bible College (Valley Forge Christian College), 292–3
Northwest Ordinance, 219, 334, 340
Notes on the State of Virginia (Jefferson), 13, 75, 76, 84, 85, 86–7, 88, 89, 90, 94, 100n34, 241, 245, 247
Nozick, Robert, 278n24

oaths, 173, 175–6, 296; for holding office, 176–9, 191–2
Observations on the Nature of Civil Liberty (Price), 88–9
O'Connor, Sandra Day, 335, 336, 337, 338
O'Hair, Madalyn Murray, 217–18; *Freedom Under Siege*, 218
Ohio Supreme Court, 212
Old World, 31, 33
One Woman's Flight (McCollum), 217–18
O'Neill, James M., 227
opinion(s), 10–11, 12–13, 16, 17, 163; cannot be coerced, 118–19; civil rights distinct from (Va. Statute), 204; freedom of, 70, 113, 132n12; and freedom of religion, 60–1; vs. practice, 13–14; religion as system of, existing in mind, 61–6, 163, 204, 205, 213, 247–8

Paine, Solomon, 37–8
Paine, Thomas, 47, 49, 214
Palmer, Robert E., 298–9
pantheism, pantheists, 57, 63, 65, 68
paper money, 124, 125, 126, 137n64
Parker, Isaac, 184, 185, 186, 192
Parker, Samuel, 173–4, 175, 192
parochial-school aid (parochiaid), 5, 211, 215, 219–21, 222, 223, 224, 283, 315; indirect, 222, 227
parochial-school aid (parochiaid) cases, 316–17, 318–20, 323, 324, 325, 328, 334, 335, 336, 337–8, 339–41
parochial schools, 214; public welfare benefit of, 320
Parsons, Theophilus, 181, 182–4, 192, 195n41
Parson's Cause, 82–3

Passamaquoddy Indians, 191
Pawtucket, R.I., 304–5, 306, 314–15, 321–3, 333
Pendleton, Edmund, 84, 91, 112
Penn, William, viii, 33–5, 37; *The Great Case of Liberty of Conscience*, 33–4
Pennsylvania, viii, 3, 36; freedom of religion in, 34–5, 37, 110, 117, 151; religious diversity in, 27, 89
pentacostalism, 67, 71; *see also* evangelicalism; sects
"per se" rule, 332, 334
perfection (spiritual): public policy and, 257–8
persecution (religious), 31, 33, 192–3; in American colonies, 30, 32, 33; in England, 36–7, 55, 56–7; in Virginia, 141–2, 160
person: concept of, 277n17; theory of, 278n22
petitions: in struggle for religious liberty in Virginia, 146–56, 159, 160, 162
Pfeffer, Leo, 15, 223, 225, 227, 252; *God, Caesar, and the Constitution*, 225
Phelps, Martin, 184
Philosophical Fragments (Kierkegaard), 281n43
philosophical theology, 44
philosophical toleration, 261, 262–3
philosophy, 258, 267; as basis for political conception of justice, 276n15; democracy and, 71; meaning of, in Rawles, 263–4; "need" for justification of liberal democracy in, 259, 260, 261–4, 272–4; and politics, 269–70, 277n19; priority of democracy to, 257–82; and religion, 62, 69; self in, 270–1
Pietism, Pietists, 37–8, 207, 210
Pilgrims, 28
Pinckney, Charles, 207, 208
Plato, 58, 73n28, 277n16; *Republic*, 45; Theory of Recollection, 269, 281n43
Platonism, 58
Plumer, William, 214
pluralism: invoked in Supreme Court religion cases, 328, 330; Jeffersonian religious liberty and, 201–35; political, 94; *see also* religious pluralism
pocket veto, 293, 294
Pocock, John, 247

poetic theology, 44
political freedom: and type of person created by democratic institutions, 269
political institutions: presuppose doctrine
of nature of human beings, 260–1, 263
political philosophy: of Jefferson, 80–1
political rights, 203
political theology, 44; of Jefferson, 47, 75–
107, 239; liberal, 257; and morality,
238; and philosophy, 260, 269–70,
277n19; and redemption, 45–6; and religion, 75–6, 238, 251, 257, 324–5,
328–9, 341; religious, 45–6, 47, 204; religious freedom and desacralization of,
43–73; religious/philosophical legitimation of, 264–8; Restoration (England),
55–61; and social theory, 261–3
polygamy, 204, 289
polytheism, 63
pope, 45, 50; authority of, 176, 177
Port Act (1784), 125
Potter, Henry, 203
Powell, Lewis F., Jr., 314, 328, 336, 337,
338–40
pragmatism, 259, 260, 264, 280n33
prayer: public, 228
prayer in public schools, 5, 7–8, 217, 222,
316; opposition to, 223, 224, 306; as
political issue, 324; Supreme Court
cases, xi, 7–8, 19, 328, 336–7, 341
preachers: inspiration of, 150–1; licensing
of, 143; symbolic function of, in Virginia struggle for religious liberty,
153–4, 156
preferences, 266, 280n33
Presbyterianism: in Virginia, 160
presbyterians (England), 55
Presbyterians, 90, 202, 208, 211; in American colonies, 24, 26, 30, 35, 41n9, 83–
4; and assessment bill (Va.), 123, 130;
and establishment (Va.), 115–16; and
Virginia Statute, 206, 222–3; and Virginia struggle for religious liberty,
149–50, 152, 154–5, 157–8
Price, Richard, 65; *Observations on the Nature of Civil Liberty*, 88–9
"priestcraft," 58, 62, 63, 64, 73n28
priesthood of all believers, 45–6, 47, 51, 54
Priestley, Joseph, 47, 61, 65

priests, 63, 69; hatred of, 50, 54, 55, 58,
60, 66
Prince, James, 178
Princeton [college], 110, 154
privacy: in religion, 45, 48
privilege: Anglicanism, 27; as component
of establishment, 12, 13, 17–18; difficulty of resolution of, 19–20
Prohibition, 226
property, church: ownership of, 186–7; tax
exemption for, 227 (*see also* tax exemption of religious entities)
property rights: of Established Church
(Va.), 157
Protestant denominations: multiple establishment of (Va.), 243
Protestant Reformation, 45–6, 47, 49
Protestantism, 66, 68; and applicability of
First Amendment to states, 5–6; as basis of Constitution, 210; office holding
and privileging of religion, 18; and religious liberty, 215–16; religious politics
and, 47
Protestants, 35, 221; and aid to parochial
schools, 227; and disestablishment, 210;
exclusion of Catholics and Jews in establishment of, 207–8; office holding
restricted to, 203–4; and religion in
public schools, 224; restriction of tax
support to (Mass.), 180, 181–2
Protestants and Other Americans United
for Separation of Church and State,
221, 222, 292, 324, 327
psychoanalysis, 258
public education, 75–6
public good, 129; and private rights, 127,
128–9
public-interest groups, 313
public lands: grants of, to churches, 287,
291–3
public office: exclusion of non-Establishment Church persons from, 57, 59; *see
also* religious test for public office
public officials: free exercise of religion by,
12–13
public peace: laws on religion in preservation of, 174, 204–5, 247
public policy, 77; conscience and, 257–8,
259; and law, 175; and spiritual perfec-

tion, 257–8; in Supreme Court religion cases, 320

public religion, 7, 76; *see also* national religion

public school movement, 211

public schools, 224; compulsory Bible reading in, 205–6; Protestantism in, 210; religion in, 19; religious instruction in, 210–12; *see also* prayer in public schools

public welfare: benefit of parochial schools, 320; public worship and, 179, 183

Puritanism, 31, 57

Puritans, 28, 29, 245

purpose, effect, and entanglement standard, 298, 299; *see also* three-part test

purpose criterion (establishment clause cases), 316, 317, 318, 319, 334, 336

Quakers, 3, 25, 26, 29, 32–5, 39–40, 41n9, 103n65, 134n28, 148, 162; in England, 55

quietism, 48, 53

Quine, Willard, 258

racial segregation, 211

Randolph, Edmund, 83, 85, 95; *History of Virginia*, 157

"rational basis" test, 335

rationalism, viii, 174; Enlightenment, 257, 258, 259, 260, 262, 273; individualistic, 258, 259; in religious liberty in Virginia, 161–3

rationalists, viii, 206

rationality, 264; innate, 258; moral intuitions grounded in, 265; rationalist theory of, 281n43; standard, 330

Rawls, John, 259, 261–8, 269–70, 271, 273, 276n15, 277n17, 277n21, 278n24, 278n29, 281n39; "Justice as Fairness," 261; *A Theory of Justice*, 261, 264–5, 278n21, 279n29

"Rawlsian self," 282n45

Reagan, Ronald, 12–13, 237–8, 242, 251–2, 253, 306, 311n105, 324; federal court appointments of, 314

Reagan administration, 341; and conservative causes, 313–14

reason, 13, 267, 280n33; Enlightenment idea of, 258; and religion, 248–9; *see also* mind

redemption: politics and, 45–6

Redlich, Norman, 306

Reed, Stanley, 220

reflective equilibrium, 264, 270, 271, 279n29

Rehnquist, William H., 292–3, 314, 317, 319–20, 335, 337, 338, 340, 341

relativism, 266

released-time programs, 217, 224, 316

religion: as cause of factionalism, 129; and civil society, 118–21; and civil virtue, 237–55; in colonial America, 23–42; common denominator of, 239–40; compulsory, 7, 92; and conscience, 258; definitions of, 13–14, 68; of democracy, 216; experimental, 162; and government, 82, 95–6, 117, 251 (*see also* state: and religion); government aid to, 201, 227, 289, 290, 291; government use of, for secular ends, 301; moderate (reasonable), 58–9, 62–3, 64, 66; and morality, 116, 183, 211, 239–41, 245, 246, 249–50, 251–2, 253; as morality, 89–90; and persuasive-coercive distinction, 3–4; politicization of, 139; and politics, 75–6, 238, 251, 257, 324–5, 328–9, 341; protection of, 14; public, 7, 76, 239; public acknowledgment of, 323; in public schools, 19, 210–12, 306; redefinition of, 60–1, 66, 67, 69, 163; role of, 237–8, 323; society's need for, 15–17; as system of opinions formed in mind, 61–6, 163, 204, 205, 213, 247–8; in thought of Jefferson, 15, 16–17, 18–19, 58, 63–4, 65, 66, 67–8, 95–6, 213, 218, 248–9, 257–8, 263; unspecificity as defining character of, 71; in Virginia Statute, 93–4

religion cases (Supreme Court), 4–5, 313–49; 1984 term, 323–4

Religion in America (Baird), 213

"religionless religion," 202

religious beliefs: as opinions, 66, 67, 69, 70–1

religious celebrations: constitutionality of government involvement in, 304–6

religious conformity: resistance to, in American colonies, 31–40
religious controversy, 190–1
religious experience: and opinions/beliefs, 60–6
religious freedom (liberty), vii–viii, ix, 20, 51, 52, 57, 210, 211, 225, 228, 247; in American colonies, 3, 26–7, 32–3, 37; bases of denial/affirmation of, 60; basis of civil liberties in, 252; becoming free-·dom of religion, reason, opinion, 54, 55; Catholic theory of, 226; and civil capacities, 11–13; civil liberty and, 110–12; concern for, in Supreme Court religion cases, 323, 328, 330; and deist-humanist school, 16; and desacraliza-tion of politics, 43–73; early struggles over, in Virginia, 140–56; in First Amendment, 10–11; and freedom from religion, 67; as issue of social relation-ships, 162; Jeffersonian, 201–35; in Massachusetts, 172, 179, 191; nationali-zation of Jeffersonian, 202, 204–29; as natural right, 83, 85–6, 92, 93, 97, 246; for sake of religion, 82; state laws guar-anteeing, 285; in thought of Jefferson, 9, 75, 76–7, 81, 83, 84–92, 93, 94, 96, 97, 131n12, 244; in thought of Madi-son, 30, 40, 55, 110–12, 113, 117, 118–24, 129, 190–3, 203, 206–7, 212, 219, 307; unity with church-state separation, 285–312; in Virginia Declaration of Rights, 81–2; in Virginia Statute, ix–x, 68, 69–71
religious pluralism: American Catholics and, 226; tensions of, 227–8; in thought of Jefferson, 89–90, 91, 94; in Virginia, 152–3, 161
religious proclamations by government, 287, 302–6, 323
religious societies: tax-supported (Mass.), 180–1, 183–5, 186
religious taxation, viii, 8, 104n79, 283, 285, 290–1; forbidden, 306; as issue, 210, 223; in Massachusetts, 179–87, 192; suspended (Va.), 113, 146; see also assessment (Va.); parochial school aid
religious test for public office, 57, 204, 224; forbidden in Constitution, 229,

286, 298; Maryland, 207–8; in Massa-chusetts, 175–9
religious traditions: Jefferson's comparison of, 240
republic (American): religious foundation of, 242–3
Republic (Plato), 45
republican convictions: Madison and crisis of, 109–38
republican government, 237; protection of rights in, 126–30
Republican Party, 209
republican tradition: public religion as ba-sis of, 239
republicanism, 81; of Virginia dissenters, 155, 157
Republicanism, 214–15
Republicans: defense of Jefferson, 76
revivalism, 38, 66, 67, 70
Rhode Island, viii, 3, 31; Anglicanism in, 28; religious freedom in, 32–3, 35, 37, 39, 151
Rice, Charles, 331
Rice, John Holt, 91
Richardson, Joseph, 189, 190, 192
Richmond News Leader, 206
right: conception of, 281n39
right, religious: attacks on incorporation, 5–6
right to disbelief, 223–4; see also freedom from religion
rights of conscience, 161, 173, 242; "di-vine," 297, 298; in thought of Jeffer-son, 76, 81, 84–5, 86–9, 93, 97, 131n12; in thought of Madison, 110, 112, 118–19, 130; see also sovereignty of conscience
rights of man, 16; see also natural right(s)
Rives, William Cabell, 285; Letters and Other Writings of James Madison, 286
Roane, Spencer, 313
Roberts, Owen, 5, 14
Robertson, Pat, 326
Roe v. Wade, 314, 330, 341
Roman Empire, 43–4
Romanism a Menace to the Nation (Crow-ley), 215
Rome, 43
Rorty, Richard, 70, 71

Ruffner, William H., 211
Rush, Benjamin, 76, 95
Rutledge, Wiley B., x, 218–20, 222, 227, 283, 286
Ryland, Garnett: *The Baptists of Virginia*, 160–1

Sabbatarian law case, 323, 325–6, 327, 328, 329, 334, 336, 337, 341
sacerdotalism, 67, 68
sacraments, 45–6, 50, 62
St. Bartholomew's Day (1662), 55
Saltonstall, Leverett, 185, 189
salvation, 45, 49–50
Salvation Army, 8
salvation history: U.S. place in, 96, 97, 239
Sandel, Michael, 259, 260, 272, 273, 276n15, 278n22, 280n36, 281n39, 282n45; *Liberalism and the Limits of Justice*, 264–8
Sartre, Jean-Paul, 277n17
Scanlon, T. M., 278n21, 278n22
Schaff, Philip, x
Schiller, Johann von, 272
School District of the City of Grand Rapids v. *Ball*, 291, 325, 332–3, 334, 335, 337–8, 339–40, 341
Schwenkfelders, 35
Scotland, 55, 57, 64
Scottish Common Sense School, 240
Scottish Rite Masons, 221, 223
Scripture, 17, 162, 173, 175, 178, 224
Scudder, Samuel, 181
sectarianism, 19, 66, 70–1; and tolerance, 211
sects, 11, 16, 53–4, 63, 67; in English Restoration, 51–3, 55, 59; freedom of, 69; intolerance of, when in power, 210–11; multiplicity of, 129, 130, 191–2; Pentecostal, 69–70; radical, 61, 62
Secular City, The (Cox), 329
secular humanism, 67, 68, 70; as religion, 19, 225, 328–9
secular political faith, 257
secular sphere: basis of civil virtue in, 242
secularism, 202, 217, 218, 238; and absolute separation of church and state, 225; in schools, 328–9
secularists, 220

secularization, 238
self (the), 258, 259; essential unity of, 281n39; sense of, 276n12; theory of, 258, 260–2, 263, 264–8, 270–1, 273, 278n24, 282n45; and legitimation; *see also* historicity of self
self-interest, 278n21, 278n22
Semple, Robert Baylor: *The History of the Rise and Progress of the Baptists in Virginia*, 159
Separate Baptists, 82, 83–4; in Virginia, 141, 142, 151, 156, 159
separation: distinct from Christian theology, 223; equal, 12; and freedom, 77, 81; of religious and political covenants, 228; rights of, 78, 79
separation of church and state, xi, 57, 64, 118, 201, 203–4, 206, 228; and aid to parochial schools, 220–1, 283; Catholics and, 208, 225–7; in Constitution, 66; in deist-humanist thought, 15–16; ecclesiastical encroachments on, 294–5; Jefferson and, 76–7, 93, 95–6, 97, 216, 229, 239; Madison's contribution to, 122, 306–7; mandated in First Amendment, 301; in Massachusetts, 180; as matter of law, 213, 214; as national issue, 215; and religious instruction in public schools, 212; in Restoration England, 56; secularism and, 225; unity of religious freedom and, 285–312; in Virginia, 147, 149, 150, 154, 159; Virginia Statute basis of, vii–viii, ix–x, *see also* church-state relations
Separation of Church and State in the United States (Yost and Johnson), 224
Separation of Religion and Government, The (Swancara), 218
separationism, 224, 227, 327; in Supreme Court religion cases, 317, 323, 332, 337
Separatists: American colonies, 37–8
Seventh-Day Adventists, 202, 217, 224, 228
Shaftesbury, Earl of (Anthony Ashley Cooper), 58
shared religious belief: and civil virtue, 251–3; necessity of, to human societies, 273–4; not essential to democratic society, 257

Shaw, Lemuel, 174, 175, 186, 192
Shays's Rebellion, 137n64
Singer, C. Gregg: *A Theological Interpretation of American History*, 18
Sixtus V., pope, 50
skepticism, 63, 174–5, 279n31
slavery, 29, 161, 205; and struggle over religious liberty (Va.), 143, 144, 145, 162–3; in thought of Jefferson, 87, 100n34
Sloan v. *Lemon*, 320
Smith, Al, 203, 222, 226
Smith, Samuel Stanhope, 242–3
Smylie, James, 237
social institutions: change over time, 275n11; as experiments in cooperation, 274
social organization, 163
social policy: authority for, 263–4
social theory, 261–2, 265, 270, 272, 281n40; false philosophical presuppositions in, 272; polarization of, 258–9
society: and religion, 15–17, 23–4, 26; well-ordered, 282n45
Society for Promoting Christian Knowledge, 24
Society for the Propagation of the Gospel, 24, 27, 28–9, 38
Socinianism, 62, 63, 67, 68
Socinians, 65–6
sociology, 262
Socratism, 267, 269, 281n43
South Carolina, viii, 30; Anglicanism in, 26; establishment in, 208
Southcott, Joanna, 63
sovereignty of conscience: as basis of civil unity, 242, 244–6, 247–9, 251–2, 253
Speech on Conciliation with America (Burke), 64
Spirit of God, 47–8, 51–3, 55, 63, 151; freedom of, 70; primacy of, 54; in Protestantism, 66; unmediated, 58, 61, 62, 71
Stallo, Johann B., 212
Stamp Act, 27
Stamp Act Congress, 27
Standing Order of Federalist-Congregationalists, 209, 210
state: police power of, 226; and religion, 117, 146, 162, 183, 212, 216, 226–7; *see also* government
state aid to churches and religion, 201, 227, 289, 290, 291; *see also* parochial-school aid; religious taxation
state church, viii, 117
states: applicability of First Amendment to, 287, 288, 331–2, 333; establishment decided in, 206–7; power of, to make decisions about religion, 5–6, 8
Stevens, John Paul, 317, 336–7
Stewart, Potter, 222
Story, Joseph, 190, 192, 334, 340
Strauss, Leo, 280n34
Stuart, Archibald, 136n56
Stuarts (royal family, England), 56
Sullivan, William M., 279n29
Summary View of the Rights of British America, A (Jefferson), 79, 80
Sumner, Charles, 214
Sunday laws, 214, 224, 316
Sunday mail, 207, 209
Supreme Court, x, 3, 4, 6, 14, 174, 204, 212, 217, 238; Jeffersonian religious liberty in, 218–20; Madison's "Detached Memoranda" in decisions of, 285–6, 287–306; Madison's "Memorial and Remonstrance" in, 283, 285
Supreme Court religion cases, 5, 19, 225, 313–49; accommodation in, 318–23; establishment clause cases, 314–18; federal support for parochial schools, 283, 285; 1984 term, 323–41; school prayer, 7–8; separation of church and state, 221–2, 228–9
Swancara, Frank: *Thomas Jefferson versus Religious Oppression*, 218; *The Separation of Religion and Government*, 218
Synagogue Council of America, 217, 306

Taft, Alphonso, 212
tax exemption of religious entities, xi, 8, 227, 287, 293–5, 298, 306, 316
taxation for religious purposes, *see* religious taxation
taxation without representation, 39, 185
Taylor, Charles, 259, 260–1, 275n12
Taylor, James Barnett, 160
Tea Act, 110

teachers of religion: tax support for (Mass.), 180, 181–2
"Ten-Thousand Name Petition," 159
Test Act (England), 57, 64, 65
Thayer, V. T., 220
theist materialism, 54
Theist school, 17–19
theocracy, 303
Theological Interpretation of American History, A (Singer), 18
theology, 44, 59, 262, 279n31; Catholic, 177; "fuzzy," 282n45; Jefferson's view of, 77, 90–1, 95, 97, 240–1
Theory of Justice, A (Rawls), 261, 264–5, 278n21, 279n29
"theory of the moral subject," 266, 278n22
Thomas Jefferson Memorial Foundation, 203
Thomas Jefferson versus Religious Oppression (Swancara), 218
three-part test (establishment clause litigation), 299, 317, 319, 320, 321, 323, 334–5, 337–9
Tillich, Paul, 13–14
Tindal, Matthew, 63
Tocqueville, Alexis de, 210; *Democracy in America*, x
Toland, John, 63
tolerance, 57, 59, 265, 268, 269; in American colonies, 31, 32–3; repressive, 64; and sectarianism, 211
toleration, 51, 52, 91, 134n33; in American colonies, 26, 29–30, 37, 85, 162; applied to philosophy (Rawls), 261–2, 263, 279n31; leads to pragmatism, 259; Locke's theory of, 176–7; in thought of Jefferson, 263, 267–8; in thought of Madison, 112–13; in Virginia Declaration of Rights, 81–2
Toleration, regime of (England), 56–7, 58, 59
toleration act (Va., proposed), 142, 143–4
Toleration Act of 1689 (England), 36–7, 57, 64, 84–5, 143, 144; *see also* Act of Toleration
Torcaso v. *Watkins*, 19, 225
trade regulation, 125
Treatise on Government (Locke), 59
Treaty of Paris, 114, 115

Trinitarians, 191, 192; and Harvard College, 188; and tax-supported religion in Massachusetts, 185, 186
Truman, Harry S., 221
truth, 31, 215, 264, 282n43; and establishment, 121, 122; and freedom of religion, 89, 91, 93, 274n2; and justifiability, 258–9; Platonic, 270
Tucker, Josiah, 65, 68
Tuckerman, Joseph, 178
tuition tax credits, 8, 315

"ultimate concern" (concept), 14
Unger, Roberto, 259; *Knowledge and Politics*, 272
Unification Church, 11, 312n112
Unitarianism, 16, 64, 65, 66, 68, 174–5, 211, 214; of Jefferson, 213
Unitarians, 17, 65–6, 90, 202, 224; and Harvard College, 188–9, 190; as heirs of Jefferson, 215–16; and tax-supported religion in Massachusetts, 185, 186, 187, 191, 192; and Virginia Statute, 228
United Presbyterian Church, 222–3
United States: as Christian nation, 221, 295–6; Jefferson's faith in, 78; place of, in salvation history, 96, 97, 239; religious foundation of, 242–3
U.S. Department of Justice, 324
United Synagogue of America, 217
universal human faculty, 257–8
universalism, 19, 69
Universalists, 172–3, 174, 186, 189, 191; and disestablishment, 208–9
University of Virginia, vii, 61, 90, 221, 298; religion at, 9, 10
Utah, 5, 289

Valley Forge Christian College v. *Americans United for Separation of Church and State*, 292–3
Vatican Council, 226; Second, 77, 226
Vidal v. *Girard's Executors*, 295–6
Vilas, William F., 214
Virgin Birth (doctrine), 173, 174
Virginia, viii, 5, 52, 57, 66, 114, 126; Anglicanism in, 2–3, 24, 25, 29, 35; church-state struggle in, 127–8, 130; constitution, 81, 111–12, 121–2, 125,

Virginia (*cont.*)
131n12, 163; disestablishment in, 112,
149–50, 156–7, 208, 285; episcopal
church without bishop in, 55; government pay for teachers in, 295; impact of
Virginia Statute on, 204–6; Jefferson
and, 78, 79, 81; moderate religion in,
64; moral atmosphere of, 75; Old Dominion, 161; religious liberty in, 81–6,
88, 140–63, 192, 202, 219, 220, 224;
Supreme Court of Appeals, 205; and
Virginia Statute, 109–38, 139
Virginia General Assembly, 3, 8, 65–6, 68,
91–2, 109, 113, 114–5, 123, 124, 141,
143, 149, 243; and assessment bill, 146,
147
Virginia Convention, 78, 83; of 1774, 79;
of 1776, 102n49, 145–6
Virginia Council of State, 113–14
Virginia Foundation for the Humanities
and Public Policy, vii, xi
Virginia Gazette, 84–5, 143
Virginia House of Delegates, 83
Virginia Resolutions of 1798, 122
Virginia Statute for Religious Freedom,
vii–xi, 1–22, 84, 201, 202, 285, 286,
306; admonitory (final) paragraph, viii,
ix; alleged contradiction in, 247–8; bill
for establishing, 1, 9, 84, 86, 92, 109,
113, 150, 152, 315; contemporary applications of, 4–8, 11–13; criticism of,
75; desacralization of politics in understanding of, 45, 52; Dissenters and,
139–69; dissenting traditions in, 156–
61; enabling clause, 92; enacting clause,
viii, ix; enactment of, 6–13, 123; ethos
of, 13–14; free-exercise clause, 11–13;
frequenting and supporting clauses, 7–
8; fundamental premise of, 61–6; God
in, 86–7; historical context of, 66–70;
incorporated into Declaration of Independence, 81; Jefferson and, vii–xi, 3,
4, 7, 109, 140, 156; legacy of, 96; Madison and, 1, 3, 7, 92–3, 109–38, 156,
222; name of Jesus Christ in, 295, 296;
nationalization of, 202, 203, 204–29;
passage of, 92–3, 123–4, 125, 128, 130,
146; political/religious indifference in,
57; preamble, viii–ix, 60, 61, 65, 70–1,
92, 219, 274n2; and public debate on

religion in society, 78; reconsideration
of, in religion and civil virtue, 237–55;
significance of, 1–3; and slavery, 163;
text of, xvii–xviii
Voltaire, François Marie Arouet, 63
voluntary system of church finance, 113,
116, 210, 241, 298

Walker, James, 190
Wall, Thomas J., 198n119
"wall of separation" metaphor (Jefferson),
x, 4, 202, 209, 218, 227, 289, 315, 340;
attempts to breach, 341; Catholic danger to, 219; and conflict in church-state
relations, 217–18; dispute over meaning of, 227–9; as interpretation of First
Amendment, 222; meaning of, in U.S.,
218–20; misleading, 340; and religion
in public schools, 224; in Supreme
Court religion cases, 318, 321, 322
Wallace, George C., 326, 331, 333
Wallace v. Jaffree, 291, 325, 326–7, 328–9,
330–1, 333, 334, 336, 337, 339, 340,
341
Walz v. Tax Commission, 286, 289, 293–4,
298, 299, 306, 316, 329
Walzer, Michael, 263
War of 1812, 122, 301
Warren, Earl, 222
Warren Court, 313
wars of religion, 48, 50–1
Washington, George, 3, 78, 87, 115; reli-
gious proclamations of, 303, 304–5
Washington Legal Foundation, 313
Weber, Max, 273
Weber, Paul J., 12
Webster, Daniel, 96, 178, 189–90, 192
Weigle, Luther A., 223–4
welfare state, 228
West Indies, 29
Whigs, 56, 57, 59, 62, 63, 64
White, Byron, 317, 318, 337
White, Morton, 204
Whitehead, John W., 5–6, 8, 10, 18–19,
326
William and Mary Quarterly, 285
William III, king of England, 36, 57
Williams, Bernard, 281n43
Williams, J. Paul, 17
Williams, Roger, viii, 31–3, 35, 37, 38, 70,

209, 221–2, 227; and relation of religion and civic virtue, 249–52, 253
Wilson, Charles H., 326
Winstanley, Gerrard, the Digger, 54
Wirt, William, 96
Wisconsin v. *Yoder,* 11
Witherspoon, John, 110, 131n9, 222
Wolman v. *Walter,* 317, 318, 319, 328, 332, 338, 339
Word of God, 44, 46–7, 49, 50–1, 52–4; preaching of, 139, 143, 153–4; struggle over, in Virginia struggle for religious liberty, 155–6
world view: religious, 15–16, 24; in struggle for religious liberty in Virginia, 152–3
World War II, 296
worship: finance of (Mass.), 179–87

Yale College, 28
"Year of the Bible," 12, 311n105
Yost, Frank H., and Alvin W. Johnson: *Separation of Church and State in the United States,* 224

zealots, 37; in American colonies, 31
Zorach v. *Clavson,* 223
Zwingli, Ulrich, 45–6